SWITZERLAND

Rick Steves'

SWITZERLAND

AVALON
TRAVEL

CONTENTS

Top Destinations in Switzerland

ZÜRICH

APPENZELL

BERN & MURTEN

LUZERN & CENTRAL SWITZ.

BERNER OBERLAND

LAKE GENEVA & FRENCH SWITZ.

❹

PONTRESINA, SAMEDAN & ST. MORITZ

❶

ZERMATT & THE MATTERHORN

❷

❸

LUGANO

BUS

Scenic Rail Journeys:

❶ Golden Pass
❷ William Tell Express
❸ Bernina Express
❹ Glacier Express

INTRODUCTION

Little, mountainous, efficient Switzerland is one of Europe's most appealing destinations. Wedged neatly between Germany, Austria, France, and Italy, Switzerland melds the best of all worlds—and adds a healthy dose of chocolate, cowbells, and cable cars. Fiercely independent and decidedly high-tech, the Swiss stubbornly hold on to their quaint traditions, too. Join the cheesemakers high atop an alp, try to call the shepherds on an alphorn, and hike through some of the world's most stunning mountain scenery.

This book breaks Switzerland into its top big-city, small-town, and rural attractions. It gives you all the information and

suggestions necessary to wring the maximum value out of your limited time and money. If you plan three weeks or less in Switzerland, this lean and mean little book has all the information you need...unless you're a skier. This is a fair-weather book—it focuses on the highlights of summertime fun (but for basic info for a winter visit, see the Switzerland in Winter chapter).

Experiencing Europe's culture, people, and natural wonders economically and hassle-free has been my goal throughout three decades of traveling, tour guiding, and writing. With this guide-book, I pass on to you the lessons I've learned.

The book includes a balance of cities and villages, mountain-top hikes and lake cruises, thought-provoking museums and sky-high gondola rides. It covers the predictable biggies while mixing in a healthy dose of Back Door intimacy. Along with Luzern, the Matterhorn, and the Glacier Express, you'll experience windswept

Map Legend

½ Viewpoint	✈ Airport	Pedestrian Zone
▲ Mountain Peak	Cable Car	●—●—● Mtn. Lift
⊕ Tourist Info	Gondola	----- Railway
▲ Mountain Hut	Ⓜ Metro	•⊞⊞⊞• Mtn. Rail
⛫ Castle	Ⓑ Bus Stop	o⊞⊞⊞o Funicular
⌂ Church	⊷ Boat Stop	Stairs
)(Mtn. Pass	Ⓟ Parking	----- Trail/Path
◉ Fountain	- - - - Walk/Tour Route	) (Tunnel
		·········· Ferry/Boat Route

Use this legend to help you navigate the maps in this book.

Roman ruins and ramble through traffic-free alpine towns. I've been selective, including only the top destinations. For example, the country is dotted with alpine villages—but Gimmelwald is a cut above.

The best is, of course, only my opinion. But after spending a third of my adult life exploring and researching Europe, I've developed a sixth sense for what travelers enjoy. Just thinking about the places featured in this book makes me want to yodel.

About This Book

Rick Steves' Switzerland is a personal tour guide in your pocket. This book is organized by destinations. Each destination is a mini-vacation on its own, filled with exciting sights, strollable neighborhoods, homey, affordable places to stay, and memorable places to eat.

In the following chapters, you'll find these sections:

Planning Your Time suggests a schedule for how to best use your limited time.

Orientation includes specifics on public transportation, helpful hints, local tour options, easy-to-read maps, and tourist information.

Sights describes the top attractions and includes their cost and hours.

Self-Guided Walks take you through interesting neighborhoods.

Sleeping describes my favorite hotels, from good-value deals to cushy splurges.

Key to This Book

Updates

This book is updated regularly. For the latest, visit www.rick steves.com/update. For a valuable list of reports and experiences—good and bad—from fellow travelers, check www .ricksteves.com/feedback.

Abbreviations and Times

I use the following symbols and abbreviations in this book:

Sights are rated:

▲▲▲	Don't miss
▲▲	Try hard to see
▲	Worthwhile if you can make it
No rating	Worth knowing about

Tourist information offices are abbreviated as **TI,** and bathrooms are **WCs.** To categorize accommodations, I use a **Sleep Code** (described on page 22).

Like Europe, this book uses the **24-hour clock.** It's the same through 12:00 noon, then keep going: 13:00, 14:00, and so on. For anything over 12, subtract 12 and add p.m. (14:00 is 2:00 p.m.).

When giving **opening times,** I include both peak season and off-season hours if they differ. So, if a museum is listed as "May-Oct daily 9:00-16:00," it should be open from 9:00 a.m. until 4:00 p.m. from the first day of May until the last day of October (but expect exceptions).

For **transit** or **tour departures,** I first list the frequency, then the duration. So, a train connection listed as "2/hour, 1.5 hours" departs twice each hour, and the journey lasts an hour and a half.

Eating serves up a range of options, from inexpensive *Stübli* to fancy restaurants.

Connections outlines your options for traveling to destinations by train and bus. In car-friendly regions, I've also included route tips for drivers.

The **Switzerland in Winter** chapter provides tips for enjoying the Alps in snow, and describes some uniquely Swiss holiday traditions.

The **Switzerland: Past and Present** chapter introduces you to some key people and events in this nation's complicated past, making your sightseeing that much more meaningful.

The **appendix** is a traveler's tool kit, with telephone tips, useful phone numbers, transportation basics (on trains, buses, boats, car rentals, driving, and flights), recommended books and films, a festival list, a climate chart, a handy packing checklist, a hotel

INTRODUCTION

reservation form, and survival phrases in German, French, and Italian.

Browse through this book, choose your favorite destinations, and link them up. Then have a great trip! Traveling like a temporary local, you'll get the absolute most of every mile, minute, and dollar. As you visit places I know and love, I'm happy that you'll be meeting some of my favorite Swiss people.

Planning

This section will help you get started on planning your trip—with advice on trip costs, when to go, and what you should know before you take off.

Travel Smart

Your trip to Switzerland is like a complex play—easier to follow and really appreciate on a second viewing. While no one does the same trip twice to gain that advantage, reading this book in its entirety before your trip accomplishes much the same thing.

Design an itinerary that enables you to visit sights at the best possible times. Note festivals, holidays, and specifics on sights, including the days when sights are closed. Whether you're traveling by public transportation (trains, buses, and boats) or by rental car, read up on my tips in the appendix. A smart trip is a puzzle—a fun, doable, and worthwhile challenge.

Be sure to mix intense and relaxed periods in your itinerary. To maximize rootedness, minimize one-night stands. It's worth a long train ride (or drive) after dinner to be settled into a town for two nights. Hotels are more likely to give a better price to someone staying more than one night. Every trip—and every traveler— needs slack time (laundry, picnics, people-watching, and so on). Pace yourself. Assume you will return.

Perhaps more than anywhere else in Europe, weather plays a huge factor in your sightseeing in Switzerland. The mountains are stunning—when it's not raining. But bad weather needn't ruin a trip. Switzerland has plenty of rainy-weather options. And it's so small and has such a slick train network that you can easily double-back later to visit the mountaintop hideaway that was clouded over your first time through.

Be flexible. For maximum spontaneity, consider traveling without room reservations (realizing that this comes with some risk). For example, you might plan on three days split between the city of Bern and the mountainous Berner Oberland region. If it's raining as you approach the area, head for Bern. If it's sunny, make a beeline for the mountains, then hit Bern on your way out of the area. To help decide, tune into TV stations and websites that show the weather in various parts of the country. Many high-altitude observation decks have 24-hour cameras that pan slowly back and forth, showing you exactly what you'll see when you get up top (for example, www.swisspanorama.com for the Berner Oberland, www.zermatt.ch for Zermatt).

Reread this book as you travel, and visit local TIs. Upon arrival in a new town, lay the groundwork for a smooth departure; write down (or print out from an online source) the schedule for the train, bus, or boat you'll take when you depart. Drivers can study the best route to their next destination.

Get online at Internet cafés or your hotel, and buy a phone card or carry a mobile phone: You can find tourist information, learn the latest on sights (special events, English tour schedule, etc.), book tickets and tours, make reservations, reconfirm hotels, research transportation connections, and keep in touch with your loved ones.

Enjoy the friendliness of the Swiss people. Connect with the culture. Set up your own quest for the richest hot chocolate, cheeriest window box, biggest cowbell, or most densely packed stack of firewood. Slow down and be open to unexpected experiences. Ask questions—most locals are eager to point you in their idea of the right direction. Keep a notepad in your pocket for confirming prices, noting directions, and organizing your thoughts. Wear your money belt, learn the currency, and figure out how to estimate prices in dollars. Those who expect to travel smart, do.

Trip Costs

Five components make up your trip cost: airfare, surface transportation, room and board, sightseeing and entertainment, and shopping and miscellany.

Airfare: A basic round-trip flight from the US to Zürich can cost $1,000-1,600, depending on where you fly from and when (cheaper in winter). If your trip extends beyond Switzerland, consider saving time and money by flying into one city and out of another; for instance, into Zürich and out of Paris.

Surface Transportation: For a two-week whirlwind trip of most of my recommended destinations, allow $600 per person for public transportation. This covers a second-class, 15-consecutive-day Swiss Saverpass, plus high-mountain trains and lifts, and reservation fees for scenic trains. For a two-week car rental, tolls, gas, and insurance, allow $500 per person (based on two people sharing). Leasing is worth considering for trips of two and a half weeks or more. Car rentals and leases are usually cheapest if arranged from the US. You can purchase a Swiss railpass before you leave home, or wait until you arrive in Switzerland—most of the passes

Budget Tips

Switzerland is pricey, but there are ways to stretch your dollars. For example, you can cut down on restaurant costs by having scenic picnics or seeking out self-service cafeterias (often attached to department or grocery stores), which offer delicious food at a fraction of the cost of dining out.

Many expensive alpine lifts offer discounted "early bird" tickets for the first trip of the day. Train trips get cheaper when you choose the right railpass (for help, see page 375); the Swiss Pass is a swinging deal for most travelers.

Save on Sightseeing with the Swiss Pass

The Swiss Pass railpass—offering consecutive-day or flexi-day coverage of Switzerland's trains, boats, and buses, and a 50 percent discount on lifts—also covers admission to more than 400 museums.

The Swiss Pass doubles as a Swiss Museum Pass (which otherwise costs about 165 SF) to cover certain museum admissions, but only during its validity period. For a consecutive-day pass, that means from the day you activate your pass (i.e., use it for the first time) until the last day it's valid for travel. If you have a flexipass, visiting a museum can use up a day of your pass. To get the most out of a flexipass, use it to visit a museum either on the same day you arrive at that destination or on the day you depart. Unlike flexipasses for most other countries, the validity of a Swiss flexipass ends with your last used-up travel day; for more

are sold at Swiss train stations. Swiss railpasses come in such a wide selection that many travelers save money with a pass, even for short visits. For more on public transportation and car rental, see the appendix.

Room and Board: You can thrive in Switzerland on an average of $145 a day per person for room and board. This allows an average of $20 for lunch, $40 for dinner, $5 for snacks, and $80 for lodging (based on two people splitting the cost of a $160 double room that includes breakfast). Students and tightwads can enjoy Switzerland for as little as $55 a day ($30 per hostel bed, $25 for meals and snacks).

Sightseeing and Entertainment: Figure $10-15 per sight, and about $50 for each major alpine lift. Though hiking is free, lifts to some of the best high-altitude trails aren't. An overall average of $30 a day works for most. Don't skimp here. After all, this category is the driving force behind your trip—you came to sightsee, enjoy, and experience Switzerland.

Shopping and Miscellany: Figure $5 per coffee, beer, and ice-cream cone. Shopping can vary in cost from nearly nothing to

information, see page 375.

The following sights, which are described in this book, are free with the Swiss Pass (for a full list of museums covered by the Swiss Pass as well as the Swiss Museum Pass, see www.museums pass.ch):

Zürich—Swiss National Museum and Rietberg Museum.

Luzern—Rosengart Collection, Depot History Museum, Bourbaki Panorama, Glacier Garden, Richard Wagner Museum, Museum of Art Luzern, Museum of Natural History, and the Alpineum, plus Fortress Fürigen Museum nearby in Stansstad. (The Swiss Transport Museum is 50 percent off with the pass.)

Bern—Museum of Fine Arts, Paul Klee Center, and Einstein Museum.

Near Murten—Roman Museum in Avenches.

Interlaken—Town History Museum/Museum of Tourism.

Near Interlaken—Ballenberg Open-Air Folk Museum in Brienz.

Zermatt—Matterhorn Museum.

Appenzell Region—Appenzell Museum and Appenzell's two modern art museums, and folk museums in Stein and Urnäsch.

Lausanne—Collection de l'Art Brut, Olympic Museum (closed for renovation until late 2013), and City History Museum.

Lake Geneva Region—Château de Chillon.

French Swiss Countryside—Gruyères' Castle, H. R. Giger Museum, and Tibet Museum.

a small fortune, though good budget travelers find that this has little to do with assembling a trip full of lifelong and wonderful memories.

Sightseeing Priorities

Depending on the length of your trip, and taking geographic proximity into account, here are my recommended priorities:

3 days:	Berner Oberland
5 days, add:	Luzern and Central Switzerland
7 days, add:	Bern and Lake Geneva area, connecting with Golden Pass scenic rail journey
10 days, add:	Zermatt and Appenzell, linking with Glacier Express train
14 days, add:	Lugano and Pontresina area, connecting with Bernina Express and William Tell Express train rides
16 days, add:	Zürich and Murten
21 days, add:	More day trips (French Swiss countryside), more hikes, and time to slow down

INTRODUCTION

Switzerland at a Glance

▲▲**Zürich** Bustling cosmopolitan city—Switzerland's largest by far—with upscale shops and a charming riverside old-town quarter full of pointy church spires and pealing bells.

▲▲**Luzern and Central Switzerland** Touristy yet worthwhile town of historic wooden bridges, picturesque streets, and vintage steamships that ply lovely Lake Luzern, ringed by mountains with stunning vistas accessible by high-altitude lifts.

▲▲▲**Bern** Cozy capital of Switzerland tucked in a sharp river bend, with arcaded shopping promenades, medieval clock towers, and museums devoted to Albert Einstein and artist Paul Klee.

▲▲**Murten** Quaint, small walled town sitting right on the German/French linguistic fault line, with nearby Roman ruins and museum in Avenches.

▲▲▲**Gimmelwald and the Berner Oberland** Rustic village spectacularly perched on a cliff in this mountainous region—popular for its alpine towns and scenic hikes, lifts, and train rides—with touristy Interlaken as the gateway.

▲**Zermatt and the Matterhorn** Glitzy ski resort still sporting some traditional old-fashioned touches, in a valley at the foot of the famous Matterhorn.

▲▲**Appenzell** The most traditional Swiss region, known for pastoral scenery, small towns, cows, folk museums, and, just a cable-car ride away, the rustic retreat at the cliffs of Ebenalp.

▲▲**Lake Geneva and French Switzerland** Small-but-sophisticated lakeside city of Lausanne, Switzerland's best castle experience at Château de Chillon, the cute cheese-making center of Gruyères, and pleasant scenery of the surrounding countryside.

▲**Lugano** Leading city of Italian-speaking Switzerland, with a tidy if dull urban core, scenic boat trips on Lake Lugano, and mountain lifts to lakeside peaks.

▲**Pontresina, Samedan, and St. Moritz** Romansh-speaking mountain resort region, anchored by three towns: touristy Pontresina, humble Samedan, and swanky St. Moritz.

▲▲**Scenic Rail Journeys** Four famous train rides, each offering panoramic views and crisscrossing the country.

The map on page 11 and the two-week itinerary on the previous two pages include everything listed here (except Murten), plus modifications for a longer or shorter trip.

When to Go

The "tourist season" runs roughly from May through September. Summer (July-Aug) has its advantages: the best weather, snow-free alpine trails, very long days (light until after 21:00), and the busiest schedule of tourist fun. In late May, June, September, and early October, travelers enjoy fewer crowds, milder weather, and the ability to grab a room almost whenever and wherever they like.

During the *Zwischenzeit* ("between time"—that is, between summer and ski seasons, roughly April, early May, late Oct, and Nov), the cities are pleasantly uncrowded, but the weather can be iffy, and resort towns such as Zermatt and Mürren are completely dead (with most hotels and restaurants closed).

During ski season (Dec-March), mountain resorts are crowded and expensive, while cities are quieter (some accommodations and sights are either closed or run on a limited schedule). The weather can be cold and dreary, and nighttime will draw the shades on your sightseeing before dinner. But Christmastime traditions (such as colorful markets and special holiday foods) can warm up your trip at a chilly time of year.

Pack warm clothing for the Alps, no matter when you go—the weather can change suddenly.

Know Before You Go

Your trip is more likely to go smoothly if you plan ahead. Check this list of things to arrange while you're still at home.

You need a **passport**—but no visa or shots—to travel in Switzerland. You may be denied entry into certain European countries if your passport is due to expire within three to six months of your ticketed date of return. Get it renewed if you'll be cutting it close. It can take up to six weeks to get or renew a passport (for more on passports, see www.travel.state.gov). Pack a photocopy of your passport in your luggage in case the original is lost or stolen.

Book rooms well in advance if you'll be traveling during peak season (July and August) and any major **holidays or festivals** (see page 391).

Call your **debit- and credit-card companies** to let them know the countries you'll be visiting, to ask about fees, and more (see page 15).

Do your homework if you want to buy **travel insurance**. Compare the cost of the insurance to the likelihood of your using it and your potential loss if something goes wrong. Also, check

INTRODUCTION

Switzerland's Best Two-Week Trip by Train

Day	Plan	Sleep in
1	Arrive Zürich Airport, head to Appenzell	Appenzell or Ebenalp
2	All day for Appenzell and Ebenalp	Appenzell or Ebenalp
3	Leave early for Luzern	Luzern
4	Luzern	Luzern
5	Boat, then bus to Lugano along William Tell Express route	Lugano
6	Bernina Express to Pontresina area	Pontresina
7	Pontresina area (with St. Moritz and Samedan)	Pontresina
8	Take Glacier Express; if weather's good, head for Zermatt; if weather's bad, consider going straight to Lausanne (see below)	Zermatt
9	Zermatt and hikes, Matterhorn-view lifts	Zermatt
10	If weather's good, spend more time in Zermatt and go late to Lausanne; if weather's bad, leave early for Lausanne	Lausanne
11	Take the Golden Pass to the Berner Oberland. If weather's good, go early; if weather's bad, linger in Lausanne/ Lake Geneva area and leave late	Berner Oberland (Gimmelwald or Mürren)
12	All day for lifts and hikes in the Berner Oberland	Gimmelwald or Mürren
13	More time in the Berner Oberland	Gimmelwald or Mürren
14	Early to Bern, then on to Zürich	Zürich
15	More time in Zürich, or fly home	

Notes

Zermatt isn't worth the trip in bad weather. If your reservations are flexible, consider skipping that leg and going straight to Lausanne (take the Glacier Express only to Brig, then change for Lausanne).

To connect Luzern and Lugano, follow the William Tell Express route, but don't spend extra for the official tourist package-trip.

If you have extra time in Switzerland, I'd suggest spending it in (listed in order of priority): Murten and Bern, Zürich, Lausanne and the Lake Geneva area, Lugano (relaxing) or the Luzern area (day trips). For a short trip of a week or so, I'd just focus on the Berner Oberland, Luzern, and Bern. (If you're trying to decide between focusing on the Berner Oberland or the more famous Zermatt/Matterhorn region, see the sidebar on page 202.)

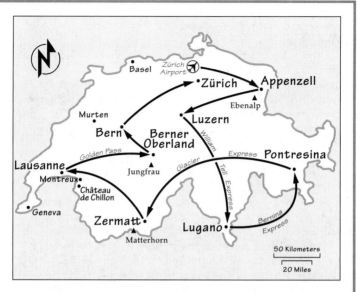

Railpass: The best railpass for this itinerary is a Swiss Pass, specifically the 15-consecutive-day Swiss Saverpass ($400 second class, $600 first class, prices are per person for 2 or more traveling together, solo travelers 26 or older pay about 15 percent more, confirm latest prices at www.ricksteves.com/rail; figure an additional $130 total in reservation fees for all the scenic rail journeys). This pass doesn't cover mountain lifts, but it does earn you a 50 percent discount on most of them.

By Car: Although this itinerary is designed for public transportation, it can be done by car with a few modifications. Obviously, you won't take the scenic rail trips. Instead, drive from Appenzell straight to the Pontresina area, then continue through Tirano and on to Lugano (via Lake Como in Italy). From Lugano, drive to Zermatt (crossing again through Italy) and resume the above itinerary, visiting Luzern at the end before returning to Zürich. The French Swiss countryside and the area around Murten merit more time if you have a car.

Beyond Switzerland: Switzerland, right in the middle of Western Europe, splices neatly into a multicountry trip by car or train. For instance, the Appenzell region is a likely gateway to Germany's Bavaria or Austria's Tirol. Italy's Lake Como is a stone's throw from Lugano or Ticino (in fact, the Bernina Express bus drives right alongside it)—and Milan is not much farther. If you're in Lausanne, you're literally looking at France (across Lake Geneva), and a handy train ride whisks you to Lyon or Chamonix. And big Swiss cities are efficiently connected by night trains and fast day trains to destinations in all of these countries and beyond.

whether your existing insurance (health, homeowners, or renters) covers you and your possessions overseas. For more tips, see www .ricksteves.com/insurance.

If you're bringing a mobile device, you can download free information from **Rick Steves Audio Europe,** featuring hours of travel interviews and other audio content about Switzerland (via www.ricksteves.com/audioeurope, iTunes, or the Rick Steves Audio Europe free smartphone app; for details, see page 387).

If you're planning to **rent a car** in Switzerland, bring along your driver's license.

If you'll be traveling by train, consider getting a **railpass** (a particularly good idea in Switzerland), but research your options first (see page 375 and www.ricksteves.com/rail for specifics).

To take one of the popular **scenic trains** during high season (July-Aug), you may want to reserve ahead. See page 315 for details and advice.

Because **airline carry-on restrictions** are always changing, visit the Transportation Security Administration's website (www .tsa.gov/travelers) for an up-to-date list of what you can bring on the plane with you...and what you must check.

Practicalities

Emergency Telephone Numbers: In Switzerland, dial 112 for medical or other emergencies. For police, dial 117. If you get sick, do as the Swiss do and go to a pharmacist for advice. Or ask at your hotel for help; they know of the nearest medical and emergency services.

Theft or Loss: To replace a passport, you'll need to go in person to the US embassy (see page 373). If your credit and debit cards disappear, cancel and replace them (see "Damage Control for Lost Cards" on page 17). File a police report, either on the spot or within a day or two; it's required when submitting an insurance claim for lost or stolen railpasses or travel gear, and can help with replacing your passport or credit and debit cards. For more information, see www.ricksteves.com/help. Precautionary measures can minimize the effects of loss: Back up photos and other files frequently, and use passwords to protect any sensitive data on your electronic devices.

Borders: Although Switzerland isn't in the European Union, it does belong to the Schengen Zone, which means border controls are now a wave-through. Even so, remember that when you change countries, you must also change phone cards, stamps, and *Unterhosen.*

Time Zones: Switzerland, like most of continental Europe, is generally six/nine hours ahead of the East/West Coasts of the US. The exceptions are the beginning and end of Daylight Saving

Time: Europe "springs forward" the last Sunday in March (two weeks after most of North America) and "falls back" the last Sunday in October (one week before North America). For a handy online time converter, try www.timeanddate.com/worldclock.

Business Hours: Swiss shops are generally open Monday through Friday 9:00-18:30, Saturday 8:00-17:00, and closed Sunday. They are often open later on Thursdays; smaller shops often close at lunchtime.

Sundays have the same pros and cons as they do for travelers in the US (special events, limited hours, banks and many shops closed, limited public transportation, no rush hour). Saturdays are virtually weekdays, with earlier closing hours and no rush hour. Popular places are even more popular on weekends—especially sunny weekends. Many sights are closed on Monday (head for the hills).

Watt's Up? Europe's electrical system is 220 volts, instead of North America's 110 volts. Most newer electronics (such as laptops, battery chargers, and hair dryers) convert automatically, so you won't need a converter, but you will need an adapter plug with two round prongs, sold inexpensively at travel stores in the US. Avoid bringing older appliances that don't automatically convert voltage; instead, buy a cheap replacement in Europe.

Discounts: Although discounts are generally not listed in this book, youths (under 18) and students (with International Student Identity Cards) often get discounts—but only by asking. To get a teacher or student ID card, visit www.statravel.com or www.isic.org.

News: Americans keep in touch via the *International Herald Tribune* (published almost daily throughout Europe and online at www.iht.com). Another informative site is www.bbc.co.uk/news. Every Tuesday, the European editions of *Time* and *Newsweek* hit the stands with articles of particular interest to travelers in Europe. Sports addicts can get their fix online or from *USA Today*. Many hotels have CNN and BBC television channels.

Money

This section offers advice on how to pay for purchases on your trip (including getting cash from ATMs and paying with plastic), dealing with lost or stolen cards, VAT (sales tax) refunds, and tipping.

What to Bring

Bring both a credit card and a debit card. You'll use the debit card at cash machines (ATMs) to withdraw local cash for most purchases, and the credit card to pay for larger items. Some travelers carry a third card, in case one gets demagnetized or eaten by a

Exchange Rates

Switzerland, which isn't a member of the European Union, has retained its traditional currency, the Swiss franc. The international abbreviation for the Swiss franc is "CHF," but in Switzerland you might also see it abbreviated "SF" or "SFr." For simplicity, I use "SF" in this book.

1 Swiss franc (SF) = about $1.10

To convert prices in Swiss francs to dollars, add 10 percent: 20 SF = about $22, 50 SF = about $55. (Check www.oanda.com for the latest exchange rates.) One Swiss franc is broken down into 100 rappen (or centimes in French Switzerland). There are coins for one, two, and five francs, plus several coins for very small denominations of rappen. The small coin with real value is the 50-rappen (marked with "1/2" rather than "50"). It looks like a tiny dime, but is equivalent to a half-dollar. In a handful of change, it's easy to identify as the only one with ridges.

temperamental machine.

For an emergency reserve, bring several hundred dollars in hard cash in easy-to-exchange $20 bills. Avoid using currency exchange booths (lousy rates and/or outrageous fees); if you have foreign currency to exchange, take it to a bank. Don't use traveler's checks—they're not worth the fees or long waits at slow banks.

Cash

Cash is just as desirable in Europe as it is at home. Small businesses (hotels, restaurants, shops, etc.) prefer that you pay your bills with cash. Some vendors will charge you extra for using a credit card, and some won't take credit cards at all. Cash is the best—and sometimes only—way to pay for bus fare, taxis, and local guides.

Throughout Europe, ATMs are the standard way for travelers to get cash. Most ATMs in Switzerland are located outside of a bank. Try to use the ATM when the branch is open (generally Mon-Fri 8:00-17:00); if your card is munched by a machine, you can immediately go inside for help. Post offices (business hours) and train stations (long hours) usually change money as well.

To withdraw money from an ATM (*Bankomat* or *Geldautomat* in German, *distributeur* in French), you'll need a debit card (ideally with a Visa or MasterCard logo for maximum usability), plus a PIN code. Know your PIN code in numbers; there are only numbers—no letters—on European keypads. For security, it's best to shield the keypad when entering your PIN at an ATM. Although you can use a credit card for ATM transactions, it's generally more expensive because it's considered a cash advance rather than a withdrawal.

When using an ATM, try to withdraw large sums of money to reduce the number of per-transaction bank fees you'll pay. If the machine refuses your request, try again and select a smaller amount (some cash machines limit the amount you can withdraw—don't take it personally). If that doesn't work, try a different machine. Be aware that some cash machines don't issue receipts for your transactions.

It's easier to pay for purchases with smaller bills; if the ATM gives you big bills, try to break them at major museums or larger stores.

To keep your cash safe, use a money belt—a pouch with a strap that you buckle around your waist like a belt and wear under your clothes. Pickpockets target tourists, even in safe Switzerland. A money belt provides peace of mind, allowing you to safely carry your passport, credit cards, and lots of cash. Don't waste time every few days tracking down a cash machine—withdraw a week's worth of money, stuff it in your money belt, and travel!

Credit and Debit Cards

For purchases, Visa and MasterCard are more commonly accepted than American Express. Just like at home, credit or debit cards work easily at larger hotels, restaurants, and shops.

I typically use my debit card to withdraw cash to pay for most purchases. I use my credit card only in a few specific situations: to book hotel reservations by phone, to cover major expenses (such as car rentals, plane tickets, and long hotel stays), and to pay for things near the end of my trip (to avoid another visit to the ATM). While you could use a debit card to make most large purchases, using a credit card offers a greater degree of fraud protection (because debit cards draw funds directly from your account).

Ask Your Credit- or Debit-Card Company: Before your trip, contact the company that issued your debit or credit cards.

• Confirm your card will work overseas, and alert them that you'll be using it in Europe; otherwise, they may deny transactions if they perceive unusual spending patterns.

• Ask for the specifics on transaction **fees.** When you use your credit or debit card—either for purchases or ATM withdrawals— you'll often be charged additional "international transaction" fees of up to 3 percent (1 percent is normal) plus $5 per transaction. If your card's fees are too high, consider getting a card just for your trip: Capital One (credit cards only, www.capitalone.com) and most credit unions have low-to-no international fees.

• If you plan to withdraw cash from ATMs, confirm your

Why No Swiss Euros?

Though surrounded by countries enjoying the convenience of a shared currency, the Swiss have stubbornly hung on to their old franc. However, in light of the euro zone's economic troubles, it's no longer so hard to see why the Swiss have resisted the euro's siren call—indeed, the Swiss are humming an "I told you so" tune as their relatively stable economy sits unperturbed at the eye of the euro storm. But it's not just fear of instability that's kept the Swiss clinging to their francs—it's simply not worth it to them to risk changing their economic system. For example, the Swiss enjoy lower mortgage interest rates than the rest of Europe. Even more importantly, a huge part of the Swiss economy is based on providing a safe and secret place for wealthy people from around the world to stash their money. When bank fees are figured in, people who "save" in Swiss banks actually earn negative interest—they *pay* the Swiss to keep their money. Compliance with European Union regulations in order to join the euro zone would mean the end of Switzerland's secret banking industry. The Swiss are not inclined to deal such a devastating blow to their economy.

Even though Switzerland hasn't officially adopted the euro, the majority of Swiss hotels, restaurants, and shops (especially in touristy areas) accept smaller euro bills. Most businesses will not take euro coins or larger bills, and you'll usually get bad rates (and your change in Swiss francs). Many coin-operated phone booths even accept euros (marked with a big yellow €). But unless this is your last chance to use up leftover euros, spend francs in Switzerland instead—you'll save money, and they're prettier.

daily **withdrawal limit** (500 SF is usually the maximum). Some travelers prefer a high limit that allows them to take out more cash at each ATM stop, while others prefer to set a lower limit in case their card is stolen.

 • Ask for your credit card's **PIN** in case you encounter Europe's "chip-and-PIN" system; since they're unlikely to tell you your PIN over the phone, allow time for the bank to mail it to you.

Chip and PIN: If your card is declined for a purchase in Europe, it may be because of chip and PIN, which requires cardholders to punch in a PIN instead of signing a receipt. Switzerland, like much of Europe, is adopting this system, but you're unlikely to encounter a Swiss machine that won't also read your card's magnetic strip. (That said, some unstaffed gas stations may not take your American card, so don't wait until nightfall to fuel up.) If, when you're using your card, you're prompted to enter your PIN but don't know it, ask if the cashier can swipe your card and print a receipt for you to sign instead; if not, just pay cash.

Dynamic Currency Conversion: If merchants offer to convert your purchase price into dollars (called dynamic currency conversion, or DCC), refuse this "service." You'll pay even more in fees for the expensive convenience of seeing your charge in dollars.

Damage Control for Lost Cards

If you lose your credit, debit, or ATM card, you can stop people from using it by reporting the loss immediately to the respective global customer-assistance centers. Call these 24-hour US numbers collect: Visa (410/581-9994), MasterCard (636/722-7111), and American Express (623/492-8427).

At a minimum, you'll need to know the name of the financial institution that issued you the card, along with the type of card (classic, platinum, or whatever). Providing the following information will allow for a quicker cancellation of your missing card: full card number, whether you are the primary or secondary cardholder, the cardholder's name exactly as printed on the card, billing address, home phone number, circumstances of the loss or theft, and identification verification (your birth date, your mother's maiden name, or your Social Security number—memorize this, don't carry a copy). If you are the secondary cardholder, you'll also need to provide the primary cardholder's identification-verification details. You can generally receive a temporary card within two or three business days in Europe (see www.ricksteves.com/help for more information).

If you promptly report your card lost or stolen, you typically won't be responsible for any unauthorized transactions on your account, although many banks charge a liability fee of $50.

Tipping

Tipping in Switzerland isn't as automatic and generous as it is in the US—but for special service, tips are appreciated, if not expected. As in the US, the proper amount depends on your resources, tipping philosophy, and the circumstances, but some general guidelines apply.

Restaurants: Tipping is an issue only at restaurants that have table service. If you order your food at a counter, don't tip.

At restaurants that have a waitstaff, service is included, although it's common to round up the bill after a good meal (usually 5-10 percent; so for an 18.50-SF meal, pay 20 SF). Give the tip directly to your server. Rather than leaving coins on the table, the Swiss usually pay with paper, saying how much they'd like the bill to be (for example, for an 8.10-SF meal, give a 20-SF bill and say *"Neun Franken"*—"Nine francs"—to get 11 SF change).

Taxis: To tip the cabbie, round up. For a typical ride, round up your fare (for instance, if the fare is 13 SF, pay 15 SF). If the cabbie hauls your bags and zips you to the airport to help you catch your flight, you might want to toss in a little more. If you feel like you're being driven in circles or otherwise ripped off, skip the tip.

Special Services: At hotels, if you let the porter carry your luggage, it's polite to tip a franc for each bag (another reason to pack light). If you like to tip maids, leave a franc per overnight at the end of your stay.

In general, if someone in the service industry does a super job for you, a small tip of a franc or two is appropriate...but not required.

When in doubt, ask. If you're not sure whether (or how much) to tip for a service, ask your hotelier or the TI; they'll fill you in on how it's done on their turf.

Getting a VAT Refund

Wrapped into the purchase price of your Swiss souvenirs is a Value-Added Tax (VAT) of 8 percent (one of the lowest in Europe). You're entitled to get most of that tax back if you purchase more than 300 SF (about $330) worth of goods at a store that participates in the VAT-refund scheme. Typically, you must ring up the minimum at a single retailer—you can't add up your purchases from various shops to reach the required amount.

Getting your refund is usually straightforward and, if you buy a substantial amount of souvenirs, well worth the hassle. If you're lucky, the merchant will subtract the tax when you make your purchase. (This is more likely to occur if the store ships the goods to your home.) Otherwise, you'll need to:

Get the paperwork. Have the merchant completely fill out the necessary refund document. You'll have to present your passport. Be sure to retain your original sales receipt.

Get your stamp at the border or airport. Process your VAT document at your last stop in Switzerland with the customs agent who deals with VAT refunds. Before checking in for your flight, find the local customs office, and be prepared to stand in line. It's best to keep your purchases in your carry-on for viewing, but if they're too large or dangerous to carry on (such as Swiss Army knives), have your purchases easily accessible in the bag you're about to check, ready to show the customs agent. You're not supposed to use your purchased goods before you leave. If you show up at customs wearing your new Swiss watch, officials might look the other way—or deny you a refund.

Collect your refund. You'll need to return your stamped document to the retailer or its representative. Many merchants work with a service, such as Global Blue (www.global-blue.com) or Premier Tax Free (www.premiertaxfree.com), that has offices at major airports, ports, or border crossings (after check-in and security, probably strategically located near a duty-free shop). These services, which extract a 4 percent fee, can usually refund your money immediately in cash or credit your card (within two billing cycles). If the retailer handles VAT refunds directly, it's up to you to contact the merchant for your refund. You can mail the documents from home or, more quickly, from your point of departure (using a stamped, self-addressed envelope you've prepared or one that's been provided by the merchant). You'll then have to wait—it can take months.

Customs for American Shoppers

You are allowed to take home $800 worth of items per person duty-free, once every 30 days. You can also bring in duty-free a liter of alcohol. As for food, you can take home many processed and packaged foods: vacuum-packed cheeses, dried herbs, jams, chocolate, oil, vinegar, and honey. Fresh fruits and vegetables and most meats are not allowed. Any liquid-containing foods must be packed in checked luggage, a potential recipe for disaster. To check customs rules and duty rates, visit www.cbp.gov.

Sightseeing

Sightseeing can be hard work. If you're spending time in urban Switzerland, use these tips to make your museum visits meaningful, fun, efficient, and painless.

Plan Ahead

Set up an itinerary that allows you to fit in all your must-see sights. Most sights keep stable hours, but you can easily confirm the latest by asking the TI or checking museums' websites.

Don't put off visiting a must-see sight—you never know when a place will close unexpectedly for a holiday, strike, or restoration. On holidays (see list on page 391), expect reduced hours or closures. In summer, some sights may stay open late. Off-season, many museums have shorter hours.

When possible, visit key sights in the morning (when your energy is best) and save other activities for the afternoon. At sights, hit the highlights first, then go back to other things if you have the time and stamina.

Study up. To get the most out of the self-guided walks and sight descriptions in this book, read them before your visit.

At Sights

Here's what you can typically expect:

Major museums and sights may require you to check daypacks

and coats, usually for free (though many museum lockers require a 1- or 2-SF coin deposit—don't forget to take your coin from the back of the locker door before leaving). The checkrooms are generally safe, but if you have something you can't bear to part with, stash it in a pocket or purse. To avoid checking a small backpack, carry it under your arm like a purse as you enter. From a guard's point of view, a backpack is generally a problem while a purse is not.

Flash photography is often banned, but taking photos without a flash is usually allowed. Look for signs or ask. Flashes damage oil paintings and distract others in the room. Even without a flash, a handheld camera will take a decent picture (or buy postcards or posters at the museum bookstore). If photos are permitted, video cameras generally are OK, too.

Museums may have special exhibits in addition to their permanent collection. Some exhibits are included in the entry price, while others come at an extra cost (which you may have to pay even if you don't want to see the exhibit).

Expect changes—artwork can be on tour, on loan, out sick, or shifted at the whim of the curator. To adapt, pick up any available free floor plans as you enter, and ask museum staff if you can't find a particular item.

Many sights rent audioguides, which generally offer excellent recorded descriptions in English (about $5). If you bring along your own pair of headphones and a Y-jack, you can sometimes share one audioguide with a companion and save money.

Important sights may have an on-site café or cafeteria (usually a good place to rest and have a snack or light meal). The WCs at sights are free and nearly always clean (it's smart to carry tissues in case a WC runs out of TP).

Many sights sell postcards that highlight their attractions. Before you leave a sight, scan the postcards and thumb through the biggest guidebook (or skim its index) to be sure you haven't overlooked something that you'd like to see.

Most sights stop admitting people 30-60 minutes before closing time, and some rooms may close early (often about 45 minutes before the official closing time). Guards usher people out, so don't save the best for last.

Every sight or museum offers more than what is covered in this book. Use the information in this book as an introduction—not the final word.

Sleeping

Accommodations in Switzerland are fairly expensive but are normally very comfortable and come with a cold buffet breakfast. Plan on spending about $130-180 for a double room in a hotel or $100-

120 for a double (with the bathroom down the hall) in a small guesthouse.

I favor hotels and restaurants that are handy to your sightseeing activities. I've scoured the options and presented you with the best values, from dorm beds to fancy doubles with all the comforts.

A major feature of this book is its extensive listing of good-value rooms. I like places that are clean, central, relatively quiet at night, reasonably priced, friendly, small enough to have a hands-on owner and stable staff, run with a respect for Swiss traditions, and not listed in other guidebooks. (In Switzerland, for me, six out of these eight criteria mean it's a keeper.) I'm more impressed by a convenient location and a fun-loving philosophy than flat-screen TVs and shoeshine machines. I've also thrown in a few hostels and other cheap options for budget travelers. The very best values are family-run places with showers down the hall and no elevator.

Book your accommodations well in advance if you'll be traveling during busy times. See page 391 for a list of major holidays and festivals in Switzerland; for tips on making reservations, see page 24.

Travel Review Websites: TripAdvisor (www.tripadvisor.com) and similar review websites are popular tools for finding hotels, but have drawbacks. To write a review, people need only an email address—making it easy to hide their true identity. If a hotel is well reviewed in a guidebook or two, and also gets good ratings on TripAdvisor, it's probably a safe bet—but I wouldn't stay at a hotel based solely on a TripAdvisor recommendation.

Rates and Deals

I've described my recommended accommodations using a "Sleep Code" (see the sidebar, next page). Prices listed are for one-night stays in peak season, include breakfast, and assume you're booking directly (not through a TI or online hotel-booking engine). Using a booking service costs the hotel about 20 percent and logically closes the door on special deals. Book direct.

Given the economic downturn, hoteliers are willing and eager to make a deal. I'd suggest emailing several hotels to ask for their best price. Comparison-shop and make your choice.

As you look over the listings, you'll notice that some accommodations promise special prices to my readers who book direct. To get these rates, you must mention this book when you reserve, and then show the book upon arrival. Some readers with ebooks have reported difficulty getting a Rick Steves discount. If this happens to you, please show this to the hotelier: Rick Steves discounts apply to readers with ebooks as well as printed books.

Sleep Code

1 Swiss franc (SF) = about $1.10

Price Rankings

To help you easily sort through my hotel listings, I've divided the accommodations into three categories based on the price for a double room with bath during high season:

$$$ Higher Priced
$$ Moderately Priced
$ Lower Priced

I always rate hostels as $, whether or not they have double rooms, because they have the cheapest beds in town. Prices can change without notice; verify the hotel's current rates online or by email. For other updates, see www.rick steves.com/update.

Abbreviations

To pack maximum information into minimum space, I use the following code to describe accommodations in this book. Prices listed are per room, not per person. When a price range is given for a type of room (such as double rooms listed for 100-130 SF), it means the price fluctuates with the season, size of room, or length of stay; expect to pay the upper end for peak-season stays.

S = Single room (or price for one person in a double).
D = Double or twin room. Double beds (which can be two twins sheeted together) are usually big enough for nonromantic couples.
T = Triple (generally a double bed with a single bed moved in).
Q = Quad (usually two double beds; adding an extra child's bed to a T is usually cheaper).
b = Private bathroom with toilet and shower or tub.
s = Private shower or tub only (the toilet is down the hall).

According to this code, a couple staying at a "Db-150 SF" hotel would pay a total of 150 Swiss francs (about $165) for a double room with a private bathroom. Unless otherwise noted, breakfast is included, hotel staff speak basic English, and credit cards are accepted.

If I mention "Internet access" in a hotel listing, there's a public terminal in the lobby for guests. If I specify "Wi-Fi," you can generally access it in public areas and often (though not always) in your room, but only if you have your own laptop or other Wi-Fi device. If you see "cable Internet," it means you can get online in your room with your laptop, provided you have (or borrow) an Ethernet cable to plug in.

In general, prices can soften if you do any of the following: offer to pay cash, stay at least three nights, or mention this book. You can also try asking for a cheaper room or a discount, or offer to skip breakfast.

A triple is cheaper than a double and a single. While hotel singles are expensive, rooms in simpler guesthouses often have a flat per-person rate. Hostels and dorms always charge per person. Especially in smaller pensions, people staying several nights are most desirable. One-night stays are sometimes charged extra.

Types of Accommodations
Hotels

Swiss hotels are, generally speaking, clean, comfortable, and efficiently run by English-speaking staff.

Smoking is prohibited in many Swiss hotels, some by law (depending on the region) and some by choice. Nearly all the hotels I list are completely non-smoking, and all of them offer non-smoking rooms. If it's important to you to have a non-smoking room, ask for one.

If you suspect night noise will be a problem (if, for instance, your room is over a nightclub), request a quiet room in the back or on an upper floor.

If you're arriving early in the morning, your room probably won't be ready. You should be able to safely check your bag at the hotel and dive right into sightseeing.

Most rooms have a sink and TV. For environmental reasons, towels are often replaced in hotels only when you leave them on the floor. In cheaper places, they aren't replaced at all, so hang them up to dry and reuse.

Hoteliers can be a great help and source of advice. Most know their city well, and can assist you with everything from public transit and airport connections to finding a good restaurant, the nearest launderette, or an Internet café. But even at the best places, mechanical breakdowns occur: Air-conditioning malfunctions, sinks leak, hot water turns cold, and toilets gurgle and smell. Report your concerns clearly and calmly at the front desk. For more complicated problems, don't expect instant results.

To guard against theft in your room, keep valuables out of sight. Some rooms come with a safe, and other hotels have safes at the front desk. Use them if you're concerned.

Checkout can pose problems if surprise charges pop up on your bill. If you settle your bill the night before you leave, you'll have time to discuss and address any points of contention (before 19:00, when the night shift usually arrives).

Above all, don't expect things to be the same as back home. Keep a positive attitude. Remember, you're on vacation. If your

Making Reservations

Given the good value of the accommodations I've found for this book, I'd recommend that you reserve your rooms in advance, particularly if you'll be traveling during peak season (especially for mountain resorts during summer weekends). Book several weeks ahead, or as soon as you've pinned down your travel dates. Note that some national holidays jam things up and merit your making reservations far in advance (for a list of holidays and festivals, see page 391).

Phoning: To call Switzerland from the US or Canada, dial 011-41 and then the local number. (The 011 is our international access code, and 41 is Switzerland's country code.) If you're calling Switzerland from another European country, dial 00-41-local number. (The 00 is Europe's international access code.) To make calls within Switzerland, just dial the local number. For more tips on calling, see page 367.

Requesting a Reservation: To make a reservation, contact hotels directly by email, phone, or fax. Email is the clearest and most economical way to make a reservation. Or you can go straight to the hotel website; many have secure online reservation forms and can instantly inform you of availability and any special deals. But be sure you use the hotel's official site and not a booking agency's site—otherwise you may pay higher rates than you should. Most recommended hoteliers are accustomed to guests who speak only English.

The hotelier wants to know these key pieces of information (also included in the sample request form in the appendix):
- number and type of rooms
- number of nights
- date of arrival
- date of departure
- any special needs (e.g., bathroom in the room or down the hall, twin beds vs. double bed, air-conditioning, quiet, view, ground floor, etc.)

When you request a room, use the European style for writing dates: day/month/year. For example, for a two-night stay in July 2013, I would request: "2 nights, arrive 16/07/13, depart 18/07/13." (Consider in advance how long you'll stay; don't just assume you can tack on extra days once you arrive.) Make sure you mention any discounts—for Rick Steves readers or otherwise—when you make the reservation.

hotel is a disappointment, spend more time out enjoying the city and mountains you came to see.

Pensions

Compared to hotels, pensions (small guesthouses) and rooms in private homes give you double the cultural intimacy for half the price. While you may lose some of the conveniences of a hotel—

Confirming a Reservation: If the hotel's response includes its room availability and rates, it's not a confirmation. You must tell them that you want that room at the given rate. Many hoteliers will request your credit-card number for a one-night deposit to hold the room. While you can email your credit-card information (I do), it's safer to share that personal info by phone call, fax, two successive emails, or secure online reservation form (if the hotel has one on its website).

Canceling a Reservation: If you must cancel your reservation, it's courteous to do so with as much advance notice as possible. Simply make a quick phone call or send an email. Family-run hotels lose money if they turn away customers while holding a room for someone who doesn't show up. Understandably, many hotels bill no-shows for one night.

Cancellation policies can be strict: For example, you might lose a deposit if you cancel within two weeks of your reserved stay, or you might be billed for the entire visit if you leave early. Internet deals may require prepayment, with no refunds for cancellations. Ask about cancellation policies before you book.

If canceling via email, request confirmation that your cancellation was received to avoid being accidentally billed.

Reconfirming a Reservation: Always call to reconfirm your room reservation a day or two in advance. (Don't have a TI call for you; they may take a commission.) Smaller hotels and B&B owners appreciate knowing your time of arrival. If you'll be arriving late (after 17:00), let them know. On the small chance that a hotel loses track of your reservation, bring along a hard copy of their emailed or faxed confirmation.

Reserving Rooms as You Travel: You can reserve while on the road, giving yourself the flexibility to modify your itinerary to adapt to the weather (spending rainy days in cities and sunny days in the mountains). You could call hotels a few days to a week before your stay. If everything's full, don't despair. Call a day or two in advance and fill in a cancellation. If you'd rather travel without any reservations at all, you'll have greater success snaring rooms if you arrive at your destination early in the day. When you anticipate crowds (weekends are worst), call hotels at about 9:00 on the day you plan to arrive, when the hotel clerk knows who'll be checking out and which rooms will be available.

such as lounges, in-room phones, daily bed-sheet changes, and credit-card payments—I happily make the trade-off for the lower rates and personal touches.

Small guesthouses go by several inexact German names: *Pension, Gasthaus, Gästezimmer,* even "B&B" (in French, it's also *pension*). In many parts of Switzerland, people rent out rooms *(Zimmer)* in their homes to travelers. Look for *Zimmer Frei,*

Zimmer mit Frühstück, or *Privatzimmer* signs in German-speaking areas and *chambres d'hôte* in French Switzerland. Booking direct saves both you and your host the cut the TI takes.

Don't confuse *Privatzimmer* with the *Ferienwohnung,* which is a self-catering apartment rented out by the week or fortnight.

Hostels

Switzerland has a wonderful network of hostels (*Jugendherberge* in German, *auberge de jeunesse* in French) that charge $25-35 per night for beds. Travelers of any age are welcome if they don't mind dorm-style accommodations (usually in rooms of four to eight beds) and meeting other travelers. Cheap meals are sometimes offered, and most hostels offer kitchen facilities, Internet access, Wi-Fi, and a self-service laundry. Bring a sleeping sheet or rent them as you go in most places (for a few francs). Expect youth groups in spring, crowds in the summer, snoring, and variability in quality from one hostel to the next. Family and private rooms are sometimes available on request.

Independent hostels tend to be more easygoing, colorful, fun, and informal (no membership required); see www.swissback packers.ch, www.hostelz.com, www.hostelseurope.com, www.hostels.com, and www.hostelworld.com.

Official hostels are part of Hostelling International and adhere to various rules (such as a lockout during the day and a curfew at night); they require that you either have a membership card or buy one-night guest memberships for 6 SF (www.hihostels.com). HI hostels are marked with either a triangular logo or a logo showing a tree next to a house.

Choose your hostel selectively. Hostels can be cozy mountain chalets, serene lakeside villas—or antiseptic spaces overrun by noisy school groups (most common on summer weekends and school-year weekdays). Though HI hostels are clean and predictable, they can also have an institutional feel.

Camping and Other Budget Beds

Campers can manage with *Let's Go* listings (see "Other Guide-books" on page 389) and help from the local TI (ask for a regional camping listing). Your hometown travel bookstore should also have guidebooks on camping in Europe. You'll find campgrounds just about everywhere you need them. Look for *Campingplatz* signs. You'll meet lots of Europeans, as camping is a popular, middle-class-family way to go. Campgrounds are cheap ($10 per person), friendly, safe, more central and convenient than rustic, and rarely full.

A fluffy straw bed awaits you at a number of farms that have opened their haylofts to sleepy tourists. It's a fun hostel alternative and more comfortable than you'd think (see www.schlaf-im-stroh.ch for details).

Many hotels, restaurants, and campsites provide dormitory-style accommodations. Look for the word *lager,* which indicates cheap dorm beds—often a loft lined with mattresses. These slumber mills may be less charming than cozy hostels, but they're cheap and convenient.

For serious hikers and climbers, mountain huts are an essential alpine experience. Don't expect ski-lodge comfort: These practical, adventurous places are simple, offering a warm place to sleep and (usually) breakfast and dinner. Most mountain-hut guests are long-distance hikers, connecting one hut to another along an extended hiking trail. You'll pay about $30 a night for your bunk and a little more for grub (see www.sac-cas.ch for more information).

Eating

The Swiss eat when we do and enjoy a straightforward, no-nonsense cuisine. Specialties include delicious fondue, rich chocolates, a melted cheese dish called raclette, *Rösti* (hash browns), fresh dairy products (try *Birchermüesli* for breakfast), 100 varieties of cheese, and Fendant—a good, crisp white wine.

Restaurants and Budget Options

When restaurant-hunting, choose a spot filled with locals, not the place with the big neon signs boasting, "We Speak English and Accept Credit Cards." Venturing even a block or two off the main drag leads to higher-quality food for less than half the price of the tourist-oriented places. Locals eat better at lower-rent locales.

Different kinds of restaurants offer different experiences. Hotels often serve fine food. A *Gaststätte* is a simple, less expensive restaurant. A *Weinstübli* (wine bar) or *Bierstübli* (tavern) usually serves food. Mountain huts—called *Hütte*—generally have hot chocolate and hearty meat-and-potato meals. Smoking is no longer allowed inside Switzerland's eateries (though a few places skirt the laws with enclosed verandas for smokers).

If you're not too hungry, order from the *kleine Hunger* (small hunger) section of the menu. Many restaurants offer half-portions, which is a great relief on your budget (although two people save even more by sharing one full portion).

Most restaurants tack a menu onto their door for browsers and have an English menu inside. If you ask for the *Menü* (or *menu* in

French), you won't get a list of dishes; you'll get a fixed-price meal of several courses. If you simply want a list of what's cooking, ask for *die Speisekarte* (dee SHPIE-seh-kar-teh; *la carte* in French).

Only a rude waiter will rush you. Good service is relaxed (slow to an American). To wish others "Happy eating!" offer a cheery *"En Guete!"* When you want the bill, request the *"Rechnung, bitte."* (See the the survival phrases in the appendix for more tips.)

Swiss restaurants are expensive, but there are several excellent budget alternatives. The Co-op and Migros grocery stores are the hungry hiker's best budget bet; groceries, while about 50 percent more than US prices, are a huge savings over any restaurant. These supermarkets often come with cheap non-smoking self-service cafeterias, with good food at much lower prices than restaurants with table service. In most big cities, you'll find Manor ("mahn-NOR") department stores, which usually feature wonderful self-service eateries called "Manora"—with lush salad bars, tasty entrées, and fresh-squeezed juices (I've listed several specific Manora locations in this book). Bakeries are another great place for a snack or affordable light meal.

Swiss Cuisine

Here at a crossroads of Europe, the food has a wonderful diversity: heavy *Wurst*-and-kraut Germanic fare; delicate, subtle French cuisine; and pasta dishes *all'Italiana*.

Aside from clocks and banks, Switzerland is known for its cheese. Gruyère cheese is hard, with a strong flavor; Emmentaler is also hard, but milder (and looks like what we call "Swiss cheese"). Appenzeller is the incredibly pungent cheese from the northeast of Switzerland, with a smell that verges on nauseating...until you taste it. Two of Switzerland's best-known specialties are cheese-based.  *Käsefondue* is usually Emmentaler and Gruyère cheese melted with white wine, garlic, nutmeg, and other seasonings. You eat it with a long fork, dipping cubes of bread into it. Raclette is cheese slowly melted on a special dish; as it softens, scrape a mound off and eat it with potatoes, pickled onions, and gherkins. (In restaurants, raclette often comes as little slices of cheese already melted.)

Another must-try dish, most typical in the mountains of the German-speaking areas, is *Rösti:* traditional hash browns with alpine cheese, often served with a bit of bacon or ham, or with an egg cracked over it...yum.

Despite all the cheese and potatoes, the Swiss tend to be

health-conscious; after all, they invented muesli. While the dry muesli served at every breakfast buffet is unremarkable, *Birchermüesli*—a yummy mixture of fresh yogurt, fresh fruit, and juice-soaked oats—is worth seeking out in supermarket delis and on café menus. Menus often feature a *Fitnessteller* ("fitness plate")—usually a large mixed salad that comes with a steak, chicken, or fish. *Bio* means organically grown (a *Biolädeli* is a store that sells organic products).

Of course, each region has its own specialties. In French-speaking Switzerland, white wine and heavy cream are used in many dishes, and horsemeat (formerly imported from Eastern Europe, now imported from the US, New Zealand, and Australia) is common. The cuisine in eastern Switzerland (Pontresina, St. Moritz) uses chestnuts in many forms, wild mushrooms, and air-dried beef. Southwestern Switzerland (Zermatt area) specializes in all kinds of cheese, and their favorite white wine is Fendant.

Swiss wine is good, but expensive because of high production costs and mostly small vineyards. The Swiss certainly have plenty of wine-making experience—they've been growing grapes since Roman times. Since Swiss wine is not well-known outside of the country, and very little is exported, this is your chance to try the local *Wein/vin/vino*. About two-thirds of the production is white, and much of that is made from the Chasselas (a.k.a. Fendant) grape. The dry, white Fendant is great with cheese dishes. Fruity St. Saphorin wines from the slopes above Lake Geneva rank among the best Swiss whites. If you're in Murten, sample Vully wine (both red and white) from sunny lakeshore vineyards. Dôle, a light-bodied red wine made from the Pinot Noir grape, is popular for sipping.

Menus list drink size by the "deci"—a deciliter (dl, tenth of a liter). In German-speaking areas, order wine by the *Glas* (glass) or *Viertel* (quarter liter, or 8 oz.). Order it *süss* (sweet), *halb trocken* (medium), or *trocken* (dry); *weiss* (white), or *rot* (red). You can say, "*Ein Viertel Weisswein* (white wine), *bitte* (please)." For fun, try ordering the same thing in colloquial Swiss German: *"Ä Viertel Wiisewyy, bitte"* (ih FEER-tehl VEE-seh-vee, BIT-teh).

In French Switzerland, wine comes either by *le verre* (a glass, 1-2 dl), *la carafe* (3 dl or 5 dl), or *la bouteille* (bottle). Order by requesting *"Un verre de vin blanc, s'il vous plaît"* (or *"vin rouge"* if you prefer red). In the Ticino region, *un boccalino* is a small, decorated eight-ounce ceramic jug filled with the local red wine.

Swiss beer is surprisingly good and inexpensive. Most of the beer is light, golden-colored lager, but you'll also find other types, such as *Hefeweizen* and *Dunkel* (dark) beers. Each pub has one brand of a local beer on tap, with others available in bottles. Feldschlössen is the largest brewery in the country, and you'll see

Swiss Chocolate:
The Souvenir that Disappears

Of Switzerland's well-known icons—watches, banks, gadgety knives, booze-bearing mountain dogs—only one makes would-be visitors salivate in anticipation: chocolate. There's nothing like the taste and feeling of a square of Swiss chocolate slowly melting over your tongue. As you travel in Switzerland, treat your taste buds and sweet tooth to their own adventure.

But why does *Swiss* chocolate hold such cachet? The answer dates back to 1819, when François-Louis Cailler first figured out how to mechanize chocolate production and set up a factory near Lake Geneva. After Cailler, other innovative chocolatiers (many whose brands are still sold today) continually improved the quality of Swiss chocolate by pioneering new techniques—most notably, the invention of milk chocolate and the process that makes solid chocolate smooth.

However, it wasn't until the 1890s that Swiss chocolate really began to take off, when the Golden Age of Swiss tourism spurred a Golden Age of Swiss chocolate. Chocolate companies cleverly targeted vacationers (and well-to-do foreign students in Swiss boarding schools), who returned home with a chocolate habit and chocolatey gifts for friends and family. By the 1910s, about 75 percent of the chocolate produced here was being exported—and tiny Switzerland had a solid 55 percent chunk in the world's chocolate export market.

Today, Swiss chocolate is still a highly desired souvenir, and what had been a small collection of "manufactories" has become a $1.8 billion industry. The Swiss, who affectionately refer to chocolate as *schoggi*, provide no small domestic demand: The average Swiss eats 22 pounds of chocolate a year—the highest per-capita consumption in the world.

The industry's success is also due to rigorous quality standards. These regulations are upheld by Chocosuisse, an umbrella association of manufacturers that's actively involved in ensuring goodness with every nibble or chomp off a Swiss chocolate

its red-castle logo all over. But the Swiss are loyal to their local brews; for example, in the Appenzell region, Appenzeller is the beer of choice. The standard size, measured in centiliters (cl), is a *Stange* (33 cl); the smaller size is called a *Herrgöttli* (20 cl). Beer mixed with lemon-flavored pop is called a *Panaché*. In summer, this lightly sweet, sudsy drink is more refreshing than straight beer.

Instead of Coke, try a local favorite: Rivella, a carbonated, vitamin-rich soft drink made with 35 percent milk serum. Its unusual (but not unpleasant) taste doesn't resemble milk at all; it's more like chewable vitamins. It comes in four colors: red is regu-

bar. Chocosuisse regulates most steps of the production process, from where the ingredients are grown to the design and maintenance of high-tech machines. Only chocolate actually produced in the country is granted the honor of being called Swiss-made.

When looking for high-quality chocolate, notice the way the chocolate breaks (a clean break with no crumbles is best), how it melts (like butter?), how it feels in your mouth (the smoother the better), and whether it leaves any gritty, unchocolatey aftertaste.

Of course, the only way to know what you like best is to try lots of different kinds (in the name of science!). The vast variety of chocolate flavors available in any Swiss supermarket—let alone a specialty chocolate shop—is staggering. The big-name brands—such as Lindt, Toblerone, and Cailler—are everywhere; keep your eyes peeled for lesser-known brands like Läderach, a favorite among many Swiss. If you prefer milk chocolate, look for bars marked *Vollmilch* or *Alpenmilch*; dark chocolate fans want the *edelbitter* or *dunkeler* stuff, and *weisse Schokolade* is white chocolate. Bars with percentages printed on them are boasting their high cocoa content (the higher the number, the more bitter the chocolate). Common additions include *Haselnuss* (hazelnuts), *Mandeln* (almonds), *Trauben* (grapes/raisins), and *Joghurt* (guess). Connoisseurs watch for seasonal flavors, determined by holidays and what fruit's in season. If you're planning on bringing home gifts, poll your recipients to make sure you know who prefers what, and who's up for trying some of the more exotic options, such as Läderach's pepper-strawberry bar.

Switzerland offers surprisingly few worthwhile sights for the choco-curious. You can ride the Chocolate Train (see page 267), which combines three Swiss greats—rail travel, panoramic Alps views, and chocolate noshing—and stops for a visit at the Cailler factory in the hills above Lake Geneva (see page 272). But for my favorite Swiss chocolate experience, I simply pack along some of my favorite bars on a high mountain hike.

lar; blue is low-calorie; green is mixed with green tea; and yellow is soy-based. Tap water, which many waiters aren't eager to bring you, is *Leitungswasser* (*l'eau du robinet* in French). Ask for it by name, or you'll receive—and be charged for—*Mineralwasser* (*mit/ohne Gas*, with/without carbonation).

As an alternative to hot chocolate, try Ovomaltine. The Swiss have a fondness for this hot drink—a malt-derived vitamin supplement, flavored with chocolate so kids will drink it. (In the US, our Ovaltine is an Asian variation on this drink—considered by the Swiss to be a cheap copy.)

And, of course, there's chocolate. The Swiss changed the

INTRODUCTION

How Was Your Trip?

Were your travels fun, smooth, and meaningful? If you'd like to share your tips, concerns, and discoveries, please fill out the survey at www.ricksteves.com/feedback. I value your feedback. Thanks in advance—it helps a lot.

world in 1875 with their invention of milk chocolate. Stroll the chocolate aisle of a grocery store and take your pick.

Traveling as a Temporary Local

We travel all the way to Switzerland to enjoy differences—to become temporary locals. You'll experience frustrations. Certain truths that we find "God-given" or "self-evident," such as cold beer, ice in drinks, bottomless cups of coffee, hot showers, and bigger being better, are suddenly not so true. One of the benefits of travel is the eye-opening realization that there are logical, civil, and even better alternatives. A willingness to go local ensures that you'll enjoy a full dose of Swiss hospitality.

Europeans generally like Americans. But if there is a negative aspect to the Swiss image of Americans, it's that we are big, loud, aggressive, impolite, rich, superficially friendly, and a bit naive.

My Swiss friends (and Europeans in general) place a high value on speaking quietly in restaurants and on trains. Listen while on the bus or in a restaurant—the place can be packed, but the decibel level is low. Try to adjust your volume accordingly to show respect for their culture.

While the Swiss look bemusedly at some of our Yankee excesses—and worriedly at others—they nearly always afford us individual travelers all the warmth we deserve.

Judging from all the happy feedback I receive from travelers who have used this book, it's safe to assume you'll enjoy a great, affordable vacation—with the finesse of an independent, experienced traveler.

Thanks, and happy travels—*gute Reise!*

Back Door Travel Philosophy
From *Rick Steves' Europe Through the Back Door*

Travel is intensified living—maximum thrills per minute and one of the last great sources of legal adventure. Travel is freedom. It's recess, and we need it.

Experiencing the real Europe requires catching it by surprise, going casual..."Through the Back Door."

Affording travel is a matter of priorities. (Make do with the old car.) You can eat and sleep—simply, safely, and comfortably—anywhere in Europe for $120 a day plus transportation costs (allow more for bigger cities). In many ways, spending more money only builds a thicker wall between you and what you traveled so far to see. Europe is a cultural carnival, and time after time, you'll find that its best acts are free and the best seats are the cheap ones.

A tight budget forces you to travel close to the ground, meeting and communicating with the people. Never sacrifice sleep, nutrition, safety, or cleanliness to save money. Simply enjoy the local-style alternatives to expensive hotels and restaurants.

Connecting with people carbonates your experience. Extroverts have more fun. If your trip is low on magic moments, kick yourself and make things happen. If you don't enjoy a place, maybe you don't know enough about it. Seek the truth. Recognize tourist traps. Give a culture the benefit of your open mind. See things as different, but not better or worse. Any culture has plenty to share.

Of course, travel, like the world, is a series of hills and valleys. Be fanatically positive and militantly optimistic. If something's not to your liking, change your liking.

Travel can make you a happier American, as well as a citizen of the world. Our Earth is home to seven billion equally precious people. It's humbling to travel and find that other people don't have the "American Dream"—they have their own dreams. Europeans like us, but, with all due respect, they wouldn't trade passports.

Thoughtful travel engages you with the world. In tough economic times, it reminds us what is truly important. By broadening perspectives, travel teaches new ways to measure quality of life.

Globetrotting destroys ethnocentricity, helping us understand and appreciate other cultures. Rather than fear the diversity on this planet, celebrate it. Among your most prized souvenirs will be the strands of different cultures you choose to knit into your own character. The world is a cultural yarn shop, and Back Door travelers are weaving the ultimate tapestry. Join in!

SWITZERLAND

Switzerland is one of Europe's richest, best organized, most expensive countries. Like the Boy Scouts, the Swiss count cleanliness, neatness, punctuality, tolerance, independence, thrift, and hard work as virtues...and they love pocketknives. The country is an enjoyable mix of bucolic peace and daring adventure. Around every alpine turn, you feel you could get a glimpse of Heidi milking a cow or James Bond schussing past on skis.

Nearly half of Switzerland—Europe's most mountainous country—consists of uninhabitable rocks and rugged Alps. It seems that any flat land (and quite a bit of hilly land) is cultivated into tidy little farms. While landlocked, Switzerland has more than its share of clear rivers and big, beautiful lakes with a striking mountain backdrop (such as

Lake Geneva, Lake Murten, Lake Luzern, and Lake Lugano—all covered in this book).

Despite the country's small size, Switzerland is unusually diverse. Its wild geography has kept people apart historically, helping its many regions maintain their distinct cultural differences.

The abbreviation for Swiss Federal Railways—in German, French, and Italian

Switzerland has four official languages: German, French, Italian, and Romansh (an obscure Latin dialect).

And yet, regardless of which language is spoken, the entire country is unmistakably Swiss. Everyday things like the post office, train station, or familiar products have the same signage and logos, but in different languages. And everywhere you go, you'll

Switzerland: Western Europe's Linguistic Crossroads

You'd be forgiven for thinking of Switzerland as a "German" country. The heart of Switzerland, with about three-fifths

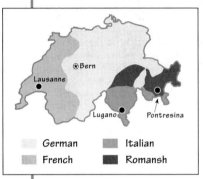

of the population and most of the famous cities and sights, is linguistically (as well as culturally) Germanic. But even here, Germans and Austrians don't feel quite at home. As if keeping alive an archaic code for insiders, the Swiss speak to each other in the lilting, fun-to-listen-to Swiss German, a.k.a. *Schwyzertütsch,* then switch seamlessly to standard German (or English) when interacting with outsiders.

Surrounding the German-speaking core is a more colorful Romance language-speaking fringe—French (to the west), Italian (to the south), and Romansh (tucked in the southeastern mountains). Switzerland's biggest canton, officially trilingual, is its linguistic melting pot: the southeastern region called Graubünden (in German), Grigioni (in Italian), and Grischun (in Romansh).

Subtle differences in cuisine, climate, and landscape seem to match the linguistic boundaries. German-speaking Switzerland enjoys a vigorous efficiency reminiscent of Germany's. The pace in genteel French-speaking Switzerland is a bit mellower, the cuisine and lifestyle more refined, resembling France's. And the relatively balmy Italian-speaking canton of Ticino comes with a touch of chaos and lust for life that's not far removed from Italy proper (which surrounds it on three sides). You can spend a week in Switzerland and feel almost as if you've traveled from Paris to Munich to Rome... without ever crossing a border.

notice a dedication to order and organization that distinguishes Swiss culture. It's refreshing to visit a predictable place where, once you've got the gist of things in one city, you generally know what to expect in the next.

That sort of orderliness doesn't happen by itself. The Swiss jealously guard their way of life. If you accidentally drop a scrap of paper on the ground, someone might cross the street to be sure you pick it up. As if belonging to an exclusive club that's careful about admitting new members, the Swiss strike some visitors as a bit standoffish—polite but not gregarious, welcoming but perhaps

Switzerland Almanac

Official Name: The Confoederatio Helvetica, or Switzerland, has a different name in each of its four official languages: Schweizerische Eidgenossenschaft (German), Confédération Suisse (French), Confederazione Svizzera (Italian), and Confederaziun Svizra (Romansh). Locals shorten those to "die Schweiz," "la Suisse," "la Svizzera," and "la Svizra."

Population: Switzerland has 7.6 million people (similar to the population of Washington State); 65 percent speak German as their main language, 18 percent speak French, 10 percent speak Italian, and about 1 percent speak Romansh. About 23 percent of Swiss residents come from other countries and range from EU businesspeople to immigrant workers. The populace is 42 percent Catholic, 35 percent Protestant, 2 percent Orthodox, 4 percent Muslim, and 17 percent other or unspecified.

Latitude and Longitude: 47°N and 8°E, similar latitude to Quebec, Canada.

Area: 16,000 square miles; twice the size of New Jersey, or half the size of South Carolina.

Geography: Switzerland sits at the crossroads between northern and southern Europe. The Alps are Europe's high point and continental divide, from which the major rivers flow—Rhine, Rhône, Danube, and Po. Switzerland's highest point is the 15,200-foot Monte Rosa (specifically, the summit called Dufourspitze), along the Italian border. Though Switzerland is mostly mountainous, the center of the country consists of rolling hills and large lakes.

Biggest Cities: One in seven Swiss lives in or near Zürich (pop. 370,000 in the city; 1 million in the metropolitan area). Geneva has 178,000 people, and Basel has 165,000. The capital is Bern (pop. 123,000).

Economy: Like a fine watch, Switzerland's economy just keeps on ticking. The Gross Domestic Product is $325 billion, similar to that of Washington State. Its per-capita GDP of

a bit suspicious. If you find the Swiss to be a little buttoned-down, remember that the payoff is a beautiful country where the trains run on time, the streets are clean, and every flower petal is perfectly in place.

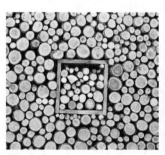

While it's one of Europe's most progressive "big-government" countries—with high taxation, ample social services, and liberal drug policies—Switzerland's devotion to order and predictability also gives it a sometimes surprising conservative streak. Traditional mind-sets

$43,000 is among Europe's highest (but still 9 percent less than the US). The franc is strong, workers are highly skilled, and unemployment is less than half the European Union average. Blessed with hydropower and using nuclear technology, Switzerland generates 99 percent of its electricity with virtually no oil.

Currency: 1 Swiss franc (SF) = 100 rappen/centimes = about $1.10.

Government: Founded in 1291 as a confederation of cantons, the country is still a model of federalism, balancing the needs of its different linguistic/ethnic groups. No single political party (or two or even three parties) dominates. The president, chosen by the legislature, serves for just one calendar year. The two-house Federal Assembly consists of the 46-seat Council of States and the 200-seat National Council, elected for four-year terms.

Flag: Switzerland's white cross on a distinctively square red background may have been the inspiration for the red-on-white symbol of the International Red Cross. It's one of only two recognized flags that are perfect squares (the other being the flag of Vatican City).

The Average Swiss: He or she has 1.46 children and will live to be 81. A typical Swiss man serves at least 260 days of compulsory service in the military. The average woman spends two hours a day on housework. He or she travels about 1,300 miles a year on a train, the equivalent of crossing the country six times. Every month, the average Swiss drinks a quart of alcohol and eats nearly two pounds of chocolate.

persist in the remote mountain hamlets—for example, women weren't guaranteed the right to vote in federal elections until 1971 (and, until 1990, could still be barred from local elections).

Historically, Switzerland is one of Europe's oldest democracies. Born when three states (cantons) united in 1291, over time the Swiss Confederation grew to the 26 cantons of today. The "CH" decal on cars doesn't stand for chocolate...but for "Confoederatio Helvetica," the country's official title (using the Latin name avoids linguistic controversy). The country is named for the Celtic Helvetii tribe that lived here back in Roman times. (Stamp collectors know to identify a Swiss stamp by looking for the word *Helvetia*.) The Confederation government is decentralized, and cantonal loyalty is very strong.

Similar to US states, each canton is semi-independent. Just as we debate "states' rights," the Swiss wrangle with just how much autonomy to allow cantons. Considering that each comes with not only its own political concerns, but also its own dialect and cultural heritage, cantonal independence is particularly important and delicate.

With the exception of the Protestant Reformation (see sidebar on page 52), Swiss history has been pretty quiet...and that's just how the Swiss like it. They're happy to be high and dry in the mountains, watching from above the fray as the tides of history swirl around them (for an overview, see the Switzerland: Past and Present chapter). Stubbornly independent, or maybe just smart, Switzerland loves its neutrality and stayed out of both world wars. But it's far from lax when it comes to national defense—on the contrary, the Swiss are legendary for their military readiness. A vast reserve army and a countryside embedded with hidden fortresses have earned Switzerland its unique ability to preserve its right to self-determination well into the 21st century, even though it's surrounded by bigger, stronger nations. Through the tumult of the 20th century, no foreign invaders dared to try cracking this nut.

Even so, for more than a century and a half, a different kind of invasion—of tourists—has descended on Switzerland each summer (for hiking season, all summer long but busiest July-Aug) and each winter (for ski season, roughly Christmas through Easter). You'll share the trails and lifts with a deluge of international visitors—from Europe, the US, and the rest of the world. Because several Bollywood movies have used the Swiss Alps as a stand-in for Kashmir, Switzerland is popular with tourists from India. And Middle Eastern visitors flock here to escape the heat. Locals report a spike in Middle Eastern tourists in the weeks leading up to the sacred, month-long observance of Ramadan...when their numbers drop to virtually zero, as Muslims go back home to spend time with their families.

Though not a European Union member—that neutrality thing again—Switzerland conforms to EU standards to stay competitive. Major Swiss moneymakers include banking (especially secret, private accounts from around the world), insurance, watches (from top-of-the-line pieces to inexpensive Swatches), chemicals and pharmaceuticals, chocolate (Nestlé is the biggest producer), tourism, and precision instruments. Swiss-made equipment helps produce everything from clothing to ballpoint-pen tips to parts for the Mars Exploration Rover. Swiss ingenuity is nowhere more apparent than in the famous Swiss Army knives, which come in sizes big and small, with as many—or as few—tools as any arm-chair MacGyver could need.

Perhaps owing to its economic might, Switzerland has earned a reputation for being one of Europe's most expensive countries. A night on the town can be a major splurge. Locals call sitting on the pavement around a bottle of wine "going out." Hotels with double rooms for less than $100 are rare. Even dormitory beds are expensive. If your budget is tight, be sure to chase down hostels (many have private rooms for couples and families), and keep your eyes peeled for *Matratzenlagers* ("mattress dorms"). Hiking is free, though most major alpine lifts cost at least $50.

Switzerland has more than its share of cosmopolitan cities. My favorites—Zürich, Luzern, Bern, Lausanne, and Lugano—are

covered in this book. Each one offers an enticing, I-could-live-here glimpse of the appealing and uniquely Swiss urban quality of life: efficient trams and buses gliding around town, manicured pedestrian zones teeming with locals enjoying their cities, crystal-clear rivers and lakes made accessible by scenic cruise boats, eclectic restaurants offering a tasty range of both Swiss and international cuisine, and low-key but generally compelling museums. While Switzerland lacks a world-class metropolis on par with Paris or Rome, all of its cities are surprisingly engaging—especially if bad weather keeps you from heading for the hills.

But let's face it: Travelers don't flock to Switzerland for its cities. Spend most of your time getting high in the Alps. You can climb onto a train in one of Switzerland's most bustling stations and, within an hour or two, step off into an idyllic time-warp world where traditional culture still thrives. Alpine villages (such as Gimmelwald) and towns (such as Appenzell) give you a taste of rural Switzerland, and are the perfect base for pastoral countryside hikes or riding lifts to dramatic cut-glass alpine panoramas.

If you're in the countryside on a

SWITZERLAND

Understanding the Alps

Switzerland's snowy, rugged mountains are its claim to fame—and most likely the main reason for your visit. Fortunately, you don't have to be a mountain climber to see the Alps up close, as the Swiss transportation system is as remarkable as its mountains. Its cog railways, gondolas, and cable cars whisk you up into the type of scenery that's only accessible in some countries by ropes, pitons, and crampons.

The Alps were formed by the collision of two continents. About 100 million years ago, the African plate began pushing north against the stable plates of Europe and Asia. In the process, the sediments of the ancient Tethys Ocean (which occupied the general real estate of the modern Mediterranean) became smooshed between the landmasses. Shoving all this material together made the rocks and sediments fold, shatter, and pile on top of each other; over millennia this growing jumble built itself up into today's Alps. Up in the mountains, look for folds and faults in the rocks that hint at this immense compression, which is still happening today: The Alps continue to rise by at least a millimeter each year (while erosion wears them down at about the same rate).

The current shape of the mountains and valleys is the handiwork of at least five ice ages over the last two million years. Glaciers flowed down the mountain valleys, scooped out Switzerland's beautiful alpine lakes, and carried rocks far away from where they had formed. The Alps were the first mountains extensively studied by geologists, and many of the geological terms that describe mountains originated here. Once you learn how to recognize a few of the landforms shaped by glaciers, you can easily spot these features when you visit other alpine areas. Study glacier exhibits to train your eye to recognize what you're seeing.

Glaciers are big and blunt, so they make simple, large-scale marks on the landscape. If a valley is U-shaped (with steep sides and a rounded base), it likely was scoured out by a glacier. Switzerland's Lauterbrunnen Valley and California's Yosemite Valley are classic examples.

A **cirque** (French for "circus") is the amphitheater-like depression carved out at the upper part of a valley by a glacier. If two adjacent cirques erode close to each other, a sharp steep-sided ridge forms, called an **arête** (French for "fishbone"). Cirques and arêtes are common in mountains with glaciers. More rarely, when three or more cirques erode toward one another, a pyramidal peak is created, called a **horn.** The Matterhorn is the world's most famous example. Glaciers flowed down all sides of this mountain, scooping material away and creating the distinctive sharp peak.

A common feature left behind by retreating glaciers is a **moraine,** a pile of dirt and rocks carried along on the glacier as it advanced, then dumped as the glacier melted. The Lindenhof in Zürich, a hilltop square once crowned with forts to defend the town, perches on a moraine.

Alpine glaciers can only originate above the snowline, so if you see any of these landforms (U-shaped valleys, cirques, horns, or moraines) in lower elevations, you know that the climate there used to be colder. The effects of a warming climate have profoundly hit the glaciers of Switzerland, which have lost at least a third of their volume since the 1950s. Some studies project that at that rate most glaciers in Switzerland could virtually disappear by the end of the century, affecting water storage and hydroelectric power generation.

In higher elevations, mountainsides have become less stable due to the melting of permafrost. A heat wave in 2003 caused several rockfalls on the Matterhorn, resulting in trail closures and the evacuation of dozens of climbers trapped on the summit. The ski resort of Pontresina built a dam in 2002 to protect the town from a potential landslide from its nearby mountain.

Another consequence of the warming climate is that winter weather no longer reliably produces snow at altitudes that it did in the past—which is bad news for Switzerland's huge ski industry. Seeing a future of ever-warmer winters, the Swiss are putting their ingenuity to the test. This goes beyond snow machines: Many resorts are investing hugely in new spas, convention centers, and other attractions that don't require snow.

With their acute awareness of their alpine climate's fragility, the Swiss are especially keen to explore green technology—even high up in the Alps. For example, in 2009, the Monte Rosa mountain refuge opened in the Alps near Zermatt. Unlike the rustic, stone-hut chalets that dot other alpine areas, this one is a futuristic-looking, high-tech building that gets 90 percent of its energy from solar power. The Monte Rosa hut is considered an example of how Switzerland's technological innovation can help keep its mountains white and its valleys green.

Sunday, you'll most likely enjoy traditional music, clothing, and culture. At the end of a day of hiking, you can retreat to a village enclave preserving a colorful, rustic, rural way of life. Because the Swiss government values the traditional lifestyles, it subsidizes families who raise cows and make cheese the old-fashioned way. In the spring and again in the fall, you might be lucky enough to see a parade of cows on their way up to or back down from the high-mountain pastures. For the whole story, see the sidebar on page 170.

The cows have also had a big impact on Swiss cuisine—especially cheese. Two of the most revered Swiss cheeses are the smooth Gruyère cheese (from the town of Gruyères) and the stinky Appenzeller cheese (from the region of Appenzell). In these areas, you can watch the cheese being made—just as it has been for centuries...or at modern facilities using technology to carry out the same age-old processes (including robots that tenderly  rub and flip each aging wheel of cheese). Cheese shops (*Käserei* in German) sell a fragrant festival of mold, perfect for picnicking or for making two famous Swiss culinary specialties: fondue (a pot of cheese melted into wine) or raclette (cheese melted over potatoes and other vegetables). But after a few days of cheese plates for breakfast, cheese sandwiches for lunch, and cheese specialties for dinner, even the biggest cheese-lovers might find they need a dairy detox. For more on Swiss cuisine, see page 28.

Switzerland's public transportation system is tops, whether you want to go across the country or straight up into the mountains. The country is crisscrossed with fine autobahns and arguably Europe's most efficient rail system. Boats ply the tranquil waters of the country's many lakes, and PostBuses (operated by the post office) pick you up in the rare situations that trains let you down. You can even go *through* the mountains, thanks to long tunnels (but you'll miss the views). Try the variety of fun cogwheel trains, funiculars, and cable cars that deliver you—no matter the season—from sunny valleys up to dizzying heights and snowy vistas. For a rundown of your options—from cable cars to gondolas to funiculars—see the sidebar on page 379.

Switzerland's best attraction might just be hiding between the cities and the villages: In this land of dramatic mountains and picture-perfect farms, perhaps more than anywhere else in Europe, the journey is the destination. The Swiss Railway markets several scenic journeys that run along the country's prettiest

routes, many with special panoramic trains designed to maximize views (for details, see the Scenic Rail Journeys chapter). But don't let the tourist hype give you tunnel vision. A sunny day spent on a train just about anywhere in Switzerland can rank as a memorable trip-capper.

From its famous efficiency, to its unique mingling of the modern and the traditional, to its flat-out spectacular scenery, Switzerland delights the Swiss...and their visitors.

SWITZERLAND

ZÜRICH

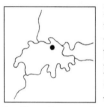

Zürich is one of those cities that tourists tend to skip right through. Since it's a transportation hub, people fly in or change trains here, but don't give stopping a serious thought. The local graffiti jokes: *Zürich = zu reich, zu ruhig* ("too rich, too quiet"). But even though you won't find a hint of Swiss Miss in Switzerland's leading city—and with limited time, I'd certainly spend it up in the mountains—Zürich is surprisingly comfortable and enjoyable for a quick visit.

Zürich was founded by the Romans as a customs post (in prehistoric times, people lived on pilings near the shores of Lake Zürich). Roman Turicum eventually became Zürich. It gained city status in the 10th century, and by the 19th century it was a leading European financial and economic center. Today, thanks largely to Switzerland's long-term economic and political stability, Zürich is a major hub of international banking. Assuming you've got the money to enjoy it, Zürich is by many measures the world's most livable city. Its 370,000 people (1 million in greater Zürich) are known for their wealth and hard work. Zürich is the only place in Switzerland where you'll see men in ties running in the streets.

Planning Your Time

While Luzern and Bern provide more charming urban experiences, Zürich is worth a quick visit. With two weeks in Switzerland, I'd spend a day here. Begin by visiting the impressive Swiss National Museum, then wander along the river, using my self-guided walk, and take a river/lake cruise. With less time, do only the self-guided walk; with more time, take your pick of the many museums.

Orientation to Zürich

Zürich sprawls around the northern tip of the long, skinny Lake Zürich (Zürichsee). The grand Bahnhofstrasse cuts through the city's glitzy shopping center—a 15-minute walk along here connects the train station and the country's top historical museum (Swiss National Museum) with the lakefront. Across the Limmat River is the Niederdorf neighborhood, a vibrant, cobbled, Old World zone of colorful little shops, cafés, and restaurants.

Tourist Information

A helpful TI is located in the great hall of the train station (under the fat blue angel; May-Oct Mon-Sat 8:00-20:30, Sun 8:30-18:30; Nov-April Mon-Sat 8:30-19:00, Sun 9:00-18:30; tel. 044-215-4000, www.zuerich.com). Pick up their city guide and map, browse the racks of brochures, and ask about their daily walking tours.

For a whirlwind visit, consider the **ZürichCARD**, which covers transportation by train, tram, bus, and boat (including trips to the airport and up to the Uetliberg viewpoint); admission to most of the city's museums (usually permanent exhibits only); half off the city walking tour; and freebies in many restaurants (20 SF/24 hours, 40 SF/72 hours, sold at TI). The one-day card will pay for itself if you do the walking tour and at least one museum in a day. The TI also sells a 24-hour transit pass (8.20 SF).

Tours: You can see Zürich on a two-hour **guided walk** (similar to the self-guided walk in this chapter; 20 SF, half-price with Swiss Pass or ZürichCARD; leaves from TI April-Oct daily at 15:00, Sat-Sun also at 11:00; Nov-March Wed and Sat-Sun at 11:00, Sat also at 15:00). On weekends from June to August there's also a one-hour version (15 SF, no discounts, departs at 17:30). If you'd rather ride than walk, consider the **trolley** tour with headphone commentary (2 hours, 33 SF, daily at 9:45, 12:00, and 14:00 year-round, leaves from bus lot behind train station). The TI has details on these and several other tours.

Arrival in Zürich

The slick **train** station (with a TI, lockers, and shopping mall) is on the north end of downtown; to reach most of my recommended hotels, cross the Walche-Brücke bridge in front of the station. If arriving by **plane** at Zürich Airport, see page 68.

Getting Around Zürich

On the trams and buses, a ticket good for one short ride (within five stops) costs 2.60 SF (1-hour ticket-4.10 SF, 24-hour transit pass-8.60 SF, www.zvv.ch). You can buy tram/bus tickets from ticket machines at stops, at public-transit booths (marked ZVV), and at the train station. You can't buy tickets on board, and it's a 100-SF fine if you're caught without one. All transportation is covered by the Swiss Pass and ZürichCARD, described earlier.

Helpful Hints

Medical Help: The **Permanence** drop-in clinic on the main floor of the train station offers on-the-spot medical aid (daily 7:00-22:00, Bahnhofplatz 15, tel. 044-215-4444). A dentist is on the lower level.

Internet Access: Internetcafe.ch, a five-minute walk from the station, has plenty of services but steep prices (3 SF/10 minutes, Mon-Fri 7:00-23:00, Sat 8:00-23:00, Sun 10:00-22:00, Uraniastrasse 3, tel. 044-210-3311, www.internetcafe.ch). Cheaper Internet is available at the hole-in-the-wall **Global Prepaid Card Center,** five minutes from the station, but away from town and not on the way to anything (5 SF/hour, Mon-Sat 10:00-22:00, Sun 10:30-20:00, Konrad Strasse 3, tel. 044-440-7500).

Baggage Storage: The train station has plenty of lockers (small locker-6 SF, large locker-9 SF).

Laundry: There is no central launderette in town, but many hotels will do laundry by request for a fee.

Bikes: A city program called "Züri rollt" allows you to borrow a bike for free (must leave passport and 20-SF deposit, daily 8:00-21:30, can bring bikes back as late as 23:00 but it'll cost you 10 SF—same as overnight rental; across from train station, next to the Swiss National Museum). Other locations around town are open only in summer (May-Oct) with roughly the same hours—look for *Züri rollt* or *Velogate* signs. Popular bike paths line the lake from Zürich. For more info, ask the TI or visit www.zuerirollt.ch.

Self-Guided Walk

Welcome to Zürich

If you're blitzing Zürich from the train station, this walk is a great way to connect the city center's main sights. It crisscrosses the river en route to the boat dock for a lazy lake-cruise finale (or a quick tram ride back to the station). Allow about an hour.

❶ Train Station

Zürich's central station has a great energy. This major European

Switzerland's Clear-Headed Drug Policy

Like many of its neighbors, Switzerland has a progressive drug policy that aims to reduce the overall harm to its society, rather than focus on punishing users. Even by European standards, the country's approaches to soft and hard drugs are unusually pragmatic.

In 2002, Switzerland legalized marijuana use. When polls showed that more than 30 percent of the country had used marijuana, the parliament decided to decriminalize the drug, rather than criminalize a third of its population. But, while not wanting to clog its prisons with petty pot smokers, the country doesn't want to be known as another Holland, either. So the laws, which vary between cantons, remain a bit ambiguous: The Swiss can possess and use pot, but they can't sell it. Each spring, there's a push for stricter control. Word gets out that Switzerland is no haven for pot, and then things ease up.

Unlike marijuana, hard drugs remain absolutely illegal. Still, Swiss laws treat addicts as people needing medical help, rather than as criminals. Even in classy Zürich, you can see evidence of this policy. For instance, across the river from the station, on the far side of the Walche-Brücke bridge, there's a big, yellow, nondescript vending machine selling safe, government-subsidized syringes to heroin junkies. Go ahead, buy a box—it's about the cheapest souvenir you can purchase in Zürich.

hub handles 2,000 trains a day, including InterCity expresses to many major capitals. Built in 1870, its vast main hall was once lined with tracks. Today, it hosts a farmers' market (Wed 10:00-20:00) and community hall—busy with concerts, exhibitions, and even "beach" volleyball. The station sits above a vast underground modern shopping mall (Mon-Fri until 21:00, Sat-Sun until 20:00).

Above you, find the fat blue angel, Zürich's "Guardian Angel," protecting all travelers. The angel was placed here in 1997 to celebrate the 150th anniversary of the Swiss rail system. To the angel's right, just across the street, is the **Swiss National Museum** (Schweizerisches Landesmuseum). It's the best museum in town, offering an essential introduction to Swiss history (described later, under "Sights in Zürich"). Consider touring this museum before starting the walk.

• *From the station hall, follow the six white lines that lead to*

ZÜRICH

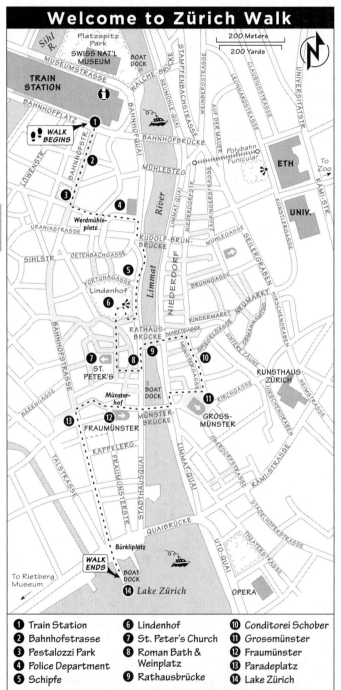

Welcome to Zürich Walk

1. Train Station
2. Bahnhofstrasse
3. Pestalozzi Park
4. Police Department
5. Schipfe
6. Lindenhof
7. St. Peter's Church
8. Roman Bath & Weinplatz
9. Rathausbrücke
10. Conditorei Schober
11. Grossmünster
12. Fraumünster
13. Paradeplatz
14. Lake Zürich

Bahnhofplatz (also well-signed). The station fronts Zürich's main shopping boulevard, the...

❷ Bahnhofstrasse

Mile-long Bahnhofstrasse, stretching from the train station to the lake, is lined with all the big-name shops (though it's become a bit "hamburgerized"). Cross the street (watch for silent trams), but before heading on down, look back at the station.

The facade of the station is a huge triumphal **arch,** built in 1871 to symbolize the triumph of industry. In the Industrial

Age, Zürich emerged as Switzerland's leading city. Presiding over all this triumph is Helvetia, the personification of Switzerland. The Helvetii were the Celtic tribe that the Romans defeated in 58 b.c. to gain control of what is now Switzerland. Romans described them as "very good warriors with an affinity for bright and shiny metal." Helvetia was adopted as a symbol of the Swiss confederation in 1848, when the diverse cantons that banded together to create Switzerland needed some symbol of unity to transcend all their linguistic and regional differences. Helvetic ethnic heritage is the one thing all Swiss cantons have in common. (The "CH" you see on Swiss bumper stickers stands for the Latin "Confoederatio Helvetica.")

Helvetia is flanked by allegories of river travel (the goddess sitting on a boat) and rail travel (another goddess sitting on a train), reminding us that Zürich has long been a transportation hub. Zürich's river, the Limmat, starts from the lake and eventually flows into the Rhine and then (in Rotterdam) out to sea.

The statue of **Alfred Escher** honors the man who spearheaded the creation of the infrastructure that allowed Switzerland to function efficiently within its mountains and connected this country with the rest of Europe. Without Escher, it's quite possible Switzerland would never have become such an economic powerhouse.

• *Start strolling down Bahnhofstrasse. In two blocks (on the right), you'll see...*

❸ Pestalozzi Park

The only park along this pedestrian- and tram-only boulevard is dedicated to Zürich's most important teacher, Johann Heinrich Pestalozzi (1746-1827). He promoted the notion, still prevalent in today's Switzerland, that a good education should be available

for everyone—not only for sons of rich families. Parks like this are rare in central Zürich because of sky-high property values, which are among the most expensive in the world.

In the park's far corner gurgles a copy of a Parisian **Wallace Fountain.** If you have a big head, good luck getting a drink from here. More than 1,200 fun and fresh fountains are sprinkled around town, spouting water that's as good as bottled mineral water (the city regularly checks its quality). This is a blessing in a town where restaurants charge for a glass of tap water. Tourist brochures brag that Zürich is Europe's most "fountainous" city.

• *From the green fountain, head left a couple of blocks, passing through Werdmühleplatz and following white signs to* Stadtpolizei. *Duck into the grand building facing the river, Zürich's...*

❹ Police Department

Enter for a free peek at a fine example of Swiss Jugendstil: an amazing wall and ceiling painting by Swiss artist Augusto Giacometti. Giacometti's famous *Hall of the Flowers* (*Blüemlihalle,* 1926), awash in vibrant orange and red, reflects the relief and joy the artist felt when World War I ended. (Augusto's nephew, Alberto, is the more famous Giacometti, much appreciated for his tall, skinny statues.)

Cost and Hours: Free, daily 9:00-11:00 & 14:00-16:00, they may ask for your ID; if the building is closed, you can get a good look from the always-open lobby—but no photos are allowed.

• *From the terrace, cross the street to the riverside, then head to the right; without crossing the river, cross Uraniastrasse just where it becomes Rudolf-Brun-Brücke (glance to your left to see a piece of the old city ramparts). Take the stairs down to the boardwalk below the Schweitzer Heimatwerk folk-crafts shop, and walk along the street called...*

❺ Schipfe

Back when the city's trade depended on river traffic, this small riverside street was Zürich's harbor. Today it retains its old river-merchant ambience. You'll pass a fun riverside eatery (the recommended Restaurant Schipfe 16) and an arcade.

• *Twenty yards before the ugliest bridge in Switzerland, head up the stairs for two blocks, and then climb to the right up Pfalzgasse. You'll enjoy a great view from another park...*

❻ Lindenhof

Important forts and strategic buildings stood on this square—perched atop a mound of glacial debris—from Roman times through the Carolingian era. The statue commemorates the local women who cleverly defended the town in 1292. Their men were engaged in another battle when the Habsburgs encircled the city. The women put on armor and made like a big, rowdy army, tricking the Habsburgs into thinking the whole city was prepared to attack.

When Zürich became a free city in the 13th century, the townspeople destroyed the fort here and established a law forbidding any new construction. The citizens realized that whoever lived on this hill would rule over the city—and they didn't want any more rulers. Today, this is a people's square, where locals relax under linden trees (for which the square is named) and enjoy the commanding city view.

Survey Zürich beyond its river. The **university** (behind the green spire) is the largest in Switzerland, with 25,000 students. Left of that is Zürich's renowned **technical college,** the ETH (Eidgenössische Technische Hochschule—the Federal Institute of Technology), with 15,000 students. The ETH has graduated 25 Nobel Prize winners, including Albert Einstein and Wilhelm Röntgen (who discovered X-rays). The ETH terrace offers a great city viewpoint (which you can visit later by riding the little Polybahn funicular). Lining the far side of the river, the **Niederdorf** is a lively restaurant, café, and bar district. On a clear day, you

can see the Alps behind the twin domes of the Grossmünster.

• *Take the stairs at the back of the park, just left of the chess players, down to Strehlgasse, and go left on Glockengasse, around the golden bell. Continue down tiny Robert-Walser-Gasse toward St. Peterhofstatt. You'll pass a characteristic eatery, Reblaube Gaststube, made famous by visits from Goethe in 1779. He'd meet here for long, wine-fueled discussions with the minister of...*

❼ St. Peter's Church (St. Peterskirche)

Founded in the seventh century, this church—Zürich's oldest—has one of Europe's largest clock faces (28 feet in diameter). The town watchman used to live above the clock. If he spotted a fire, he would ring the alarm and hang a flag out of the window facing the blaze. This system seems to have worked—Zürich never suffered a devastating fire. In the 18th century, this church's preacher, Johann Kaspar Lavater (1741-1801), was so well loved that people reserved their seats for Sunday Mass.

• *Continue past the church on Schlüssel-gasse and take the first left, down the narrow Thermengasse ("Bath Lane"). Look under your feet through the grid at the lit-up excavations of a **Roman bath**, discovered by accident in 1984. You're standing over studs that elevated the floor, which was heated from below.*

The lane empties out on...

❽ Weinplatz

This pleasant spot was a wine market in centuries past (notice the grape picker on the fine little fountain). A wall mural inside the Barchetta bar (facing the river) shows the medieval river action circa 1570, including a mill on the bridge that raised drinking water to pipes that led to nearby buildings. Note the dock here for the riverboat-bus (described later, under "Sights in Zürich").

The city's oldest bridge, the ❾ **Rathausbrücke**, goes back to Roman times, but now looks more like a concrete pier.

• *Cross the bridge, passing the 17th-century, Renaissance-style City Hall, which faces a fancy Neoclassical police station, and walk a block uphill to Marktgasse, the gateway to the bustling...*

▲▲Niederdorf

A district of colorful streets, fun shopping, restaurants, and nightlife, the Niederdorf neighborhood continues to the left along narrow Niederdorfstrasse, which was the leading com-mercial street before the old city wall was torn down to create Bahnhofstrasse. The Starbucks a block down from here faces a charming square. You can explore this area now...or, better yet, tonight (you'll find some dining suggestions later, under "Eating in Zürich").

To continue our walk, go in the opposite direction (right), heading up **Münstergasse**. Dada enthusiasts know that in 1916, at the Cabaret Voltaire (#26), this "anti-art" art movement was born. At #19, pop into Schwarzenbach, which still advertises "merchan-dise from the colonies" out front and sells things the old-fashioned way inside (in loose bags, by the weight). Inhale. Pick up 100 grams of dried bananas from Togo or some Thai sticks...of coco-nut, of course. Across the street, Zürich's popular ❿ **Conditorei Schober**, a riot of silk flowers, serves famously good (and expen-sive) hot chocolate and champagne truffles.

• Farther up the street is the...

⓫ ▲Grossmünster

Literally the "big cathedral," this is where Huldrych Zwingli—whose angry religious fervor made Martin Luther seem mellow—sparked the Reformation in German-speaking Switzerland. The domes of its towers (early examples of Neo-Gothic) are symbols of Zürich. They were rebuilt following a 1781 fire, and after much civic discussion, were left a plain stone color.

Cost and Hours: Free, daily March-Oct 10:00-18:00, Nov-Feb 10:00-17:00, pick up English story of the Swiss Reformation, www.grossmuenster.ch.

Touring the Church: Step inside and sit down. Let the strength and purity of the 12th-century Romanesque architecture have its way with you. The simple round arches seem strong, and the wide triumphal arch separating the nave from the altar makes you feel like a winner. The impact of the architecture is made stronger because it's uncluttered—Zwingli's reforms led to a clean sweep of Catholic decor in 1519.

In the front are three **choir windows** by Augusto Giacometti (c. 1933). Mary and the Baby Jesus (at her feet) meet two of the three kings bearing their gifts, while angels hover above with offerings of flowers. In the **crypt** (stairs below altar), you'll see an original 15th-century statue of Charlemagne (a copy now fills its niche on the river side of the church exterior). For a sweeping city view, climb the 187 steps to the top of the **Karlsturm,** one of the church's twin towers (4 SF, Mon-Sat 10:00-17:00, Sun 12:30-17:30, Nov-Feb daily until 16:30).

Leaving the church, go right and into the corner, where a door leads to a fine Romanesque **cloister** ringed with fanciful 12th-century carvings (free, Mon-Fri 10:00-18:00, closed Sat-Sun). Upon entering, take 10 steps to the left and meet the sculptor (self-portrait on the highest arch).

• Cross back over the river to another tall-steepled church.

⓬ ▲▲Fraumünster

This was founded as an abbey church for a convent in 853, when Zürich was little more than a village. The current building, which sits on the same footprint as its Carolingian predecessor, dates from 1250. With the Reformation of Zwingli, the church was taken by the Zürich town council in 1524 and—you know the drill—gutted

Switzerland's Zwingli Reformation

Today's Evangelical Reformed Church of Switzerland was founded by Huldrych Zwingli (1484-1531), who preached in Zürich from 1519 through 1531. A follower of the humanist philosopher Erasmus of Rotterdam, Zwingli believed that the true foundation of the church was based on preaching the Holy Scriptures freely— in the people's language, rather than in Latin. In 1522, most of German-speaking Switzerland embraced Zwingli's ideas...and that required leaving the Roman Catholic Church.

In 1517, when Zwingli was 33, German church reformer Martin Luther posted his revolutionary *95 Theses* (which questioned the practice of selling forgiveness, salvation, church offices, and so on). Within two years, sellers of indulgences were refused entry to Zürich. As the Reformation swept Switzerland, things heated up. In 1523, rioters were storming churches, and authorities called for an orderly removal of all images in Zürich houses of worship (except stained-glass windows, which were destroyed).

The new, reformed Swiss church let priests marry. (Zwingli, like Luther, promptly took advantage of this freedom.) Fancy Masses were replaced by simple services. At Zürich's main church, the Grossmünster, preachers studied Latin, Greek, and Hebrew in order to translate the Bible into the people's German. In 1531, the Zwingli Bible (the first complete Bible translated into German) was published. It's still used today (like the King James Bible is in English).

Zwingli gave the Swiss church an unusual austerity: no altar, no pictures, and for a while, not even any music. Church services focused on preaching. Holy Communion was celebrated only on holidays. This puritanical simplicity permeated Swiss society in general. Zwingli was no fan of the "separation of church and

to fit Zwingli's taste. Today, it's famous for its windows by Chagall.

Cost and Hours: Free, Mon-Sat 10:00-18:00, Sun 12:00-18:00, Nov-March daily until 16:00, occasional evening concerts, www.fraumuenster.ch.

Touring the Church: Enter the Fraumünster for a look at its claim to fame— a collection of 30-foot-tall stained-glass windows by Marc Chagall (1887-1985), the Russian-born French artist. Chagall gave an exhibit in Zürich in 1967. It was such a hit that the city offered the world-famous artist a commission. To their surprise, the 80-year-old Chagall accepted. Chagall designed the windows to stand in the church's spacious choir (zone behind the altar; underutilized in Protestant-style worship)—a space where he intuitively felt his unique mix of

state." Pushing for a theocracy, he established an ironclad city law: The government's duty was to oversee public worship, and only preaching that was true to the Bible was to be tolerated.

But Zwingli's reforms were by no means universally supported. It was a mess: Switzerland's Protestant movement split over baptism. Luther and Zwingli split over the Eucharist (is Christ's body really *in* the bread, or there only in a spiritual sense?). And, as old-school Catholics predicted, putting the Bible into the hands of regular people brought chaos—enabling every Tom, Dick, and Hans to "carve his own path to hell." Switzerland was embroiled in a religious civil war, as Protestant cantons fought Catholic ones. In 1531, while fighting as a "citizen soldier," Zwingli was killed in battle. His friend and partner Heinrich Bullinger succeeded him as the leader of German-speaking Swiss Protestantism.

Bullinger collaborated with John Calvin as Swiss Protestantism matured. The Protestant focus on preaching promoted the translation and interpretation of the Bible. Everyone was reading the Bible directly, which promoted literacy. The Reformation provided a basis for the autonomous community spirit, strong work ethic, and high literacy of a prosperous Switzerland for the future. The Swiss church became a place where equals would meet and worship God. Zwingli's heritage included transferring the notion of social charity from a church phenomenon to the responsibility of any self-respecting modern state. The foundations of Swiss democracy and its present social policies are rooted in Zwingli's teaching. And these Swiss reformers planted the seeds of what became the Presbyterian Church in the United States.

religious themes could flourish.

For the next three years, Chagall threw his heart and soul into the project, making the sketches at his home on the French Riviera, then working in close collaboration with a glassmaking factory in Reims, France. After the colored panes were made, Chagall personally painted the figures on with black outlines, which were then baked into the glass. Chagall spent weeks in Zürich overseeing the installation and completion.

His inimitable painting style—deep colors, simple figures, and shard-like Cubism—is perfectly suited to the medium of stained glass. Blending Jewish and Christian traditions, Chagall created a work that can make people of many faiths comfortable.

The five windows depict Bible scenes, culminating in the central image of the crucified Christ. From left to right, they are as follows:

1. The Prophets (red): The prophet Elisha (bottom) looks up to watch a horse-drawn chariot carry his mentor Elijah off to heaven. Farther up, Jeremiah (blue in color and mood) puts his hand to his head and ponders the destruction of wicked Jerusalem. Up in heaven (top), a multicolored, multifaceted God spins out his creation, sending fiery beams down to inspire his Prophets on earth. This window is artificially lit, as it's built into an interior wall.

2. Jacob (blue—Chagall's favorite color): Jacob (bottom, in deep purple amid deep blue) dreams of a ladder that snakes up to heaven, with red-tinged angels ascending and descending, symbolizing the connection between God above and Jacob's descendants (the Children of Israel) below.

3. Christ (green): The middle, and biggest, window depicts the central figure in God's plan of salvation—Jesus Christ, who, as the Messiah, fulfills the promises of the Old Testament prophets. Mother Mary suckles baby Jesus (bottom) amid the leafy family tree of Jesus' Old Testament roots. The central area is an indistinct jumble of events from Christ's life, leading up to his crucifixion. The life-size ascendant Christ is crucified in a traditional medieval pose, but he's surrounded by a circle that seems to be bearing him, resurrected, to heaven. Chagall signed and dated the work (1970).

4. Zion (yellow): King David (bottom right) strums his harp and sings a psalm, while behind him stands his mistress Bathsheba, who gave birth to Solomon, the builder of Jerusalem's temple. At the end of history, an angel (top) blows a ram's horn, announcing the establishment of a glorious New Jerusalem, which descends (center), featuring rust-colored, yellow, and green walls, domes, and towers.

5. The Law (blue): Moses, with horns of light and the Ten Commandments (top), looks sternly down on lawbreaking warriors on horseback wreaking havoc. At the bottom, an angel (in red) embraces the prophet Isaiah (very bottom) and inspires him to foretell the coming of the Messiah (in red, above the angel).

Everyone comes away with a different interpretation of this complex work, which combines images from throughout the Bible. The tall, skinny windows seem to emphasize the vertical connection between heaven above and earth below, both bathed in the same colored light. Some think Chagall used colors symbolically: Blue and green represent the earth, while red and yellow are heavenly radiance. But all recognize that the jumble of images—evoking the complexity of God's universe—reaches its Point Omega in the central window, celebrating the idea of salvation through Christ's crucifixion.

• *From the church, veer left into the square (away from the river), and head toward the blue building (Restaurant Zunfthaus zur Waag). Follow the small lane to its left, passing the recommended Zeughauskeller restaurant as you round the corner into busy...*

⓭ Paradeplatz

Survey the scene: The train station is a 10-minute walk to your right up Bahnhofstrasse, and the lake is a few minutes to your left, down the classiest stretch of Bahnhofstrasse. On the square is Sprüngli, Zürich's top café for the past century. Its "Luxemburgerli" *macarons*—little cream-filled, one-inch *macaron*-meringue hamburgers—are a local favorite (you can buy just a couple; if you buy 100 grams,

you'll get a selection of 12). It also sells elegant finger-sandwich lunches, either in its café (upstairs/outside) or to go (perfect for a lakeside snack). Across the square is Credit Suisse, with a luxurious ground floor full of fancy shops worth a look. A bit farther up Bahnhofstrasse (at #31) is the fine little **Beyer Clock and Watch Museum** (8 SF, Mon-Fri 14:00-18:00, closed Sat-Sun). The watchmaker's personal collection is in the basement of his watch shop.

• *Turning left, follow Bahnhofstrasse to the boats and riverside terrace at Bürkliplatz. We'll finish this walk at...*

⓮ Lake Zürich (Zürichsee)

Lake Zürich is 17 miles long, 2.5 miles wide, and—because it's relatively shallow—warm enough for swimming in the summer. From

here, you can enjoy the lakeside promenade (a fine strolling path 3 miles in either direction; left is sunnier and more interesting) or a short cruise. To go back to the station, catch tram #11 (from the inland side, across the street) or the riverboat-bus (both boat options described next).

Sights in Zürich

Cruises on Limmat River and Lake Zürich—You have two basic boat-ride options: 1) small, low-floating buses that take commuters and joy-riding visitors up and down the river and to points nearby on the lake; and 2) big, romantic ships taking tourists on longer rides around Lake Zürich. All boats leave from Bürkliplatz (lake end of Bahnhofstrasse) and are covered by both Swiss Passes and Eurailpasses (but a cruise costs a flexi-day, which is no problem if you're already using that day for a train trip to or from Zürich).

None of the boats comes with commentary.

The low-to-the-water riverboat-buses (designed to squeeze under the bridges) make a one-hour loop around the Zürich end of the lake and down the river to the train station and Swiss National Museum. They can be handy for connecting the lake and the museum (4.10 SF for any ride, short or long, buy ticket on boat, also covered by 24-hour transit pass and ZürichCARD; April-late Oct daily 2/hour, first boat generally at 13:00 Mon-Fri but at 10:00 Sat-Sun and daily July-Aug; last boat generally at 17:30 but at 21:00 May-Sept, schedule posted at pier 6, www.zvv.ch).

The big, touristy, lake-only boats are run by the Lake Zürich Navigation Company (8.20 SF for basic 1.5-hour trip; April-Oct daily 2/hour 11:00-18:30, May-Sept until 19:30; Nov-March daily at 13:00 and 14:30 plus Sat-Sun at 10:00 and 16:00, www.zsg.ch). They also offer longer trips, jazz and dinner cruises, and so on. The ticket kiosk is near pier 3; boats depart from piers 1 through 6.

▲▲Swiss National Museum (Schweizerisches Landes-museum)—This massive museum, in a Neo-Gothic castle next to the train station, provides a solid background on Swiss history and identity. If Zürich is your first stop in Switzerland, visiting here for a primer on all things Swiss can help put the rest of your trip in context. Even if you're not staying the night in Zürich, the museum can be a worthwhile rainy-day excursion from Luzern, Appenzell, Bern, or even Interlaken (especially if you have a railpass).

By the late 19th century, it was clear that the world was changing, and the Swiss wanted to protect their unique heritage. A national competition was held, and Zürich (promising to provide a piece of land, pay for construction, and donate an impressive collection) won the privilege of hosting the country's national museum. Much of the museum was renovated in 2009; here's hoping that its remaining dusty corners get the same great treatment.

Cost and Hours: 10 SF, covered by Swiss Pass, Tue-Sun 10:00-17:00, Thu until 19:00, closed Mon, audioguide-5 SF, mandatory bag check in free lockers upstairs from gift shop (across from entrance), Museumstrasse 2, café in courtyard, tel. 044-218-6511, www.musee-suisse.ch.

◑ Self-Guided Tour: Up on the first floor, after you've left your things in a locker, pop into the room with a model of the Battle of Murten (see page 132) and just off it, a smaller room displaying very old Swiss coins. Then, following *Rundgang* signs, weave your way through the building. Everything is well-explained in English, either on the wall or on information sheets in each room.

The museum's main exhibits are organized thematically. The **historical section** kicks off with an exhibit called "Niemand War Schon Immer Da" ("nobody's been here forever")—a look at the (pre-) history of the Swiss people from the perspective of immigration and emigration. The exhibit's implication that there's no such thing as a native Swiss is a controversial claim in a nation perennially concerned with what right-wing parties call *Überfremdung*—"over-foreignization" (see the wall of anti-immigration political posters, some from the present day). From here, follow Swiss history through the Reformation and humanist movement into the Enlightenment, then step into the grand main hall recounting and celebrating Swiss unity (with a gigantic clock-like wheel holding a bit of every Swiss cliché, from chocolate to holey cheese). The parts describing the nation's 20th-century history are surprisingly interesting, with pictures documenting the waaaay late-in-the-game movement for women's suffrage (not fully achieved until 1990) and videos featuring interviews with those who lived through World War II (the exhibit openly admits that "neutral" Switzerland traded mostly with Axis powers, clamped down on the press, and didn't recognize Jews as refugees).

Next, an exhibit chronicling Switzerland's **economic development** addresses what you may have been wondering for a while—how'd they end up with so much money? After a series of fragrant wood-paneled rooms reconstructed from historical buildings, you can detour up the **weapons tower** *(Waffenturm)*, with an impressive array of weapons, uniforms, and military equipment. On the way up you'll pass a dimly lit floor holding Switzerland's largest collection of costumes, traditional garments, and decorative textiles.

Back on the main *Rundgang* path, the model living rooms and sauna-scented wooden rooms continue down to the ground floor. There you'll find the final exhibit, the **Collections Gallery,** with a bevy of pre-Reformation church art (all the fancy stuff the Protestants gutted from churches so they could concentrate). A highlight is the oldest panoramic painting of Zürich, still recognizable five centuries later.

Platzspitz Park—What used to be a riverside hangout for drug addicts has been cleaned up, and—apart from a rusty needle here and there—is now a safe, friendly place for a scenic picnic. From here, you can take a riverboat-bus down the river and around the lake (described earlier).

Cost and Hours: Free, park open daily May-Sept 6:00-21:00, Oct-April 8:00-17:00, behind train station and Swiss National Museum, clean WC.

▲▲**Kunsthaus Zürich**—It's worth the tram/bus ride up here to see Switzerland's top collection of modern art. The renovated modern wings are great, but you'll find most of the gems in the musty older rooms, with works by Swiss artists (Alberto Giacometti, Johann Heinrich Füssli, and Ferdinand Hodler), as well as international greats such as Munch, Picasso, Kokoschka, Beckmann, Corinth, Monet, and Chagall. The younger generation is also represented, with pieces by Rothko, Merz, Twombly, Beuys, Bacon, and Baselitz.

Cost and Hours: 14 SF, free on Wed, not covered by Swiss Pass, Tue-Sun 10:00-18:00, Wed-Fri until 20:00, closed Mon, free English audioguide, mandatory bag check downstairs in lockers— 2-SF deposit, café; tram #3, #5, #8, or #9, or bus #31 to Kunsthaus stop, Heimplatz 1; tel. 044-253-8484, www.kunsthaus.ch.

Rietberg Museum—Filling historic villas set in a beautiful park, this museum houses art from Asia, Africa, the Americas, and the South Pacific.

Cost and Hours: 16 SF, covered by Swiss Pass, Tue-Sun 10:00-17:00, Wed-Thu until 20:00, closed Mon, English audio-guide-5 SF, tram #7 to Museum Rietberg stop, Villa Wesendonck, Gablerstrasse 15, tel. 044-206-3131, www.rietberg.ch.

Zürich Zoo—With 360 species, an impressive Madagascar rain forest hall, and a huge indoor exhibit, the city's zoo is a kid-friendly, fun place to see locals at play.

Cost and Hours: 22 SF, daily March-Oct 9:00-18:00, Nov-Feb until 17:00, tram #6 from Bahnhofstrasse in front of the station, direction: Zoo, ride to last stop, Zürichbergstrasse 221, tel. 084-896-6983, www.zoo.ch.

Uetliberg—If you want to see Zürich from above, take the excursion train that climbs from the main train station to this little mountain peak, high atop the city and lake. Buy your ticket at the station, then go downstairs to find the little red-orange S10 train on track 2 (16 SF round-trip, covered by ZürichCARD, 2-3/hour, runs 6:30-24:00, 20 minutes, www.zvv.ch). From the Uetliberg station, it's a moderately steep, 10-minute climb up a paved pedestrian road to a hotel and a tall observation tower overlooking the city. The view is particularly striking at sunset. Sunny summer weekends bring hordes of families with strollers. You can do the whole trip in about 1.5 hours.

Sleeping in Zürich

High season in Zürich is May, June, September, and October. In this business-oriented city, rooms may be cheaper on weekends and pricier during festivals and conventions (September can be particularly busy). Most hotels keep their room rates closely tied to fluctuating demand: For the best deals, check their websites and book in advance.

Most of my listings are near the train station, ideal for those passing through or leaving on an early-morning train or plane (for train connections to Zürich's airport, see page 67).

Sleep Code

(1 SF = about $1.10, country code: 41)
S = Single, **D** = Double/Twin, **T** = Triple, **Q** = Quad, **b** = bathroom, **s** = shower only. Unless otherwise noted, credit cards are accepted, English is spoken, and breakfast is included. Prices may not include the extra 2.50 SF per person per night hotel tax.

To help you sort easily through these listings, I've divided the accommodations into three categories, based on the price for a standard double room with bath during high season:

$$$ Higher Priced—Most rooms 200 SF or more.
 $$ Moderately Priced—Most rooms between 140-200 SF.
  $ Lower Priced—Most rooms 140 SF or less.

Prices can change without notice; verify the hotel's current rates online or by email. For other updates, see www.ricksteves.com/update.

East of the Limmat River
Across the River from the Train Station

With this efficient, handy neighborhood as your home base, you're a quick stroll away from the train station, Swiss National Museum, riverboat-bus dock, a huge underground mall of services and shops (under the station), and the Niederdorf restaurant and nightlife zone (down Stampfenbachstrasse). To reach these hotels, exit the train station from the huge hall with the "Guardian Angel" sculpture and the TI. Cross the river on the Walche-Brücke bridge, and use the map on page 62 to find your hotel.

$$ Hotel Bristol, run by Martin Hämmerli and his friendly staff, offers 56 modern, cozy rooms an eight-minute walk from the station. This is a business-quality place with family-run warmth. The staff at the reception desk are helpful and happy to answer travel questions (Sb-150-190 SF, small Db-160-195, big Db-190-240 SF, Tb-210-260 SF, Qb-230-285 SF, superior Qb-280-360 SF, lower prices are for Nov-April, 5 percent discount if you reserve direct and show this book, pay Internet access, free cable Internet, possibly free Wi-Fi, laundry-15 SF, Stampfenbachstrasse 34, tel. 044-258-4444, fax 044-258-4400, www.hotelbristol.ch, info@hotel bristol.ch).

$$ Hotel Leoneck offers 80 modern yet kitschy, bovine-themed rooms at a decent price. The hotel, with its cheery lobby and fine attached Crazy Cow restaurant (daily 6:30-22:30, www.crazycow.ch), somehow manages to make Swiss cows seem

ZÜRICH

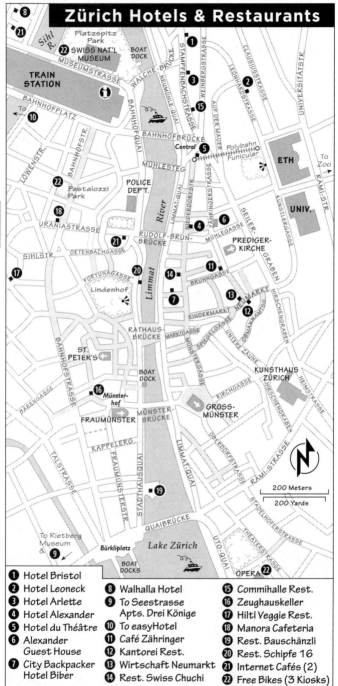

Zürich Hotels & Restaurants

200 Meters
200 Yards

1 Hotel Bristol
2 Hotel Leoneck
3 Hotel Arlette
4 Hotel Alexander
5 Hotel du Théâtre
6 Alexander Guest House
7 City Backpacker Hotel Biber
8 Walhalla Hotel
9 To Seestrasse Apts. Drei Könige
10 To easyHotel
11 Café Zähringer
12 Kantorei Rest.
13 Wirtschaft Neumarkt
14 Rest. Swiss Chuchi
15 Commihalle Rest.
16 Zeughauskeller
17 Hiltl Veggie Rest.
18 Manora Cafeteria
19 Rest. Bauschänzli
20 Rest. Schipfe 16
21 Internet Cafés (2)
22 Free Bikes (3 Kiosks)

cool. Enjoy the moo-velous mural in your room (Sb-120-170 SF, Db-170-230 SF, Tb-230-280 SF, Qb-280-320 SF, family rooms, ask for 10 percent Rick Steves discount when you reserve, breakfast-18 SF, many have balcony, elevator; free Internet access, cable Internet, and Wi-Fi; some street noise—ask for quieter back room, Leonhardstrasse 1, tel. 044-254-2222, fax 044-254-2200, www.leoneck.ch, info@leoneck.ch, Herr Gold). From the Walche-Brücke bridge, it's a 12-minute uphill walk, or take tram #6 or #10 from the station (direction: Bahnhof Oerlikon, two stops to Haldenegg, look for Crazy Cow restaurant). You can also take tram #10 directly from the airport (30 minutes).

$$ Hotel Arlette is a bit forgettable, but its 30 rooms are comfortable, functional, and centrally located in a quiet neighborhood (Sb-135-185 SF, Db-175-250 SF, air-con, pay Internet access, pay Wi-Fi, Stampfenbachstrasse 26, tel. 044-252-0032, fax 044-252-0923, www.arlette-beim-hauptbahnhof.com, hotel.arlette@bluewin.ch, Schlotter family).

In the Niederdorf

The atmospheric, cobblestoned old town of Zürich lies across the river and a short walk from the station. During the day, it's busy with shoppers and workers on lunch breaks; at night, the restaurants and clubs keep the pedestrian streets vibrant. To reach the Niederdorf on foot from the train station, cross the Bahnhofbrücke bridge, go through the square called Central (beware of the silent trams), and head to the right along Niederdorfstrasse.

$$$ Hotel Alexander is a good business-class hotel in a very central location offering a decent value, especially if you book well in advance (Sb-150-180 SF, Db-210-230 SF, pricier if demand is high, 10 percent discount if you show this book, extra bed-30 SF, may not include breakfast, air-con, free Internet access and Wi-Fi, Niederdorfstrasse 40, tel. 044-251-8203, fax 044-252-7425, www.hotel-alexander.ch, info@hotel-alexander.ch).

$$$ Hotel du Théâtre occupies a renovated little trapezoid-shaped theater. The 50 thespian-themed rooms are small but luxurious, with triple-paned windows that keep out street noise. The breakfast room/lounge overlooks the Polybahn funicular (Sb-155-210 SF, Db-205-250 SF, breakfast-18 SF, free Internet access, pay Wi-Fi, Seilergraben 69, Centralplatz, tel. 044-267-2670, www.hotel-du-theatre.ch, info@hotel-du-theatre.ch).

$$ Alexander Guest House is the annex to (and one block away from) the Hotel Alexander, listed earlier. Its 20 rooms, all with twin beds, are basic and uninspiring, but they're also clean, quiet, and perfectly fine (Sb-95-120 SF, Db-140-160 SF, ask for 10 percent Rick Steves discount when you book, extra bed-25 SF, free Internet access at Hotel Alexander, pay Wi-Fi, contact through Hotel Alexander—where you'll also have breakfast, Zähringerstrasse 16).

Hostel: $ City Backpacker Hotel Biber, buried right in the middle of the Niederdorf action three floors above a restaurant, offers the cheapest backpacker beds in the old center, with a cool ambience aimed at young travelers (65 bunks in 4- to 6-bed dorms for 36 SF each, S-75 SF, D-114 SF, towels-3 SF, sheets-3 SF, private rooms include sheets, no breakfast, pay Internet access, free Wi-Fi, lockers, kitchen, terrace, street noise at night, no curfew, no membership needed, reception open daily 8:00-11:00 & 15:00-22:00, 8-minute walk from station at Niederdorfstrasse 5, tel. 044-251-9015, www.city-backpacker.ch, sleep@city-backpacker.ch).

West of the Limmat River
Near the Train Station

$$$ Walhalla Hotel, just behind the train station, has 48 modern, spacious rooms (Sb-171 SF, Db-245 SF, Tb-300-350 SF, family room-350-400 SF, cheaper on weekends, free Wi-Fi, Limmatstrasse 5, tel. 044-446-5400, fax 044-446-5454, www.walhalla-hotel.ch, walhalla-hotel@bluewin.ch). Their guest house annex, around the corner, rents 26 simpler but ample rooms for less (Sb-127-147 SF, Db-194-224 SF).

Farther from the Center

$$ Seestrasse Apartments Drei Könige offers studios with kitchenettes for a good price in a classy neighborhood near the Rietberg Museum. The units are in a stately Art Nouveau building rented out by the fancy Hotel Ascot down the street, and the lake is a five-minute walk away (Sb-150-180 SF, Db-180-220 SF, prices vary with demand—generally cheaper on weekends, breakfast-32 SF at Hotel Ascot, free Wi-Fi, Seestrasse 65, tel. 044-283-1777, www.seestrasse-apartments.ch, info@seestrasse-apartments.ch). From the station, take tram #7 to the Museum Rietberg stop, and cross the street to #65.

$ easyHotel is a decent value in this pricey town, with small, modern rooms located away from all the sights but still only a 10-15-minute walk from the station. Although the base rate is fairly cheap (Db-90-120 SF), you'll pay for each additional service—breakfast, Internet access, baggage storage, Wi-Fi, extra towels, room-cleaning service if staying 3 or more nights, and so on—which can add up (Zwinglistrasse 14, toll tel. 0900-327-994—1.50 SF/minute, www.easyhotel.com, zuerich@easyhotelschweiz.ch). From the station, take bus #31 (direction: Schlieren Zentrum) to the Kanonengasse stop, walk away from station one block down Kanonengasse, then right on Zwinglistrasse to #14.

ZÜRICH

Eating in Zürich

East of the Limmat River

In the Niederdorf

The Niederdorf is Zürich's dining district, and the traffic-free Niederdorfstrasse is its restaurant row. And though the countless eateries lining this main drag don't offer the best values, the people-watching is hard to beat. Browse the street and survey the eating options (including many colorful ethnic places). All of these recommendations are within a few minutes' walk of this spine of Zürich's people zone. Many of the venerable guild houses—no longer economic powers—are now convivial traditional restaurants.

Café Zähringer is an artsy, bohemian co-op with a passion for serving reasonably priced healthy food to people who take time to keep life in balance. Linger in the stay-awhile interior, or enjoy the leafy seating out on the square—a block from where Lenin lived before heading back to Russia (25-SF daily specials, always good veggie and vegan plates, organic produce, salads, also meat dishes and wok dishes, famously good coffee, Mon 18:00-22:00, Tue-Fri 12:00-15:00 & 17:00-22:00, Sat-Sun 12:00-22:00, Zähringerplatz 11, tel. 044-252-0500). You may happen to notice the sweet smell of an herb not on the menu.

Kantorei Restaurant serves well-presented modern Mediterranean cuisine with an Italian touch in a classy but unpretentious setting. Sit inside or out on the quiet, atmospheric square next to a fountain (30-40-SF plates, 20-25-SF lunch specials, daily 11:30-14:00 & 17:30-22:30, proud of its wine list, good vegetables, Neumarkt 2, tel. 044-252-2727).

Wirtschaft Neumarkt, tucked away in the old town, offers creative international dishes and prides itself in using only healthy ingredients such as organic vegetables, salads, and additive-free meat, which justifies the higher prices. The interior is unremarkable—eat outdoors here. In good weather, the restaurant's long and fun-loving garden is packed with in-the-know locals eating well under chestnut trees. The upper garden is best—but may be filled with diners who knew to make reservations (30-40-SF plates, lunch specials, Mon-Sat 11:30-14:00 & 18:00-24:00, closed Sun except June-Aug, extensive wine list and good beer on tap, Neumarkt 5, tel. 044-252-7939).

Restaurant Swiss Chuchi is a busy place popular with tourists and locals for traditional cheese dishes. They offer a fun selection of cheese and meat fondues. The 25-30-SF fondue is splittable if you order another dish or a salad (daily 11:30-24:00, indoor and outdoor seating, follow your nose to Rosengasse 10 on Hirschenplatz, tel. 044-266-9666).

Across the River from the Train Station

Commihalle Restaurant, near several recommended hotels, is part of a popular Italian chain. Their 36-SF "Tavolata" special—ideal for big eaters—gets you an antipasto buffet, pasta dish, main meat dish, and dessert-buffet finale (available only Tue-Sat 18:30-21:30). The interior is plain but dressy, and there's outdoor seating (filling 20-SF pastas, no pizza, always a good vegetarian option, daily 11:00-24:00, Stampfenbachstrasse 8, tel. 044-250-5960).

West of the Limmat River

Off Bahnhofstrasse

Zeughauskeller fills an atmospheric 500-year-old armory with medieval battle gear (William Tell's crossbow?) and happy eaters enjoying typically Swiss cuisine. Their fun, accessible menu offers traditional meals, including lots of soft meats (but no cheese, which the Swiss don't like to smell unless they're eating it). *Kalbsgeschnetzeltes*—calf's liver with *Rösti* (35 SF)—is a house specialty and a local fave. There's outdoor seating, but the interior has all the character and stays cool even when it's hot (18-30-SF plates, daily 11:30-23:00, plenty of beer and wine, kid-friendly, near Paradeplatz at Bahnhofstrasse 28—go down In Gassen lane to find entrance, tel. 044-220-1515).

Hiltl Vegetarian Restaurant is a popular treat for vegetarians. In 1898, Ambrosius Hiltl was fighting rheumatoid arthritis. His doctor said, "No more meat," so Ambrosius established the world's first vegetarian restaurant. Today his great-great-great-grandson Rolf carries on the family tradition. Historic photos decorate the walls, but the loyal clientele's attention is on the enticing buffet and friendly conversation. At dinner, along with the salad buffet, there's an Indian buffet (endorsed by Indian tourists). Fill your plate, which is sold by the weight—generally 25-30 SF per hearty meal. At lunch, the salad bar is cheaper, but with fewer Indian options. The à la carte menu comes with delightful salads, curries, and fancy fruit juices. Hiltl's food is legendary for its freshness and lack of preservatives (daily 6:00-23:00, 2 blocks off Bahnhofstrasse where it kinks at Sihlstrasse 30, tel. 044-227-7000).

Manora, a cafeteria at the Manor department store on Bahnhofstrasse, is reliably good and fast. Choose between a fresh salad bar (big plate-12 SF) and a variety of main dishes (10-15 SF). It's popular with residents—eat early or late (Mon-Sat 9:00-20:00, closed Sun, fifth floor, Bahnhofstrasse 75).

Along the Limmat River

Restaurant Bauschänzli is both a fancy riverside restaurant and a sloppy beer garden (a block inland from the boat docks at

Bürkliplatz). Filling a small island on the river, its fun-loving and popular self-serve restaurant offers Zürich's best beer-garden experience—like a Munich *Biergarten* without the kraut. Help yourself to the reasonably priced salad bar and the beer and wine from big casks (grab the glass or carafe of your choice). *Citro* (lemonade) is mixed with lager to make a shandy (known here as a *Panaché*).
Süssmost is apple juice. The garden is open daily in good weather generally May through mid-September (call ahead if it's raining), followed in fall by a raucous Oktoberfest (15-40-SF plates, daily 11:00-23:00, live Bulgarian folk band plays Euro-folk music daily as locals dance—15:00-17:00 & 19:00-22:30, Stadthausquai 2, tel. 044-212-4919, reserve only for the fine-dining restaurant).

ZÜRICH

Restaurant Schipfe 16, gorgeously and peacefully situated on the river with an old-town view, is part of a city-run organization providing work for hard-to-employ people. It was originally a soup kitchen, but the location was just too charming to stay that way, so it's now open to the general public. Don't expect polished service; instead, feel good that you're contributing to a worthy cause and enjoying healthy and decent food at a great price. The best seats are right along the river (lunch only, 21-23-SF two-course daily specials, Mon-Fri 10:00-16:00, closed Sat-Sun, Schipfe 16, tel. 044-211-2122).

Zürich Connections

By Train

From Zürich by Train to: Luzern (2/hour, 1 hour), **Interlaken** (2/hour, 2 hours, change in Bern or Spiez), **Bern** (3/hour, 1 hour), **Murten** (1-2/hour, 1.75 hours, 1-2 transfers), **Appenzell** (2/hour, 1.75 hours with transfer in Gossau or 2.25 hours with transfer in St. Gallen), **Lausanne** (2/hour, 2.25 hours), **Zermatt** (at least hourly, 3.5 hours, 1-2 changes), **Chur** (2/hour, 1.25-1.5 hours), **Lugano** (hourly, 2.75 hours, half with easy change in Arth-Goldau), **Berlin** (roughly hourly, 8.25-9 hours, 1 transfer; several overnight options, including 1 direct, 11.5-12.5 hours), **Munich** (3/day direct, 4.25 hours; more with transfers, 5-6 hours), **Frankfurt** (6/day direct, 4 hours, more with transfers), **Vienna** (2/day direct, 8 hours; 1 night train, 9 hours), **Paris** (4/day direct, 4.5-5 hours). Train info: toll tel. 0900-300-300 (1.19 SF/minute), or www.rail.ch.

By Plane

Smooth, compact, and user-friendly, **Zürich Airport** has three levels and is an eye-opening introduction to Swiss efficiency. The ground floor features baggage claim (free baggage carts) and the train station (with train info and ticket desk). The main level has a top-end food court, Migros and Co-op supermarkets, fancy souvenir shops, post office (easy to mail things home—pack light), mobile-phone shops, banks, ATMs, and lockers. The upper level has departures, TI, lockers, and Internet kiosks. Eateries and ATMs are plentiful before and after the security checkpoint. For flight information, call the automated toll number: 0900-300-313 (2 SF/minute, press 2 for English).

The train station underneath the airport can whisk you about anywhere you'd want to go in Europe, including **downtown Zürich** (6.40 SF, 10-15 minutes, leaves every 10 minutes 5:00-24:00, much cheaper than the 50-60-SF taxi ride). Your train ticket into Zürich is good for one hour on all city public transportation.

Sleeping at the Airport: Since most of my recommended accommodations are near the station, and the train connection to the airport is so fast and frequent, there's little reason to sleep at the airport. But if you're catching an early-morning flight and are up for a splurge, consider the **$$$ Radisson Blu Hotel** (Db-around 325 SF, tel. 044-800-4040, www.radissonblu.com /hotel-zurichairport).

From Zürich Airport by Train to: Luzern (2/hour, 1.25 hours, most with change in Zürich), **Interlaken** (2/hour, 2.25 hours, transfer in Bern or Spiez), **Bern** (2/hour, 1.25 hours), **Murten** (2/hour, 2 hours, transfer in Bern, Fribourg, or Neuchâtel), **Appenzell** (2/hour, 1.5 hours, transfer in Gossau), **Lausanne** (2/ hour, 2.5 hours, some with change in Biel), **Zermatt** (1-2/hour, 3.5 hours, 1-2 changes), **Chur** (2/hour, 1.75-2 hours, change at Zürich main station), **Lugano** (hourly, 3 hours, 1-2 changes), **Munich** (4/ day direct, 4-4.25 hours, more with 2-4 changes, 4.75-5.5 hours).

LUZERN
and CENTRAL SWITZERLAND

 Luzern has long been Switzerland's tourism capital. Situated on the edge of a lake, with a striking alpine panorama as a backdrop, Luzern was a regular stop on the "Grand Tour" route of Europe during the Romantic era, entertaining visitors such as Mark Twain, Goethe, and Queen Victoria. And with a charming old town, a pair of picture-perfect wooden bridges, a gaggle of fine museums, and its famous weeping lion, there's still enough in Luzern to earn it a place on any Swiss itinerary.

Luzern also makes a fine home base for exploring the surrounding region, known as Central Switzerland (Zentralschweiz). A wide variety of boat trips, mountain lifts, and other excursions make fun day trips.

Planning Your Time

Many visitors home-base in Luzern for a week of side-trips. While I'd rather settle in the high country instead, Luzern itself is worth at least a full day and two nights. To get the most out of your day, begin with the TI's two-hour walking tour, or follow the self-guided walk in this chapter. Then hit the museums that interest you most: Art buffs flock to the Rosengart Collection for its Picasso exhibit; gearheads will have a ball at the Swiss Transport Museum; and rock hounds dig the Glacier Garden. In the late afternoon, take a peaceful boat trip on Lake Luzern, then wander the town's scenic bridges at sunset. With extra time and good weather, head up to Mount Pilatus.

Luzern

Luzern (loot-SERN, "Lucerne" in English) is a charming midsize city with about 60,000 residents (and a metropolitan area sprawling to almost 200,000). The town grew up around a monastery and is said to have been founded here because an angel shone a heavenly spotlight on the site (the name "Luzern" is derived from *lucerna*, Latin for "lamp").

Luzern sits where the Reuss ("royce") River flows out of Lake Luzern. Its English name is Lake Lucerne, but the Swiss call it the Vierwaldstättersee—"Lake of Four Forest States," since it lies at the intersection of four of Switzerland's cantons (political units similar to US states).

South of the river is the train station and the bustling new town (Neustadt), and north of the river is the quaint, traffic-free old town (Altstadt). The river is spanned by a series of pedestrian bridges, including two classic wooden ones: the Chapel Bridge, with its famous stone water tower, and the Mill Bridge. Museums, restaurants, and hotels are scattered on both sides of the Reuss River.

Orientation to Luzern

Tourist Information

Luzern's helpful, modern TI is right inside the train station (mid-June-mid-Sept daily 8:30-19:30; May-mid-June and mid-Sept-Oct Mon-Fri 8:30-18:30, Sat-Sun 9:00-19:30; Nov-April Mon-Fri 8:30-17:30, Sat-Sun 9:00-13:00; Bahnhofstrasse 3, tel. 041-227-1717, phone not answered on weekends, www.luzern.org).

At the TI, pick up the free, informative *City Guide* (with a Visitors Card, described below) and browse through their other literature. Confirm the details for their walking tour (described later, under "Tours in Luzern"). The TI provides a free room-booking service (with some great last-minute deals) and sells tickets to various activities around town, such as boat trips. If you have kids (or are one), ask about the pedal boats.

Sightseeing Passes: The **Swiss Pass** covers most of Luzern's attractions. The free **Visitors Card** *(Gästekarte)*, which comes inside the *City Guide* brochure (available at TI and some hotels), gives minor discounts to most of Luzern's sights. When you check into your Luzern hotel, have them stamp the Visitors Card. Remember to carry it with you and ask for the discount when buying entry tickets. For most, the Visitors Card is enough, but avid museumgoers can consider the **LucerneCard,** which includes unlimited travel on local trains and buses (but not boats), as well as half off the walking tour and entry fees to most area museums (19 SF/24 hours, 27 SF/48 hours, 33 SF/72 hours). Buying this card makes sense only if you don't have a Swiss Pass (which already covers many Luzern attractions) and plan on doing a lot of sightseeing.

Arrival in Luzern

Luzern's train station is user-friendly. The TI is on the town side of the station, next to Burger King, just off track 3. Most other important services are down the escalators at the front of the tracks, in an underground shopping mall called RailCity. There you'll find the ticket desks, WCs, ATMs, lockers, a convenient self-service cafeteria, a long-hours grocery store, and lots of other shops and restaurants. If all the other stores in town are closed (such as on Sun), head for RailCity.

In front of the train station is Bahnhofplatz (where buses fan out in every direction) and the pleasant lakefront.

Helpful Hints

Medical Help: Permanence is a welcoming drop-in medical clinic open 24/7 at the train station (downstairs in RailCity, near Co-op grocery store).

Festival: The **Lucerne Festival** draws musicians and fans each year from mid-August to mid-September (www.lucerne festival.ch).

Internet Access: An Internet point is inside the **TI** (4 SF/10 minutes). The cheaper **Inside** is downstairs in RailCity, inside an Indian take-out restaurant (3 SF/15 minutes, 8 SF/hour, Mon-Sat 9:00-22:00, Sun 10:00-21:00). Free Internet terminals and Wi-Fi are available at the city **library** *(Stadtbibliothek),* situated upstairs in the same building as the Bourbaki Panorama (Mon 13:30-18:30, Tue-Fri 10:00-18:30, Thu until 20:00, Sat 9:30-16:00, closed Sun, Löwenplatz 10, tel. 041-417-0707, www.bvl.ch). In theory, free public Wi-Fi should be available throughout the old town, though as of my last visit, they were sill working out the kinks.

Post Office: The main post office *(Hauptpost)* is kitty-corner from the train station (Mon-Fri 7:30-18:30, Sat 8:00-16:00, closed Sun).

Laundry: Take your dirty laundry to **Jet Wasch** (21 SF wash and dry, Mon-Fri 8:00-12:00 & 14:00-18:00, Sat 10:00-16:00, closed Sun, Bruchstrasse 28, tel. 041-240-0151, www.jet wasch.ch). Ask nicely and they may deliver.

Bike Rental: You can rent bikes at the train station and enjoy Luzern's delightful lakeside cycling paths (25 SF/half-day, 33 SF/day, 5 SF less with Eurailpass or Swiss Pass; at SBB counter #21 downstairs in RailCity—signage gives no indication they have bikes, but they do; www.sbb.ch/mobilitaet).

Cinema: In Switzerland, movies are shown in their original language with subtitles. The Bourbaki Panorama building has several screens. The IMAX-like Filmtheater at the Swiss Transport Museum shows first-run movies in the evening.

Water Fountains: Luzern is proud of its clean drinking water and its more than 200 public fountains, each with a fun design and spouting potable water. In the summer, make like the locals, who take full advantage of these fountains, refilling their water bottles again and again.

Getting Around Luzern

Except for the Swiss Transport Museum, all of the sights, hotels, and restaurants recommended in this chapter are within easy walking distance from the station. The Swiss Transport Museum is a 30-minute walk around Lake Luzern. To get there without the hike, catch a bus or boat (summer only) to the Verkehrshaus stop. Buses and all boats depart from Bahnhofplatz, in front of the train station. The TI's free city map and *City Guide* brochure both include a map of bus routes. On the bus, the stops for all the major sights are announced.

Public transportation prices in Luzern depend on which zones you travel in; a single ticket within the primary zone (Zone 1) costs 2.80 SF. A short ride of up to six stops—which covers the trip from the town center to the Swiss Transport Museum or the Lion Monument—costs 2.20 SF. A day pass is 10 SF. All public transit in Luzern is covered by the Swiss Pass (and, except for boats, by the LucerneCard). Transit info: www.vbl.ch.

Tours in Luzern

Walking Tour—A two-hour tour in both English and German is offered every morning in summer (18 SF, departs from TI at 9:45, daily May-Oct, only Wed and Sat Nov-April).

Tourist Train—This tacky little train does a 40-minute circuit of the city's sights, departing from Hotel Schweizerhof (12 SF, kids-5 SF, buy tickets from driver, headphone commentary, daily Easter-Oct, runs hourly 11:00-19:00 June-Aug, less frequently outside summer, tel. 041-220-1100, www.citytrain.ch).

Local Guide—**Ursula Korner** is a good guide (160 SF/2 hours, tel. 041-248-6048, ursula.korner@ko5ive.com). The TI has a list of other guides.

Self-Guided Walk

Reuss River Stroll

This self-guided orientation stroll will give you a brief overview of the town—you'll walk up along the Reuss River, across one of

Luzern's famous wooden bridges, then back through the old town.

• *Begin at Bahnhofplatz, the busy zone between the lake and the train station. Stand in front of the big stone arch.*

❶ **Bahnhofplatz:** This is the transportation hub of Luzern— and all of Central Switzerland. From the area in front of the station, buses zip you anywhere in town. Along the lakefront, you can catch a boat for a lazy cruise around Lake Luzern. And underneath you is the extensive RailCity shopping mall, honeycombed with pedestrian passageways leading to different parts of town. The big stone **arch** was the entrance of the venerable old train station—built in the late 19th century when Switzerland became a top tourist spot, with Luzern as its main attraction. But it burned down in 1971 and was replaced with the modern station. Today, the arch hides vents for the huge underground parking lot below. This is a popular evening meeting spot for city teens.

• *The huge modern building with the big overhanging roof (on your right, with your back to the station) is the...*

❷ **Culture and Conference Center (Kultur-und-Kongress-zentrum):** This building, finished in 1998 by Parisian architect Jean Nouvel, features a concert hall that hosts the Luzern Festival, one of Switzerland's biggest music events. It also holds the **Luzern Museum of Art** (Kunstmuseum Luzern; described later, under "Sights in Luzern").

Lake water is pumped up, into, through, and out of this building; if you were to wander around its far side, you'd see open channels that go right through the middle of the structure (blocked by benches, so distracted visitors don't fall in), as well as a big pond. The architect claims the design recalls earlier times, when this area was swampland...but it more likely recalls his own original plans for the building. Nouvel wanted to put the center out in the middle of the lake. When he was voted down by the people of Luzern, he decided to surround it with water anyway. The plaza under the roof (which reflects the lake and weather, further incorporating the building into the surrounding environment) is a busy community space popular for open-air concerts.

• *Now walk in the opposite direction from the conference center, across*

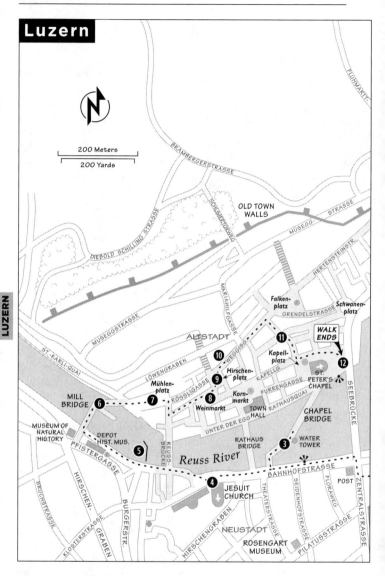

the busy street. Stroll Bahnhofstrasse along the river until you have a good view of Luzern's most famous landmark, the wooden...

❸ **Chapel Bridge (Kapellbrücke):** Luzern began as a fishing village. By the 13th century, traffic streaming between northern and southern Europe went through nearby Gotthard Pass, and Luzern became a bustling trading center. In the first half of the 14th century, this bridge was built at an angle, to connect the town's medieval fortifications. The bridge was part of the

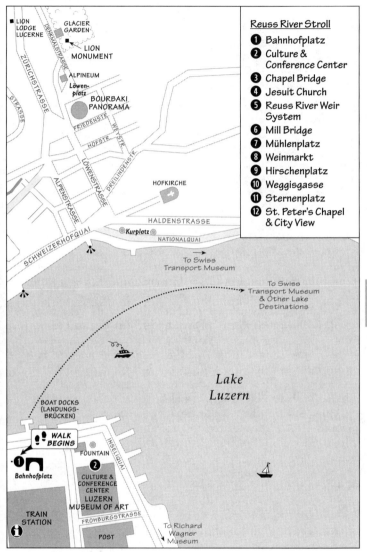

LUZERN

city defense system, so the "window" openings facing the lake are smaller than those on the inland side, giving defenders more cover. The octagonal stone **Water Tower** (Wasserturm, pictured on next page) was built around 1300.

In the 17th century, the bridge was decorated with paintings depicting the development of the town, as well as its two patron saints. In 1993, a leisure boat moored under the bridge caught fire, and before long, Luzern's wooden landmark was in flames.

(A plaque before the start of the bridge tells the story.) When you venture onto the bridge, you'll notice the wood is a lighter color—that is, newer—in the middle. Chapel Bridge was painstakingly rebuilt, but many of its famous paintings were lost. Those still remaining under the wooden roof at the ends of the bridge are restorations of the 17th-century originals; those in the middle were in storage during the fire and were therefore saved. Boats are no longer allowed under the bridge, it's now strictly non-smoking, and tiny security cameras are everywhere.

• *Wander out onto the bridge itself.*

Study the colorful **paintings** overhead. The coats of arms on the paintings tell you which aristocratic families sponsored them. Painting #1 features a legendary and formidable giant, an icon of Luzern you'll see all over town. This big boy dates back to the Middle Ages, when mammoth bones discovered locally were mistakenly identified as the bones of a 15-foot-tall human giant. Painting #2 shows an angel shining a divine light on the place where the town would be born, and where, in the eighth century, a monastery was founded. Painting #3 shows Luzern circa 1400— see how the bridge was already part of the city fortifications. Painting #6 shows a bigger city, as it looked in 1630. In the middle, a painting features the town's patron saint, Mauritius (a plaque midbridge tells why he matters to Luzern). Paintings #9 and #10 remain charred black—a reminder of the tragic fire.

Any swans out? Residents say they originated as a gift from the French king Louis XIV, in appreciation for the protection he got from his Swiss Guards. Today, local children make sure the swans get their daily bread.

• *Head back to the train-station end of the bridge, and continue up the river. Enter the big, white...*

❹ **Jesuit Church (Jesuitenkirche):** This was the first major Baroque church in Switzerland, built 1666-1677 (free, daily 6:00-18:30). It's dedicated to the great missionary Francis Xavier, a co-founder of the Jesuit order, who's shown on the facade baptizing Asians (depicted looking like Native Americans). Luzern's music school uses the church's pipe organ for practice—if you're lucky, you may catch an impromptu concert.

Even though Luzern was a relatively small town back then, the pope wanted to establish a strong presence in Central Switzerland to empower the area's Catholics during the tense times of the Protestant Reformation. The interior of the church once dripped with Baroque stucco. It's been retouched in the lighter Rococo style (c. 1750). Rich as it looks, there's no real marble here—what you see on the altar, pulpit, and side-chapel altars is

stucco made from ground-up marble laid smoothly and economically upon a wooden foundation.

The decorations on the ceiling celebrate the life (and afterlife) of Xavier. After the missionary dies, you see him heaven-bound (in the center). In an exuberant setting that includes both this church and Luzern's landmark Chapel Bridge, the pope's representative and townsfolk gather to wish him Godspeed. Xavier's cart is pulled by an elephant, a leopard, and a camel, all commemorating his mission trips to the exotic Far East. Riding his chariot into heaven, he anticipates a hero's welcome.

In the second niche up on the right, you can meet the only Swiss saint: Brother Klaus, a 15th-century hermit monk who lived in the nearby mountains. He was a great peacemaker between the cantons and is considered the original Swiss isolationist. Since Klaus' time, Switzerland has employed this ethic of avoiding pointless entanglement in foreign squabbles. The statue wears Klaus' original robe. His walking stick hovers just over the altar.

• *Back outside, continue strolling downriver toward Luzern's other wooden bridge. You'll pass the recommended Opus Restaurant and iron pedestrian bridge (at the narrowest crossing spot, marking the location of Luzern's first bridge in the 12th century). Stop at the spiky fence partially damming up the river.*

❺ **Reuss River Weir System:** This big river flows out of the lake. Lake Luzern's main source of water is snowmelt, which

trickles in from streams coming off the surrounding mountains. The water drains out of the lake here on its way to the Rhine. Luzern is responsible for controlling the flow of water and preventing the flooding of lakeside villages by maintaining the lake level. In the mid-19th century, the city devised and built a simple yet ingenious extendable dam (*Nadelwehr*, "spiked weir"). When the water is highest (in the spring), they remove spikes to open the flow; as the summer wears on and the water level drops, they gradually broaden the dam to keep the flow steady. In the winter, they close the dam entirely to keep the lake level high enough for boats.

• *Continuing along the river, you'll pass the Depot History Museum on your left (described later, under "Sights in Luzern") before coming to the wooden...*

❻ Mill Bridge (Spreuerbrücke): Unlike the rebuilt Chapel Bridge, this one's original—and the city is determined to keep it that way (try to find the low-profile security cameras). Before you cross the bridge, pause to appreciate the first of the bridge's fine 17th-century paintings, which shows Luzern's favorite giant again, with the blue-and-white city and cantonal banners under the double eagle of the Holy Roman Empire—a reminder that

the emperor granted free status to the city. The flip side shows Judgment Day, with some going to heaven and others to hell. As you cross the bridge, notice that each painting includes a skeleton. Townsfolk crossed the bridge daily, and these scenes provided vivid reminders that nobody, in any walk of life, can escape death (an especially poignant message in times of war and plague, when these were painted). Like the other wooden bridge, this bridge was part of the city fortification—its downstream defending wall is higher.

Midway across is a little 16th-century chapel, built to guard against destruction by flood. A line of family crests on the door frame acknowledges the volunteers who, over the years, have kept the chapel decorated according to the season. Since 1987, this has been the work of Frau Segesser. While you're paused here, notice the serious woodwork.

The wide stretch at the end of the bridge was to accommodate wagons delivering grain or whatever else was to be milled. Once upon a time, 10 mills churned here—this was the medieval industrial center of Luzern. The "Spreu" in the bridge's name means "chaff" (the sheath surrounding the wheat), which was separated from the wheat at the mill. You can see sketches of these mills as you leave the bridge (on the red wall on the left). A turbine that generated power in 1889 sits quiet on the left, and the tradition of harnessing water power continues here. The stream of water spurting into the air (on the right) indicates that the modern hydroelectric plant—underwater beneath you—is engaged. It creates enough power for 1,000 households.

• *After crossing the bridge, turn right to find yourself in...*

❼ **Mühlenplatz:** This square, which is traffic-free in summer, marks the entrance to the old town. The recommended, riverfront Hug bakery on your right is a good place for lunch or a snack. Across the square, a fun facade tells the story of the wine god Bacchus (to the right of the river murals, above the Italian restaurant at Mühlenplatz 12).

• *At the top of the square (under the Swiss Marilyn Monroe), head right on Kramgasse, then take the first left onto Weinmarktgasse, which leads to...*

❽ **Weinmarkt:** In medieval Luzern, this square served as a marketplace for wine (as the name implies). At first glance, the big

mural on the green building at the top of the square seems to depict the Last Supper, but it's actually the Wedding Feast at Cana, where Jesus turned water into wine. On the right (as you face the mural), the facade of a now-gone pharmacy comes with a wise saying, *Amor medicabilis nvllis herbis* (roughly, "No medicine can cure a broken heart"). Across the square is a building with a secret message hiding in the strange zigzags on its modern shutters. Start at the top left and read: W-E-I-N-M-A-R-K-T. The soldiers on the fine 15th-century fountain are there to remind visitors that this town is tough and strong.

• *Leave the square on the left side of the big mural, then walk several yards to...*

❾ **Hirschenplatz:** This square hasn't always been a square—notice the footprints of two former buildings in the middle. It's named for the Hirschen ("Deer") Restaurant, with the elaborate golden sign. Across from that, try to guess who used to have a shop in the big green building. Yep—the jeweler (see all the rings?). To the right of that building, look for the painting of a famous German writer with the legend *"Goethe logierte hier 1779."* Goethe—the "German Shakespeare"—visited Luzern and stayed in a hotel on this corner. To the left of the building with the rings, the grand facade on the Dornach House, from 1899, celebrates the 400-year anniversary of the last battle against the Germans. Switzerland has enjoyed a durable understanding that there can be disagreements—but no wars—with its historically aggressive and militaristic neighbor to the north.

Continue out of the square onto the busy ❿ **Weggisgasse.** As you stroll, consider that every building in the old town—whether new or rebuilt—is required to offer residential apartments to prevent this historic zone from becoming only office space and touristy shops.

• *After two blocks, you'll come to the Manor department store, with the recommended, tasty, and convenient Manora self-service cafeteria on the top floor. Turn right after Manor and walk one block to...*

⓫ **Sternenplatz:** This tiny square is dominated by the colorful facade of the Restaurant Fritschi. The paintings feature symbols from Luzern's annual Mardi Gras celebration—the city's biggest event, called Fasnacht here. Pictured near the top of the building are the restaurant owners, Mr. and Mrs. Fritschi, celebrating Fasnacht by wearing masks and throwing oranges. Flanking them are their trusty servants, a nanny and a jester—who, in this case, bear a striking resemblance to the Fritschis. Below them is the story of Fasnacht: The cock calls at 5:00 in the morning the Thursday before Ash Wednesday (on the left), and the people get up to frighten winter away. Mr. and Mrs. Fritschi arrive on their wagon to kick off the festivities (on the right). Flying around the scene are oranges—traditionally tossed from the Fritschis to their adoring fans. Once rare here in winter, oranges are special to the festivities, as they mark the beginning of spring.

Continue down the street at the bottom of the square (Hans-Holbein-Gasse), and you'll come upon a colorful fountain with masks of Herr and Frau Fritschi and their servants. Continue to the riverfront, walking around ⓬ **St. Peter's Chapel,** the namesake of Chapel Bridge—which you've arrived at once again. Enjoy the classic Luzern view: the Chapel Bridge and Water Tower, with Mount Pilatus hovering in the background.

• *From here you may want to take a...*

Lakefront Stroll: Consider walking from here along the lakefront, past the National Hotel toward the Swiss Transport Museum. The delightful pathway was built during the tourism boom in the 19th century, when this part of the bay was filled in and fancy resort hotels went up—giving this city the nickname "Monte Carlo of Switzerland." Simply follow the tree-lined waterfront promenade (Nationalquai) that begins near the Hofkirche (the big church with the pointy spires). Believe it or not, Luzern's wooden Chapel Bridge used to stretch all the way to that church.

LUZERN

Sights in Luzern

If you'll be doing a lot of sightseeing here, review your options for saving money: Many Luzern sights are covered by the Swiss Pass; your stamped Visitors Card (free from your hotel) gives you minor discounts at many attractions—remember to ask about these when buying tickets; and the LucerneCard offers half-price entry to most major attractions in town but is only worthwhile if you plan to pack your days with sightseeing (see page 70 for details).

Museums

Luzern is charming enough that simply strolling the streets and bridges and cruising the lake would be enough for a happy day of sightseeing. But the city also offers some fine museums, especially if you're into modern art.

▲▲**Rosengart Collection (Sammlung Rosengart Luzern)**—In the 1930s and 1940s, wealthy resident Siegfried Rosengart palled around with all-star modern artists, financing and collecting their works. This museum displays the fruits of his labor. The building's three floors boast works from all the big names from the late 19th and early 20th centuries, with an emphasis on the art of Pablo Picasso and Paul Klee.

Cost and Hours: 18 SF, covered by Swiss Pass, daily April-Oct 10:00-18:00, Nov-March 11:00-17:00; well-written but brief and overpriced 2.50 SF English booklet—instead borrow English info sheets when you buy your ticket; a few blocks from the train station in the new town up Pilatusstrasse at #10, tel. 041-220-1660, www.rosengart.ch.

Touring the Museum: The ground floor features an extensive **Picasso** collection, including 32 paintings and some 100 drawings, watercolors, and graphic and sculptural works. Near the Picassos are several dozen black-and-white candid photographs of the artist (from a rotating collection of 200), by American David Douglas Duncan. This exhibit makes the museum a ▲▲▲ experience for Picasso fans. I've seen a pile of Picassos, but never have I gotten as personal with him as I did here. Duncan's intimate photos of the artist and his family capture the very human personality of this larger-than-life genius. The photos—taken in Picasso's later years, and many featuring his wife Jacqueline—provide insight into his artistic process, as well as his lifestyle, showing him at work and at play. As a fly on the wall of his chaotic studio, you'll see Picasso in the bathtub, getting a haircut, playing dress-up, moving to a new house, horsing around with his kids, entertaining his guest Gary Cooper, and getting a ballet lesson from Jacqueline. The excellent English descriptions (borrow when you buy your ticket) are essential for getting the stories behind the photos.

In the basement are 125 small works by **Paul Klee,** displayed chronologically by room number so you can follow the evolution of his career. Watch as Klee discovers colors and blossoms from a doodler and, at times, watercolor artist into a mature painter.

The museum also has works by Braque, Monet, Renoir, Miró, Chagall, Cézanne, Matisse, Modigliani, and Pissarro.

Depot History Museum (Depot Historisches Museum Luzern)—This cluttered old museum is a "depot" for the accumulated bric-a-brac of Luzern's past, housed in one of Luzern's oldest surviving buildings, which was long used to store military weapons and uniforms. Their collection is too big to display effectively, so they've come up with an innovative concept: Throw all of their archived stuff together and display it on three crowded floors. Wander through shelves of old weapons, stained-glass windows, sculptures, and old-fashioned tourism posters. The items are displayed without much rhyme or reason, and each is labeled with a barcode—use your scanner (included with entry) on whichever one you're interested in. You can then read about its history in English on your handheld screen.

Cost and Hours: 10 SF, covered by Swiss Pass, Tue-Sun 10:00-17:00, closed Mon, Pfistergasse 24, tel. 041-228-5424, www .hmluzern.ch.

▲▲**Swiss Transport Museum (Verkehrshaus)**—This enormous complex, across the lake from the train station, includes hundreds of exhibits in several buildings, covering virtually all modes of transportation. It's a fun excursion, but it's pricey, a bit dated (the giant country map is nothing when you've Google-Earthed), and a little overwhelming, demanding at least a half-day. If you're in town for only one day, I'd skip this and enjoy the muse-

ums and ambience in the old town. But if you have a second day, have your kids in tow, or are obsessed with trains, planes, and automobiles, this can be time well spent.

Cost and Hours: 28 SF, half-price with Swiss Pass, daily April-Oct 10:00-18:00, Nov-March 10:00-17:00, tel. 041-370-4444, recorded info tel. 0848-852-020, www.verkehrshaus.ch.

Films and Shows: In addition to the exhibits, the museum has a wide variety of shows and demonstrations (pick up a schedule—and inquire about English-speaking events—as you enter). These include a planetarium show (included in entry price) and the Filmtheater—an IMAX in every way but name (the museum's IMAX contract has expired). The film costs 18 SF or 38 SF for a combo-ticket that includes the museum; showings take place from 11:00 to 17:00 and sometimes in the evenings (www.film theater.ch).

Getting There: From downtown, it's a 30-minute **walk** to the museum, most of it along a beautiful promenade (described earlier, under "Lakefront Stroll"; the museum is at Lidostrasse 5). This is a pleasant walk, even if you're not going to the museum. To make a beeline to the museum, take **bus** #6, #8, or #24 from the station, and get off at the Verkehrshaus stop (the stop is announced, plus you'll see the huge, barrel-shaped, can't-miss-it theater, covered by 2.20-SF short ride ticket). For a more scenic approach, catch a **boat** in front of the train station (direction: Verkehrshaus, 2/hour, 10 minutes each way, 11.20 SF round-trip).

Touring the Museum: Starting in the first building, you'll come across a 30-minute show about the Gotthard Tunnel. Then wander through endless halls of train engines and tram cars. Cross from the train hall into the **Road Transport Hall.** It holds a warehouse stacked floor to ceiling with 80 vehicles dating from 1860 to 2005, including horse carriages, bicycles, and automobiles. At the interactive car theater, you can select the vehicle you want to see.

As you exit, you'll be face-to-face with jetliners and surrounded by pavilions devoted to more vehicles (such as planes, boats, motorcycles, spaceships, and high-mountain lifts). Many of the exhibits are interactive, such as the parasailing simulator,

where you lie down on a smoothly gliding platform and peer down at the countryside below.

Upstairs in the boat and cable-car building, be sure to seek out the **Swiss-arena,** an enormous (more than 2,000 square feet) aerial photograph of Switzerland (follow signs that look like a Swiss map in a CBS-style eye). This photo map, spread out on the floor like laminated linoleum, is detailed enough to show virtually every single building within the country's borders. Slide on the Swiss slippers, borrow a map and magnifying glass, and glide across Switzerland, looking for the places you've visited so far.

Richard Wagner Museum—This museum is a 10-minute walk along the lakefront, south of the train station and housed in a building where the composer once lived.

Cost and Hours: 8 SF, covered by Swiss Pass, mid-March-Nov Tue-Sun 10:00-12:00 & 14:00-17:00, closed Mon and off-season, café, Richard Wagner Weg 27, tel. 041-360-2370, www .richard-wagner-museum.ch.

Luzern Museum of Art (Kunstmuseum Luzern)—Located in the lakefront cultural center by the train station, this museum features special exhibits of contemporary art.

Cost and Hours: 16 SF, covered by Swiss Pass, Tue-Wed 10:00-20:00, Thu-Sun 10:00-18:00, closed Mon, Europaplatz 1, tel. 041-226-7800, www.kunstmuseumluzern.ch.

Museum of Natural History (Natur-Museum)—With an emphasis on interactive exhibits, this is a great place to bring kids.

Cost and Hours: 6 SF, covered by Swiss Pass, Tue-Sun 10:00-17:00, closed Mon, near the end of the Mill Bridge next to the Depot History Museum at Kasernenplatz 6, tel. 041-228-5411, www.naturmuseum.ch.

Löwenplatz

North of the old town, Löwenplatz has a must-see monument and a pair of fun attractions (Glacier Garden and Bourbaki Panorama). While the area may, for good reason, set off your "tourist-trap" alarms, I appreciate these sights for their historical significance. They composed the original 19th-century tourist center of Luzern and were designed back when tourism was new. Behind the tacky souvenir shops, they retain some of their Victorian-era charm.

I've listed Löwenplatz's sights in descending order of respectability. If you're doing the Glacier Garden and Bourbaki Panorama, and you don't have a Swiss Pass or LucerneCard, you might as well buy the 21-SF **Lionpass** combo-ticket, which saves you 3 SF.

Getting There: It's a 10-minute walk from the old town or a short bus ride across the river from the station. Take bus #1, #19, #22, or #23 two or three stops north from the train station (covered by 2.20-SF short ride ticket). When you get off the bus, you'll see the round Bourbaki Panorama across the street; the lion and the Glacier Garden are one long block farther up the hill, on a lane away from the busy street.

▲**Lion Monument (Löwendenkmal)**—This famous monument is an essential stop if you're visiting Luzern—if only because when you get back home, everyone will ask you, "Did you see the lion?" Free and open from sunrise to dusk, the huge sculpture (33 feet long by 20 feet tall) is carved right into a cliff face, over a reflecting pool in a peaceful park. Though it's often overrun with tour groups, a tranquil moment here is genuinely moving: The mighty  lion rests his paws on a shield, with his head cocked to one side, tears streaming down his cheeks. In his side is the broken-off end of a spear, which is slowly killing the noble beast. (Note the angle of the spear, which matches the striations of the rock face, subtly suggesting more spears raining down on the lion.) This heartbreaking figure represents the Swiss mercenaries who were killed or executed defending the French king in the French Revolution. The inscription reads, *Helvetiorum fidei ac virtuti*—"To the loyalty and bravery of the Swiss."

▲**Bourbaki Panorama**—Here's your chance to get right in the middle of a great painting—literally. In the 19th century, before the dawn of cinema, modern people were hungry for visual entertainment. Uniform panorama theaters like this were built all over Europe and hosted various gigantic paintings, which were rolled up and taken on road trips. This 360-degree painting (a 33-foot-tall wraparound canvas with a circumference of 360 feet) tells the story of the culminating battle of the Franco-Prussian War. The 1.50-SF booklet explains it all and makes for a good souvenir.

Upon arrival, request an English playing of the 12-minute soundtrack of the battle. Spend your waiting time enjoying the fine first-floor exhibit about 19th-century entertainment. When the English narration starts, be on the second-floor viewing platform to savor all 360 degrees of the dramatic conclusion of the Franco-Prussian War. For three days in February of 1871, the 87,000-man French Army—led by the panorama's namesake, General Bourbaki—trudged through the snow across the Swiss border, near Neuchâtel. Once in Switzerland, they gave up their weapons and surrendered to the Swiss—who, the story goes, took excellent care of the French, nursing them back to health before sending them home.

The Bourbaki Panorama was painted by Edouard Castres, who was actually there (as a Red Cross volunteer) on that frigid morning. The 1881 painting was thoroughly refurbished in 2000, when several life-size figures were added to the foreground. Sound effects fill the hall while you view the painting. The museum exhibit gives more background on the Franco-Prussian War and Bourbaki's army, as well as details about this and other panorama paintings.

Cost and Hours: 12 SF, covered by Lionpass combo-ticket and Swiss Pass; April-Oct Tue-Sun 9:00-18:00, Mon 13:00-18:00; Nov-March Tue-Sun 10:00-17:00, Mon 13:00-17:00; Löwenplatz 11, tel. 041-412-3030, www.bourbakipanorama.ch.

Glacier Garden (Gletschergarten)—This complex is a strange sort of mini-theme-park with an eclectic hodgepodge of exhibits, most loosely relating to alpine geology. Although the various pieces don't quite hang together (such as the fun but out-of-place Hall of Mirrors), it adds up to a pleasant, if overpriced, activity.

Cost and Hours: 12 SF, covered by Lionpass combo-ticket

LUZERN

and Swiss Pass, daily April-Oct 9:00-18:00, Nov-March 10:00-17:00, Denkmalstrasse 4, tel. 041-410-4340, www.gletschergarten.ch.

Touring the Garden: Pick up the English info booklet as you enter, and follow the numbers on the confusing one-way path. First, you'll walk through the **glacier-grinded grounds** that give the garden its name. While geologists would get a thrill out of this, it was just a bunch of holes to me. Then enter the **museum,** with exhibits about glacial processes and a dramatic slideshow that gives you an idea of what this area once looked like. The slideshow takes you back in time, starting 16,000 years ago—at the end of the last Ice Age, when Luzern was emerging from beneath the Reuss Glacier—to 20 million years ago, when this region was a subtropical sea. You'll see lots of rocks with fossils and with the tracks of former sea creatures. Downstairs are huge 3-D reliefs of late-18th-century Luzern, and the Alps and lakes of Central Switzerland. Back upstairs, cross directly into the **Amrein's House,** an old chalet with some original furnishings and models of traditional Swiss buildings. As you leave, you have the option of hiking up the steep **Tower Walk,** which leads to another old chalet and an observation tower.

At the end, be sure to visit the **Hall of Mirrors.** This undeniably enjoyable attraction, made in 1896 for a national exhibition in Geneva, is a delightfully low-tech fun house. You'll grope your way through twisting corridors—with mirrors on all sides—decorated like a Disneyfied Alhambra. It's confusing, dizzying, and claustrophobic, but goofy fun. As you run into yourself (literally) again and again, you'll lament the poor sap who has to clean the smudge marks off all those mirrors (walk slowly, and see if you can make it through without hitting yourself). As you leave, giggling and nauseated, you may find yourself wondering, "So, what exactly did that have to do with glaciers?"

Alpineum—This disappointing attraction, overshadowed by its substantial gift shop, displays a handful of paintings and reliefs of famous Swiss mountain peaks and panoramas. The exhibit includes miniature models of traditional houses, trains, boats, people, and cows. Though it's now a musty, outmoded tourist trap, imagine how stunning this would have been in an age before movies and mountain lifts—when you had to climb the mountains yourself to get these views. Visit this only if you have a Swiss Pass, which gets you in for free.

Cost and Hours: 6 SF, covered by Swiss Pass but not Lionpass combo-ticket, April-Oct daily 9:00-18:00, closed Nov-March, English explanations, Denkmalstrasse 11, tel. 041-410-6266, www.alpineum.ch.

Sleeping in Luzern

Luzern accommodations are expensive. I've listed two classic (and renovated) hotels—one big (the Waldstätterhof) and one smaller (Hotel des Alpes), a handful of small, basic hotels, and two good backpacker options. These are all centrally located (except Backpackers Luzern). To avoid nighttime noise from city streets, ask for a room on a high floor.

$$$ Hotel Waldstätterhof is a grand old hotel across the street from the train station, with reasonable rates for its high level of comfort. Its 99 bright, spacious rooms come with all the amenities (June-Oct: Db-260 SF, Nov-May: Db-170 SF, pricier suites, free Internet access, pay Wi-Fi, Zentralstrasse 4, tel. 041-227-1271, fax 041-227-1272, www.hotel-waldstaetterhof.ch, info@hotel-waldstaetterhof.ch).

$$$ Hotel des Alpes is a good bet if you want to sleep right on the river in the old town. Its lobby hides above a busy restaurant, but the 45 rooms are fresh and modern, with new bathrooms. Pricier riverfront rooms come with beautiful views (riverview rooms: Sb-160 SF, Db-255 SF; back-side rooms: Sb-135 SF, Db-205 SF, less in winter; a few rooms have balconies for the same price, free Wi-Fi and Internet access, Furrengasse 3, tel. 041-417-2060, fax 041-417-2066, www.desalpes-luzern.ch, info@desalpes-luzern.ch).

$$ Hotel Baslertor and its cheaper annex, **Hotel Pension Rösli** (across the street), offer well-located rooms for various budgets. The Baslertor's 30 rooms, with old, dark furnishings, are

---

Sleep Code

(1 SF = about $1.10, country code: 41)
S = Single, **D** = Double/Twin, **T** = Triple, **Q** = Quad, **b** = bathroom, **s** = shower only. Unless otherwise noted, credit cards are accepted, English is spoken, and breakfast is included.

To help you sort easily through these listings, I've divided the accommodations into three categories, based on the price for a standard double room with bath during high season:

  $$$ Higher Priced—Most rooms 200 SF or more.
  $$ Moderately Priced—Most rooms between 100-200 SF.
  $ Lower Priced—Most rooms 100 SF or less.

Prices can change without notice; verify the hotel's current rates online or by email. For other updates, see www.ricksteves.com/update.

LUZERN

Luzern Hotels & Restaurants

LUZERN

more expensive and come in several sizes (Sb-100-150 SF, budget Db-100-150 SF, small Db-125-175 SF, medium Db-150-200 SF, large Db-175-225 SF, Qb and Quint/b rooms available, ask for 10 percent Rick Steves discount when you reserve and show book upon arrival, extra bed-25 SF, elevator, free Internet access in business center, free Wi-Fi, atmospheric breakfast room, plush public spaces, small, solar-heated swimming pool). The Rösli pension—an older building with lower ceilings—has nine rooms with even older furnishings and no elevator (Db-100-150 SF). Both hotels charge 18 SF per person extra for breakfast. Roland runs a tight ship (with strict cancellation policies), staffing both hotels from the Baslertor reception desk (Pfistergasse 17, tel. 041-249-2222, fax 041-249-2233, www.baslertor.ch, info@baslertor.ch).

$$ Hotel Goldener Stern is a solid value, offering 16 perfectly pleasant rooms over a restaurant and with some street noise (Sb-100 SF, smaller top-floor D-140 SF, Db-160 SF, Tb-190 SF, Qb-220 SF, prices drop for longer stays or when slow, tiny elevator, pay Internet access, free Wi-Fi, Burgerstrasse 35, tel. 041-227-5060, fax 041-227-5061, www.goldener-stern.ch, hotel@goldener-stern .ch, Amrein family).

$$ Hotel Alpha, once a convent-run boarding house for village girls, is now popular with students. It offers 50 big, bright,

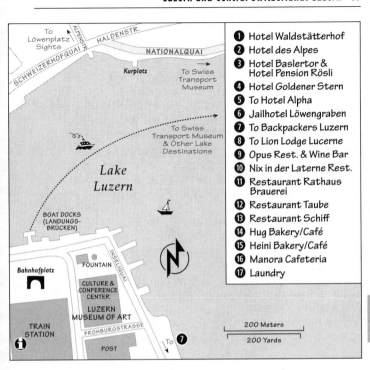

1. Hotel Waldstätterhof
2. Hotel des Alpes
3. Hotel Baslertor & Hotel Pension Rösli
4. Hotel Goldener Stern
5. To Hotel Alpha
6. Jailhotel Löwengraben
7. To Backpackers Luzern
8. To Lion Lodge Lucerne
9. Opus Rest. & Wine Bar
10. Nix in der Laterne Rest.
11. Restaurant Rathaus Brauerei
12. Restaurant Taube
13. Restaurant Schiff
14. Hug Bakery/Café
15. Heini Bakery/Café
16. Manora Cafeteria
17. Laundry

institutional rooms, most with the toilet down the hall, and none with phones or TVs. Although it's located in a pleasant residential area, it still has some street noise from the nearby school and playing field—even at night (S-75 SF, twin D-108 SF, twin Db-150 SF, T-159 SF, pay Internet access and Wi-Fi, comfy lounges and TV room, Zähringerstrasse 24, at intersection with Pilatusstrasse, tel. 041-240-4280, fax 041-240-9131, www.hotelalpha.ch, info@hotel alpha.ch). It's a 10-minute walk or an easy bus ride from the train station (take bus #1, #2, or #10, get off at Pilatusplatz, and—with Hotel Anker at your back—walk past the Marilyn bar 2 blocks).

$$ Jailhotel Löwengraben is a theme hotel renting clean but small, spare cells in the renovated former city prison on a nondescript street a few steps from the heart of the old town. As much an experience as a place to sleep, it has 133 beds in 56 cells (3 double beds, but the vast majority—logically—are twins). Cells, which can be a bit stuffy, come with cot-like beds, tiny barred windows, and reinforced doors—so it really does feel like a prison (except for the mod but teeny WCs). It's a fun experience, but hardly a good value, given how spartan the rooms are. It's noisy on weekends, as it's above a club. On the upside, the club waives its 15-20-SF cover charge for hotel guests—if you can't beat 'em, join 'em (S-100 SF, Sb-110 SF, D-150 SF, Db-170 SF, T-210 SF, Tb-240 SF, Qb-300

SF, people who actually did time here enjoy sleeping in the four wardens' suites-190-220 SF for two people; prices drop in shoulder season, all rooms about 10 SF less per person off-season; free Wi-Fi but no Internet terminals, Löwengraben 18, tel. 041-410-7830, fax 041-410-7832, www.jailhotel.ch, hotel@jailhotel.ch).

$ Backpackers Luzern is calm and well-run, sharing a modern, blocky building with student dorms *(Studentenheim)* in a peaceful residential area a 15-minute walk south of the train station. The place has 30 rooms (each with a balcony), a pair of kitchens for guests, a welcoming lounge, no curfew, Internet access (6 SF/hour), and laundry (9 SF/load for full service). The walk to the center is mostly along the lake, through pretty parks and next to a fine beach (32 SF/person in 4-bed rooms, 37 SF/person in 2-bed rooms, D-80 SF, T-105 SF, includes sheets, no breakfast but nice kitchen, reception open 7:30-10:00 & 16:00-23:00, elevator, free Wi-Fi, Alpenquai 42, tel. 041-360-0420, fax 041-360-0442, www.backpackerslucerne.ch, info@backpackerslucerne.ch).

$ Lion Lodge Lucerne, located near the Lion Monument, is laid back but well-maintained, with decent-sized rooms (32-34 SF/person in 4- to 6-bed rooms, 36 SF/person in 2-bed rooms, D-72-90 SF, Db-90 SF, includes sheets, no breakfast, kitchen, pay Internet access, verandas; take bus #1 direction: Maihof to Wesemlinrain stop, then cross street to Zürichstrasse 57; for location see map on page 88, tel. 041-410-0144, www.lionlodge.ch, info@lionlodge.ch).

Eating in Luzern

While eateries along the river are pricey and a bit touristy, if you have one evening in Luzern, that's where you'll make the best memories. Here's a selection of places with decent prices, many with great riverfront ambience.

Dining in Style

Opus, next to the big Jesuit Church, is both a trendy wine bar and a good restaurant. Pair your wine with meat, fish, and vegetarian dishes with international flair (25-40 SF); the lush and varied salad bar ("antipasti buffet"—a small plate piled high makes a light and healthy dinner for 19 SF); or your choice of dried meats and cheeses (20-30 SF, choose and cut your own fresh bread to go with it). They always have a couple dozen bottles of wine open and available by the glass. Sit in the upscale, colorful interior; in the candlelit and extremely romantic wine cellar; or out front, right on the river (open long hours daily, Bahnhofstrasse 16, tel. 041-226-4141).

Romantic **Nix in der Laterne** has a white-tablecloth-dressy interior and great outside seats right on the fast-rushing river. In keeping with their philosophy of making everything from scratch using fresh seasonal ingredients, they offer a brief chalkboard menu that the server explains (35-45-SF plates, 20-SF lunches, daily 11:00-22:00, reservations smart for dinner, Reusssteg 9, tel. 041-240-2543).

Traditional Swiss Sit-Down Restaurants

Restaurant Rathaus Brauerei is a lively microbrewery with an ideal riverfront location and a young, helpful staff. It's clearly a local favorite for its Seidel Rathausbier, brewed in such small quantities that you can only get it here. They serve their beer to ladies in a two-deciliter "elegant flute." Special seasonal brews are on the menu board, along with salads, "gourmet" pretzel sandwiches, 22-30-SF dishes, Swiss-style mac-and-cheese (21 SF), and the daily three-course special (25 SF on weekdays, 30-35 SF on weekends)—available until it's sold out (open long hours daily, Unter der Egg 2, tel. 041-410-5257).

Restaurant Taube is popular for serving "grandma's cooking" (great spot for a good *Rösti*, 26 SF) and for its riverside seating—not for its lackluster service (20-SF two-course lunches, Mon-Sat 11:30-14:00 & 17:30-22:30, closed Sun, Burgerstrasse 3, tel. 041-210-0747).

Restaurant Schiff has scenic riverfront tables in the old town with good, traditional Swiss food, relatively reasonable prices, and a fun, accessible menu (plenty of salads, pizzas, most main dishes 25-35 SF, open long hours daily with food served until 23:00, music many evenings, across the river from Jesuit Church, Unter der Egg 8, tel. 041-418-5252).

Fast and Affordable

Bakeries: Luzern has several bakery chains with many inviting branches that serve both takeaway sandwiches and treats and light sit-down meals. Consider these two: **Hug Bakery/Café** has a cuddly location overlooking the river at the old-town end of the Mill Bridge, smack in the middle of the sightseeing action. People come for a drink, snack, or dessert, or to settle in for a meal. The selection includes basic traditional Swiss dishes (some plates come with *Rösti*, 20 SF) and two-course lunch deals (18-25 SF) to enjoy at outdoor tables with river views or in the splendid glassed-in terrace (Mon-Sat 7:00-18:30, until 23:00 in good summer weather, Sun 8:00-17:00, Mühlenplatz 6). The cheap takeaway salads, pastries, and sandwiches are made to order for the inviting riverside benches just a few steps away. The similarly priced (but not as classy) **Heini Bakery/Café** has four locations in Luzern, including one in the old town half a block down from the Manor department store on

Falkenplatz (Mon-Fri 7:00-18:00, Thu until 21:00, Sat 7:00-17:00, Sun 9:00-18:00).

Self-Service Cafeteria: **Manora,** a cafeteria on the fifth floor of the Manor department store in the old town, is ideal for a tasty, efficient lunch. Choose between a fresh salad bar (big plate-11 SF) or a variety of main dishes (6-15 SF). In good weather, climb the stairs to the outdoor terrace, with great views over the rooftops of Luzern to the lake and Mount Pilatus. This place is packed with locals and very crowded during peak times—eat early or late, and send your travel partner up top to claim an outdoor table while you buy the food (Mon-Wed 9:00-18:30, Thu-Fri 9:00-21:00, Sat 8:00-16:00, closed Sun, smoking allowed on roof, Weggisgasse 5).

Luzern Connections

Luzern is marvelously well-situated, with convenient connections to anywhere in the country. Note that Luzern is on both the Golden Pass and the William Tell Express scenic rail lines (see the Scenic Rail Journeys chapter).

From Luzern by Train to: Zürich (2/hour, 1 hour), **Zürich Airport** (2/hour, 1.25 hours, some with change in Zürich), **Bern** (3/hour, 1-1.5 hours, some with change in Olten), **Interlaken** (2/hour, 2 hours direct, 2.5 hours with 1-2 changes), **Lausanne** (hourly direct, 2.25 hours), **Appenzell** (2/hour, 2.75 hours, change in Herisau or in Zürich and Gossau), **Lugano** (hourly, 2.5 hours, half with change in Arth-Goldau), **Chur** (hourly, 2.25 hours, change in Thalwil). Train info: toll tel. 0900-300-300 (1.19 SF/minute), or www.rail.ch.

Central Switzerland: Day Trips from Luzern

Luzern is perched on the edge of a super-scenic lake and ringed by family-friendly mountain peaks that are easily conquerable for a price. All of this makes the city a perfect springboard for alpine excursions. The following side-trips are all popular and include a boat cruise, a hidden military fortress, and two of the most famous and most accessible mountain lifts from Luzern: Mount Pilatus and Mount Rigi.

Planning Your Time

While it's possible to combine most of these adventures (the fortress, a mini-lake cruise, and the Pilatus mountain lift—up one side and down the other) into one jam-packed day trip, you won't have much time to enjoy any one sight. For a more relaxed day (especially in good weather), focus on Pilatus. Note that the fortress is open only on weekends from April through October. Confirm all schedules and logistics at the TI before embarking.

Boats of Note: These boats can help you connect the excursions in this chapter—**Stansstad** (Fortress Fürigen) **to Alpnachstad** (where you catch the Pilatus cogwheel train; 7 boats/day, 22 minutes, 1 steamboat/day mid-July–mid-Aug, 11 SF); **Stansstad to Luzern** (9 boats/day, 1 hour, 2 steamboats/day mid-July–mid-Aug, 18.40 SF, 35 SF round-trip); **Alpnachstad to Luzern** (7 boats/day, 1.5 hours, 1 steamboat/day mid-July–mid-Aug, 25 SF). For boat information, see www.lakelucerne.ch.

Tell-Pass: If you're home-basing in Luzern for several days, consider the Tell-Pass. This pass includes two days of free rides on lifts, boats, and several area train lines in a seven-day period, and half-price rides on the other five days (180 SF, 144 SF with Swiss Pass; buy at TIs, train stations, and boat docks; April-Oct only, www.tell-pass.ch). A longer version gives you 5 free days in a 15-day period and half-price rides on the other 10 days (246 SF, 197 SF with Swiss Pass). A Tell-Pass doesn't make sense if you have a consecutive-day Swiss Pass (as opposed to a flexipass).

Lake Luzern

Lake Luzern—the most touristed in Switzerland—has a variety of boat routes and destinations (35 stops in all). Cruises range from

a one-hour sampler tour (around Luzern's "harbor") to a full-blown, 5.5-hour exploration (to Flüelen, at the far end of the lake, and back again). Some routes are round-trip; others are designed for you to get out, explore, and then take the next boat back. Romantics will want to hitch a ride on one of the five old-fashioned paddleboat steamers.

In summer, a "villa and castle cruise" makes a one-hour, 16.40-SF round-trip sightseeing swing around Luzern's corner of the lake (4/day, Sun only in spring and fall, leaves from pier). Better yet, a more dramatic two-hour excursion takes you from Luzern to Weggis or Vitznau (under Mount Rigi, across the lake), then back to Luzern (also part of William Tell Express route, 35

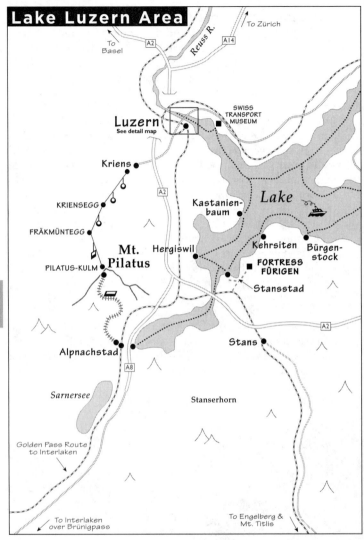

Lake Luzern Area

To Zürich
To Basel
Reuss R.
A2
A14
Luzern
See detail map
SWISS TRANSPORT MUSEUM
Kriens
KRIENSEGG
A2
FRÄKMÜNTEGG
Kastanien-baum
Lake
PILATUS-KULM
Mt. Pilatus
Hergiswil
Kehrsiten
Bürgen-stock
FORTRESS FÜRIGEN
Stansstad
A2
Alpnachstad
A8
Stans
Sarnersee
Stanserhorn
Golden Pass Route to Interlaken
To Engelberg & Mt. Titlis
To Interlaken over Brünigpass

SF round-trip to Weggis, 42 SF to Vitznau). For most, a two-hour circle is about as much of a scenic cruise as the lake deserves. The Luzern TI sells tickets and can offer advice on which trip best fits your schedule.

Boats leave from the lake piers in front of the Luzern train station. They're operated by the Lake Lucerne Navigation Company (tel. 041-367-6767, www.lakelucerne.ch). These boats are free with a Eurailpass or Swiss Pass (but remember that if you're using a flexipass, the boat trip costs a flexi-day). Doing the lake cruise on

the day you arrive or depart—when you're already using a flexi-day for your train transportation—is a smart plan.

Mount Pilatus

Looming behind Luzern, Pilatus (7,000 feet), worth ▲, is a dramatic backdrop to the city and also an enjoyable destination. While legend dictates that it's named for Pontius Pilate—whose body is supposedly in one of its lakes, kicking up a fuss if disturbed—it more likely comes from a Latin word meaning "cloudy." It's also said to be infested with dragons.

Getting There

You can ascend Pilatus (to the summit, called "Pilatus Kulm") in two ways: by cogwheel train (the world's steepest, at 48 percent grade, up the east side straight to the summit) or gondola/cable car (in three stages, up the north side, with a chance to stop at Fräkmüntegg for a luge ride or ropes course). For maximum views, go up one way, down the other—in good weather, the view's spectacular on both sides in both directions. If you're interested in  the luge at Fräkmüntegg, it makes a little more sense to take the gondola and cable car up, since the luge course has shorter lines and offers a discount earlier in the day. Otherwise, take the cogwheel train up, as it's a bit more dramatic to ride it uphill than down (and the gondola ride down catches more afternoon light than the cogwheel does on the east side). For more advice, ask at your hotel or Luzern's TI.

Cost: A round-trip to the top and back, no matter how you go, costs 66 SF from the base of the mountain (with your choice of cogwheel train or gondola/cable car for each leg; does not include transportation between Luzern and the cogwheel train or gondola stations). Swiss Pass holders go for half-price, and Eurailpass holders get a 30 percent discount (46 SF round-trip). Don't throw your ticket away when you board, as you'll have to scan it several times until you exit at the last station.

If you're staying in Luzern and traveling without a Swiss Pass, it makes sense to get either the popular **Golden Round Trip** package or **Silver Round Trip** package (both offered May-mid-Oct only). These include transportation from Luzern to the base of the mountain, as well as lifts up and down the mountain. The Golden Round Trip includes a lazy, 1.5-hour boat trip between Luzern and the cogwheel base station (94 SF); the cheaper Silver Round Trip pays for a train trip, not boat, between Luzern and the cogwheel station (74 SF).

By Train: The cogwheel train leaves from the lakeside town of Alpnachstad. To reach Alpnachstad from Luzern, take either the S5 train (2/hour, 20 minutes, 6.20 SF) or the boat, which leaves from the dock opposite the train station (7/day, 1.5 hours, 1 steamboat/day mid-July-mid-Aug, 25 SF). The cogwheel train runs mid-May–mid-Nov only (1-2/hour daily, first train up at 8:15; last train up usually at 17:10 but at 17:50 July-Aug, last train down at 17:45 but at 18:45 July-Aug, shorter operating times in Nov, 30 minutes up, 40 minutes down; for the best views going up, take a downhill-facing seat on the right side, www.pilatus.ch).

By Gondola/Cable Car: The gondola leaves from the town of Kriens, virtually a suburb of Luzern. To reach Kriens, catch city bus #1, which departs frequently from in front of Luzern train station (15-minute ride, direction: Kriens, stop: Linde-Pilatus). After getting off the bus, walk 10 minutes to the gondola station, following *Pilatus* signs (to return to Luzern from the gondola station, follow the white signs for *Luzern bus* and hop on bus #1; you don't want the bus stop in front of the station).

The gondola runs continuously (daily April–mid-Oct 8:30-17:30, off-season until 16:45 but closes for maintenance mid-Oct-mid-Nov and mid-Dec-mid-Feb, www.pilatus.ch). If you already have a pink-and-blue round-trip ticket, you can skip the ticket line, but you'll still need to show it to an attendant to get the card that lets you through the turnstile. The gondola stops at Krienseregg (recreation area with trails and playground) and then Fräkmüntegg (total trip 30 minutes). From Fräkmüntegg, it's another seven minutes in a cable car to the observation platform at Pilatus Kulm.

Activities on Pilatus

At Fräkmüntegg

This spot, on the north slope of Pilatus, is a summer-fun zone. If the weather's good, stop here to zip down the nearly mile-long

Fräkigaudi, Switzerland's longest **luge ride** (1 ride-8 SF, 5 rides-36 SF, 11 rides-72 SF, multi-ride cards transferrable and include free ride before 12:00, open daily May-late Oct 10:00-12:00 & 13:15-17:00, until 17:30 with no midday break Sat-Sun and daily July-Aug, closes if rainy, no rain refunds, expect lines on sunny weekends, www .rodelbahn.ch). A nearby **tubing course** runs on a dry track during similar hours, even in terrible weather (1 hour-15 SF, 1.5 hours-20 SF, 2 hours-25 SF). At the fun **Suspension Rope Park** (Seilpark), you can test your agility high up on 10 rope courses with varying degrees of difficulty (27 SF includes three hours on the course plus material and instruction, family discounts—but no kids under 8 years or 4 feet, May-late Oct daily 10:00-17:00, open in good weather off-season, www.pilatus-seilpark.ch).

At the Summit

Hotel Bellevue acts as the visitors' center, with a good information office, restaurants, a souvenir shop, and Internet terminals. Hotel Pilatus-Kulm's three restaurants have the original furnishings from 1889; there's also a modern self-service cafeteria. The terrace below is full of free and comfortable deck chairs.

Hiking: These walks lead to great viewpoints. I've listed them roughly in order of difficulty, from easiest to most strenuous. All leave from the summit, Pilatus Kulm.

Two short **"Dragonpaths"** along the ridge beyond Hotel Pilatus-Kulm lead through tunnels to various viewpoints in the rock. These paths come with signs illustrating dragon tales by the famous Swiss artist Hans Erni.

A 10-minute hike above Hotel Bellevue takes you up to **Esel** ("Donkey," commemorating the pre-cable-car days, when Queen Victoria came up to Pilatus on the back of a donkey). Below Esel hides an impressive part of Switzerland's anti-aircraft defense system. Find the gray, round structures within the imitation rock. Modern missiles behind the camouflage point to the skies. The biggest radar in Switzerland towers above Hotel Pilatus-Kulm in an off-limits military zone.

Hiking to **Tomlishorn** (35 minutes), you'll spot more camouflaged military installations. Stop at the yellow *Echo* sign and shout your message out to the world. Somebody out there keeps yelling it back.

A 1.5-hour hike leads to the 6,700-foot cross-capped summit of **Matthorn** (not Matterhorn). This hike is moderately strenuous—generally uphill, with lots of ups and downs. A visitors' book invites you to sign and leave your impressions on this breathtaking spot.

Sleeping at the Summit: You can spend the night on the summit of Pilatus. Linger outside to enjoy the views with the marmots and mountain goats...or head inside for the hotels' free nightly entertainment: movies and a disco on alternating nights. **$$$ Hotel Bellevue** is a modern, round building with 28 rooms—clean and bright, with Nordic-style furniture (Sb-150 SF, Db-220 SF). **$$$ Hotel Pilatus-Kulm** is a historic building from 1900 (Sb-170-240 SF, Db-220-300 SF, price depends on demand). Both hotels come with a big breakfast, have Wi-Fi, and share contact information (tel. 041-329-1212, fax 041-329-1213, www.pilatus.ch, hotels@pilatus.ch).

Mount Rigi

This long, shelf-like mountain, across the lake from Luzern, provides sweeping views of Central Switzerland (and, on a clear day,

Germany and France, too). Even though it's at a lower altitude than Pilatus (5,900 feet), this so-called "Queen of the Mountains" boasts the first cog railway in Europe and claims to offer the best vistas in the area. Compared with Mount Pilatus, Rigi has virtually no tour groups (since its summit hotel doesn't court them). Still, the top can be busy between 10:00 and 15:00.

Getting There

You can reach the top of Rigi from either its "front" (west) or "back" (east) side. Hourly cogwheel trains chug up to the summit from base stations on both sides (hikers can hop off on the way up or down). The west side also has a cable-car option.

If you're staying in Luzern, coming up the west side makes the most sense, as it gives you an excuse to take a scenic boat ride to the base of the mountain. This route also has better views than the east face and lets you go one direction by train and the other by cable car.

Figure five to six hours for the total round-trip from Luzern. The schedules and prices listed here are for mid-March through November (less frequent in winter; confirm at Luzern TI, or check www.rigi.ch).

Cost: No matter how you go, the price from the base of the mountain to Rigi Kulm is 40 SF one-way, 64 SF round-trip, plus the cost of getting from Luzern to the cogwheel train or cable-car stations at the base of the mountain (with a Swiss Pass, the whole trip is free, from Luzern all the way to the top of Rigi). The cogwheel train and cable-car prices are half-price with a Eurailpass; the train trip from Luzern to Arth-Goldau (east-side cogwheel train) and the boat trips to Vitznau (west-side cogwheel train) and Weggis (cable car) are also included in your pass (but you'll have to use one of your flexi-days).

From the West: From Luzern's dock, hourly boats leave for Weggis (cable car, 45-minute ride) and continue to Vitznau (cogwheel train, one-hour ride). From **Vitznau,** the red cogwheel train chugs to the summit, "Rigi Kulm," in 30 minutes (hourly, daily 8:35-22:05, for the best views up, sit on the side closest to the station). From **Weggis,** a 10-minute cable-car ride lifts you up to the

Rigi Kaltbad point (2/hour—but essentially hourly, since boat connection is hourly; Mon-Fri 6:45-18:50, Sat-Sun 8:20-18:50); to reach the tippy-top of Rigi, connect to the red cogwheel train from Vitznau (or hike up; takes about 1.5 hours). For variety, take the train up and cable car down (or vice versa, though the train is arguably more dramatic as an uphill ride). Either way, you get to the summit in the same amount of time (1.5 hours from Luzern).

From the East: If you're visiting Rigi from the north, east, or south (not from Luzern), it can make sense to ascend the "back" side of the mountain, from the town of Arth-Goldau ("behind" Rigi, also accessible by 30-minute train from Luzern), where a blue cogwheel train takes you up to the summit (hourly, daily 8:00-18:10, 40-minute ride).

Activities on Rigi

The mountain is laced with more than 60 miles of hiking trails and other attractions to while away an afternoon (all well-described in the *Rigi-Guide* pamphlet, available at Luzern's TI and on local boats and trains). From the Rigi Kulm station, it's a short, steep climb (5 minutes) past the hotel to the top of the mountain.

Hiking: Serious hikers can do the whole thing on foot (well-marked trails start at Weggis, Vitznau, and Arth-Goldau; about 3-4 hours uphill from Weggis or Vitznau), but I'd save my legs for a shorter walk up top, where the views are. The classic Rigi hike is between the summit at Rigi Kulm and the cable-car station at Rigi Kaltbad (I prefer it as a downhill stroll; you can shorten the walk by meeting the train at the scenic Staffel stop).

Rigi has a few other good hiking options, including a 45-minute walk down from the summit to a working cheese farm (Alpkäserei Chäserenholz); from there you can cross the hill to the Staffel train stop to avoid the steep hike back up to the summit. For a longer hike from the *Alpkäserei*, continue down Rigi's "back" ridge to the Obere Schwändihütte, then across the mountain to the Klösterli stop, where you can visit the cute Chapel of Maria-of-the-Snow before hopping on the blue cogwheel train (1.5 hours from the summit to Klösterli stop). You can also hike along sections of the Mark Twain trail, which traces his route up the mountain (as described in *A Tramp Abroad*), with excerpts from his account signposted along the way.

Sleeping at the Summit: Stay overnight and watch the sun rise, accompanied only by the sounds of the wind and the ringing of a few cow and goat bells. **$$$ Rigi Kulm Hotel** is a large, recently remodeled inn set just below the summit (Sb-150-200 SF, Db-228-320 SF, prices depend on room size and views, free Wi-Fi, café and restaurant, tel. 041-880-1888, fax 041-855-0055, www.rigikulm.ch, hotel@rigikulm.ch, Käppeli family).

Fortress Fürigen Museum of War History

The Fortress Museum of Fürigen (Festung Fürigen Museum zur Wehrgeschichte) shows you another face of the country and the reason why Switzerland has been able to remain peaceful and neutral: its elaborate and secret system of bunkers and fortresses. Unfortunately, this fascinating exhibit is open only on weekends, April through October.

Cost and Hours: 5 SF, covered by Swiss Pass, April-Oct Sat-Sun 11:00-17:00, closed Mon-Fri and Nov-March, tel. 041-618-7340, www.nidwaldner-museum.ch.

Getting There: Fortress Fürigen is near the lakefront town of Stansstad (on Kehrsitenstrasse), below the village of Fürigen, not far from Luzern. It's an easy trip from Luzern by **train** (2/hour, 17 minutes, direction: Engelberg, 6.20 SF one-way). From the train station in Stansstad, walk 15 minutes, following brown signs to *Festungsmuseum* or *Kehrsiten* (down Bahnhofstrasse to Stanserstrasse, cross and follow signs, right on Achereggstrasse, left swimming-pool sign and tennis courts, and finally along the lake).

You can also get to Stansstad from Luzern by **boat** (9/day, 1 hour, 2 steamboats/day mid-July-mid-Aug, 18.40 SF one-way, 35 SF round-trip). From Stansstad's boat dock, walk 10 minutes up to the main street (Achereggstrasse) and keep left, following the brown signs for *Festungsmuseum*.

Drivers arriving in Stansstad can follow white signs to *Kehrsiten* for lakeside parking (1 SF/hour, free WC, 5-minute walk along lake to museum entrance).

Touring the Fortress: Enter through an innocent-looking wooden barrack (pick up the loaner English booklet as you go in). The bunker is always chilly, but no worries: Visitors are loaned original Swiss Army coats. Put on your coat, grab the English brochure that explains each room, and you're on your way. The radio station was placed near the entrance to assure clear reception. The living quarters were gas-proof, complete with specially sealed doors and devices to monitor the air for poison. The museum is a petting zoo of 20th-century weaponry. Visitors can fiddle with and even aim guns, knowing all the ammo is now imaginary. Think of the photo op: you, in a Swiss military uniform, manning a cannon.

Historical photographs take you back to World War II. Fortress Fürigen was built in 1941 as part of a new military strategy: to protect Switzerland with fortresses hidden in the Alps, called *Réduitfestung* (roughly "shelter fortress"—see sidebar, next page). In case of a Nazi invasion, the Swiss government would

Swiss Military Readiness

Strolling through a peaceful Swiss village—charming pastoral greenery studded with rustic farmhouses between an Alp and a lake—my friend walked with me to the door of a nondescript barn. He said, "Stand here," and slid open the door to reveal a solitary, mighty gun—pointing right at me. Crossing a field, kicking a stray soccer ball back to a group of happy grade-schoolers, we came to another barn. This time I noticed the "wooden" door was actually metal, with a clever paint job.

Inside was a military canteen, now selling snacks to civilians, and a steel ladder leading down into a military-gray world that felt like a vast submarine. A network of passages, just big enough for heavily armed soldiers to race down single file, led to a series of gun barns and subterranean command rooms with charts locating other installations in the area.

Switzerland may be famous for its neutrality, but it's anything but lax defensively. Travelers marvel at how Swiss engineers have conquered their Alps with the world's most-expensive-per-mile road system. But no one designs a Swiss bridge or tunnel without also designing its destruction. Each comes with built-in explosives, so, in the event of an invasion, the entire country can be blasted into a mountain fortress.

Even today, you can't get a building permit without an expensive first-class bomb shelter worked into the plan. Old tank barriers (nicknamed "Toblerones" for their shape) stand ready to be dragged across the roads to slow any invasion. Sprawling hospitals are dug into mountains, still ventilated to be kept dry and ready for use. And halfway up alpine cliffs, Batcave-type doors can slide open, allowing fighter jets to zoom into action from hidden airstrips cut out of solid rock. If you're approaching a mountain pass by car, look for the explosive patches ominously checkering the roads near the summit.

The end of the Cold War in 1989 brought changes even to neutral Switzerland. Western armies began cutting back on their military spending, and Switzerland followed suit, with deep cuts in its defense budget. The Swiss Army met its tighter budget in part by closing many of the 15,000 hidden fortresses that protected the country's strategic roads, train lines, and mountain passes. Some of the forts, such as Fortress Fürigen, have been turned into tourist attractions no more formidable than medieval castles.

retreat to a secret bunker in the Berner Oberland, and Swiss troops would abandon the border regions and gather around this alpine stronghold. Fortress Fürigen was meant to protect roads and rail lines that led from Luzern and Zürich along Lake Luzern into the Berner Oberland. This was one of a network of fortresses in the area. After World War II, they were retooled with a new focus: the threat of the Soviet Union and nuclear war.

Big guns in the fortress could shoot more than six miles, and machine guns protected the immediate access routes to the bunker. This fortress could house and feed 100 people for three weeks. But in 1990, with the end of the Cold War, the practical Swiss decommissioned the fortress, refit it with vintage WWII and early Cold War gear, and opened it to the curious public.

BERN and MURTEN

Enjoy urban Switzerland in the charming, compact capital of Bern. Ramble the ramparts of Murten, Switzerland's best-preserved medieval town, and resurrect the ruins of an ancient Roman capital in nearby Avenches.

If you like cute, small towns (as I do), make Murten your home base. Otherwise, spend the night in busier Bern.

Planning Your Time

On a quick trip, big Bern and little Murten—about a half-hour apart by train or car—are each worth a half-day. Either makes a fine day trip or overnight stop.  Murten, while easy by train, is even better by car. With a car, I'd sleep in Murten.

Bern is a convenient stop between other destinations (such as going from the Berner Oberland to Murten or Zürich). If you're day-tripping, put your bag in a locker at the Bern station, spend a few hours taking my self-guided "Welcome to Bern" walk and visiting some museums, then catch a late-afternoon train to your next stop. You could combine the destinations in this chapter by ending your busy Bern day in Murten, where you can spend the evening wandering the walls and savoring a lakeview dinner. In the morning, linger in Murten or move on to your next destination.

Bern

Stately but human, classy but fun, the Swiss capital gives you the most delightful look at urban Switzerland. Bern's top attractions are window-shopping and people-watching in lively market squares and along streets lined with cozy, covered arcades. But there's more to this city: Enjoy Bern's excellent museums, quaint-for-a-capital ambience, and delightful river scene. In this city (and canton), look for flags "bearing" the symbol of the local mascot—a roaring bear.

The city, founded in 1191, has managed to avoid war damage and hasn't burned down since a great fire swept through in 1405. After the fire, wooden buildings were no longer allowed, and Bern took on its gray-green sandstone complexion (with stones quarried from nearby). During its 12th- and 13th-century growth spurt, the frisky town grew through two walls. Looking at the map of the city contained within a bend of the Aare River, you can get a sense of how it started with a castle at the tip of the peninsula, and expanded with a series of walls—each defending an ever-bigger city from its one land-accessible side. The clock tower marks the first wall (1218). A generation later, another wall was built (in 1256, at today's prison tower). The final wall—where today's train station sits—was built in 1344.

In 1353, Bern became the eighth canton to join the Swiss Federation. Its power ended with the conquest by Napoleon in 1798. But in 1848, Bern rose again to become the Swiss capital.

Today, the German-speaking town has about 123,000 people (two-thirds Protestant and one-third Catholic). Its pointy towers, sandstone buildings, and colorful fountains make Bern one of Europe's finest surviving medieval towns.

Orientation to Bern

User-friendly Bern is packed into a peninsula bounded by the Aare River. The train station is located where the peninsula connects to the mainland. From there, a handy main drag leads gradually downhill, straight through the middle of town past most of the major sights, to the tip of the peninsula (across a bridge and finally to the Bear Park).

Tourist Information

Start your visit at the TI, on the ground floor inside the **train station** (Mon-Sat 9:00-19:00, Sun 9:00-18:00, tel. 031-328-1212, www.berninfo.com). Pick up a free map of Bern (and maps for any other Swiss cities you'll be visiting), and browse through their free brochures: general information booklet, museum guide, bus and walking tour info, transit map, quarterly events and exhibits listings, and informative leaflets on various sights. There's a second TI near the **Bear Park** (June-Sept daily 9:00-18:00; March-May and Oct daily 10:00-16:00; Nov-Feb Fri-Sun 11:00-16:00, closed Mon-Thu).

Arrival in Bern

By Train: Bern's bustling train station is a thriving multistory mall. The trains almost get lost. On the upper level, you'll find a Migros grocery store (daily 8:00-21:00) and a pharmacy (daily 6:30-22:00). The ground floor has lockers (6 SF) and WCs (2 SF, both near the TI in the far-back corner), and the lower level has a Co-op grocery store (Mon-Sat 6:00-22:00, Sun 7:00-22:00). From the station, it's a 30-minute downhill stroll through the heart of town to the Bear Park and up to the rose garden. My "Welcome to Bern" self-guided walk lays out the most interesting route.

By Car: The old town is essentially car-free (only service vehicles and public transit allowed), so leave your car near the train station *(Bahnhof)*. Drivers approaching by freeway should follow *Bern Zentrum* signs, then *Bahnhof* and *Bahnhof Parking* to find the huge pay garage behind the station (45-minute metered parking outside, all-day lot inside, 2-4 SF/hour, depending on time of entry). While not the cheapest option, it's the easiest for a quick visit. From here, you're just an escalator ride away from the TI and Switzerland's capital.

Helpful Hints

Blue Monday: Most of Bern's museums are closed on Monday. But you can still follow my self-guided walk, tour the cathedral (and climb its tower), tour the Zytglogge-Turm, watch the parliament in action (generally possible Mon afternoons), ogle the beasts at the Bear Park, and go for a swim in the river.

Internet Access: The **TI** has an Internet terminal (12 SF/hour); you can also get online at **Thalia Bookstore,** on the lower level of the Loeb department store on Spitalgasse, two blocks from the station (1 SF/6 minutes, 4 SF/30 minutes; pay at cashier, then take receipt to info desk near terminals behind escalators; Mon-Wed 9:00-19:00, Thu 9:00-21:00, Fri 9:00-20:00, Sat 8:00-17:00, closed Sun, tel. 031-320-2020).

Bookstore: Stauffacher is huge, with an entire floor of English books, a fine travel section, and an inviting café with a terrace and good salads (Mon-Fri 9:00-19:00, Thu until 21:00, Sat 9:00-17:00, closed Sun, a block from the train station at Neuengasse 25-37, tel. 031-313-6363, www.stauffacher.ch). They also offer pay Internet access, but only to customers (1 SF/6 minutes, 4 SF/30 minutes). A second branch is on the lower level of the train station (Mon-Sat 7:00-22:00, Sun 9:00-22:00).

Laundry: Jet Wash is located at Dammweg 43 (self-service, 5-8 SF to wash, 6 SF to dry, Mon-Sat 7:00-21:00, Sun 9:00-18:00, get there on bus #20, mobile 077-417-9502).

Bike Rental: The **"Bern rollt"** program offers free loaner bikes for a half-day during the summer at three very central locations: at the train station (on Milchgässli), south of the train station (on Hirschengraben), and in the old center (on Zeughausgasse, near the Zytglogge-Turm). Just leave your photo ID and a 20-SF deposit and take off with the bike of your choice (first 4 hours free, then 1 SF/hour, daily in summer 7:30-21:30, tel. 079-277-2857, www.bernrollt.ch). Try the "Swiss Flyer," a clever little electric-motor-powered bike, or even a scooter or skateboard.

BERN AND MURTEN

Getting Around Bern

The city is walkable, though the buses and trams can be handy. A standard single ticket costs 4 SF, a shorter trip *(Kurzstrecke)* runs 2.20 SF, and a day pass is 12 SF (all covered by Swiss Pass). The bus info center is across Bubenbergplatz from the station (Mon-Fri 8:30-18:00, closed Sat-Sun, tel. 031-321-8844, www.bernmobil.ch). Buy tickets from the machines located at bus and tram stops (they take coins and credit cards—including US cards).

Here's the best plan for exploring the town: Walk from the train station to the far end of town, then catch bus #12 back to the station (2.20 SF, bus usually runs about every 6 minutes).

Tours in Bern

Walking Tours—These leave daily from April through October at 11:00 from the TI at the train station (1.5 hours, 20 SF, German and English together). The TI also offers a four-hour **iPod audio-guide** (18 SF).

Local Guide—**Marie-Therese Lauper** is a charming and hard-working independent guide (prices vary, mobile 079-700-0880, amthlauper@sunrise.ch).

Self-Guided Walk

Welcome to Bern

This orientation walk begins at the train station and ends at the Bear Park, at the far end of town. From the Bear Park, you can catch bus #12 or browse your way back to your starting point, which is the...

❶ Train Station

The station is a bright and airy shopping center, with a TI (in the far-back corner), an exchange desk open long hours, and all the shops you could need. Stepping outside, you enter the big square called Bahnhofplatz. The old town was sealed off here with a forti-fied wall, which was replaced in the 19th century by the train sta-tion. Today all city buses and trams come and go from the station.

Bern's vision is to create a car-less city. The city was ripped up and new tram lines were put in for the Euro 2008 soccer tourna-ment. And the "Bern rollt" program (government-subsidized and staffed by otherwise hard-to-employ people) provides free loaner bikes and even skateboards.

Across the square stands the **Holy Ghost Church** (Heilig-geistkirche). Notice the gray-green Bernese sandstone, quarried nearby, used for the church and surrounding buildings. Because this stone is porous and easily eroded by water, Bern's buildings are designed with characteristic oversized eves. Even newer buildings (like these) are built with the same stone to maintain architectural harmony, as dictated by city law.

• *From the train-station TI, cross Bahnhofplatz, walk 50 yards, and turn left (around the church) onto Spitalgasse. This marks the start of one long street (with four names). The spine of both the peninsula and our walk, this street rambles downhill through the heart of town to the bridge and Bear Park.*

Notice the first of Bern's 11 historic **fountains,** the Bagpiper. These colorful 16th-century fountains are Bern's trademark. The city commissioned them for many reasons: to brighten the cityscape of gray-stone buildings, to show off the town's wealth, and to remind citizens of great local heroes and events. They also gave artists something to work on after the Reformation deprived them of their most important patron, the Catholic Church.

Shopping opportunities abound under the more than three miles of arcades that line Bern's lanes. Stores run the gamut from affordable to high-end, where prices are so steep, there's no danger of buying anything—my kind of shopping (stores generally open Mon-Fri 9:00-18:30, Thu until 21:00, Sat 9:00-16:00, closed Sun). In German, the slang for the corridor under these arcades is *Rohr* (pipe). To stroll through the town is to *rohren* (go piping).

• *Continue "rohren" down Spitalgasse until you reach...*

❼ Bärenplatz

In summer, a market is held on this square (Mon-Fri 8:00-18:00, Sat 8:00-16:00, busiest on Tue and Sat mornings, closed Sun; Tue and Sat only in Nov-March). The street runs under the **Prison Tower** (Käfigturm)—once a part of the city wall (c. 1256). Renovated from 1641 to 1644, the tower served as a prison until 1897 (*Käfig* means "cage"). Notice how the hand on the clock really is a hand—and how it was built in a slower-paced era, when just an hour hand told time precisely enough. The bears on the tower are from Bern's coat of arms. Live ones await you at the end of this walk.

To the left (50 yards), you'll see the **Dutch Tower** (Holländerturm). Swiss soldiers were famous mercenaries who fought all over Europe. Returning from a battle in the Netherlands, the soldiers brought back the habit of smoking. But smoking was forbidden within the city walls of Bern, so they hid in this tower to smoke secretly. Locals joke that now that a new, modern-day smoking ban has come to Bern, this tower may regain its historic function.

Farther left at the far end of the square is a modern, controversial, and mossy **fountain** by the Swiss surrealist Meret Oppenheim. Made in 1983, it symbolizes growth and life, and is supposed to demonstrate communication between an object of art

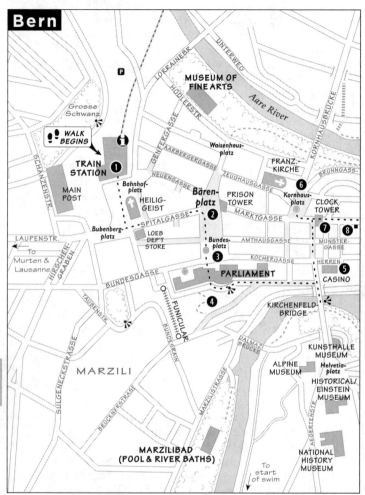

and the beholder. It worked well...too well, in fact, as most citizens immediately communicated their dislike and wanted it destroyed. But Bern's politicians proved braver than expected, and the fountain survived. Time has transformed Oppenheim's gray concrete column into a multicolored pillar decorated with moss, grass, and flowers. Residents like it only in the winter, when it's covered with ice. The grand building beyond the fountain—once the city orphanage—is the police station.

As each of the town's successive walls and moats was torn down, it provided Bern with vast, people-friendly swaths of land that function as elongated "squares"—popular today for markets and outdoor cafés. This is a top place to be seen in the evening.

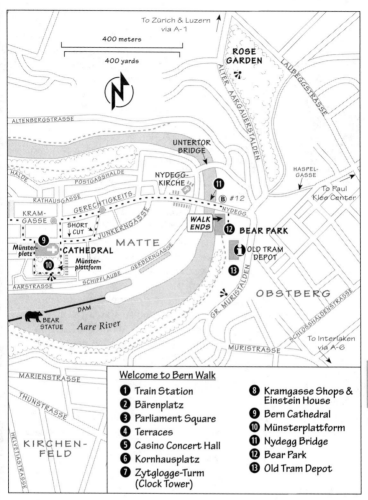

To Zürich & Luzern
via A-1

ROSE
GARDEN

ALTER AARGAUERSTALDEN

LAUBEGGSTRASSE

400 meters

400 yards

N

ALTENBERGSTRASSE

UNTERTOR
BRIDGE

HALDE

POSTGASSHALDE

NYDEGG-
KIRCHE

HASPEL-
GASSE

RATHAUSGASSE

GERECHTIGKEITS-

KRAM-
GASSE

SHORT
CUT

JUNKERNGASSE

MATTE

(11)

(B) #12

NYDEGG

WALK
ENDS

To Paul
Klee Center

(12) BEAR PARK

Münster-
platz

(9)

(10)

CATHEDRAL

Münster-
plattform

GERBERNGASSE

(13)

OLD TRAM
DEPOT

AARSTRASSE

SCHIFFLAUBE

OBSTBERG

BEAR
STATUE

DAM

Aare River

GR. MURISTALDEN

SCHLOSSHALDENSTRASSE

To Interlaken
via A-6

MARIENSTRASSE

MURISTRASSE

THUNSTRASSE

Welcome to Bern Walk

KIRCHEN-
FELD

HELVETIASTRASSE

(1) Train Station
(2) Bärenplatz
(3) Parliament Square
(4) Terraces
(5) Casino Concert Hall
(6) Kornhausplatz
(7) Zytglogge-Turm
(Clock Tower)

(8) Kramgasse Shops &
Einstein House
(9) Bern Cathedral
(10) Münsterplattform
(11) Nydegg Bridge
(12) Bear Park
(13) Old Tram Depot

BERN AND MURTEN

• With your back to the modern fountain, stroll to the end of Bärenplatz, filled with market stalls and lined with fun places to eat (see "Eating in Bern," later). The big building you'll see from the square is the...

❸ Parliament (Bundeshaus)

You may brush elbows with some high-powered legislators, but you wouldn't know it—everything looks very casual for a national capital. Check out the statuary: The woman on the top of the building represents political independence, the one on the left (under the "1291") stands for freedom, and the one on the right (1848) symbolizes peace. The fine granite plaza in front of the parliament (built in 2004 to replace a parking lot) is a favorite spot

for demonstrations and markets. The 26-squirt fountain (one for each canton) is a real kid-pleaser (and makes for fun photos) on a hot summer day. Facing the square on the left is the Swiss National Bank—this country's Fort Knox, with half the Swiss gold stock buried under the square (the rest is in Zürich).

Walk through the passageway to the right and drop into the **welcome center** at the back of the building, where you can pick up some of their generous literature on the Swiss government. Its bicameral system was inspired by the US Constitution, with one big difference: Executive power is shared by a committee of seven, with a rotating ceremonial president and a passion for consensus. This is a mechanism to avoid power grabs by any single individual...a safeguard that the Swiss love.

Touring the Parliament: When parliament is in session, the **galleries** are open to the public, so you can watch the action (free; parliament generally in session Mon afternoon, Tue and Thu mornings, and all day Wed; must leave ID at entrance, lines to get in can be long, no photos). When parliament is not in session, you can take a free, guided, hour-long English **tour** of the building (tours run Mon-Sat at 11:30 and 15:00; spaces for individuals may also open up on group tours Mon-Sat at 9:30, 13:00, 15:00, and 16:00, Thu also at 17:00, 18:00, and 19:00; sign up the day before by calling 031-322-8522, www.parlament.ch, besucherdienst@parl .admin.ch).

• *Beyond the back of the parliament building are...*

❹ Terraces

From here, you have a commanding view over the Aare River and Bern's biggest swimming pool, the **Marzilibad**. On a clear day, you can see the Eiger, Mönch, and Jungfrau—the highest peaks in the Berner Oberland—and the far less imposing "mountain" of Bern, the **Gurten** (with the view tower poking up above its forested summit). The Gurten is the city's favorite recreation spot, offering music festivals in summer and very modest skiing opportunities for children in winter.

Follow the terrace walls left a few hundred yards to Kirchenfeld Bridge. Walk out to the center for great river views (many museums are just across the bridge; the best options are described later, under "Sights in Bern"). The ❺ **Casino** isn't for gamblers—it's the home of Bern's Symphony Orchestra.

• *Backtrack across the bridge, and with your back to the river, follow the tram tracks down another swath of land created by the removal of a city wall, to...*

❻ Kornhausplatz

This square is ornamented by the colorful fountain of an **Ogre** (*Chindlifresser,* "child-eater"). Two legends try to explain this grue-some sight. It's either a folkloric representation of the Greek god Chronos, or a figure that was intended to scare children off the former city walls.

The building behind on the left used to be the granary and now houses the modern public library and the huge **Kornhauskeller** restaurant. If the restaurant is open, wander down the stairs and head inside—even if you're not eating here, you must take a peek at this magnificent subterranean place. Once the vast city wine cellar, now a recommended Italian restaurant, this cellar was built in high Baroque style (1718) and renovated with paintings inspired by the Pre-Raphaelites in 1897. The 12 columns show traditional costumes of Bernese women.

• *Back on Kornhausplatz, step under the clock tower where Marktgasse becomes Kramgasse to see the fancy clock ornamenting its downhill side.*

❼ Zytglogge-Turm

Bern's famous clock tower was part of the original wall marking the first gate to the city (c. 1250). The clock, which dates back

to 1530, performs four minutes before each hour: The happy jester comes to life, Father Time turns his hourglass, the rooster crows (in German, that's "kee-kee-ree-kee" rather than "cock-a-doodle-doo"), and the golden man on top hammers the bell. Apparently, this nonevent was considered quite entertaining five centuries ago.

To pass the time waiting for the action, read the TI's leaf-let explaining what's so interesting about the fancy old clock (for example, the golden hour hand is an hour behind for half the year because of the modern innovation of Daylight Saving Time). You can determine the zodiac, today's date, and the stage of the moon—look at the black-and-gold orb.

Under the clock are the old regional measurements (Swiss foot, the bigger Bernese foot, and the *Elle,* or "elbow," which was the distance from the elbow to the fingertip) and the official meter and double meter. It took a strong man like Napoleon to bring consistency to measurements in Europe, and he replaced the many goofy feet and elbows of medieval Europe with the metric system used today (c. 1800).

Touring the Tower: Enthusiasts can tour the medieval mechanics—early Swiss engineering at its best—and see the bellows that enable the old rooster to crow (12 SF, 50-minute tour, May-Oct daily at 14:30, buy ticket from guide or at TI).

• *Continue your stroll down the main drag. At this point, you enter the older part of town, where bigger department stores are replaced by quainter shops and galleries on...*

❽ Kramgasse

Bern has wide streets like this one, but not many true squares. In the Middle Ages, craftsmen exhibited their goods on the sidewalks under simple roofs. Eventually, these were formalized, buildings were expanded, and arcades evolved. Today, though the arcades are privately owned, owners must keep them clean and allow public access.

Most shops are underneath the arcades, but don't miss the ones in the **cellars** that you can access only from the main road. The cellars, marked by old-time hatches, were originally for storing potatoes and coal, and later, wine. People said "merry Bern" was floating on wine, just as Venice was floating on water. The merry times ended in 1798, when the French invaded (and drank all the wine). The cellars were once again used for potatoes, and the city got a new nickname: "sad Bern." Napoleon's soldiers not only liberated Bern from its wine, but also from the tremendous treasury the city was known for. Napoleon used money looted from Bern to finance his Egyptian crusade.

The apartment that Einstein called home between 1903 and 1905, during some of his happiest and most productive years, is now the **Einstein House** museum (200 yards from the clock tower, on the right, at Kramgasse 49). See period furniture, the

original spiral staircase entrance, Einstein's Patent Office desk, photos, and manuscripts. The museum doesn't do much for me, but I guess everything's relative (6 SF, 4.50 SF with Swiss Pass; April-mid-Dec daily 10:00-17:00; Feb-March Mon-Sat 10:00-17:00, closed Sun; closed mid-Dec-Jan; tel. 031-312-0091, www.einstein-bern.ch). Die-hard fans may also want to visit the Einstein Museum, located in the Historical Museum of Bern (see page 121).

• *Just below Einstein's apartment, 20 yards past the Samson Fountain, turn right and crawl through the narrow Münstergässchen to the...*

❾ Bern Cathedral

Bern's 15th-century Münster, Catholic-turned-Protestant, is capped with a 330-foot-tall tower, the highest in Switzerland (finished in 1893). The late-Gothic church was dedicated to St. Vincent of Zaragoza.

The current **interior** is very plain, but it was once adorned with 26 separate little chapels and altars dedicated to Mary and various saints. An ornate screen separated the priests from the worshippers. But when the Reformation came to town in 1528, all this was swept away. The iconoclasts believed that images distracted worshippers from focusing on God, so they destroyed the distasteful decoration. The new center of attention was the pulpit, where Protestant preachers shared the word of God—not in Latin, but in the people's language.

This church's **main portal,** with its striking gold-leaf highlights, seems pretty un-Protestant. It probably survived because its theme, the Last Judgment, showed that no matter how rich you are or what rank you have in Church hierarchy, anyone can end up in hell (an idea Protestants dug). Condemned people are popping in the flames like lottery balls. Notice the humorous details in the commotion of people heading to hell (especially what the little green devil is doing to the sinful monk).

Cost and Hours: Cathedral entrance is free, audioguide-5 SF; May-mid-Oct Mon-Sat 10:00-17:00, Sun 11:30-17:00; mid-Oct-April Mon-Fri 12:00-16:00, Sat 10:00-17:00, Sun 11:30-16:00; last entry 30 minutes before closing, tel. 031-312-0462, www.berner muenster.ch.

Climbing the Tower: You can pay 5 SF to huff up the spiral staircase (344 steps) to a viewpoint at the base of the open-work steeple (same hours as cathedral, last entry 30 minutes before closing). From this 210-foot-high vantage point, you enjoy a behind-the-scenes look at the varied courtyards and rooftop gardens hidden behind the conformist building facades. Don't forget to turn around to appreciate an up-close look at the tower's carved figures. Marie-Thérèse Lauper works up here every day, watching over the church, answering questions, and giving visitors a chance to peek at her **bells**—including the largest bell in Switzerland, a 10.5-ton beauty cast in 1611 and called Susanne (named by a bell-ringer after his sizeable girlfriend). This bell was so heavy that it took eight men to swing her. The bells are no longer rung by hand, after a drunken bellringer was killed by a swinging clapper. If

Albert Einstein in Bern

The man who changed how we see our universe made his greatest discoveries during the eight years he lived in Bern (1901-1909). Raised in Germany, Albert Einstein (1879-1955) went to college in Zürich, hoping to land a job teaching math and physics. But the young grad's GPA and resume were mediocre, so he took a temp job instead in Bern's Patent Office, inspecting and registering inventions.

Twenty-three-year-old Albert and his new bride Mileva (his brainy college sweetheart) rented a second-floor apartment at Kramgasse 49 (today's Einstein House), where Mileva soon gave birth to their first son, little Hans Albert. Einstein punched the clock at the Patent Office and spent his spare time reading, hiking the Bernese countryside, and thinking. At night, he'd join with his mates—the self-named "Olympia Academy"—to smoke, drink beer, and talk math and philosophy. Outwardly, he led an ordinary life, but his thoughts were always on science's Big Questions. At home, in pubs, or at work he'd scribble down equations and ideas, filing them in his self-described "Department of Theoretical Physics"—a desk drawer in his office.

Then, one warm spring day, as Einstein walked on the outskirts of Bern, it all started coming together. So began his *annus mirabilis*—the miracle year of 1905—in which the 26-year-old unknown amateur physicist quickly wrote five papers that would shock and perplex the world. Published in a major physics journal, they touched on a variety of subjects—such as how molecules move and how light can appear as either a wave of energy or as a beam of tiny particles.

The most famous and unsettling paper, his theory of special relativity, described a world in motion. A person on a moving train and someone who's stationary see the world from different perspectives—that's the classic principle of relativity described by Galileo and Newton. But Einstein said there's an exception to the rule—light, whose speed always remains constant whether it's on a moving train or on the ground. So a person on a moving train and one at rest will never agree on what they observe...yet they're both right. The discrepancies only become obvious as the train travels close to the speed of light. Then, while the person on the train thinks everything is normal, the one on the ground sees the train shrink, train clocks slow down, and the person on the

you're up here when the Prayer Bell rings, you may feel the tower sway (while smaller than Susanne, this bell's weight isn't centered within the tower).

• *Head behind the cathedral to a terrace overlooking the river, the...*

❿ Münsterplattform

Starting in the 14th century, this terrace was built from all kinds

train stops aging!

Einstein's papers initially drew little interest and a measure of skepticism. (Einstein did get a promotion in the Patent Office—from "technical expert third class" to "technical expert second class.") But over time, other physicists grasped the significance of Einstein's work, seeing how he took earlier findings, wove them together, and did the math that explained it all. Subsequent experiments proved that, in fact, even Einstein's most bizarre assertions were correct. Time on a fast-moving jet really does slow down (hence, those interminable intercontinental flights).

Einstein was invited to lecture at the local university, though he was still working nine-to-five at the Patent Office. In his spare time, he worked on his next project, general relativity. He theorized that gravity is not a force that attracts things but a curving of space—like a bowling ball on a soft mattress—that affects the motion of nearby objects. In 1909, Einstein's growing reputation won him a job offer to teach in Zürich, and he quit the Patent Office and left Bern for good.

Einstein would never again approach the creative level of his days in Bern. (In 1922, he won the Nobel Prize for his work done during the 1905 *annus mirabilis*.) Albert and Mileva split, and he remarried to a cousin. When Hitler took power in Germany (1933), Einstein—a pacifist and a Jew—left Europe for America. His curly black hair had turned white, and his aging face later became a pop-culture icon of genius—complete with pipe, moustache, basset-hound eyes, and halo of frizzy white hair (which he backcombed in order to look sufficiently unkempt).

In 1939, Einstein wrote a letter to President Roosevelt theorizing that the tiniest particle of matter could be converted into an enormous amount of energy. The principle was one he'd discovered back in 1905—that energy is equivalent to mass times the speed of light squared (a very big number). And so, $E = mc^2$ became the atomic bomb, from an idea hatched in the pubs and arcaded streets of Bern.

If you're curious to learn more, Bern has two sights about its brightest mind: the Einstein House in the town center, and the Einstein Museum just across the river (both described in this chapter).

BERN AND MURTEN

of "recycled" stones from older buildings. Archaeologists even unearthed some heads of statues that were victims of Reformation iconoclasts. Look down on the Aare (find the bear out on the breakwater). Notice the security nets beneath you. The platform used to be the favorite place for suicides—to the terror of the people living below. The Pavilion Café offers a scenic spot under a chestnut tree for a bite or a drink on a sunny day. The pavilion opposite is a tiny branch of the city library, providing park-goers with books, boules, and table tennis. This little park is frequented by pot smokers, and nobody seems to care. Behind the café, the "vertical tram" has been carrying passengers up and down since 1896 (1.20 SF).

With your back to the river, return to the main drag (now called Gerechtigkeitsgasse) via Kreuzgasse. (Or, for a quieter stretch of street, turn right down Junkerngasse, go about 50 yards, then take the alley to your left called Obere Gerechtigkeitsgässchen.) On the **Fountain of Justice** on the main street, a blindfolded figure of Justice triumphs over the mayor, pope, sultan, and emperor. Along this stretch of the street, a grate reveals a bit of the stream that used to flow open down the middle of the peninsula, providing people with a handy disposal system.

• *From here, it's straight on through the oldest part of town to the bridge at the end of the old town, called...*

⓫ Nydegg Bridge

Look downstream from the Nydegg Bridge. To your left is the site of the original town castle (now a church). The small bridge below is the oldest in Bern (and, until 1844, the only bridge crossing the Aare here). Above on the ridge, just behind and to the right of the pointy spire, is the Rosengarten restaurant (described at the end of this walk). Now cross the street to the other side of the bridge, and look just upstream. You can see the original Lindt chocolate factory, evoking an age when this stretch of river was lined with mills powering the industrial zone of Bern—tanneries, shipyards, lumber mills, and so on. The area is now routinely flooded when the river runs high. As you look upstream, notice the peaceful path along the left bank, a nice place for a walk.

• *Continue across the bridge to reach the...*

⓬ Bear Park (BärenPark)

The symbol of Bern is the bear, and some lively ones frolic along this terraced hillside, to the delight of locals and tourists alike. Since 1857, Bern had been housing its bears in big, barren, concrete pits *(Bärengraben).* But thanks to  the agitation of the B.L.M. (Bear Liberation Movement), a reluctant city government was forced to replace the pits with posher digs. In 2009, the last of the pit bears died, and later that year, three-year-old brown bears Finn (a male from Finland) and Björk (a female from Denmark) moved to this new space; soon they welcomed their female cubs, Ursina and Berna. This ursine family enjoys much better conditions than their fore-bears, including a fishing channel next to the river—though they can still access the larger pit, which is now a historic monument.

Cost and Hours: Free, circuit around park open daily 24 hours, shop open daily 8:30-16:30, bus #12, tel. 031-357-1515, www .baerenpark-bern.ch. For info on guided tours by bear keepers, call 031-357-1525.

• *Behind the Bear Park is the...*

⓭ Old Tram Depot

This depot hosts a tourist center (TI, brewery restaurant/café with terrace). Its excellent 3-SF "Bern Show," complete with an animated town model and marching Napoleonic-era soldiers, illustrates the history and wonders of Bern (20 minutes, uncom-fortable benches, show in English once hourly—see schedule—or ask for a printed script; June-Sept daily 9:00-18:00; March-May and Oct-Nov daily 10:00-16:00; Dec-Feb Fri-Sun 11:00-16:00, closed Mon-Thu).

From here, a seven-minute hike up the moderately steep, cobbled pathway takes you to the rose garden and **Restaurant Rosengarten,** which offers a grand city view and basic, reasonably priced food (for details, see page 126).

From the Old Tram Depot, it's an easy trip on bus #12 back to the train station (2.20 SF). If wandering back through town, be sure to get off into the quieter side lanes, which have a fascinating and entertaining array of shops and little eateries.

More Sights in Bern

▲▲**The Berner Swim and Marzilibad**—For something to write home about, join Bern's merchants, students, and carp in a float down the Aare River. The Bernese, proud of their very clean river and their basic ruddiness, have a tradition—sort of a wet, urban *paseo.* On summer days, they hike upstream 5 to 30 minutes, then float back down to the excel-lent (and free) riverside baths and pools (Marzilibad) just below the Parliament building.

The process is easy: Hike up the paved riverside sidewalk as far as you like, then take the steps leading into the water whenever you want to "put in." As you approach Marzilibad, just stroke over to the shore to grab one of the several poles placed to help people exit the river. The locals make it look easy, but this can be dangerous—the current is swift. If you miss the last pole, you're history.

If a float down the river is a bit much for you, enjoy the Marzilibad, a well-equipped public swimming pool and park with picnic spots, restaurant, lockers, wading pools, games, and more.

▲▲Museum of Fine Arts (Kunstmuseum)—Featuring 800 years of art, this three-story museum offers a unique opportunity to see the best of Swiss artists, from romantic folk art to the Jugendstil movement. You'll find old masters in the basement, 19th-century works on the ground floor, and 20th-century stuff upstairs.

Cost and Hours: 7 SF, extra for temporary exhibits, covered by Swiss Pass, no English on wall captions but English sheet for temporary exhibits, Tue 10:00-21:00, Wed-Sun 10:00-17:00, closed Mon, no photos, 4 blocks north of station, Holdergasse 12, tel. 031-328-0944, www.kunstmuseumbern.ch.

▲▲Paul Klee Center (Zentrum Paul Klee)—With his wavy building mirroring the wavy landscape of the Bern countryside, Italian architect Renzo Piano celebrates the creative spirit of Swiss-born artist Paul Klee (1879-1940). Klee wasn't just a great painter—he was an interdisciplinary explosion of creative energy. The center, which fosters music and theater as well as the visual arts, has a  mission: to bring art to the people. For instance, a huge zone is devoted to a children's creative workshop that includes painting and a shadow theater.

Cost and Hours: 18 SF for one exhibit, 23 SF for two, covered by Swiss Pass, heavily academic audioguide-5 SF, Tue-Sun 10:00-17:00, closed Mon, pick up free English-language booklet, mandatory lockers require refundable 1-SF coin deposit, Monument im Fruchtland 3, tel. 031-359-0101, www.zpk.org.

Getting There: Take bus #12 from the train station to its last stop, Zentrum Paul Klee (6-10/hour, stops right at center).

Children's Workshops: 15 SF for 1-hour workshop at 12:00, 14:00, or 16:00, no advance reservations.

Touring the Museum: The Klee collection is in the building's middle wave. This cultural center keeps about 200 of Klee's pieces on display (out of a collection of 4,000). It's the best place in the world to experience and learn about this modernist painter of lively, almost childlike art. Artistically, you can't put Klee in a box. His paintings—mostly from the 1920s and 1930s—are playful yet enigmatic. His art is full of symbolism...or maybe we just think so. He experimented in pointillism, as you'll see in the piece *Ad Parnassum*.

Insula Dulcamara (Bittersweet Island) is a good example of Klee's enigmatic hieroglyph style. It's a puzzle—he pairs opposites:

man, woman; air, water. It's 1938... is that a submarine on the horizon evoking the rise of fascism? Perhaps the black figures are death, floating in an eternal spring-like landscape. Kids love Klee, and they always teach the art snobs a thing or two with their interpretations.

Downstairs you'll find cafés, an art database, a movie about building the museum, a cozy hangout, and the children's workshop.

▲**Einstein Museum**—Fans of the genius will want to visit this "museum" (essentially the second floor of Bern's Historical Museum), devoted to Einstein and his times. It's more interesting and informative than the Einstein House downtown, but it's also overpriced (as admission also includes the rest of the Historical Museum)—unless you're a serious Einstein fan, have a Swiss Pass, or are a Swiss history buff, it's probably not worth the money.

Photos and displays explain Einstein's accomplishments and complicated personal life, and place him within his historical context. His concepts are nicely illustrated, and everything is well-explained in English (the 5-SF audioguide is not necessary). The mirrored stairway up to the second floor prepares your brain to expand your ideas about space and time.

Cost and Hours: 18 SF, includes entrance to Historical Museum, covered by Swiss Pass, Tue-Sun 10:00-17:00, closed Mon; across bridge from Parliament at Helvetiaplatz 5—take tram #6, #7, or #8; tel. 031-350-7711, www.einsteinmuseum.ch.

Other Bern Museums—Near the Historical Museum are the Alpine, Communication, Natural History, Rifle, and Kunsthalle (contemporary art) museums—appealing mainly to visitors with those specific interests; the TI produces a good free pamphlet describing all the museums. The Natural History Museum is fun for kids (all covered by Swiss Pass except Rifle Museum, most open Tue-Sun 10:00-17:00, closed Mon, take trams #6, #7, #8, or #19 across the bridge, www.museen-bern.ch).

Sleeping in Bern

As Switzerland's capital, Bern hosts not only tourists but also waves of businessmen and politicians, keeping room rates here rather high; conventions and other events can drive demand and prices

BERN AND MURTEN

Sleep Code

(1 SF = $1.10, country code: 41)
S = Single, **D** = Double/Twin, **T** = Triple, **Q** = Quad, **b** = bathroom,
s = shower only. Unless otherwise noted, credit cards are
accepted, English is spoken, and breakfast is included.

    To help you easily sort through these listings, I've divided
the accommodations into three categories, based on the price
for a double room with bath during high season:

  $$$ **Higher Priced**—Most rooms 180 SF or more.
   $$ **Moderately Priced**—Most rooms between 100-180 SF.
    $ **Lower Priced**—Most rooms 100 SF or less.

   Prices can change without notice; verify the hotel's
current rates online or by email. For other updates, see www
.ricksteves.com/update.

radically higher. Every place listed here is about a 5- to 10-minute
walk from the train station.

$$$ Hotel Goldener Schlüssel is the oldest inn in down-
town Bern, but it's been completely and nicely renovated. Its 34
small, Euro-style rooms have modern sliding-glass-door bath-
room pods. The high-ceilinged back rooms are quieter and more
expensive, as the front rooms facing Rathausgasse get café and
disco noise from across the street (Sb-140-165 SF, Db-180-240 SF,
Db suite-300-380 SF, Tb-240-285 SF, Qb-260-290 SF, extra bed-
50 SF, elevator, free Internet access, Wi-Fi, Rathausgasse 72, tel.
031-311-0216, fax 031-311-5688, www.goldener-schluessel.ch, info
@goldener-schluessel.ch).

$$$ Hotel Continental has institutional corridors, but its 40
Nordic-flavored rooms are bright, and the cheery breakfast room
features a sun terrace (Sb-120-170 SF, Db-190-230 SF, Tb-240-
300 SF, cheaper Fri-Sun, save 15 SF by skipping breakfast, elevator, free Internet access, pay Wi-Fi, Zeughausgasse 27, tel.
031-329-2121, fax 031-329-2199, www.hotel-continental.ch, info
@hotel-continental.ch).

$$ Hotel National offers 46 rooms—some basic, others much
nicer. It's a simple, old-school, hardwood-floor time warp of a
place with a classic elevator. There's some street noise, and inward-
facing rooms can be noisy on Friday and Saturday, so request a
quiet room. For the best prices, book far in advance (S-65-90 SF,
Ss-100-125 SF, D-130 SF, Ds-150-170 SF, Ts/Qs family room-
235-300 SF, extra bed-30-45 SF, elevator, free Internet access and
Wi-Fi, Hirschengraben 24, tel. 031-381-1988, fax 031-381-6878,

www.nationalbern.ch, info@nationalbern.ch).

$ Backpackers Hotel Glocke rents the cheapest beds in the old town. Your group always gets its own dorm, and the two upper floors have no dorms—just basic but adequate private rooms. All the rooms are stacked directly above a nightclub; fortunately, the reception desk provides a basket of free earplugs (bunk in 6-bed dorm-35 SF, bed in bunkbed D-47 SF, S-74 SF, D with one big bed-110 SF, Db-142 SF, T-144 SF, Tb-174 SF, Q-176 SF, includes sheets, towels-3 SF but included for private rooms, dorms have lockers and sinks, no breakfast but nice kitchen, elevator, pay Internet access, free Wi-Fi in lounge, laundry, no membership necessary, no curfew, reception open 8:00-12:00 & 15:00-22:00, 10-minute walk from station or take tram #9 to Zytglogge stop, Rathausgasse 75, tel. 031-311-3771, fax 031-311-1008, www.bern backpackers.com, info@bernbackpackers.com).

$ Bern Youth Hostel is a big, institutional place below the Parliament building near the river. It's well-run and adult-friendly (bunk in 4- to 6-bed dorm-35-39 SF, S-65 SF, D-93 SF, Ds-106 SF, includes sheets and breakfast, nonmembers pay 6 SF extra/ night, dinner-16 SF, pay Internet access, free Wi-Fi, lockers, laundry, game room, reception open 7:00-12:00 & 14:00-24:00, Weihergasse 4, tel. 031-326-1111, www.youthhostel.ch/bern, bern@youthhostel.ch).

Eating in Bern

In the Old Town

Traditional Swiss Cuisine

Restaurant Harmonie, owned by the Gyger family since 1915, is one of the oldest and most traditional places in town. It offers filling Swiss cuisine and is the favorite lunch spot for the country's politicians, with both inside seating and outdoor tables on a leafy patio (daily specials, 30-50-SF plates, Mon-Fri 8:00-23:30, closed Sat-Sun, Hotelgasse 3, tel. 031-313-1141).

Restaurant Lötschberg, a new local favorite, serves old-style Swiss cuisine in a fun, modern space with a hip clientele that's not limited to the twentysomething crowd. One long wall is lined with the place's large variety of Swiss wines (25-SF *Rösti*, good salads, 17-20-SF lunch specials from 12:00-14:00, open Mon-Sat 9:00-late, Sun 11:00-23:00, Zeughausgasse 16, tel. 031-311-3455).

Budget Option: At **Housi's Brot-Loube** (the bakery around the corner from Restaurant Harmonie), you can pick up sandwiches—they'll warm them up for you—along with salads, drinks, and pastries for a picnic at the nearby Münsterplattform (Mon-Fri 6:30-18:30, closed Sat-Sun, Münstergasse 74, tel. 031-311-2771).

Bern Hotels & Restaurants

1. Hotel Goldener Schlüssel
2. Hotel Continental
3. Hotel National
4. Backpackers Hotel Glocke
5. Bern Youth Hostel
6. Restaurant Harmonie & Housi's Brot-Loube
7. Restaurant Lötschberg
8. Tibits Cafeteria
9. Gourmanderie Moléson
10. Mishio Restaurant
11. Ristorante Luce
12. Kornhauskeller Rest.
13. Markthalle Eateries
14. Restaurant Rosengarten
15. Altes Tramdepot Restaurant
16. Schwellenmätteli & Rist. Casa
17. Internet Access (in Loeb Dep't Store)
18. Stauffacher Bookstore
19. To Launderette
20. Free Bikes (3 Locations)

International Cuisine

Tibits, a busy self-service buffet in the train station building, offers a huge variety of vegetarian-only salads and sandwiches, plus two different hot dishes. Help yourself to a plate and pile it on. The price is by weight: An average helping will cost you about 20 SF (4.20 SF/100 grams, 7.50 SF for soup and bread, variety of sandwiches for 8 SF, fresh fruit juices for 7 SF, Mon-Wed 6:30-23:30, Thu-Sat 6:30-24:00, Sun 8:00-23:00, Bahnhofplatz 10, tel. 031-312-9111).

Gourmanderie Moléson is a long, skinny, classy bistro serving dishes with a French flair, including fondue, *tartes flambées* (Alsatian flatbread—25-30 SF), vegetarian meals, two-course lunch deals (30 SF), and 30-50-SF dinner plates. It has a dressy and very Swiss interior with tables that tumble out onto the street (Mon-Fri 11:30-14:30 & 18:00-23:30, Sat 18:00-23:30, closed Sun, Aarbergergasse 24, tel. 031-311-4463).

Mishio is a fresh, mod Thai place with a Japanese name (go figure) and a terrace overlooking the lively Bärenplatz (20-25-SF plates, a few francs cheaper for takeout, Mon-Fri 9:00-18:30, Thu until 20:00, Sat 8:00-16:00, closed Sun, Bärenplatz 2, tel. 031-313-1121).

Ristorante Luce brings the cooking of Italy's Emilia Romagna

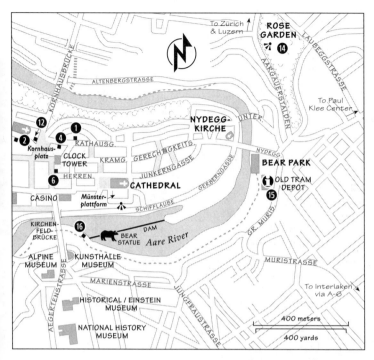

region to Bern. With a venerable dining hall and great seating on the square, it's popular and known as a good value (20-25-SF hearty pastas, salads, usually no pizzas, daily 11:30-23:00, Zeughausgasse 28, tel. 031-310-9999). The same owners run a somewhat cheaper pizzeria across the street.

Kornhauskeller, decorated with colorful mural paintings, is a splurge. It's in the palatial cellar of the old granary, originally built to house the state's wine cellar. This dressy, pricey Mediterranean place offers lunch specials and a fine antipasto bar for those on a budget. Make a meal out of the 19-SF or 27-SF plate, telling the man behind the buffet exactly what you'd like. Even if you don't dine here, step into the cellar to take a look (35-45-SF plates, Mon-Sat 11:45-14:30 & 18:00-24:30, Sun 18:00-23:30, Kornhausplatz 18, tel. 031-327-7272).

Budget Option: **Markthalle** is a fun jumble of eateries in the city's inviting old market hall, a short walk from the train station. With a wide range of choices (including Japanese, Italian, Turkish, Indian, Chinese, Mexican, bakeries, and wine bars), it's like a funky, classy food court—by far the best dining experience for budget eaters, and a fun nightlife stop for anyone (7-10-SF plates, many places offer lunch specials, most open Mon-Sat 9:00-late, closed Sun, Bubenbergplatz 9).

Across the River

Restaurant Rosengarten, perched on top of the hill above Nydegg Bridge, is good for city views. During the day, come for lunch, or for tea and cake with grannies (19-SF two-course lunch special on weekdays). At night, you'll dine with couples enjoying the fresh seasonal menu (20-40-SF dinner plates, March-Nov daily 9:00-24:00, closed Dec-Feb, moderately steep walk up cobbled Alter Aargauerstalden, or take tram #10 from the old town, tel. 031-331-3206).

Altes Tramdepot, in the Old Tram Depot above the Bear Park, offers seating in their big, bright, and boisterous microbrewery, or on their leafy terrace overlooking the town and river. Quick and not too expensive, it's popular, serving good-time food and Swiss specialties (fast and healthy 16-24-SF lunch plates, 20-35-SF dinner plates, daily 11:00-24:00, bus #12 to Bärengraben stop, reserve in evening for outdoor view seating, tel. 031-368-1415).

Schwellenmätteli Restaurant is a chance to join trendy locals for a meal or drink while sitting directly over the river. This mod restaurant/lounge has classy tables inside and out. At the tip of the pier is a lounge complete with sofas, mattresses, and a glass floor that lets you see the river racing underneath. The outdoor dining area and bar is open only in nice weather. The cuisine is modern Mediterranean, and also features local trout (30-40-SF main dishes, Mon-Sat 9:00-24:00, Sun 9:00-23:00, 15-minute riverside stroll from Bear Park to Dalmaziquai 11, or take stairs and path below Kirchenfeld Bridge down to river, reservations smart for dinner, tel. 031-350-5001). **Ristorante Casa,** their Italian restaurant across the parking lot, is also good (similar hours but closed Mon and open only for dinner on Sat).

Bern Connections

From Bern by Train to: Murten (hourly, 35 minutes), **Lausanne** (2/hour, 70 minutes), **Interlaken** (2/hour, 55 minutes, some with change in Spiez), **Luzern** (3/hour, 1-1.5 hours, some with change in Olten), **Zürich** (3/hour, 1 hour), **Zürich Airport** (2/hour, 1.25 hours), **Fribourg** in Switzerland (4/hour, 20-30 minutes), **Zermatt** (hourly, 2.25 hours, transfer in Visp), **Montreux** (2/hour, 1.5 hours, transfer in Lausanne), **Lugano** (hourly, 3.75 hours, transfer in Luzern or Zürich), **Appenzell** (hourly, 3 hours, transfer in Gossau), **Munich** (roughly hourly, 5.75-6.25 hours, 1-2 changes), **Frankfurt** (hourly, 4 hours, some with change in Basel), **Freiburg** in Germany (hourly, 1.75-2 hours, few direct, most with change in Basel), **Salzburg** (roughly hourly, 6.5-9 hours, 1-4 changes), **Paris** (1-2/hour, 4.5-6 hours, 1 direct train in morning and 1 in evening, otherwise 1-3 changes). Train info: toll tel. 0900-300-300 (1.19 SF/minute) or www.rail.ch.

Route Tips for Drivers

Interlaken to Bern: From Interlaken, catch the autobahn (direction: Spiez, Thun, then Bern). Circle Bern on the autobahn, taking the fourth Bern exit, *Neufeld Bern*. Signs to *Bern Zentrum* take you to Bern Bahnhof (train station). Turn right just before the station into the Bahnhof Parkplatz (described earlier, under "Arrival in Bern").

Bern to Murten: From the station, drive out of Bern following signs for *Lausanne,* then follow the green signs to *Neuchâtel* and *Murten.* The autobahn ends 20 miles later, in Murten.

Murten

The finest medieval ramparts in Switzerland surround the 5,000 people of Murten (pronounced MOOR-ten; if you say MURR-ten, you might get a quizzical look). You're on the linguistic cusp of Switzerland: 25 percent of Murten speaks French; a few miles to the southwest, nearly everyone does (French-speakers call the town Morat).

Murten is a totally endearing mini-Bern with lively streets, the middle one nicely arcaded with breezy outdoor cafés and elegant shops (many closed Mon). Its castle is romantic, overlooking Lake Murten and the rolling vineyards of gentle Mont Vully in the distance. Spend a night here and have dinner with a local Vully wine, white or rosé. Murten is touristed, but seems to be enjoyed mostly by its own people.

Make time for nearby Avenches (see end of chapter). Though quaint today, the town was once a powerful Roman capital—as its ruins attest.

Orientation to Murten

Tourist Information

Murten's TI is just inside the city walls at the far end of town from the train station (Easter-Sept Mon-Fri 9:00-12:00 & 13:00-18:00, Sat-Sun 10:00-12:00 & 13:00-17:00, Oct-Easter shorter hours and closed weekends, Französische Kirchgasse 6, tel. 026-670-5112, www.murtentourismus.ch). Get a free map and walking guide, and ask about sights, biking, and boat trips.

Arrival in Murten

By Train: To reach the town from the station (a 5-minute walk), exit to the right, take the first left, and walk up Bahnhofstrasse, then turn right through the town gate. Murten is a tiny town, and a delight on foot.

By Car: You can park overnight in the old town for free (18:00-10:00). During the day, don't park inside the gates; Murten's brown-clad parking cops are infamous. Park in the lot near the castle and Co-op supermarket (1.80 SF/hour, pay at machine inside by elevator). Get the latest advice on parking from your hotelier.

Helpful Hints

Internet Access: Try **A&A Computer** (12 SF/hour, Mon-Fri 9:00-12:00 & 14:00-19:00, Sat 9:00-16:00, closed Sun, behind train station, past Peugeot garage, at Engelhardstrasse 6, tel. 026-670-0520). The TI has info on Wi-Fi hotspots in the middle of town.

Post Office: It's across the street from the train station.

Baggage Storage: Leave your bags at the **train station,** with the kind folks at the left-luggage counter (5 SF/bag, daily 6:00-22:15).

Laundry: There's none in town.

Local Guide: Mary Brunisholz, an American who married into this part of Switzerland, is an excellent guide with a car (150-200 SF/half-day, mobile 078-601-7040, mary.brunisholz @vtxnet.ch). The TI has a list of other guides.

Self-Guided Walk

Welcome to Murten

This introductory walk will give you the lay of the land and a lesson on the historic 15th-century Battle of Murten.

• *Start your walk just below the town's main gate at the public school, where you see a statue of the feisty town hero...*

Adrian von Bubenberg

Burgundy was the aggressive power of the day, and this Murten native stopped the power grab of the 15th century by beating Charles the Bold. Adrian von Bubenberg stood here and looked across the lake at the distant peaks of the Jura Mountains—the historic border between the Swiss and the French (more on the battle a little later).

The earliest Swiss clockmakers were from those Jura Mountains. Look at the

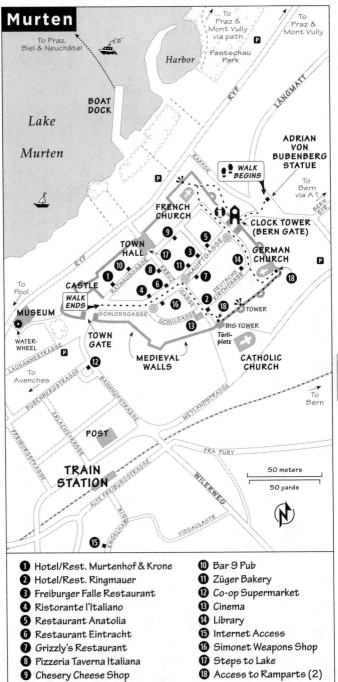

Murten

1 Hotel/Rest. Murtenhof & Krone
2 Hotel/Rest. Ringmauer
3 Freiburger Falle Restaurant
4 Ristorante l'Italiano
5 Restaurant Anatolia
6 Restaurant Eintracht
7 Grizzly's Restaurant
8 Pizzeria Taverna Italiana
9 Chesery Cheese Shop
10 Bar 9 Pub
11 Züger Bakery
12 Co-op Supermarket
13 Cinema
14 Library
15 Internet Access
16 Simonet Weapons Shop
17 Steps to Lake
18 Access to Ramparts (2)

BERN AND MURTEN

clock tower—where's the little hand? As part of its lease, the restaurant below takes responsibility for hand-winding the clock each day, as it has since 1712. That's the Bern gate—so called because it opens up onto the road to Bern. The tiny grated window in the mighty door is a security window.

• *Rather than enter the gate, go right instead (along the wall, not downhill). Head along the outside of the wall, around the first turret, and look for the cannonballs, left in the wall to remind townsfolk of their incredible victory over the Burgundians—like an Alamo with a happy ending.*

Stroll up to the wall along the...

Lakeview Terrace

Across the way is Mont Vully (mohn voo-yee)—one big vineyard and a mecca for lovers of Swiss white wine. The lowlands to the right—a rich former lakebed—are the heart of the fertile Three Lakes Region (lakes Biel, Neuchâtel, and Murten). The lush farmland is called the "vegetable garden of Switzerland" for its soil, which yields more than 60 varieties of produce.

The ancient Celtic Helvetii tribe recognized the fertility of this land and settled here. The Romans likewise made this land a priority in establishing their colony of Helvetia (the origin of Switzerland's official name, Confoederatio Helvetica).

• *Check out the small...*

French Church

Foreseeing a showdown with Burgundy, Adrian von Bubenberg had the town walls strengthened. As three-quarters of the towns-people were German-speaking, they took a vote and decided to tear down the French church to get more stones. (This little church was rebuilt for the French-speaking community six years after its big one was demolished.) As the Calvinist Reformation swept through Catholic Switzerland in the early 16th century, churches like this were stripped of their rich paintings, sculptures, and stained glass. Elaborate altars were replaced with simple, Bible-topped tables, and pulpits became the focus. The emphasis was teaching the word of God. In this church, about the only exceptions to the "no distractions" rule are the tiny stained-glass coats of arms—heraldry of the wealthy families who helped fund its construction (church open sporadically, closed Nov-Feb).

• *From here, we'll cross to the other side of town. Walk past the TI and the clock tower, and go up the lane to the library (on right, #31).*

Library

Notice that along with being a "Bibliothek," the library is also a "Ludothek." This means that parents can check out toys and games for their children, rather than spend their hard-earned money keeping massive places like Toys "R" Us in business. Across the street, the little **Web Hüsli** is one of the few buildings that survived a 14th-century fire that burned down the wooden town; before then, most houses looked like this one. After the fire, future building was limited to the characteristic yellow Jura stone (like the library). Around the corner (left), just past the town's morgue, is the public WC.

• *Continue straight ahead to the...*

German Church

Murten's German church, built in 1710, is also post-Reformation Protestant simple. As the town is on the border between two cantons (Bern and Fribourg), for 400 years its rule was shared: Every five years, it would flip between cantons. Arrangements like this didn't sit well with Napoleon, and around 1800, he made it firmly a part of nearby Fribourg.

Inside, notice the big stucco relief (center of ceiling) with two seals: the bear for Bern and the three castles for Fribourg. The Protestant passion for Bible study is also evident in this church. Explore the choir (two rows of seats on each side for big shots) behind the altar. Find Adrian von Bubenberg's seat. (Hint: The window above shows the war hero in red, with his victorious local yokels in their alpine red-knit hats...underdogs whupping the Burgundians.) The pulpit was carved in 1460 from a single oak tree. Notice the two prime seats on either side of the altar; the one to the preacher's right was for the leader of Bern or Fribourg—depending on who happened to be ruling that year.

• *Leaving the church, hook left around the back. Finger the limestone and sandstone tombstones, quarried from Mont Vully for noble families. Then climb the creaky stairs onto the ramparts and walk about 50 yards to the...*

Ramparts

Murten's only required sightseeing is to scramble the ramparts (free, open daily until 21:00). Survey the town, and note the uniformity of Murten. Paint your place the wrong color, and you may be instructed to redo it—at your own expense. Scanning the countless chimneys, think of the enforced conformity that comes with living in a small town (and find the one oddball). Telephone and electricity wires are all underground. Look back at the roof of the German church. The six-sided "star of David" isn't a Jewish symbol in this case, but recalls the star that guided the wise men to Bethlehem on the first Christmas.

• *Continue to the **tower**. Climb the steps for a commanding town and lake view.*

With your back to the lake, look inland and imagine the

action on June 22, 1476. Mighty Charles the Bold, with his 20,000 well-armed Burgundians, was camped on the hill (the one with the divided forest) for 10 days, laying siege to the town of 2,000. Runners were sent out from the town to gather help. A makeshift army of about 10,000 villagers gathered on the hills to the left. Just as George Washington attacked when the Redcoats were celebrating Christmas, the Swiss swooped in as the Burgundians were still hung over from a big Midsummer Night's Eve bash. The Battle of Murten was fought in pouring rain—a muddy, bloody mess. Almost all 20,000 Burgundians were slaughtered—many driven into the lake with their armor to drown (try swimming in a coat of mail). For centuries, French bones would wash ashore. Charles the (no-longer-so-) Bold barely got away on a very fast horse.

This victory demonstrated to the Swiss the advantages of *E Pluribus Unum,* and the assemblage of the many still-fiercely independent Swiss cantons into the Helvetic Confederation snowballed. In this sweet little corner, an influential battle in European history had been fought. Burgundian power ebbed, and Europe got to know a new nation...Switzerland.

• *Walk a bit farther along the wall and descend at the next tower (across from Café-Pension Ringmauer).*

The stairs lead to a fine old **clock** mechanism from 1816. Once powering the big clock in the City Hall tower, it spent decades in a to-be-assembled pile (à la Ikea), gathering dust in an attic. Finally, in 1991, a town resident—recognizing a good challenge—reassembled it into perfect working order. Notice how the gearbox powers three different clock faces, and how the old hand crank raises the stones that power the clock. The white face determines the clock's time, which rings on the quarter-hour.

• *Step outside the wall, where you'll see the Catholic church (1886), private gardens along the wall, and evidence of how the wall was constructed in several distinct stages.*

The first phase was built with large river stones, some arranged in a neat fishbone pattern. Later, the town ran out of money, and the next stage shows pebbles and rubble mixed with a rough concrete. And finally, when the town prospered again, they finished the wall with finely cut sandstone.

• *Walk back into town, stopping on the first corner at the fire station-turned-community-cinema.*

Contributors are thanked with their names on the door. Notice what's playing tonight (in Switzerland, movies are subtitled, not dubbed, to accommodate a two-language audience). At this corner, spin slowly, admiring the town's fine shutters.

• *Then, continue a block to the...*

Main Street

In the 19th century, Murten's townsfolk used one of three water fountains on this street. Enjoy the colorful store signs as they still hang out their shingles in the traditional fashion. Bakery and *pâtis-serie* competition on this street is fierce. Drop into one for regional specialties: *Nidlechueche,* a sweet, doughy cream tart; and *Seelander Zwetschen,* a chocolate-covered prune truffle with liqueur.

Near the top of the main street, **Simonet Weapons** sells all the latest knives by Victorinox. There's the green "stay-glow," and even a model with a USB flash drive for the outdoorsman with a laptop. At the top of the street (#16), Murten's oldest house has fine paintings under its eaves. There's some nice *Schmuck* (jewelry) two doors to the right.

• *Farther to the right, at the top of town, step into...*

Murten Castle

The town castle, which houses the police station in a former prison (closed to the public), shows off an impressive gun from 1882 and a lovely lake view. The nearby museum is not worth your time or money, but outside it is a func-tioning water mill; from there, you're a short stroll from the lakeside.

Activities in Murten

Lake Activities—To get down to Murten's lazy lakefront, find the access just past the castle, at Rathausgasse 17 (a block from Hotel Murtenhof), or go out the gate by the TI and take a left down the hill. Just past the grassy breakwa-ter is Pantschau, a big park, which is flanked by cheap self-service eateries (such as La Chaloupe, with salad bar and crêpes) and the Beach House (with better lakeside seating). There's mini-golf, wind-surfing gear rental and instruc-

tion, an open-air summer film fest, and a fine lakeside promenade. Buy tickets for cruises (described next) at the kiosk at pier 1.

One-Hour Lake Murten Cruise (with Hiking Option): Boats go about six times a day through the summer (19 SF, covered by Swiss Pass; mid-April-late May and late Sept-mid-Oct 5/day

Fri-Sun only, no boats Mon-Thu; no boats mid-Oct–mid-April; tel. 032-729-9600, www.navig.ch; TI can help).

Consider stopping in the small town of Praz on the French-speaking shore. From there you have two good options: You could hike through vineyards up Mont Vully—where a bench and a pretty lake and Alp views await—and return on the lake with your same ticket. Or you can walk from Praz two hours back to Murten, clockwise around the lake (12.20 SF one-way for boat from Murten to Praz).

Half-Day Three Lakes Cruise: Consider sailing on all three of the region's lakes (connected by canals) and stopping at several small medieval villages along the way. Two boat companies make the round-trip once a day—one originates in Murten, the other in Biel (3.25-4.25 hours each way, 54 SF for one-way ticket, "day card" covers round-trip—69 SF for Murten-based boat, 78 SF covers both boat companies, both covered by Swiss Pass). One boat leaves Murten at 10:00, arrives in the town of Biel at 14:10, then turns around just a half hour later and heads back along the same route, leaving Biel at 14:40 and arriving in Murten at 18:30 (runs Tue-Sun late May–late Sept, off-season runs Fri-Sun only, tel. 032-729-9600, www.navig.ch). A different boat leaves Biel at 9:45 and arrives in Murten at 13:00; it returns from Murten at 14:30—giving you about an hour and a half in town—and docks in Biel at 18:20 (runs daily April-Oct, tel. 032-329-8811, www.bielersee.ch). Ask at the TI about boat-trip discount vouchers (must choose specific day; limited number available, so be at TI when it opens)—then buy tickets at the waterfront. You can condense this full-day trip by taking the boat one way and the train the other (2/hour, 45-50 minutes, 1-2 changes).

Swimming Pool—The Olympic-size public swimming pool is outside of town next to the lake, just past the castle.

Cost and Hours: 8 SF, daily mid-June–mid-Aug 9:00-21:00, spring and fall 9:30-19:00, closed in winter and spring, www.schwimmbad-murten.ch.

Biking—The Three Lakes region has 100 miles of signposted bike paths (well-described in the TI's brochures). Pick up a free map or buy a top-notch one at the TI. The best easy ride circles the lake and Mont Vully (through vineyards and, if you like, to the summit for a good view). You can rent **bikes** at train-station ticket counters (25 SF/half-day, 33 SF/day, 5 SF less with Eurailpass or Swiss Pass, includes helmets, daily 6:00-22:15, www.rent-a-bike.ch). Ask about being dropped off with your bike—or dropping off your bike—at another station, which opens up interesting options (7 SF extra, limited to a few stations).

Nightlife in Murten

Movies—Murten's cute little community co-op theater plays movies nightly (15 SF, Schulgasse 18). Movies are shown in their original language (capital letter indicates the soundtrack language, small letters indicate subtitles—e.g., "Efd" means "English with French and *Deutsch* subtitles").

The open-air cinema hosts a lakeside summer film festival with outdoor screenings of a different movie each night (early July-early Aug, details at TI).

Pubs—There are plenty of inviting pubs and nightclubs in town. **Bar 9** sells drinks with a lake view by night (between Hotel Murtenhof & Krone and Town Hall). Along the same street, closer to the clock tower, is **Chesery,** which serves regional cheeses, as well as meats, desserts, and drinks in a classy/funky little space (cheese-12 SF/100 grams, daily 11:00-late, Rathausgasse 28, tel. 026-670-6577). The main street has an Irish bar and several other nightspots, and there's a popular bar just outside the clock tower.

Sleeping in Murten

(1 SF = $1.10, country code: 41)
This adorable town is no secret. July through mid-September (especially on weekends) is peak time—make a reservation and expect maximum prices. Where price ranges are given in the hotel listings, it means that prices vary depending on the season, type of room, or view. The nearest youth hostel is in Avenches (see page 140).

$$$ Hotel Murtenhof & Krone, a worthwhile splurge, has 57 nicely appointed rooms—each a stylish mix of old and new. This place is well-run by the Joachim family—Theodore, Jutta, and their sons Marc and Ariste (Sb-120 SF, small Db-160 SF, big Db-240 SF, Tb-220-280 SF, family rooms, mid-Sept-May ask for a 10 percent discount with this book, elevator, free Internet access, free Wi-Fi for Rick Steves readers who ask nicely, parking-18 SF/day, next to castle at Rathausgasse 1-5, tel. 026-672-9030, fax 026-672-9039, www.murtenhof.ch, info@murtenhof.ch). They have the best lakeview restaurant in town (described later, under "Eating in Murten").

$$ Hotel Ringmauer ("Ramparts") is friendly, with a fun mix of modern decor in a traditional setting in a quiet corner of town. Showers and toilets are within a dash of all 14 rooms (S-65-75 SF, D-115-135 SF, Db-135-145 SF, T-165 SF, Q-190-240 SF, attached restaurant, near town wall farthest from lake, Deutsche Kirchgasse 2, tel. 026-670-1101, fax 026-672-2083, www.ringmauer .ch, willkommen@ringmauer.ch).

Eating in Murten

Eating in Murten is a joy. I'd stroll the main drag up one side and down the other to survey the action before making a choice. For elegance and a lake view, it's the Murtenhof. There are several good options right on the lake a 10-minute walk down from the town center. Budget eaters can assemble a picnic at the Co-op grocery or find a salad bar. Bakeries make good sandwiches, but they close by about 18:00.

Anything called *Seelander* or mentioning "three lakes" is typical of this Three Lakes region. Traditional restaurants serve *Egli-Filets,* the very popular perch "from the lake" (these days actually caught in the Bodensee—Lake Constance in English—up by the German border). As this is the "vegetable garden of Switzerland," restaurants pride themselves on offering good veggies. You'll want a glass of wonderfully smooth and refreshing white Vully (voo-yee) wine with your meal (about 4 SF/glass).

Restaurant Murtenhof, perched high above the lake in the old town with a covered terrace giving diners a comfortable and classy lake view regardless of the weather, serves "updated Three Lakes cuisine" and several vegetarian choices. Sipping a glass of local white wine with the right travel partner, while gazing across the lake at hillside vineyards as the sun sets, is one of Europe's fine moments. Their fresh and tasty "catch of the day" (while not *Egli*) actually *is* from the lake (19 SF). To be sure you get the limited lakeview seating, call in a reservation. The occasional baaah-ing of sheep and goats from the field below the open windows adds a nice soundtrack to the rustic elegance (salad bar, 25-50-SF main courses, March-Nov Tue-Sun 11:00-23:00, closed Mon except mid-July-mid-Aug, closed Dec-Feb, tel. 026-672-9030).

Ringmauer Restaurant is a good bet for French cuisine and decadent desserts, offering both a dressy section (20-30-SF lunch plates, 40-50-SF dinner plates, three-/four-/five-course fixed-price meals for 60/78/88 SF) and a cheaper zone (20-SF lunch plates, 25-40-SF dinner plates, 19-SF daily special). This local favorite has outdoor seating on a quiet, picturesque lane and serves the area's top-end wine by the glass (Tue-Sat 11:30-14:00 & 18:30-21:30, closed Sun-Mon, Deutsche Kirchgasse 2, tel. 026-670-1101).

Freiburger Falle serves all the old *Fribourgeoise* traditions, such as meat on a hot stone (40 SF), fondue, and so on, hiding in a cellar under the main street. You'll eat under alphorns and castle-style chandeliers (closed one day a week—which changes, find it under the storm-cellar doors in front of the Irish pub at Hauptgasse 43, tel. 026-672-1222).

Ristorante l'Italiano is the town choice for authentic Italian cuisine. The Prozzillo family emphasizes gastronomic simplicity. As its menu makes quite clear, they don't serve pizza (18-23-SF pasta dishes, 23-33-SF meat dishes, warm food served Mon-Sat 11:30-13:30 & 18:00-21:30, off-season opens Mon at 17:00, closed Sun year-round, outside seating, Hauptgasse 11, tel. 026-672-2212).

Restaurant Anatolia is a Turkish place with fresh ingredients, good cooking, and a welcoming owner, Mehmet. Eat indoors with the fine mural of Istanbul, or watch the main-drag action from an outside table (20-30 SF, food served daily 11:00-15:00 & 17:00-23:30 in summer, shorter hours off-season, Hauptgasse 45, tel. 026-670-2868).

Restaurant Eintracht serves local cuisine from a fun menu, including old-time chef specials. If there is a down-and-dirty, horse-meat-cookin' hangout in town, this is it (17-SF lunch specials, 20-30-SF plates, half portions available, healthy specials, food served Mon-Tue and Thu-Sat 11:30-13:45 & 18:00-21:30, Sun 11:30-13:45, closed Wed, streetside seating, Hauptgasse 19, tel. 026-670-2240).

Grizzly's Restaurant, perfect for those in need of a quick trip back home, is a playful, enthusiastic place with an enticing menu of North American delicacies. The Yukon-chic interior comes with totem poles, buckskins, and rock-and-roll. The outside offers the finest seats on the main street. As the menu says, "If the meal's not ready in 10 minutes, it will be in 15. If it's not on the table in 15 minutes, have another beer" (fresh salads, trappers' spare ribs, mussels, vegetarian options, food served Tue-Sat 11:30-13:30 & 18:00-21:30, closed Sun-Mon, reservations smart, Hauptgasse 24, tel. 026-670-0787).

Pizza: Murten has two pizzerias. The one on the main street has better views, but townsfolk prefer **Pizzeria Taverna Italiana** for its better value (18-SF daily specials, 20-SF pizza and pasta, 15-SF pizzas to go, cash preferred, daily 10:00-14:00 & 17:00-22:00, near Hotel Murtenhof at Kreuzgasse 4, tel. 026-670-2122).

Bakeries: The main street has four bakeries, all with ample charm. **Züger** (at Hauptgasse 33) has a tearoom and offers daily indoor seating and pleasant outside seats. They have delicate open-face sandwiches typical of the region, and a wide variety of salads for around 16 SF (Wed-Sat and Mon 6:45-18:30, Sun 7:45-18:30, closed Tue).

Supermarket: The giant **Co-op** (with a cafeteria) towers between the train station and city center (Mon-Thu 8:00-19:00, Fri 8:00-20:00, Sat 7:30-17:00, closed Sun).

BERN AND MURTEN

Murten Connections

From Murten by Train to: Avenches (hourly, 10 minutes, direction: Payerne), **Bern** (hourly, 35 minutes), **Fribourg** in Switzerland (hourly, 30 minutes), **Lausanne** (2/hour, 1.5 hours, generally transfer in Fribourg, Payerne, or Neuchâtel), **Zürich** (1-2/hour, 1.75 hours, transfer in Bern, Fribourg, or Neuchâtel). Train info: toll tel. 0900-300-300 (1.19 SF/minute) or www.rail.ch.

Route Tips for Drivers

Murten to Lake Geneva (50 miles): The autobahn from Bern to Lausanne/Lake Geneva makes everything speedy (see the Lake Geneva and French Switzerland chapter). Murten and Avenches are 10 minutes off the autobahn; Broc, Bulle, and Gruyères are within sight of each other and the autobahn. It takes about an hour to drive from Murten to Montreux. The autobahn (direction: Simplon) takes you high above Montreux (pull off at great viewpoint rest stop) and Château de Chillon. For the castle, take the first exit east of the castle (Villeneuve); signs direct you along the lake back to the castle.

Near Murten: Avenches

Avenches, four miles south of Murten, was once Aventicum, the Roman capital of Helvetia. Today, it's a quaint little town with an ancient theater taking a bite out of it. From the town spreads a vast field of sparse Roman ruins.

With a pleasant, small-town French ambience, Avenches (ah-vahnsh) is a quieter, less expensive place to stay than Murten. Just a few minutes away by train, it also makes an easy day trip. The **TI** (Mon-Fri 8:30-12:00 & 13:30-17:30, Sat 9:30-12:30, closed Sun, Place de l'Eglise 3, tel. 026-676-9922, www.avenches.ch) and the town are a seven-minute uphill walk from the station.

Sights in Avenches

Roman Avenches

Aventicum was a Roman capital, with a population of 20,000. The Romans appreciated its strategic crossroads location, fertile land, and comfortable climate (in modern times, it's been voted the "most livable place to retire"). While the population of today's Avenches could barely fill the well-worn

ruins of their Roman amphitheater, Aventicum was once one of the largest cities of the Roman Empire. Everything sits on Roman ruins, which were nearly quarried to oblivion over several centuries; the scant remains were finally spared in the 19th century, and today, things are carefully preserved. Metal detectors must be registered here. Mothers, knowing that turning up anything ancient will bring on the archaeologists, yell at their kids, "Don't dig!" Even the benches on the main street are bits of a 2,000-year-old temple cornice.

The town has five Roman sights: the amphitheater, a lone tower, a sanctuary and a theater in a field outside of town, and a museum. While you'll pay to enter the museum, the ruins are free and always viewable.

The **amphitheater,** or arena, which once seated 18,000, is the largest Roman ruin in Switzerland (free, always open). Although the gladiator action is no more, it's still busy with an annual opera festival and other musical events. At the top of the amphitheater (just past the museum entrance), scan the surrounding countryside. All the farmland was once a walled Roman town of about 20,000 people. The **tower** on the ridge (on left)—the only one remaining of the original 73 towers—marks where the wall once stood. In the middle, past the lone standing column of the **sanctuary,** you can see the small **theater** ruins (described below).

The **Roman museum** fills a medieval tower attached to the amphitheater in town with three fascinating floors of Roman artifacts. Good students borrow the extensive English catalog, which affords a fairly intimate look at domestic life here back then. Don't miss the glass, mosaics, and a gold bust of Marcus Aurelius (A.D. 80) found in an old Roman sewer in 1939 (4 SF, covered by Swiss Pass; April-Sept Tue-Sun 10:00-17:00; Oct-March Tue-Sun 14:00-17:00; closed Mon year-round, tel. 026-557-3315, www.aventicum.org).

Perhaps the best Aventicum experience is to spend some quiet time at sunset pondering the evocative **Roman theater** (Théâtre Romaine) and **sanctuary** in the fields, a half-mile walk out of town (free, always open, tiny free car park at the site). The single column marks "Du Cigognier"—nicknamed the "stork sanctuary" (c. 1700) for the stork nest it supported. The site was a quarry until the 19th century, so almost nothing remains.

Sleeping in Avenches

(1 SF = $1.10, country code: 41)

$$$ Hotel de la Couronne is an Old World, three-star place with a modern interior. It sits grandly on the main square of little Avenches, with 21 charming, bright rooms (Sb-130-145 SF,

Db-190-220 SF, Db suite-280 SF, extra bed-65 SF, parking-25 SF/ day, free Wi-Fi, next to TI at Rue Centrale 20, tel. 026-675-5414, www.lacouronne.ch, info@lacouronne.ch).

$ The Avenches **IYHF hostel,** the only hostel in the area, is a beauty (open April-mid-Oct). Run by the Dhyaf family, it has 3- to 10-bed rooms and includes breakfast and linens, a homey TV room, table tennis, a big backyard, and a very quiet setting near the Roman theater. If you're on a tight budget and have a car or a railpass, this place is a great option (40 SF for dorm bed in 3-bed room, 38 SF in 4-bed room, 34 SF in 6- to 10-bed room, nonmembers pay 6 SF extra, lunch or dinner for 15 SF, no curfew, reception open 7:00-10:00 & 17:00-22:00, Internet access, free Wi-Fi, laundry, 3 blocks from center at medieval *lavoir,* Rue du Lavoir 5, tel. 026-675-2666, fax 026-675-2717, www.youthhostel.ch/avenches, avenches@youthhostel.ch).

GIMMELWALD
and the BERNER OBERLAND

Interlaken • Lauterbrunnen • Gimmelwald •
Mürren • Wengen

Frolic and hike high above the stress and clouds of the real world. Take a vacation from your busy vacation. Recharge your touristic batteries high in the Alps, where distant avalanches, cowbells, the fluff of a down comforter, the whistle of marmots, and the crunchy footsteps of happy hikers are the dominant sounds. If the weather's good (and your budget's healthy), ride a cable car from the traffic-free village of Gimmelwald to a hearty breakfast at the revolving Piz Gloria restaurant, 10,000 feet up on the Schilthorn. Linger among alpine whitecaps before riding, hiking, or paragliding down 5,000 feet to Mürren and home to Gimmelwald.

Your gateway to the rugged Berner Oberland is the grand old resort town of Interlaken. Near Interlaken is Switzerland's open-air folk museum, Ballenberg, where you can climb through original traditional houses gathered from every corner of this diverse country.

Ah, but the weather's fine and the Alps beckon. Head deep into the heart of the Alps, and ride the cable car to the stop just this side of heaven—Gimmelwald.

Planning Your Time

Rather than tackle a checklist of famous Swiss mountains and resorts, choose one region to savor: the Berner Oberland.

Interlaken is the region's administrative headquarters and transportation hub. Use it for business—banking, post office, laundry, shopping—and as a springboard for alpine thrills.

If the weather's decent, explore the two areas that tower above either side of the Lauterbrunnen Valley, south of Interlaken: On one side is the Jungfrau (and beneath it, the town of Kleine Scheidegg), and on the other is the Schilthorn (overlooking the villages of Gimmelwald and Mürren).

Ideally, spend three nights in the region, with a day exploring each side of the valley. For accommodations without the expense and headache of mountain lifts, consider the valley-floor village of Lauterbrunnen. But for the best overnight options, I'd stay on the scenic ridge high above the valley, in the rustic hamlet of Gimmelwald or the resort town of Mürren. I've also listed a few high-altitude options in the resort of Wengen and several other mountain towns.

For a summary of the wildly scenic activities this region has to offer (from panoramic train rides and lifts to spectacular hikes and mountain biking), see "Activities in the Berner Oberland" on page 186.

If time is limited, consider a night in Gimmelwald, breakfast at the Schilthorn, an afternoon doing the Männlichen-Wengen hike, and an evening or night train out. What? A nature-lover not spending the night high in the Alps? Alpus interruptus.

Getting Around the Berner Oberland

For more than a century, this region has been the target of nature-worshipping pilgrims. And Swiss engineers and visionaries have made the most exciting alpine perches accessible.

By Lifts and Trains

Part of the fun—and most of the expense—here is riding the many mountain trains and lifts (gondolas and cable cars).

Trains connect Interlaken to Wilderswil, Grindelwald, Lauterbrunnen, Wengen, Kleine Scheidegg, and the Jungfraujoch. Lifts connect Wengen to Männlichen and Grund (near Grindelwald); Grindelwald to First; Lauterbrunnen to Grütschalp (where a train connects to Mürren); and the cable-car station near Stechelberg to Gimmelwald, Mürren, and the Schilthorn.

For an overview of your many options, study the "Alpine Lifts in the Berner Oberland" map on page 146 and the "What's What in the Berner Oberland" sidebar on page 144. Lifts generally go at least twice hourly, from about 7:00 until about 20:00 (sneak preview: www.jungfraubahn.ch or www.schilthorn.ch).

Beyond Interlaken, trains and lifts into the Jungfrau region are only 25 percent covered by Eurailpasses, without using a flexi-

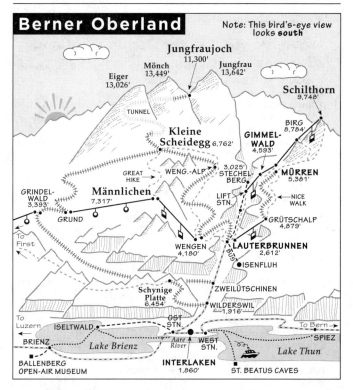

day; with the Swiss Pass, they're free up to Wengen or Mürren (uphill from there, Swiss Pass-holders pay half-price). Ask about discounts for early-morning and late-afternoon trips, youths, seniors, families, groups (assemble a party of 10 and you'll save about 25 percent), and those staying awhile. Generally, round-trips are double the one-way cost, though some high-up trains and lifts are 10-20 percent cheaper. It's possible to buy your entire package of lifts at once, but then you don't have the flexibility to change with the weather.

Popular Passes: The **Junior Card,** for families traveling with children, pays for itself in the first hour of trains and lifts (30 SF/one child, 60 SF/two or more children, lets children under 16 travel free with at least one parent, buy at Swiss train stations).

The **Berner Oberland Regional Pass** covers most trains, buses, and lifts in this area. It doesn't, however, cover the full cost of the popular and pricey Mürren-Schilthorn cable car or the train from Kleine Scheidegg up to the Jungfraujoch. While the pass may cost less than individual tickets, it's not much cheaper than a whole-country Swiss Pass (4 days-230 SF, 6 days-290 SF, 8 days-330 SF, discount with Swiss Pass, valid May-Oct, www.regiopass-berneroberland.ch).

What's What in the Berner Oberland

For such a small corner of the world, this region packs in a lot to experience. Here's a quick rundown of the place names you'll encounter.

Allmendhubel (AHL-mehnd-hoo-behl): Family-friendly village with Jungfrau views, connected to Mürren by a classic old funicular (see page 182).

Ballenberg: Swiss Open-Air Folk Museum, on Lake Brienz (see page 153).

Berner Oberland: The mountainous part of the canton of Bern, sometimes referred to as the "Jungfrau region." Everything else on this list is in the Berner Oberland (also called "Bernese Oberland" in English).

Birg (beerg): Cable-car stop between Mürren and the Schilthorn, with a trail leading steeply down to Gimmelwald and more (see page 189).

Brienz (bree-ENTS): Lake on the east side of Interlaken (Brienzersee) and the namesake town on its shore.

First (feersht): Overlook point accessible by lift from Grindelwald; endpoint of hike from Schynige Platte (see page 197).

Gimmelwald (GIM-mehl-vahlt): Wonderfully rustic time-warp village overlooking the Lauterbrunnen Valley; good home-base option (see page 168).

Grindelwald (GRIN-dehl-vahlt): Expensive resort town, not to be confused with Gimmelwald.

Grütschalp (GRITSH-alp): Station at the top of the cable car from Lauterbrunnen. It's connected by train and a trail to Mürren (see page 195).

Interlaken (IN-tehr-lah-kehn): Big town at the "entrance" to the Berner Oberland; you'll go through here to get anywhere else in this chapter (see page 148).

Jungfrau, Mönch, Eiger (YOONG-frow, munkh, EYE-gehr): Literally "Maiden, Monk, Ogre," the three major peaks of the region, from right to left (the Jungfrau's the highest, at 13,642 feet).

Jungfraubahn (YOONG-frow-bahn): Company that runs all of the trains and lifts in the area (except for the Schilthorn cable cars).

Jungfraujoch (YOONG-frow-yoke): High-altitude (11,300 feet) observation deck near the Jungfrau peak, accessible by train from Kleine Scheidegg.

Kleine Scheidegg (KLY-neh SHY-dehk): Viewpoint with breath-taking Eiger, Mönch, and Jungfrau views; has several hotels and restaurants (see page 199), plus the train station that offers pricey rides to the Jungfraujoch (page 188).

Lauterbrunnen (LOUT-ehr-broo-nehn): Small town in the middle of the Lauterbrunnen Valley. From here, a cable car goes up to Grütschalp (with connections to Mürren and Gimmelwald), the train runs up to Wengen and Kleine Scheidegg, and the PostBus goes to Stechelberg and the Schilthornbahn lift. For hotels and restaurants, see pages 165-167.

Lauterbrunnen Valley: Valley at the heart of the Berner Oberland; most towns and activities in this chapter lie in or overlook this valley.

Männlichen (MEN-leekh-ehn): Lift station on a dramatic ridge separating the region's two valleys. Connected to Wengen and also to Grund (near Grindelwald) by lifts; also the starting point of an easy hike to Kleine Scheidegg with nonstop mountain views (see page 196).

Mürren (MIH-rehn): Pleasant resort town near Gimmelwald, midway up the Schilthorn cable-car line; a good high-mountain home base for those who find Gimmelwald too small and rustic (see page 177).

Schilthorn (SHILT-horn): The 10,000-foot peak across the Lauterbrunnen Valley from the Jungfrau, reached by cable car from near Stechelberg (in the valley), Mürren, and Gimmelwald; features spectacular views and the Piz Gloria revolving restaurant made famous by a James Bond movie (see page 186).

Schilthornbahn: Cable-car company that operates the lift on the west side of the Lauterbrunnen Valley near Stechelberg, connecting the valley floor with Gimmelwald, Mürren, Birg, and the Schilthorn.

Schynige Platte (SHIH-nih-geh PLAH-teh): High-altitude observation point near the entrance to Lauterbrunnen Valley, reached by funicular from Wilderswil; starting point of a long but scenic hike to First (see page 197).

Sefinen Valley (seh-FEE-nehn): Branches off the Lauterbrunnen Valley beyond Stechelberg and Gimmelwald; good for a hike (see page 191).

Stechelberg (SHTEH-khehl-behrk): Village where the road ends at the upper end of the Lauterbrunnen Valley, about a mile beyond the Schilthornbahn cable-car station (for accommodations, see page 200).

Thun (toon): Lake to the west of Interlaken (Thunersee) and its namesake town on the lake.

Trümmelbach Falls (TRIM-mehl-bahkh): Striking series of waterfalls near Lauterbrunnen (see page 164).

Wengen (VAYNG-ehn): Resort town on Jungfrau side of Lauterbrunnen Valley with lift to Männlichen, on the train line between Lauterbrunnen and Kleine Scheidegg.

Wilderswil (VIHL-dehrs-vihl): Village near entrance of the Lauterbrunnen Valley; on the train line between Interlaken and Lauterbrunnen; has funicular to Schynige Platte and trailhead to First (see page 197).

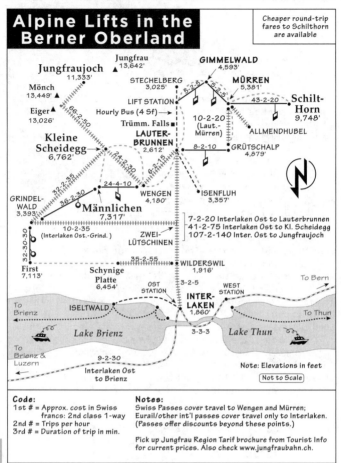

Alpine Lifts in the Berner Oberland

Cheaper round-trip fares to Schilthorn are available

GIMMELWALD 4,593'

Jungfrau ▲ 13,642'

Jungfraujoch 11,333'

STECHELBERG 3,025'

MÜRREN 5,381'

Schilt-Horn 9,748'

Mönch 13,449' ▲

LIFT STATION

43-2-20

Eiger ▲ 13,026'

Hourly Bus (4 Sf) →

10-2-20 (Laut.-Mürren)

ALLMENDHUBEL

66-2-50

Trümm. Falls

Kleine Scheidegg 6,762'

LAUTER-BRUNNEN 2,612'

8-2-10

GRÜTSCHALP 4,879'

24-2-30

6-2-15

N

32-2-35

24-4-10

WENGEN 4,180'

• ISENFLUH 3,357'

GRINDEL-WALD 3,393'

36-2-30

Männlichen 7,317'

7-2-20 Interlaken Ost to Lauterbrunnen
41-2-75 Interlaken Ost to Kl. Scheidegg
107-2-140 Inter. Ost to Jungfraujoch

10-2-35 (Interlaken Ost.-Grind.)

ZWEI-LÜTSCHINEN

32-30-30

35-2-55

• WILDERSWIL 1,916'

First 7,113'

Schynige Platte 6,454'

OST STATION

3-2-5

WEST STATION

To Bern

INTER-LAKEN 1,860'

To Brienz

ISELTWALD

To Thun

Lake Brienz

3-3-3

Lake Thun

To Brienz & Luzern

9-2-30

Interlaken Ost to Brienz

Note: Elevations in feet

Not to Scale

Code:
1st # = Approx. cost in Swiss francs: 2nd class 1-way
2nd # = Trips per hour
3rd # = Duration of trip in min.

Notes:
Swiss Passes cover travel to Wengen and Mürren; Eurail/other int'l passes cover travel only to Interlaken. (Passes offer discounts beyond these points.)

Pick up Jungfrau Region Tarif brochure from Tourist Info for current prices. Also check www.jungfraubahn.ch.

The **Jungfraubahnen Pass** covers six consecutive days of transportation in the Jungfrau region. This pass covers most trains, lifts, buses, and funiculars. It excludes the cable car connecting Stechelberg with Gimmelwald, Mürren, Birg, or the Schilthorn (but does cover the lift/train ride to Mürren via Grütschalp), and you pay half-price for the Kleine Scheidegg-Jungfraujoch train (210 SF, 160 SF with Swiss Pass, valid May–Oct, tel. 033-828-7233, www.jungfraubahn.ch).

By Car

Interlaken, Lauterbrunnen, Isenfluh, and Stechelberg are all accessible by car. You can't drive to Gimmelwald, Mürren, Wengen, or Kleine Scheidegg, but don't let that stop you from staying up in the mountains; park the car and zip up on a lift. To catch the lift to Gimmelwald, Mürren, and the Schilthorn, park at the cable-car station near Stechelberg (2 SF/2 hours, 6 SF/day, cash only; see page 169 for more information). To catch the train to Wengen or Kleine Scheidegg, park at the train station in Lauterbrunnen (2 SF/2 hours, 10 SF/9-24 hours).

Helpful Hints in the Berner Oberland

Weather: Let your plans flex with the weather. If it's good—go! Ask at your hotel or the TI for the latest info. A webcam showing live video from the famous (and most expensive-to-reach) peaks plays just about wherever you go in the area. For the current weather, you can also check www.swisspanorama .com (entire area), www.jungfraubahn.ch (for Jungfraujoch), or www.schilthorn.ch (for Schilthorn peak).

Closed Days: On Sundays and holidays (including the lesser-known religious holidays), small-town Switzerland is quiet. Hotels are open and lifts and trains run, but many stores are closed.

Off-Season Closures: Note that at higher altitudes many hotels, restaurants, and shops are closed between the skiing and hiking seasons: from late April until late May, and again from mid-October to early December.

Rainy-Day Options: When it rains here, locals joke that they're washing the mountains. If clouds roll in, don't despair. They can roll out just as quickly. With good rain gear and the right choice of trail, you can thoroughly enjoy a hike in the rain, with surprise views popping out all around you as the clouds break. Some good bad-weather options are the North Face Trail, the walk from Mürren or Allmendhubel to Grütschalp, the Sefinen Valley hike, and the Lauterbrunnen Valley walk. Also consider a visit to Trümmelbach Falls or the Lauterbrunnen Valley Folk Museum. All of these options are described in this chapter.

Local Guidebook: For an in-depth look at the area's history, folk life, flora, fauna, and for extensive hiking information, consider Don Chmura's *Exploring the Lauterbrunnen Valley* (sold throughout the valley, 8 SF).

Visitors Cards *(Gästekarten):* The hotels in various towns issue free Visitors Cards that include small discounts on some sights. Though these cards won't save you much, you can ask at your hotel for the details.

Weekend Tour Packages for Students: Andy Steves (Rick's son) runs Weekend Student Adventures, offering experiential three-day weekend tours for €250, and designed for American students studying abroad (call US tel. 425/876-2544 or see www.wsaeurope.com for details on tours of Gimmelwald and other great destinations).

BERNER OBERLAND

Skiing and Snowboarding: The Berner Oberland is a great winter-sports destination, with good snow on its higher runs, incredible variety, relatively reasonable prices, and a sense of character that's missing in many swankier resort areas. You can even swish with the Swiss down the world's longest sledding run (9 miles long, out of Grindelwald, only open when snow's good). Three ski areas cluster around the Lauterbrunnen Valley: Mürren-Schilthorn (best for experts), Kleine Scheidegg-Männlichen (busiest, best variety of runs), and Grindelwald-First (best for beginners and intermediates, but lower elevation can make for iffier snowpack). Lift tickets cost around 70 SF a day, or you can buy the two-day Sportspass Jungfrau, which covers all three areas, for about 130 SF (see www.jungfrauwinter.ch for prices and info). For more tips, see the Switzerland in Winter chapter.

Interlaken

When the 19th-century Romantics redefined mountains as something more than cold and troublesome obstacles, Interlaken became the original alpine resort. Ever since, tourists have flocked to the Alps "because they're there." Interlaken's glory days are long gone, its elegant old hotels eclipsed by the newer, swankier alpine resorts. Today, its shops are filled with chocolate bars, Swiss Army knives, and sunburned backpackers.

While European jet-setters are elsewhere, Interlaken is cashing in on a huge interest from India and the Arab world. Indians come to escape their monsoon season—especially in April and May—and to visit places they've seen in their movies. (The Alps often stand in for Kashmir, which is less accessible to film crews.) There's even a restaurant called "Bollywood" atop the Jungfraujoch. People from the hot and dry Arabian Peninsula come here just to photograph their children frolicking in the mist and fog.

Orientation to Interlaken

Efficient Interlaken (pop. 5,500) is a good administrative and shopping center. Take care of business, give the town a quick look, and view the webcam coverage of the weather higher up (at the TI)... then head for the hills.

Tourist Information

The TI, with good information on the region, is located under the 18-story skyscraper on the main street between the two train stations, a 10-minute stroll from either (May-June Mon-Fri 8:00-18:00, Sat 8:00-16:00, closed Sun; July-Aug Mon-Fri 8:00-19:00, Sat 8:00-17:00, Sun 10:00-12:00 & 17:00-19:00; Sept Mon-Fri 8:00-18:00, Sat 9:00-13:00, closed Sun; shorter hours Oct-April, Höheweg 37, tel. 033-826-5300, www.interlaken.ch). The *You Want It All* booklet is an almanac covering everything you need in Interlaken (except for some events, which are covered more thoroughly in the monthly entertainment guide). There's no point in buying a regional map, as good mini-versions of the map are included in various free transportation and hiking brochures.

Arrival in Interlaken

Interlaken has two train stations: Ost (East) and West. All trains coming from western Switzerland stop at both stations. If heading for higher-altitude villages, get off at Ost Station. For hotels in Interlaken, get off at West Station, which has a helpful and friendly information center for in-depth rail questions (Mon-Fri 9:00-12:00 & 13:30-18:20, Sat until 17:00, closed Sun, tel. 058-327-4750, www.bls.ch; ticket windows open daily 6:40-19:00). Ask about discount passes, special fares, railpass discounts, and schedules for the scenic mountain trains. There's an exchange booth next to the ticket windows and a very pricey Internet-access computer. A post office with a cluster of phone booths is a few blocks away.

It's a pleasant 20-minute walk between the West and Ost train stations; an easy, frequent train connection (2-3/hour, 3.40 SF); or a quick trip on the bus (2/hour, 10 minutes, 3.40 SF). From Ost Station, private trains take you deep into the mountainous Jungfrau region (see "Interlaken Connections," on page 160).

Helpful Hints

Baggage Storage: Both stations have lockers (small locker-4 SF, large-5 SF) as well as left-luggage counters (5 SF, West Station—daily 9:00-12:00 & 13:30-18:00, Ost Station—daily 7:00-18:30).

Laundry: Friendly Helen Schmocker's **Wäscherei** has a change machine, soap, English instructions, and a delightful riverside location (self-service daily 7:00-22:00—wash-6 SF/load, dry-about 5 SF/load; full service Mon-Fri 8:00-12:00 & 13:30-18:00, Sat until 16:00, closed Sun, drop off in the morning and pick up that afternoon—12 SF/load; from the main street take Marktgasse over two bridges to Beatenbergstrasse 5, tel. 033-822-1566).

Bike Rental: You can rent bikes (both regular and electric) at West Station (11.50 SF/2 hours, 25 SF/half-day, 33 SF/day, 5 SF less with Eurailpass or Swiss Pass, daily 9:00-18:00, www.rentabike.ch).

Flying Wheels, a short walk from Ost Station, is a hip, well-organized, family-friendly outfit that specializes in electric bikes and guided bike tours of the area. Its amiable English-speaking staff give tips on where to go and can help you pick the right bike (electric or hard-core mountain bikes—35 SF/half-day, 50 SF/day; normal mountain bikes—25 SF/half-day, 33 SF/day; 5 SF cheaper with Swiss Pass, no discount with Eurailpass, tandem electric bikes available, daily 9:00-19:00, across street from the northeast corner of Höhematte Park at Höheweg 133, tel. 033-511-2161, www.flyingwheels.ch). For info on their tours, see "Adventure Sports," later.

A short walk from West Station, **Eiger Sport** rents bikes for a little less than Flying Wheels (8 SF/hour, 10 SF/2 hours, 15 SF/3 hours, 20 SF/half-day, 30 SF/day, Mon-Fri 8:30-12:00 & 13:30-18:30, Sat 8:30-16:00; from West Station, cross river—it's on the right at Bahnhofstrasse 2, tel. 033-823-2043).

Self-Guided Walk

Welcome to Interlaken

Most visitors use Interlaken as a springboard for high-altitude thrills (and rightly so). But the town itself has history and scenic charm and is worth a short walk. This 45-minute stroll circles from the West train station, down the main drag to the big meadow, past the casino, along the river to the oldest part of town (historically a neighboring town called Unterseen), and back to the station.

• *From the West train station, walk along...*

Bahnhofstrasse: This main drag, which turns into Höheweg as it continues east, cuts straight through the town center from the West train station to the Ost train station. The best Swiss souvenir shopping is along this stretch (finer shops are on the Höheweg stretch, near the fancy hotels). At the roundabout is the handy post office (with free public WCs). At Höheweg 2, the TV in the window of the Schilthornbahn office shows the weather up top.

The 18-story **Metropole Hotel** (a.k.a. the "concrete shame of Interlaken") is by far the town's tallest building. Step right into the main lobby (through the second set of doors) and ride the elevator to the top for a commanding view of the "inter-laken" area, and gaze deep into the Jungfrau region to the scenic south. A meal or drink here costs no more than one back on earth. Consider sipping a drink on the outdoor view terrace (or come back tonight—it's open very late).

• *On your right is...*

Höhematte Park: This "high meadow," or Höhematte (but

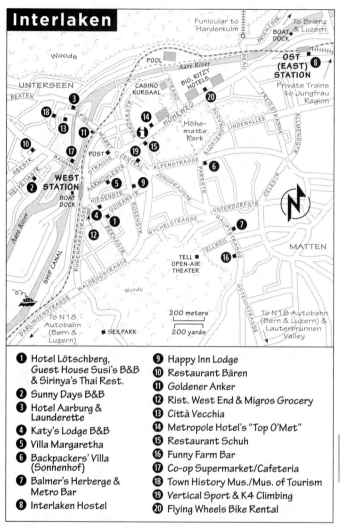

Interlaken

1. Hotel Lötschberg, Guest House Susi's B&B & Sirinya's Thai Rest.
2. Sunny Days B&B
3. Hotel Aarburg & Launderette
4. Katy's Lodge B&B
5. Villa Margaretha
6. Backpackers' Villa (Sonnenhof)
7. Balmer's Herberge & Metro Bar
8. Interlaken Hostel
9. Happy Inn Lodge
10. Restaurant Bären
11. Goldener Anker
12. Rist. West End & Migros Grocery
13. Città Vecchia
14. Metropole Hotel's "Top O'Met"
15. Restaurant Schuh
16. Funny Farm Bar
17. Co-op Supermarket/Cafeteria
18. Town History Mus./Mus. of Tourism
19. Vertical Sport & K4 Climbing
20. Flying Wheels Bike Rental

BERNER OBERLAND

generally referred to simply as "the park"), marks the beginning of Interlaken's fancy hotel row. Hotels like the Victoria-Jungfrau hearken back to the days when Interlaken was *the* top alpine resort (late 19th century). The first grand hotels were built here to enjoy the views of the Jungfrau in the distance. (Today, the *jung Fraus* getting the most attention are next door, at Hooters.)

The park originated as farmland of the monastery that pre-dated the town (marked today by the steeples of both the Catholic and Protestant churches—neither are of any sightseeing interest). The actual **monastery site** is now home to the courthouse and county administration building. With the Reformation in 1528, the monastery was shut down, and its land was taken by the state. Later, when the land was being eyed by developers, the town's leading hotels and business families bought it and established that it would never be used for commercial buildings (a very early example of smart town planning). There was talk of building a parking lot under it, but the water table here, between the two lakes, is too high. (That's why the town cemetery is up on the hillside.) Today, this is a fine place to stroll, hang out on the park benches or at Restaurant Schuh, and watch the paragliders gracefully land.

Across the street from the park, right where the path that bisects the park hits Höheweg, turn left onto the grounds of the **Casino Kursaal,** where, at the top of each hour, dwarves ring the toadstools on the flower clock. The Kursaal, originally a kind of 19th-century fat farm, is now both a casino (passport but no tie required to enter) and a convention center.

• *Follow the path left of the Kursaal to the river (huge public swimming pool just over the river). Walk downstream under the train track and cross the pedestrian bridge, stopping in the middle to enjoy the view.*

Aare River: The Aare River is Switzerland's longest. It connects Lake Brienz and Lake Thun (with an 18-foot altitude difference—this short stretch has quite a flow). Then it tumbles out of Lake Thun, heading for Bern and ultimately into the Rhine. Its level is controlled by several sluices. In the distance, a church bell tower marks a different parish and the neighborhood of Unterseen, which shares the town's name, but in German: Like the word *Interlaken, Unterseen* means "between the lakes." Behind the spire is the pointy summit of the Niesen (like so many Swiss peaks, capped with a restaurant and accessible by a lift). Stroll downstream along the far side of the river to the church spire. The delightful riverside walk is lined by fine residences. Notice that your Jungfrau view now includes the Jungfraujoch observation deck (the little brown bump in the ridge just left of the peak).

• *At the next bridge, turn right to the town square lined with 17th-century houses on one side and a modern strip on the other.*

Unterseen: This was a town when Interlaken was only a monastery. The church is not worth touring. A block away to the left, the (generally empty) **Town History Museum/Museum of Tourism** shows off classic posters, fascinating photos of the construction of the Jungfraujoch, and exhibits on folk life, crafts, and winter sports—all well-described in English (5 SF, covered by Swiss Pass, May-mid-Oct Tue-Sun 14:00-17:00, closed Mon and mid-Oct-April, Obere Gasse 26).

Return to Station: From Unterseen, cross the river on Spielmatte, and you're a few minutes' walk from your starting point. On the second bridge, notice the border between the two towns/parishes, marked by their respective heraldic emblems (each with an ibex, a wild mountain goat). A block or so later, on the left, is the Marktplatz. The river originally ran through this square. The town used to be called "Aaremühle" ("Aare mill") for the mill that was here. But in the 19th century, town fathers made a key marketing decision: Since "Aaremühle" was too difficult to pronounce for English tourists who flocked here, they changed the name to "Interlaken." Judging from the throngs of tourists on the main drag, it worked.

Sights near Interlaken

▲▲Swiss Open-Air Folk Museum at Ballenberg

Across Lake Brienz from Interlaken, the Swiss Open-Air Museum of Vernacular Architecture, Country Life, and Crafts in the Berner Oberland is a rich collection of more than 100 traditional and historic buildings brought here from every region of the country. All the houses are carefully furnished, and many feature traditional craftspeople at work. The sprawling 50-acre park, laid out roughly as a huge Swiss map (Italian Swiss in the south, Appenzell in the east, and so on), is a natural preserve providing a wonderful setting for this culture-on-a-lazy-Susan look at Switzerland.

The Thurgau house (#621) has an interesting wattle-and-daub (half-timbered construction) display, and house #331 has a fun bread museum and farmers' shop. There are daily events and demonstrations (near the east entry), hundreds of traditional farm animals (like very furry-legged roosters, near the merry-go-round in the center), and a chocolate shop (under the restaurant on the east side).

An outdoor cafeteria with reasonable prices is inside the west entrance, and fresh bread, sausage, mountain cheese, and other goodies are on sale in several houses. Picnic tables and grills with free firewood are scattered throughout the park.

The little wooden village of Brienzwiler (near the east entrance) is a museum in itself, with a lovely pint-size church.

Cost and Hours: 20 SF, covered by Swiss Pass; RailAway combo-ticket includes transportation to and from Ballenberg—41 SF from West Station, 38 SF from Ost Station, add 15 SF to return by boat instead, ticket available at both Interlaken stations; houses open daily mid-April-Oct 10:00-17:00, grounds and restaurants stay open until 18:00.

Information: Pick up a daily craft demonstration schedule at the entry, and buy the 2-SF map/guide so you'll know where you are. The more expensive picture book is a better souvenir than guide; tel. 033-952-1030, www.ballenberg.ch.

Getting There: From Interlaken, take the train from either station to Brienz (2/hour, 30 minutes, 9.20 SF one-way from West Station or get the RailAway combo-ticket—described earlier). From the Brienz train station, catch a bus to Ballenberg (10 minutes, 4.20 SF one-way). The bus back to Brienz leaves Ballenberg's east entrance on the hour, then picks up at the west entrance at :07 after the hour (after 18:00, buses leave only from the west entrance). Consider returning from Brienz by boat (boat dock next to train station, one-way to Interlaken's Ost Station-28 SF). Parking is free outside both entrances to the park.

Boat Trips

"Interlaken" is literally "between the lakes" of Thun and Brienz. You can explore these lakes on a lazy boat trip, hopping on and off as the schedule allows (free with Swiss Pass or Eurailpass but uses a flexi-day, schedules at TI or at travel center in West Station). The boats on Lake Thun (5/day in summer, 2/day spring and fall, 5-hour round-trip, 68 SF) stop at the St. Beatus caves (30 minutes away, described next) and two visit-worthy towns: Spiez and Thun. The boats on Lake Brienz (5/day July-Aug, 2-4/day off-season, 3-hour round-trip, 48 SF) stop at the super-cute village of Iseltwald and at Brienz (near Ballenberg Open-Air Folk Museum; easy bus and train connections back to Interlaken from Brienz).

The **St. Beatus caves** on Lake Thun can be visited with a one-hour guided tour (18 SF, 2/hour, April-mid-Oct daily 9:30-17:00, closed mid-Oct-March, tel. 033-841-1643, www.beatushoehlen .ch). The best excursion plan: Ride bus #21 from Interlaken (1-2/ hour, 25 minutes, 5 SF, departs West Station at :17 and :47 past the hour, direction: Thun); tour the caves; take the short, steep hike down to the lake; and return to Interlaken by boat (30 minutes, 13 SF one-way).

Adventure Sports

High-Adrenaline Trips—For the thrill-seeker with money, several companies offer trips such as rafting, canyoning (rappelling down watery gorges), bungee jumping, and paragliding. Costs range from roughly 150 SF to 200 SF—higher for skydiving and hot-air balloon rides. Interlaken's two dominant companies are **Alpin Raft** (tel. 033-823-4100, www.alpinraft.com) and **Outdoor Interlaken** (tel. 033-826-7719, www.outdoor-interlaken.ch). Other companies are generally just booking agents for these two outfits. For an overview of your options, visit www.interlakenadventure. com, or study the racks of brochures at most TIs and hotels (everyone's getting a cut of this lucrative industry).

Several years ago, two fatal accidents jolted the adventure-sport business in the Berner Oberland, leading to a more professional respect for the risks involved. Companies have very high standards of safety. Statistically, the most dangerous sport is mountain biking. Enjoying nature up close comes with risks. Adventure sports increase those risks dramatically. Use good judgment.

Indoor Climbing—**K44** is a breathtaking indoor climbing facility where you can snack or enjoy a nice cup of hot chocolate while watching hotshots practice their gravity-defying skills.

Cost and Hours: Free entry for viewing, 39 SF for one hour of climbing; open longer hours in bad weather: Mon 16:00-22:00, Tue-Fri 9:00-22:00, Sat 9:00-20:00, Sun 9:00-18:00; in good weather: Tue-Fri 9:00-18:00, Sat 9:00-16:00, closed Sun-Mon; next to—and run by—**Vertical Sport**, at the back of the park across from Hotel Savoy at Jungfraustrasse 44, tel. 033-821-2821, www.k44.ch.

Rope Courses—**Outdoor Interlaken's Seilpark** offers five rope courses of varying difficulty and height in a forest, giving you a tree-top adventure through a maze of rope bridges and zip lines.

Cost and Hours: 37 SF, family deals, must weigh between 44 and 264 pounds; June-Aug daily 10:00-18:00; April-May and Sept-Oct Mon-Fri 13:00-18:00, Sat-Sun 10:00-18:00; closed Nov-March; from Interlaken's West Station, it's a 15-minute walk—head right up Rugenparkstrasse and into the park, then look for signs; tel. 033-826-7719, www.outdoor-interlaken.ch.

Bike Tours—**Flying Wheels** offers bike tours of varying length and difficulty around the area. They also offer an interesting "bike and fly" deal: Ride your electric bike up the hill and paraglide back into Interlaken (around 200 SF). If it rains the day you're booked to go, they'll take you on a bus tour instead to a nearby indoor destination.

Cost and Hours: Interlaken-only tour—60 SF, 3 hours; Lauterbrunnen Valley up to Stechelberg—100-110 SF, 6 hours, includes picnic and Trümmelbach Falls visit; around Lake Brienz—90-100 SF, 6 hours, includes picnic; shorter tours start at 9:45, longer tours at 8:30; for contact info, see page 150.

Castles

A few impressively well-kept and welcoming old castles in the Interlaken area are worth considering for day trips by boat, bus, or car.

Thun Castle (Schloss Thun)—Built between 1180 and 1190 by the Dukes of Zähringen, the castle houses a five-floor historical museum offering insights into the cultural development of the region over a period of some 4,000 years. From the corner turrets of the castle, you are rewarded with a spectacular view of the city of Thun, the lake, and the Alps.

Cost and Hours: 8 SF, April-Oct daily 10:00-17:00, Nov-Jan

Sun only 13:00-16:00, Feb-March daily 13:00-16:00, tel. 033-223-2001, www.schlossthun.ch.

Hünegg Castle (Schloss Hünegg)—Located in Hilterfingen (farther along Lake Thun, toward Interlaken), this castle contains a museum exhibiting furnished rooms from the second half of the 19th century. The castle is situated in a beautiful wooded park.

Cost and Hours: 9 SF, mid-May-mid-Oct Mon-Sat 14:00-17:00, Sun 11:00-17:00, closed off-season, tel. 033-243-1982, www.schlosshuenegg.ch.

Oberhofen Castle (Schloss Oberhofen)—Also on Lake Thun, this place is ideal for those interested in gardens. Its beautifully landscaped park with exotic trees is a delight. The museum in the castle depicts domestic life in the 16th-19th centuries, including a Turkish smoking room and a medieval chapel.

Cost and Hours: Gardens-free, mid-May-mid-Oct daily 10:00-dusk; museum-10 SF, mid-May-mid-Oct Mon 14:00-17:00, Tue-Sun 11:00-17:00; both closed off-season, 40 minutes from Interlaken on bus #21, tel. 033-243-1235, www.schlossoberhofen.ch.

Nightlife in Interlaken

Youthful Night Scenes—For counterculture with a reggae beat, check out **Funny Farm** (past the recommended Balmer's Herberge hostel, in Matten). The young frat-party dance scene rages at the **Metro Bar** at Balmer's (bomb-shelter disco bar, with cheap drinks and a friendly if loud atmosphere). And if you're into **Hooters,** you won't have a hard time finding it.

Mellower After-Dark Hangouts—To nurse a drink with a view of the park, the outdoor tables at **Restaurant Schuh** are convenient if you don't mind the schlocky music. The **"Top O'Met"** bar and café has great indoor and outdoor view seating with reasonable prices, 18 floors above everything else in town (in the Metropole Hotel skyscraper, open nightly until late, see "Eating in Interlaken," later). **Hotel Oberland** (near the post office) has live alpine music in its restaurant (Tue at 19:00 or 20:00).

Sleeping in Interlaken

I'd sleep in Gimmelwald, or at least Lauterbrunnen (20 minutes by train or car). In ski season, however, prices go down in Interlaken, while they shoot up at most hotels in the mountains. Interlaken is not the Alps. But if you must stay here...

$$$ Hotel Lötschberg, with a sun terrace and 21 rooms, is run with lots of thoughtful touches by English-speaking Susi (Sb-135 SF, Db-178 SF, big Db-198 SF, extra bed-35 SF, family deals,

Sleep Code

(1 SF = about $1.10, country code: 41)
S = Single, **D** = Double/Twin, **T** = Triple, **Q** = Quad, **b** = bathroom,
s = shower only. Unless otherwise noted, credit cards are
accepted, English is spoken, and breakfast is included.

To help you sort easily through these listings, I've divided
the accommodations into three categories, based on the price
for a standard double room with bath during high season:

$$$ Higher Priced—Most rooms 150 SF or more.
 $$ Moderately Priced—Most rooms between 90-150 SF.
  $ Lower Priced—Most rooms 90 SF or less.

Prices can change without notice; verify the hotel's
current rates online or by email. For other updates, see www
.ricksteves.com/update.

closed Nov-mid-April, elevator, pay Internet access, free Wi-Fi,
free laundry machines, free loaner bikes; lounge with microwave,
fridge, and free tea and coffee; 3-minute walk from West Station:
leaving station, turn right, after Migros at the circle go left to
General-Guisan-Strasse 31; tel. 033-822-2545, fax 033-822-2579,
www.lotschberg.ch, hotel@lotschberg.ch).

$$$ Guest House Susi's B&B is Hotel Lötschberg's no-
frills, cash-only annex, offering three nicely furnished, cozy rooms
and four apartments with kitchenettes (Sb-119 SF, Db-151 SF;
apartment-140 SF/2 people, 250 SF/4-5 people; free Wi-Fi, hotel
closed Nov-mid-April but apartments available with 5-night stay,
same contact info as Hotel Lötschberg, above).

$$ Sunny Days B&B, run by Dave from Britain, is a homey,
nine-room place in a quiet residential neighborhood (Sb-108-140
SF, Db-120-158 SF, prices vary with size of room and view, less
in winter, 1-night stay-20 SF extra, discount for 4 or more nights,
extra bed-about 40 SF, pay Wi-Fi, patio; from West Station: exit
left out of station and take first bridge to your left, after crossing
two bridges turn left on Helvetiastrasse and go 3 blocks to #29; tel.
033-822-8343, www.sunnydays.ch, mail@sunnydays.ch).

$$ Hotel Aarburg offers nine plain, peaceful rooms over
a restaurant in a beautifully located but run-down old building
in Unterseen, a 10-minute walk from West Station (Sb-70 SF,
Db-140-150 SF, 10 SF more in July-Aug, 2 doors from launderette
at Beatenbergstrasse 1, tel. 033-822-2615, hotel-aarburg@quick
net.ch).

$$ Katy's Lodge B&B is a funky old house in a quiet, handy
location. It's not cozy, but it rents seven basic rooms at a good price.

BERNER OBERLAND

All the beds are twins—no double beds here (D-90-108 SF, T-114-126 SF, Q-140-160 SF, 6-bed room-160-180 SF, lowest prices in winter, reception open 7:00-12:00 & 14:00-20:00, garden, playground, 3-minute walk from West Station, around the corner from Hotel Lötschberg at Bernastrasse 7, mobile 078-604-6507, www.katys-lodge.ch, katyslodge@hotmail.com).

$$ Backpackers' Villa (Sonnenhof) Interlaken is a creative guesthouse run by a Methodist church group. Renovated in 2009, it's fun, youthful, and great for families, without the frat-party scene of Balmer's Herberge (listed later). Travelers of any age feel comfortable here (dorm bed in 2- to 7-bed room with free locker, sheets, and towel-37-47 SF, S-69 SF, view S-74 SF, Sb-79 SF, D-98-106 SF, view D-110-114 SF, Db-138 SF, T-135-141 SF, view T-153-159 SF, Tb-165-171 SF, Q-164-172 SF, view Q-180-188 SF, Qb-196-204 SF, view rooms have balconies and WCs, lowest prices in winter, kitchen, garden, movies, small game room, pay Internet access, free Wi-Fi, laundry, free admission to public swimming pool/spa, no curfew, no membership required, open all day, reception open 7:00-23:00, free use of public buses—bus #102 runs from hostel to either of Interlaken's stations, 10-15-minute walk from stations, across the park from the TI at Alpenstrasse 16, tel. 033-826-7171, fax 033-826-7172, www.villa.ch, mail@villa.ch).

$ Villa Margaretha, run by English-speaking Frau Kunz-Joerin, offers the best cheap beds in town. It's like Grandma's big Victorian house on a residential street. Keep your room tidy, and you'll have a friend for life (D-90 SF, T-135 SF, Q-180 SF, the three rooms share one big bathroom, 2-night minimum, apartment for 2-3 people-1,000 SF/week, closed Oct-April, cash only, no breakfast served but dishes and kitchenette available, lots of rules to abide by, go up small street directly in front of West Station to Aarmühlestrasse 13, tel. 033-822-1813, www.villa-margaretha.com, info@villa-margaretha.com).

$ Balmer's Herberge is many people's idea of backpacker heaven. This Interlaken institution comes with movies, table tennis, a launderette, bar, restaurant, tiny grocery, kitchen, bike rental, swapping library, excursions, bus pass, shuttle-bus service (which meets important arriving trains), and friendly, hardworking staff. This hive of youthful fun and activities is home for those who miss their fraternity. It can be a mob scene, especially on summer weekends (bunk in 6- to 12-bed dorm-27 SF, S-45 SF, D-74 SF, T-99 SF, Q-132 SF, these are walk-in prices—booking online costs 1-2 SF more, includes sheets and breakfast, open year-round, emailed reservations recommended at least 5 days in advance for private rooms, free Wi-Fi, pay Internet access, Hauptstrasse 23, in Matten, 15-minute walk from either train station, tel. 033-822-1961, fax 033-823-3261, www.balmers.com, mail@balmers.ch).

They also have private rooms in an adjacent guesthouse (Db-130 SF, Tb-165 SF, Qb-220 SF).

$ Interlaken Hostel, opened in 2012, isn't your cheapest option, but it's convenient (right next to the Ost train station), huge (with 220 beds), thoroughly modern, and full of daylight. It also offers plenty of amenities (bed in 6-bed dorm-39 SF, bed in 4-bed dorm-43 SF, Sb-121 SF, Db-134-138 SF, includes sheets, all rooms have sinks, restaurant, swimming pool, game room, lockers, Internet access and Wi-Fi, check-in 15:00-24:00, Untere Bönigstrasse 3, tel. 033-826-1090, www.youthhostel.ch/interlaken, interlaken@youthhostel.ch).

$ Happy Inn Lodge, above the lively, noisy Brasserie 17 restaurant, has 16 cheap backpacker rooms and two doubles with private baths; come here as a last resort only if you belong to the young-and-scrappy set (bed with bedding in 4- to 8-bed dorm-22-24 SF, S-32-60 SF, D-52-80 SF, Db-84-104 SF, breakfast-8-9 SF, no membership required, no curfew, pay Internet access, free Wi-Fi, bus pass, 5-minute walk from West Station at Rosenstrasse 17, tel. 033-822-3225, fax 033-822-3268, www.brasserie17.ch, info @happyinn.com).

Eating in Interlaken

In Unterseen, the Old Town Across the River

Restaurant Bären, in a classic low-ceilinged building with cozy indoor and fine outdoor seating, is a great value for *Rösti,* fondue, raclette, fish, traditional sausage, and salads (20-30-SF plates including fondue for one, Cordon Bleu is popular; open Tue-Thu 16:30-23:30, Fri-Sun 10:30-23:30 or later—but may close 14:00-17:30 in off-season, closed Mon; from West Station, turn left on Bahnhofstrasse, cross the river, and go several blocks to Seestrasse 2; tel. 033-822-7526).

Goldener Anker is *the* local hangout—with smokers lingering outside, a pool table inside, and a few unsavory types. If you think Interlaken is sterile, you haven't been to the "Golden Anchor." Jeannette serves and René cooks, just as they have for 25 years. This place, with its "melody rock and blues" ambience, sometimes hosts small concerts and has actually launched some of Switzerland's top bands (hearty 15-25-SF salads, fresh vegetables, 3 courses for 15-20 SF, daily from 16:00, Marktgasse 57, tel. 033-822-1672).

Ristorante West End is a reliable Italian place and a local favorite for *cucina casalinga* (20-SF pasta, 25-SF plates, no pizza, Mon-Sat 17:30-22:30, closed Sun, next to West Station and across the street from Migros at Rugenparkstrasse 2, tel. 033-822-1744).

Città Vecchia serves decent Italian with seating indoors or out, on a leafy square (16-22-SF pizzas, 20-28-SF pastas, 30-40-SF plates, daily 10:30-14:00 & 18:00-23:00, closed during the day Tue-Wed Oct-May, on main square in Unterseen at Untere Gasse 5, tel. 033-822-1754, Rinaldo).

On or near Höheweg

Interlaken's main drag, Höheweg, is lined with eateries. Tourists dampen the local ambience, but you have plenty of options.

Sirinya's Thai Restaurant is run by charming Sirinya, who serves great Thai dishes and popular spring rolls at reasonable prices (20-25-SF plates, Tue-Sat 16:00-23:30, Sun 16:00-22:00, closed Mon, at the recommended Hotel Lötschberg, General-Guisan-Strasse 31, tel. 033-821-6535).

Metropole Hotel's "Top O'Met," capping Interlaken's 18-story aesthetic nightmare, is actually a decent café/restaurant serving traditional and modern food at down-to-earth prices. For just 6 SF, you can enjoy a glass of wine and awesome views from an indoor or outdoor table (25-SF lunch deals Mon-Sat include two courses and coffee, 25-35-SF dinner plates, daily 11:30-24:00, no hot food 14:00-18:00 or after 22:00, Höheweg 37, just step into the Metropole Hotel and go up the elevator as far as you can, tel. 033-828-6666).

Supermarkets

Interlaken's two big supermarkets sell picnic supplies and also have reasonable self-service restaurants: **Migros** is across the street from West Station (Mon-Thu 8:00-18:30, Fri 8:00-21:00, Sat 7:30-17:00, closed Sun), while the **Co-op** is across the river from West Station, on your right (same hours as Migros except Mon-Thu until 19:00). The only grocery store open late at night is **Co-op Pronto** (daily 6:00-22:30, 30 yards west of TI on Höheweg).

Interlaken Connections

If you plan to arrive at Zürich Airport and want to head straight for Interlaken and the Alps, see page 68. Note that Interlaken is connected to Luzern and Montreux (on Lake Geneva) via the Golden Pass scenic rail route (see the Scenic Rail Journeys chapter).

There are a few long-distance trains from Interlaken—you'll generally transfer in Bern (for Bern connections, see page 126). Train info: toll tel. 0900-300-300 or www.rail.ch.

From Interlaken Ost by Train to: Bern (2/hour, 55 minutes, some with change in Spiez), **Spiez** (3/hour, 25 minutes), **Brienz** (2/hour, 20 minutes), **Zürich** and **Zürich Airport** (2/hour, 2-2.5 hours, most with transfer in Bern or Spiez), **Luzern** (2/hour, 2 hours direct, 2.5 hours with 1-2 changes), **Lugano** (hourly, 4.75

hours, 1-2 changes), **Zermatt** (hourly, 2.25 hours, transfer in Spiez and Visp).

From Interlaken to the Lauterbrunnen Valley: To reach the heart of the valley, drive or take the train to **Lauterbrunnen** (train leaves hourly from Interlaken's Ost Station, 20 minutes). You cannot drive to Gimmelwald (park at the cable-car station near Stechelberg and ride up on the lift; see page 169) or to Mürren or Kleine Scheidegg (park in Lauterbrunnen and take the cable car to Mürren or the train to Kleine Scheidegg). For more details, see "Lauterbrunnen Valley Connections" on page 167.

Lauterbrunnen

Lauterbrunnen is the valley's commercial center and transportation hub. In addition to its train station and cable car, the one-

street town is just big enough to have all the essential services (bank, post office, bike rental, launderette, and so on)—plus several hotels and hostels. It's idyllic, in spite of the busy road that slices it in two. Sitting under sheer cliffs at the base of the valley, with its signature waterfall spurting mightily out from the cliff (flood-lit at night), Lauterbrunnen is a fine springboard for Jungfrau and Schilthorn adventures. But for spending the night, I still prefer Gimmelwald or Mürren, perched on the ledge above the valley.

Orientation to Lauterbrunnen

Tourist Information: Stop by the friendly TI to check the weather forecast, find out about guided walks and events, and buy hiking maps or any regional train or lift tickets you need (June-mid-Sept daily 9:00-12:00 & 13:30-18:00, off-season Mon-Fri 9:00-12:00 & 13:30-17:00, closed Sat-Sun, located on the main street a block up from the train station, tel. 033-856-8568, www.mylauterbrunnen .com).

Arrival in Lauterbrunnen: The slick, modern train station has lockers and is across the main street from the cable-car station. Go left as you exit the station to find the TI. Drivers can find parking in the large multistory pay lot behind the station (2 SF/2 hours, 10 SF/9-24 hours, www.jungfraubahn.ch).

BERNER OBERLAND

Helpful Hints

Medical Help: Dr. Bruno Durrer, who has a clinic (with pharmacy) near the Jungfrau Hotel (look for *Arzt* sign), is good and very busy. He splits his time between seeing patients at his main office here, spending a couple of days a week up in Mürren, and buzzing around the region in helicopters to rescue injured adventure-seekers. He and his associate both speak English (tel. 033-856-2626, answered 24/7).

Money: Several ATMs are along the main street, including one immediately across from the train station.

Internet and Laundry: Two places are within a short walk of each other in the town center: The **Valley Hostel** is automated (Internet access-2.50 SF/15 minutes, launderette-5 SF/load, includes soap, May-Oct daily 9:00-22:00, shorter hours Nov-April, don't open dryer door until machine is finished or you'll have to pay another 5 SF to start it again, tel. 033-855-2008); **Airtime** is fully staffed (Internet access-5 minutes free, 2 SF/15 minutes, pay Wi-Fi, self-service laundry-10 SF/load, full-service laundry-25 SF/load, daily 9:00-19:00, closed Nov).

Grocery Store: The **Co-op** is on the main street across from the station (Mon-Sat 9:00-19:00, closed Sun).

Bike Rental: You can rent mountain bikes at **Imboden Bike** on the main street (25 SF/half-day, 35 SF/day; full-suspension—35 SF/half-day, 55 SF/day; daily July-Aug 8:30-20:00, Sept-June 9:00-18:30 except closed for lunch 12:00-13:00 Oct-May, tel. 033-855-2114, www.imboden-bike.ch). They work with the bike-rental shop in Mürren, allowing you to pick up a bike here and drop it off there—or vice versa (8 SF supplement).

Sports Gear: You can rent hiking boots, skis, and snowboards at the **Alpia Sports** shop (daily 8:00-12:30 & 13:30-19:00, shorter hours on weekends and in fall, closed in May, at Hotel Crystal, tel. 033-855-3292, www.alpiasport.ch).

Activities in and near Lauterbrunnen

Hikers' Loop from Lauterbrunnen—If you're staying in Lauterbrunnen, consider this ambitious but great day plan: Ride the cable car to Grütschalp, walk along the ridge to Mürren, take the cable car up to the Schilthorn and back down to Mürren, ride the funicular up to Allmendhubel, hike the North Face Trail to Gimmelwald, take the lift down to the Schilthornbahn station near Stechelberg, catch the PostBus to Trümmelbach Falls, and walk through the valley back into Lauterbrunnen. Make it more or less strenuous or time-consuming by swapping lifts and hikes (all described later in this chapter). Or rent a mountain bike and do

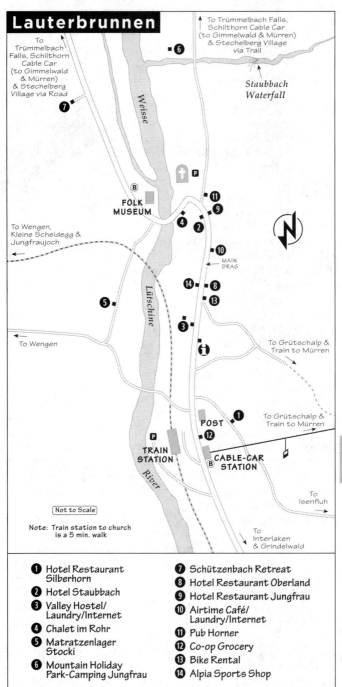

Lauterbrunnen

To Trümmelbach Falls, Schilthorn Cable Car (to Gimmelwald & Mürren) & Stechelberg Village via Road ❼

To Trümmelbach Falls, Schilthorn Cable Car (to Gimmelwald & Mürren) & Stechelberg Village via Trail

Staubbach Waterfall

Weisse

❻

❶ FOLK MUSEUM

❶❶
❾
❹ ❷

To Wengen, Kleine Scheidegg & Jungfraujoch

MAIN DRAG ❿

Lütschine

❶❹ ❽
❶❸

❺

To Wengen

❸

To Grütschalp & Train to Mürren

To Grütschalp & Train to Mürren

POST ❶

❶❷

TRAIN STATION

CABLE-CAR STATION

To Isenfluh

To Interlaken & Grindelwald

Not to Scale

Note: Train station to church is a 5 min. walk

River

BERNER OBERLAND

❶ Hotel Restaurant Silberhorn
❷ Hotel Staubbach
❸ Valley Hostel/ Laundry/Internet
❹ Chalet im Rohr
❺ Matratzenlager Stocki
❻ Mountain Holiday Park-Camping Jungfrau

❼ Schützenbach Retreat
❽ Hotel Restaurant Oberland
❾ Hotel Restaurant Jungfrau
❿ Airtime Café/ Laundry/Internet
❶❶ Pub Horner
❶❷ Co-op Grocery
❶❸ Bike Rental
❶❹ Alpia Sports Shop

a wheeled variation on this (parking your bike in Mürren for the Schilthorn trip).

▲**Trümmelbach Falls**—If all the waterfalls have you intrigued, sneak a behind-the-scenes look at the valley's most powerful, Trümmelbach Falls. You'll ride an elevator up through the mountain and climb through several caves (wet, with lots of stairs, and—for some—claustrophobic) to see the melt from the Eiger, Mönch, and Jungfrau grinding like God's bandsaw through the mountain at the rate of up to 5,200 gallons a second (that's 20,000 liters—nearly double the beer consumption at Oktoberfest). The upper area is the best; if your legs ache, skip the lower falls and ride down on the elevator.

Cost and Hours: 11 SF, daily July-Aug 8:30-18:00, April-June and Sept-mid-Nov 9:00-17:00, closed mid-Nov-March, tel. 033-855-3232, www.truemmelbach.ch.

Getting There: It's about halfway between Lauterbrunnen and the Schilthornbahn cable-car station; from either, it's a short ride on the PostBus or a 45-minute walk.

▲▲**Cloudy-Day Lauterbrunnen Valley Walks**—Try the easy trails and pleasant walks along the floor of the Lauterbrunnen Valley. For a smell-the-cows-and-flowers lowland walk—ideal for a cloudy day, weary body, or tight budget—take the PostBus from Lauterbrunnen town to the Schilthornbahn cable-car station near Stechelberg (left of river), and follow the riverside trail back for three basically level miles to Staubbach Falls, near the town church (you can reverse the route, but it's a very gradual uphill to Stechelberg). A trail was cut into the cliff to take visitors up "behind" Staubbach Falls (at the uphill end of Lauterbrunnen town). But, depending on the wind, the trail may be closed short of the actual falls.

You don't ever need to walk along the road. A fine, paved, car-free riverside path goes all the way along the valley (popular with bikers). Detour to Trümmelbach Falls (described earlier) en route (it's a 45-minute walk from the Schilthornbahn station to Trümmelbach Falls, and another 45 minutes to Lauterbrunnen). In this "Valley of Many Waterfalls" (literally), you'll see cone-like mounds piled against the sides of the cliffs, formed by centuries of rocks hurled by tumbling rivers. Look up to see BASE jumpers between Trümmelbach Falls and Lauterbrunnen.

If you're staying in Gimmelwald, try this plan: Take the Schilthornbahn lift down to the station near Stechelberg (5 minutes), then walk 1.5 hours along the river to Lauterbrunnen (side-tripping to Trümmelbach Falls after 45 minutes). To return to Gimmelwald from Lauterbrunnen, take the cable car up to Grütschalp (10 minutes), then either walk to Gimmelwald (1.5 hours) or take the train to Mürren (10 minutes). From Mürren, it's a downhill walk (30 minutes) to Gimmelwald. (This loop trip can be reversed or started at any point along the way—such as Lauterbrunnen or Mürren.)

Hang Out with BASE Jumpers—In recent years, the Lauterbrunnen Valley has become an El Dorado of BASE jumping (parachuting off cliffs), and each season thrill-seekers hike to the top of a cliff, leap off—falling as long as they can (this provides the rush)—and then pull the ripcord to release a tiny parachute, hoping it will break their fall and a gust won't dash them against the walls of the valley. (For a fascinating look at this sport, search for "BASE jumping Lauterbrunnen" at www.youtube.com.)

Some Swiss consider BASE jumpers reckless and don't respect them. But, like other adventure sports, it is getting safer and more accepted. To learn more, talk with the jumpers themselves, who congregate at the **Pub Horner,** at the upper end of town (near the waterfall). This is the grittiest place in Lauterbrunnen, providing cheap beds and meals for BASE jumpers and the only real after-dark scene in town. Locals, jumpers, and stray tourists gather here in the pub each evening (9 rooms, bunks-32 SF, D-86 SF, cheaper apartments, no breakfast, free Wi-Fi and Internet access for customers, dancing nightly from 22:00 upstairs, tel. 033-855-1673, www.hornerpub.ch, mail@hornerpub.ch, run by Gertsch Ferdinand). Their kitchen sells cheap pastas and raclette, and puts out a nightly salad bar (8-14-SF meals, BBQ dinner-15 SF in summer).

Lauterbrunnen Valley Folk Museum (Talmuseum Lauterbrunnen)—This interesting museum shows off the region's folk culture and two centuries of mountaineering from all the towns of this valley. You'll see lots of lace, exhibits on cheese and woodworking, cowbells, and classic old photos.

Cost and Hours: 3 SF, free with Visitors Card given by local hotels, mid-June-mid-Oct Tue and Thu-Sun 14:00-17:30; closed Mon, Wed, and off-season; English handout, just over bridge and below church at the far end of Lauterbrunnen town, tel. 033-855-3586, www.talmuseumlauterbrunnen.ch.

Sleeping in Lauterbrunnen

(2,612 feet, 1 SF = about $1.10, country code: 41)
$$$ Hotel Silberhorn is a big, formal, 32-room, three-star hotel that still manages to feel family-run. It has generous public spaces and a recommended, elegant-for-Lauterbrunnen restaurant just

above the quiet lift station across from the train station. Almost every double room comes with a fine view and balcony (Sb-89-109 SF, Db-159-179 SF, bigger "superior" Db-180-209 SF, Internet access, Wi-Fi, tel. 033-856-2210, www.silberhorn.com, info@silberhorn.com).

$$$ Hotel Staubbach, a big, Old World place, is one of the oldest hotels in the valley (1890). The staff is friendly, and the hotel has the casual feel of a national park lodge, with 30 simple and comfortable rooms. It's family-friendly and has a kids' play area. Rooms that face up the valley have incredible views, though you may hear the happy crowd across the meadow at Pub Horner or the church bells chiming on the hour. If the weather's bad, you can watch a DVD of my Switzerland TV show in the lounge (S-100 SF, Sb-120 SF, D-120 SF, Db-150-170 SF, Tb-210-240 SF, Qb-240 SF, closed Nov-mid-April, elevator, free Wi-Fi, 4 blocks up from station on the left, tel. 033-855-5454, fax 033-855-5484, www.staubbach.com, hotel@staubbach.com, run by American Craig and his Swiss wife, Corinne).

$ Valley Hostel is practical and comfortable, offering 70 inexpensive beds for quieter travelers of all ages, with a pleasant garden and the welcoming Abegglen family: Martha, Alfred, Stefan, and Fränzi (D with bunk beds-66 SF, twin D-66 SF, beds in larger family-friendly rooms-28 SF/person, breakfast-6 SF, rooms have no sinks, free kitchen, Internet access, Wi-Fi, coin-op laundry, reception open 8:00-12:00 & 15:00-22:00, 2 blocks up from train station, tel. & fax 033-855-2008, www.valleyhostel.ch, info@valleyhostel.ch).

$ Chalet im Rohr—a creaky, old, woody firetrap of a place— has oodles of character (and lots of Asian groups, paragliders, and BASE jumpers). It offers 50 beds in big one- to four-bed rooms that share six showers (28 SF/person, no breakfast, cash only, common kitchen, free Wi-Fi, across from church on main drag, tel. & fax 033-855-2182, www.chaletimrohr.ch, bookings@chaletimrohr.ch, Elsbeth von Allmen-Müller).

$ Matratzenlager Stocki is rustic and humble, with the cheapest beds in town (15 SF with sheets in easygoing little 25-bed co-ed dorm with kitchen, closed Nov-Dec, across river from station, tel. 033-855-1754, run by elderly Frau Graf, who often ignores the phone).

$ *Camping:* Two campgrounds just south of town provide beds in dorms and 2- and 4-bed bungalows (rentable sheets, kitchen facilities, cash only, big English-speaking tour groups). **Mountain Holiday Park-Camping Jungfrau,** romantically situated beyond Staubbach Falls, is huge and well-organized by Hans. It also has fancy cabins and mobile homes you can rent by the week (30-35-SF beds, tel. 033-856-2010, www.camping-jungfrau.ch).

Schützenbach Retreat, on the left just past Lauterbrunnen toward Stechelberg, is a simpler campground (bed in 6- and 12-bed rooms-17 SF, often full with groups, tel. 033-855-1268, www.schuetzen bach.ch).

Eating in Lauterbrunnen

At **Hotel Restaurant Oberland,** Mark (Aussie) and Ursula (Swiss) Nolan take pride in serving tasty, good-value meals from a fun menu. It's a high-energy place with lots of tourists and a huge front porch good for lingering into the evening (17-SF pizzas, 20-25-SF main courses, traditional Swiss dishes, daily 11:30-21:00, tel. 033-855-1241).

Hotel Restaurant Jungfrau, along the main street, offers a wide range of specialties, including fondue and *Rösti*, served by a friendly staff. Their terrace has a great valley view (daily 12:00-14:00 & 18:00-21:00, tel. 033-855-3434, run by Brigitte Melliger).

Hotel Restaurant Silberhorn is the local choice for a fancy meal out. Call to reserve a view table (18-SF salad plate, 23-35-SF main dishes, daily from 18:00, classy indoor and outdoor seating, above the cable-car station, tel. 033-856-2210).

Airtime Café feels like an alpine Starbucks with hot drinks, homemade treats, breakfast, simple lunches, and light early dinners (7.50-SF sandwiches made to order, 6-SF meat pies). Besides food, they offer other services, including laundry, Internet access, Wi-Fi, and an English-language swap library. They can also help you book adventure-sport activities (May-Oct daily 9:00-19:00, shorter hours off-season, closed Nov, tel. 033-855-1515, www.air time.ch, Daniela and Beni).

Lauterbrunnen Valley Connections

The valley-floor towns of Lauterbrunnen and Stechelberg have connections by mountain train, bus, and cable car to the traffic-free villages, peaks, and hikes high above. Prices and trip durations given are per leg unless otherwise noted.

From Lauterbrunnen by Train to: Interlaken (hourly, 20 minutes, 7.20 SF), **Wengen** (1-2/hour, 15 minutes, 6.40 SF), continues to **Kleine Scheidegg** (hourly, 30 minutes, 30 SF), where you change to a different train to reach the **Jungfraujoch** (2/hour, 50 minutes, 66 SF) or **Grindelwald** (2/hour, 30 minutes, 32 SF).

By Cable Car to: Grütschalp (2/hour, 10 minutes), where you can catch a train to **Mürren** (2/hour, 10 minutes); total trip time 30 minutes, total cost 10.40 SF.

By PostBus to: Schilthornbahn cable-car station (buses depart with the arrival of trains in Lauterbrunnen, 15-minute ride,

BERNER OBERLAND

4 SF, covered by Swiss Pass), continues to **Stechelberg town**.

By Car to: Schilthornbahn cable-car station (10-minute drive, parking lot: 2 SF/2 hours, 6 SF/day, cash only).

From Schilthornbahn cable-car station near Stechelberg to: Gimmelwald (2/hour, 5 minutes, 5.80 SF), continues to **Mürren** (2/hour, 10 minutes, 10.40 SF) and the **Schilthorn** (2/hour, 20 minutes, 55.20 SF). The cable car runs up from the valley station— and down from Mürren—at :25 and :55 past the hour (5:55-19:55; after 19:55, runs only once an hour until 23:45 Sun-Thu, until 24:55 Fri-Sat). From Gimmelwald to both Mürren and the valley station, the cable car runs at :00 and :30 (6:00-20:00; after 20:00 runs only once an hour).

Gimmelwald

Saved from developers by its "avalanche zone" classification, Gimmelwald was (before modern tourism) one of the poorest places in Switzerland. Its tradi-

tional economy was stuck in the hay, and its farmers—unable to make it in their disadvantaged trade—survived only on a trickle of visitors and on Swiss government subsidies (and working the ski lifts in the winter). For some travelers, there's little to see in the village. Others (like me) enjoy a fascinating day sitting on a bench and learning why they say, "If heaven isn't what it's cracked up to be, send me back to Gimmelwald."

Take a walk through the town. The huge, sheer cliff face that dominates your mountain views is the Schwarzmönch ("Black Monk"). The three peaks above (or behind) it are, left to right, Eiger, Mönch, and Jungfrau. Although Gimmelwald's population dropped in the last century from 300 to about 120 residents, traditions survive. Most Gimmelwalders have one of two last names: von Allmen or Feuz. They are tough and proud. Raising hay in this rugged terrain is labor-intensive. One family harvests enough to feed only about 15 cows. But they'd have it no other way, and, unlike the absentee-landlord town of Mürren, Gimmelwald is locally owned. (When word got out that urban planners wanted to develop Gimmelwald into a town of 1,000, locals pulled some strings to secure the town's bogus avalanche-zone building code. Today, unlike nearby resort towns, Gimmelwald's population is

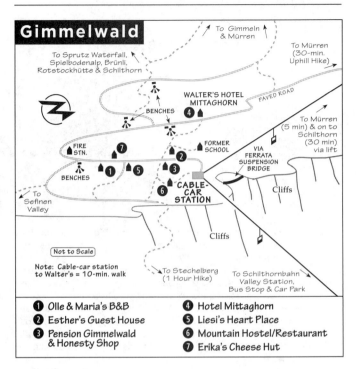

Gimmelwald

To Gimmeln & Mürren

To Mürren (30-min. Uphill Hike)

To Sprutz Waterfall, Spielbodenalp, Brünli, Rotstockhütte & Schilthorn

PAVED ROAD

WALTER'S HOTEL MITTAGHORN

4

BENCHES

To Mürren (5 min) & on to Schilthorn (30 min) via lift

FORMER SCHOOL

VIA FERRATA SUSPENSION BRIDGE

FIRE STN.

7

1 **5**

2

3

BENCHES

6

CABLE-CAR STATION

Cliffs

To Sefinen Valley

Cliffs

Not to Scale

Note: Cable-car station to Walter's = 10-min. walk

To Stechelberg (1 Hour Hike)

To Schilthornbahn Valley Station, Bus Stop & Car Park

1 Olle & Maria's B&B

2 Esther's Guest House

3 Pension Gimmelwald & Honesty Shop

4 Hotel Mittaghorn

5 Liesi's Heart Place

6 Mountain Hostel/Restaurant

7 Erika's Cheese Hut

BERNER OBERLAND

the same all year.) Those same folks are happy the masses go to touristy and commercialized Grindelwald, just over the Kleine Scheidegg ridge. Don't confuse Gimmelwald and Grindelwald—they couldn't be more different.

Thanks to the leadership of schoolteachers Olle and Maria, and their son Sven, Gimmelwald has a helpful little website (www.gimmelwald.ch), where you can check out photos of the town in different seasons, get directions for 11 of the best hikes out of town, and see all the latest on activities and rooms for rent.

Getting to Gimmelwald

To get from Lauterbrunnen to Gimmelwald, you have two options:

1. Schilthornbahn Cable Car: The faster, easier way—best in bad weather or at the end of a long day with lots of luggage—is to drive. It's 10 minutes from Lauterbrunnen (or 30 minutes from Interlaken) to the Schilthornbahn cable-car station near Stechelberg (parking lot: 2 SF/2 hours, 6 SF/day, cash only).

If you don't have a car, ride the PostBus from Lauterbrunnen to the Schilthornbahn cable-car station (buses depart with the arrival of trains in Lauterbrunnen, 15-minute ride, 4 SF, www.postauto.ch).

Swiss Cow Culture

Traditional Swiss cow farmers could make more money for much easier work in another profession. In a good year, farmers produce enough cheese to break even—they support their families on government subsidies. (Throughout the Alps, various governments support traditional farming as much for the tourism as for the cheese.) But these farmers have made a lifestyle choice to keep tradition alive and live high in the mountains. Rather than lose their children to the cities, Swiss farmers have the opposite problem: Kids argue about who gets to take over the family herd.

The cows' grazing ground can range in elevation by as much as 5,000 feet throughout the year. In the summer (usually mid-June), the farmer straps elaborate ceremonial bells on his cows and takes them up to a hut at high elevations. The cows hate these big bells, which weigh upward of 10 pounds and can cost more than 2,000 SF apiece—a proud investment for a humble farmer. When the cows arrive at their summer home, the bells are hung under the eaves.

These high-elevation summer stables are called "alps." Try to find some on a Berner Oberland tourist map (e.g., Wengernalp, Grütschalp, or Schiltalp). The cows stay at the alps for about 100 days. The farmers hire a team of cheesemakers to work at each

From Schilthornbahn, the cable car whisks you in five thrilling minutes up to Gimmelwald (2/hour at :25 and :55 past the hour 5:55-19:55; after 19:55, runs only once an hour until 23:45 Sun-Thu, until 24:55 Fri-Sat; 5.80 SF, Gimmelwald is the first stop). Note that the Schilthornbahn cable car is closed for servicing for a week in early May and also from mid-November through early December. If you're here during this time, you'll ride the cargo cable car directly from the valley floor up to Mürren, where a small bus shuttles you down to Gimmelwald.

2. Grütschalp Cable Car and Mürren Train: This is the more scenic route. Catch the cable car from Lauterbrunnen to Grütschalp. As you glide from Lauterbrunnen upward, notice the bed of the 100-year-old funicular train track that the new cable car recently replaced. At Grütschalp, a special vintage train will roll you along the incredibly scenic cliffside to Mürren (total trip from Lauterbrunnen to Mürren: 30 minutes, 10.40 SF, www.jungfraubahn.ch). From there, either walk to the middle of Mürren

alp—mostly hippies, students, and city slickers eager to spend three summer months in mountainous solitude. Each morning, the hired hands get up at 5:00 to milk the cows; take them to pasture; and make the cheese, milking the cows again when they come home in the evening. In summer, all the milk is turned into alp cheese (it's too difficult to get it down to the market in liquid form). In the winter, with the cows at lower altitudes, the fresh milk is sold as milk.

Every alp also has a resident herd of pigs. Cheesemaking leftovers (*Molke,* whey) can damage the ecosystem if thrown out—but pigs love the stuff. (The pigs parade up with the cows, but no one notices.) Cheesemakers claim that bathing in whey improves their complexion...but maybe that's just the altitude talking.

Meanwhile, the farmers, glad to be free of their bovine responsibilities in summer, turn their attention to making hay. The average farmer has a few huts at various altitudes, each surrounded by small hay fields. The farmer follows the seasons up into the mountains, making hay and storing it above the huts. In the fall, the cows come down from the alps and spend the winter moving from hut to hut, eating the hay the farmer spent the summer preparing for them.

Throughout the year you'll see farmers moving their herds to various elevations. If snow is in the way, farmers sometimes use tourist cable cars to move their cows. Every two months or so, Gimmelwald farmers bring together cows that aren't doing so well and herd them into the cable car to meet the butcher in the valley below.

and take a left down a moderately steep paved path 30 minutes to Gimmelwald, or walk 10 minutes across Mürren to catch the cable car down to Gimmelwald (5.80 SF).

Self-Guided Walk

Welcome to Gimmelwald

Gimmelwald, though tiny, with one zigzag street, offers a fine look at a traditional Swiss mountain community.

• *Start this quick walking tour at the...*

Cable-Car Station: When the lift came in the 1960s, the village's back end became its front door. Gimmelwald was, and still is, a farm village. Stepping off the cable car and starting up the path, you see a sweet little hut (pictured on next page). Set on stilts to keep out mice, the hut was used for storing cheese (the rocks on the rooftop here and throughout the town are not decorative—they keep the shingles on through wild storms). Behind the cheese hut stands the village schoolhouse, long the largest structure in town (in Catholic Swiss towns, the biggest building is the church; in Protestant towns, it's the school). But in 2010, classes ceased. Gimmelwald's students now go to school in Lauterbrunnen, and the building is being used as a chapel when the Protestant pastor makes

his monthly visit. Up and across from the station, just beyond the little playground, is the recommended Mountain Hostel and Restaurant.

• *Walk up the lane 50 yards, past the town's Dalí-esque art gallery (Who's showing in the phone booth?), to Gimmelwald's...*

"Times Square": The yellow alpine "street sign" shows where you are, the altitude (1,370 meters, or 4,470 feet), how many hours *(Std.)* and minutes it takes to walk to nearby points, and which tracks are serious hiking paths (marked with red and white, and further indicated along the way with red and white patches of paint on stones). You're surrounded by buildings that were built as duplexes, divided vertically right down the middle to house two separate families. Look for the Honesty Shop at Pension Gimmelwald, which features local crafts and little edibles for sale.

The writing on the post office building is a folksy blessing: "Summer brings green, winter brings snow. The sun greets the day, the stars greet the night. This house will protect you from rain, cold, and wind. May God give us his blessings." Small as Gimmelwald is, it still has daily mail service. The postman comes down from Mürren each day (by golf cart in summer, sled in winter) to deliver mail and pick up letters at the communal mailbox. The date on this building indicates when it was built or rebuilt (1911). Gimmelwald has a strict building code: For instance, shutters can only be painted certain colors.

• *From this tiny intersection, walk away from the cable-car station and follow the town's...*

Main Street: Walk up the road past the gnome greeting committee on the right. Notice the announcement board: one side for tourist news, the other for local news (e.g., deals on chainsaw sharpening, upcoming shooting competitions). Cross the street and peek into the big barn, dated 1995. To the left of the door is a cow-scratcher. Swiss cows have legal rights (e.g., in the winter, they must be taken out for exercise at least three times a week). This big barn is built in a modern style. Traditionally, barns were small (like those on the hillside high above) and closer to the hay. But with trucks and paved roads, hay can be moved more easily, and farm businesses need more cows to be viable. Still, even a well-run big farm hopes just to break even. The industry survives only with government subsidies (see "Swiss Cow Culture" sidebar on page 170). As you wander, notice private garden patches. Until recently, most locals grew their own vegetables—often enough to provide most of their family's needs.

• *Go just beyond the next barn. On your right is the...*

Water Fountain/Trough: This is the site of the town's historic water supply—still perfectly drinkable. Village kids love to bathe and wage water wars here when the cows aren't drinking from it. Detour left down a lane about 50 yards (along a wooden fence), passing the lovingly tended pea-patch gardens of the woman with the best green thumb in the village (on your left). Go to the next trough and the oldest building in town, Husmättli, from 1658. (Most of the town's 17th-century buildings are on the road zig-zagging below town.) Study the log-cabin construction. Many are built without nails. The wood was logged up the valley and cut on the water-powered village mill (also below town). Gimmelwald heats with wood, and since the wood needs to age a couple of years to burn well, it's stacked everywhere.

From here (at the water trough), look up at the solar panels on the house of Olle and Maria. A Swiss building code requires that new structures provide 30 percent of their own power, part of a green energy policy. Switzerland is gradually moving away from nuclear power; its last reactor is supposed to close in 2034.

• *Return to the main paved road and continue uphill.*

Twenty yards along, on the left, the first house has a bunch of scythes hanging above the sharpening stone. Farmers pound, rather than grind, the blade to get it razor-sharp for efficient cutting. Feel a blade...carefully.

A few steps farther, notice the cute **cheese hut** on the right. This is Erika's hut, and she loves to sell her alpine cheese to visitors (an arrow points to her house). Its front is an alpine art gallery with nail shoes for flower pots. Nail shoes grip the steep, wet fields—this is critical for safety, especially if you're carrying a sharp scythe. Even today, farmers buy metal tacks and fasten them to boots. The hut is full of strong cheese—up to three years old.

Look up. In the summer, a few goats are kept here (rather than in the high alp) to provide families with fresh milk (about a half-gallon per day per goat). The farmers fence off the fields, letting the goats eat only the grass that's most difficult to harvest.

On the left (at the *B&B* sign) is Olle and Maria's home. Maria runs the **Lilliput shop** (the "smallest shop with the greatest gifts"—handmade delights from the town and region; just ring the bell and meet Maria). She does a booming trade in sugar-coated almonds.

• *Fifty yards farther along is the...*

Alpenrose: At the old schoolhouse, you might see big ceremonial cowbells hanging under the uphill eave. These swing from the necks of cows during the procession from the town to the high Alps (mid-June) and back down (mid-Sept).

• *At the end of town, pause where a lane branches off to the left, leading into the dramatic...*

Sefinen Valley: All the old homes in town are made from wood cut from the left-hand side of this valley (shady side, slow-growing, better timber) and milled at a water-powered sawmill on the valley floor.

• *A few steps ahead, the road switches back at the...*

Gimmelwald Fire Station: The *Föhnwacht Reglement* sheet, posted on the fire-station building, explains rules to keep the village from burning down during the fierce dry wind of the Föhn season. During this time, there's a 24-hour fire watch, and even smoking cigarettes outdoors is forbidden. Mürren was devastated by a Föhn-caused fire in the 1920s. Because villagers in Gimmelwald—mindful of the quality of their volunteer fire department—are particularly careful with fire, the town has not had a terrible fire in its history (a rare feat among alpine villages).

Check out the other posted notices. This year's Swiss Army calendar tells reservists when and where to go (in all four official Swiss languages). Every Swiss male does a 22-week stint in the military, then a few days a year in the reserves until about age 30. The *Schiessübungen* poster details the shooting exercises required this year. In keeping with the William Tell heritage, each Swiss man does shooting practice annually for the military (or spends three days in jail).

• *Take the...*

High Road to Hotel Mittaghorn: The resort town of Mürren hovers in the distance. And high on the left, notice the hay field with terraces. These are from WWII days, when Switzerland, wanting self-sufficiency, required all farmers to grow potatoes. Today, this field is a festival of alpine flowers in season (best at this altitude in May and June).

• *Our walk is over. A peaceful set of benches, just off the lane on the downhill side, lets you savor the view. From Hotel Mittaghorn, you can return to Gimmelwald's "Times Square" via the path with the steps cutting downhill.*

Nightlife in Gimmelwald

These two places provide after-dark entertainment in Gimmelwald. The **Mountain Hostel and Restaurant,** where Petra and her staff serve drinks nightly, is lively with locals and backpackers alike. It's easy to make friends here and share travel experiences. There's a pool table and lots of youthful impromptu fun. **Pension Gimmelwald** (which is next door on the uphill side) offers a mellower scene with an old-time bar, cozy lounge, and view terrace. And from almost anywhere in Gimmelwald, you can watch the sun tuck the mountaintops into bed as the moon rises over the Jungfrau. If that's not enough nightlife, stay in Interlaken.

Sleeping in Gimmelwald

(4,593 feet, 1 SF = about $1.10, country code: 41)

Gimmelwald is my home base in the Berner Oberland. To inhale the Alps and really hold them in, you'll want to sleep high in Gimmelwald, too. Poor and pleasantly stuck in the past, the village has only a few accommodations options—all of them quirky and memorable. Rates include entry to the public swimming pool in nearby Mürren (at the Sportzentrum—see page 180).

Be warned: You'll meet a lot of my readers in this town. This is a disappointment to some; others enjoy the chance to be part of a fun extended family.

$$ At **Olle and Maria's B&B,** the Eggimanns rent two rooms—Gimmelwald's most comfortable—in their quirky but alpine-sleek chalet. Having raised three kids of their own here, Maria and Olle offer visitors a rare and intimate peek at this community (D-130 SF, Db with kitchenette-190 SF for 2 or 200 SF for 3 people, optional breakfast-20 SF, 3-night minimum, cash only, guarantee your reservation with PayPal, free Wi-Fi, laundry service; from cable car, continue straight for 200 yards along the town's only road, B&B on left; tel. 033-855-3575, oeggimann @bluewin.ch).

$$ Esther's Guest House, overlooking the village's main intersection, rents seven clean, basic, and comfortable rooms, three of which have private bathrooms and share a generous lounge and kitchen (S-55-75 SF, big D-130 SF, Db-130 SF, big T-150 SF, Tb-180-190 SF, Q-180 SF, Qb-200-210 SF, family room with private bath for up to 5 people-230 SF, cash preferred, breakfast-15 SF, 2-night minimum, pay Internet access, free Wi-Fi, low ceilings, tel. 033-855-5488, fax 033-855-5492, www.esthersguesthouse.ch, info@esthersguesthouse.ch). Esther, a bundle of entrepreneurial energy, also rents two four-person **apartments** with kitchenettes next door (3-night minimum, see website for details).

$$ Pension Gimmelwald is an old, low-ceilinged farmhouse converted into a family-style inn, with 12 simple rooms, a restaurant, and a cozy bar. Its six-bed dorm attracts more mature guests than your usual hostel. Its terrace, overlooking the Mountain Hostel, has gorgeous views across the valley (bed in 6-bed dorm-25

SF, S-60 SF, D-100 SF, T-150 SF, Q-185 SF, less in winter, 10 percent discount for 3 nights with this book, breakfast-12 SF, Wi-Fi, open June-mid-Oct and mid-Dec-mid-April, 2-minute walk up from cable-car station, tel. 033-855-1730, www.pensiongimmelwald .com, tsnewark@yahoo.com, Englishman David).

$$ At **Liesi's Heart Place,** friendly owner Liesi rents a little suite in her home with a view and terrace (Db-120 SF, Tb-150 SF, Qb-170 SF, minimum 2-night stay, at the town's water fountain find the little house about 100 feet to the left, tel. 033-841-0880, www.liesisheartplace.ch).

$ Hotel Mittaghorn is a classic creaky, thin-walled, alpine-style place with superb views. It's run by Walter Mittler, an elderly Swiss gentleman, with help from trusty Tim. The hotel has three rooms with private showers (first-come, first-served) and four rooms that share a coin-operated shower. Walter's guests-only dinner is the cheapest hot meal in the valley (S-54 SF, D-86 SF, T-129 SF, 6-SF surcharge per person for 1-night stays, cash only, simple but hearty 15-SF dinner at 19:30 by reservation only, free Internet access, open April-Oct, a five-minute climb up the path from the village center, tel. 033-855-1658,

www.ricksteves.com/mittaghorn, mittaghorn@gmail.com—email answered May-Sept only). It's necessary to reconfirm by phone the day before your arrival. If no one's there when you arrive, look for a card in the hallway directing you to your room.

$ Mountain Hostel is a beehive of activity, as clean as its guests, cheap, and friendly. The hostel has low ceilings, a self-service kitchen, a mini-grocery, a bar, a free pool table, and healthy plumbing. It's mostly a college-age crowd; families and older travelers will probably feel more comfortable elsewhere. Petra Brunner, who lines the porch with flowers, runs this relaxed hostel with the help of its guests.

Read the signs, respect Petra's rules, and leave it tidier than you found it. This is one of those rare spots where a congenial atmosphere spontaneously combusts as the piano plays, and spaghetti becomes communal as it cooks (28 SF/bed in 6- to 15-bed rooms, includes sheets, no breakfast, showers-1 SF, laundry-5 SF, pay Internet access and Wi-Fi, open mid-April-mid-Nov, 20 yards up the trail from lift station, reserve with credit card through website or by phone, tel. 033-855-1704, www.mountainhostel .com, info@mountainhostel.com). The hostel has a full-menu restaurant, described next.

Eating in Gimmelwald

Gimmelwald has two good eating options.

Mountain Hostel Restaurant is open for lunch and dinner and comes with fun, mountain-high energy and a youthful spirit (15-SF plates, popular 17-SF pizzas, daily 12:00-21:00). You can eat inside or with breathtaking views on the terrace.

Pension Gimmelwald Restaurant has a good, simple menu featuring local produce served in a rustic indoor dining room or on a jaw-dropping-view terrace. The atmosphere here is a little more jazz-and-blues mellow (13-22-SF main dishes, daily in summer 12:00-15:00 & 18:00-21:00, bar open until 23:00).

Picnic: Consider packing in a picnic meal from the larger towns. Mürren, a 5-minute cable-car ride or a 30-minute hike up the hill, has good restaurants and a grocery (see "Eating in Mürren," later). If you need a few groceries and want to skip the hike to Mürren, you can buy the essentials—noodles, spaghetti sauce, and candy bars—at the Mountain Hostel's reception desk or the little Honesty Shop at Pension Gimmelwald. Farmers post signs to sell their produce. Farmer Erika sells meat, cheese, and eggs—and sometimes bread and milk—from her picturesque hut on the town's main lane (see "Self-Guided Walk," earlier).

Mürren

Pleasant as an alpine resort can be, Mürren is traffic-free and filled with cafés, souvenirs, old-timers with walking sticks, employ-

ees enjoying incentive trips, and snap-happy tourists. Its chalets are prefab-rustic. With help from a cliffside train, a funicular, and a cable car, hiking options are endless from Mürren. Sitting on a ledge 2,000 feet above the Lauterbrunnen Valley, surrounded by a fortissimo chorus of mountains, the town has all the comforts of home (for a price) without the pretentiousness of more famous resorts.

BERNER OBERLAND

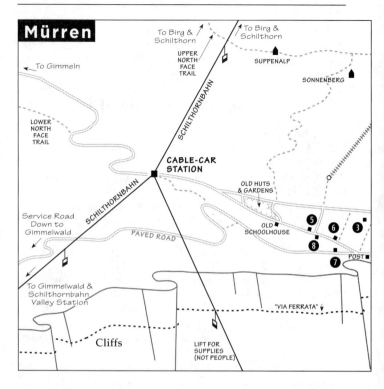

Mürren

To Gimmeln →

← To Gimmeln

LOWER
NORTH
FACE
TRAIL

To Birg &
Schilthorn

To Birg &
Schilthorn

UPPER
NORTH
FACE
TRAIL

SUPPENALP

SONNENBERG

SCHILTHORNBAHN

CABLE-CAR
STATION

OLD HUTS
& GARDENS

Service Road
Down to
Gimmelwald

SCHILTHORNBAHN

PAVED ROAD

OLD
SCHOOLHOUSE

❺

❻

❸

❽

❼ POST

To Gimmelwald &
Schilthornbahn
Valley Station

"VIA FERRATA" ↓

Cliffs

LIFT FOR
SUPPLIES
(NOT PEOPLE)

Historic Mürren, which dates from 1384, has been overwhelmed by development. Still, it's a peaceful town. There's no full-time doctor, no police officer (they call Lauterbrunnen if there's a problem), and no resident priest or pastor. (The Protestant church—up by the TI—posts a sign showing where the region's roving pastor preaches each Sunday.) There's not even enough business to keep a bakery open year-round (bread is baked down in Lauterbrunnen and shipped up to the "bakery," which is open in-season only)—a clear indication that this town is either lively or completely dead, depending on the time of year. (Holiday population: 4,000. Permanent residents: 400.) Keep an eye open for the "Milch Express," a tiny cart that delivers fresh milk and eggs to hotels and homes throughout town.

Getting to Mürren

There are two ways to get to Mürren: on the train from Grütschalp (10 minutes, connects by 10-minute cable car to Lauterbrunnen, 30-minute total trip) or on the Schilthornbahn cable car from near Stechelberg (in the valley), which stops at Gimmelwald, Mürren, and continues up to the Schilthorn. The train and cable-car stations (which both have WCs and lockers) are at opposite ends of town.

To Birg & Schilthorn

ALLMENDHUBEL

To
Grütschalp

FUNICULAR

1 Hotel Eiger & Eiger
Guesthouse

2 Hotel Edelweiss & Cafeteria

3 Hotel/Restaurant Bellevue
& Launderette

4 Hotel Jungfrau

5 Hotel/ Restaurant Blumental

6 Chalet Fontana

7 Stägerstübli Restaurant

8 Co-op Grocery

SPORT-
ZENTRUM

4

To Grütschalp &
Lift Down to
Lauterbrunnen

1

TENNIS
COURTS

2

TRAIN
STATION

Cliffs

Note:
Cable-car station to train
station = 10-min. walk

Not to Scale

Orientation to Mürren

Mürren perches high on a ledge, overlooking the Lauterbrunnen
Valley. You can walk from one end of town to the other in about
10 minutes.

Tourist Information: Mürren's TI can help you find a room
and gives hiking advice (July-mid-Sept daily 8:30-19:00, Thu until
20:00, shorter hours off-season, above the village, follow signs to
Sportzentrum, tel. 033-856-8686, www.mymuerren.ch).

Helpful Hints

Money: An ATM is by the **Co-op** grocery in the middle of town.
You can change money at the TI.

Internet Access: Connect at the **TI** (5 SF/15 minutes), at the
cable-car station inside an old gondola (5 SF/15 minutes), or
at the **Eiger Guesthouse** (4 SF/20 minutes, daily 8:00-23:00,
across from the train station).

Laundry: Hotel Bellevue has a slick and modern little self-service
launderette in its basement (5 SF/wash, 5 SF/dry, open 24/7).

Bike Rental: You can rent mountain bikes at **Stäger Sport** (25 SF/
half-day, 35 SF/day, includes helmet, daily 9:00-18:00, closed

late Oct-mid-May, in middle of town, tel. 033-855-2355, www.staegersport.ch). There's a bigger bike-rental place in Lauterbrunnen (Imboden Bike, described on page 162).

R & R: The slick **Sportzentrum** (sports center) that houses the TI offers a world of indoor activities. The pool is free with the regional Visitors Card given by area hotels (July-mid-Sept daily 8:30-19:00, Thu until 20:00, Sun until 18:00; pool and sauna generally open at 10:00 Tue-Wed and Fri, otherwise at 13:00; shorter hours off-season, closed May and Nov-mid-Dec, www.muerren.ch/sportzentrum). In season, they offer squash, mini-golf, table tennis, and a fitness room.

Yoga: Denise offers weekly yoga lessons in summer (off Chalet Fontana, mobile 078-642-3485).

Skiing and Snowboarding: The Mürren-Schilthorn ski area is the Berner Oberland's best place for experts, especially those eager to tackle the famous, nearly 10-mile-long Inferno run. The runs on top, especially the Kanonenrohr, are quite steep and have predictably good snow; lower areas cater to all levels, but can be icier. For rental gear, try the friendly, convenient **Ed Abegglen** shop (best prices, next to recommended Chalet Fontana, tel. 033-855-1245), **Alfred's Sporthaus** (good selection and decent prices, between ski school and Sportzentrum, tel. 033-855-3030), or **Stäger Sport** (one shop in Sportzentrum and another on the lower road near cable-car station, tel. 033-855-2330). For more info on snow sports, see the Switzerland in Winter chapter.

Self-Guided Walk

Welcome to Mürren

Mürren has long been a top ski resort, but a walk across town offers a glimpse into a time before ski lifts. This stroll takes you through town on the main drag, from the train station (where you'll arrive if coming from Lauterbrunnen) to the cable-car station, then back up to the Allmendhubel funicular station.

• *Start at the...*

Train Station: The first trains pulled into Mürren in 1891. (A circa-1911 car is permanently parked at Grütschalp's station.) A display case inside the station displays an original car from the narrow-gauge, horse-powered line that rolled fancy visitors from here into town. The current station, built in 1964, comes with impressive engineering for heavy cargo. Look out back, where a small truck can be loaded up, attached to the train, and driven away.

• *Wander into town along the main road (take the lower, left fork) for a stroll under the...*

Alpin Palace Hotel: This towering place was the "Grand Palace Hotel" until it burned in 1928. Today it's closed, and no one knows its future. The small wooden platform on the left—looking like a suicide springboard—is the place where snow-removal trucks dump their loads over the cliff in the winter. Look back at the meadow below the station: This is a favorite grazing spot for chamois (the animals, not the rags). Ahead, at Edelweiss Hotel, step to the far corner of the restaurant terrace for a breathtaking view stretching from the big three (Eiger, Mönch, and Jungfrau) on the left to the lonely cattle farm in the high alp on the right. Then look down.

• *Continue toward an empty lot with a grand view.*

Viewpoints: There are plans for a big apartment-hotel to be built here, but the project is waiting for investment money. Detour from the main street around the cliff-hanging tennis court. Stop at one of the little romantic shelters built into the far wall. Directly below, at the base of the modern wall, is the start of a one-mile "trail" with a steel cable (*via ferrata*), which mountaineers use to venture safely along the cliff all the way to Gimmelwald (described later). You can see the Gimmelwald lift station in the distance.

• *Return to the main street and continue to...*

"Downtown" Mürren: This main intersection (where the small service road leads down to Gimmelwald) has the only grocery store in town (Co-op). A bit farther on, the tiny fire barn (labeled *Feuerwehr*) has a list showing the leaders of the volunteer force and their responsibilities. The old barn behind it on the right evokes the time, not so long ago, when the town's barns housed cows. Imagine Mürren with more cows than people, rather than with more visitors than residents.

About 65 feet beyond the fire barn (across the street from the old schoolhouse—Altes Schulhaus), detour right uphill a few steps into the oldest part of town. Explore the windy little lanes, admiring the ancient woodwork on the houses and the cute little pea patches.

• *Back on the main drag, continue to the far end of Mürren, where you come to the...*

Cable-Car Station: The first cable car (goes directly to the valley floor) is for cargo, garbage, and the (reputedly) longest bungee jump in the world. The other takes hikers and skiers up to the Schilthorn and down to the valley via Gimmelwald.

• *Hiking back into town along the high road, you'll enter...*

Upper Mürren: You'll pass Mürren's two churches, the Allmendhubel funicular station, and the Sportzentrum (with swimming pool and TI).

• *Our walk is finished. Enjoy the town and the views.*

BERNER OBERLAND

Activities in Mürren

During ski season and the height of summer, the Mürren area offers plenty of activities for those willing to seek them out. In spring and fall, Mürren is pretty dead.

Allmendhubelbahn—A quaint-looking but surprisingly rewarding funicular (from 1912, renovated in 1999) carries nature-lovers from Mürren up to Allmendhubel, a perch offering a Jungfrau view that, though much lower, rivals the Schilthorn. At the station, notice the 1920s bobsled. Consider mixing a mountain lift, grand views, and a hike with your meal by eating at the restaurant on Allmendhubel (good chef, open daily until 18:00).

Allmendhubel is particularly good for families. The entertaining Adventure Trail children's hike—with rough and thrilling kid-friendly alpine rides along the way—starts from here. This is also the departure point for the North Face hike and walks to Grütschalp (see page 194). While at Allmendhubel, consider its Flower Trail, a 20-minute loop with nice mountain views and (from June through Sept) a chance to see more than 150 different alpine flowers blooming.

Cost and Hours: 7.40 SF one-way, 12 SF round-trip, 6 SF round-trip with Swiss Pass, mid-June–mid-Oct daily 9:00–17:00, runs every 20 minutes, tel. 033-855-2042 or 033-856-2141, www.schilthorn.ch.

Mürren Via Ferrata (Klettersteig Mürren)—Mountaineers and thrill-seekers can test their nerves on this one-mile trail along the cliff running from Mürren to Gimmelwald. A *via ferrata* ("way of iron" in Italian) or *Klettersteig* ("climbing path" in German) is a cliffside trail made of metal steps drilled into the mountainside with a cable running at shoulder height above it. Equipped with a helmet, harness, and two carabiners, you are clipped to the cable the entire way. Experienced mountaineers can rent gear (25 SF from the Gimmelwald hostel or Mürren's Intersport) and do it independently; others should hire a licensed mountain guide. For a peek at what you're getting yourself into, search *"via ferrata Switzerland Murren"* at www.youtube.com.

The journey takes about three hours. While half of the route is easily walked, several hundred yards are literally hanging over a 3,000-foot drop. I did it, and through the most dangerous sections, I was too scared to look down or take pictures. Along with ladders and steps, the trip comes with three thrilling canyon crossings—one by zip line (possible with guide only), another on a single high wire (with steadying wires for each hand), and a final stint on a terrifying suspension bridge (which you can see from the Gimmelwald-Mürren cable-car—look for it just above Gimmelwald).

Cost and Hours: 95 SF, includes gear and donation to the Mürren Via Ferrata Association, guided tours in small groups of 4-8, tel. 033-821-6100, www.klettersteig-muerren.ch.

Nightlife in Mürren

These are all good places for a drink after dinner: **Eiger Guesthouse** (a popular sports bar-type hangout with pool tables, games, and Internet terminals), **Stägerstübli** (where old-timers nurse a drink and gossip), **Hotel Blumental** (with a characteristic cellar— lively when open), and **Hotel Bellevue** (with its elegant alpine-lounge ambience). All of these places are further described under "Sleeping in Mürren" or "Eating in Mürren." In July and August, you can enjoy occasional folkloric evenings (some Wednesdays, at the Sportzentrum—listed earlier, under "Helpful Hints").

Sleeping in Mürren

(5,381 feet, 1 SF = about $1.10, country code: 41)
Prices for accommodations are often higher during the ski season. Many hotels and restaurants close in spring, roughly from Easter to early June, and may also shut down any time between late September and mid-December.

$$$ Hotel Eiger, a four-star hotel dramatically and conveniently situated just across from the tiny train station, is a good bet. Family-run for four generations, Adrian and Susanna Stahli offer all the service you'd expect in a big city hotel (plush lounge, indoor swimming pool, and sauna) while maintaining a creaky, Old World, woody elegance in its 50 rooms. Their family suites, while pricey, include two double rooms and can be a good value for groups of four or five (Db-275-315 SF with grand breakfast, view rooms-about 20 SF extra, discounts for stays of 3 nights or more, email for best deals, Wi-Fi, tel. 033-856-5454, fax 033-856-5456, www.hoteleiger.com, info@hoteleiger.com). If you opt for their five-course dinner with your reservation, it'll cost you about 50 SF extra per person.

$$$ At Hotel Edelweiss, it's all about the location—convenient and literally hanging on the cliff with devastating views. It's a big, modern building with 30 basic rooms and a busy, recommended restaurant well-run by hardworking Sandra and Daniel Kuster von Allmen (Db-145-180 SF depending on view and balcony, 10 percent discount for 2 nights, Wi-Fi, piano in lounge, tel. 033-856-5600, fax 033-856-5609, www.edelweiss-muerren.ch, edelweiss@muerren.ch).

$$$ Hotel Bellevue has a homey lounge, solid woodsy furniture, a great view terrace, the hunter-themed Jägerstübli restaurant,

BERNER OBERLAND

and 19 great rooms at fair rates—most with balconies and views (Sb-105-145 SF, viewless Db-140 SF, view Db-170-190 SF—150 SF if staying 2 nights or more in June or Sept-Oct, free Internet access and Wi-Fi, closed May and Nov, tel. 033-855-1401, fax 033-855-1490, www.muerren.ch/bellevue, bellevue-crystal@bluewin.ch, Ruth and Othmar Suter). In summer, Othmar offers a morning flowers and wildlife tour of Allmendhubel (10 SF includes funicular ride up, Sun at 9:00, 1.5 hours, meet at Allmendhubel funicular station, tel. 078-604-1401).

$$$ Hotel Jungfrau offers 29 modern and comfortable rooms and an apartment for up to six people (Sb-95-120 SF, Db-140-200 SF, lower prices are for viewless rooms, email for best deals, elevator, laundry service-15 SF, Wi-Fi, downhill from TI/Sportzentrum, tel. 033-856-6464, fax 033-856-6465, www.hoteljungfrau.ch, mail@hoteljungfrau.ch, Alan and Véronique).

$$$ Hotel Blumental has 16 older but nicely furnished rooms, a fun game/TV lounge, and a recommended restaurant (Sb-75-80 SF, Db-150-170 SF, 10 percent cheaper in Sept-Oct, higher prices are for July-Aug, outside of July-Aug book direct and ask for a 10 percent Rick Steves discount, pay cable Internet and Wi-Fi, tel. 033-855-1826, fax 033-855-3686, www.muerren.ch/blumental, blumental@muerren.ch; Ralph and Heidi, fourth generation in the von Allmen family). Their modern little chalet out back rents six rooms (Db-140-155 SF, includes breakfast in the hotel).

$$ Eiger Guesthouse offers 12 good budget rooms. This friendly, creaky, easygoing home away from home was renovated in 2009 (S-75 SF, Sb-80-95 SF, D-100-120 SF, Db-130-160 SF, bunk Q-180-200 SF, Qb-200-240 SF; special with this book: D-95 SF with a 2-night minimum year-round—making this a great deal for cheap beds in July-Aug; Wi-Fi, game room, terrace, across from train station, tel. 033-856-5460, fax 033-856-5461, www.eigerguesthouse.com, info@eigerguesthouse.com, Ema and Robert).

$ Chalet Fontana, run by charming Englishwoman Denise Fussell, is a rare budget option in Mürren, with simple, crispy-clean, and comfortable rooms (S-45-55 SF, D-75-85 SF, large D-95 SF, T-130 SF, price varies with size of room, cash only, closed Nov-April, fridge in common kitchen, across street from Stägerstübli restaurant in town center, mobile 078-642-3485, www.chaletfontana.ch, chaletfontana@gmail.com). If no one's home, check at the Ed Abegglen shop door next door (tel. 033-855-1245, off-season only). Denise also rents a family apartment with kitchen, bathroom, and breakfast (two bedrooms with 3 beds each, 140 SF/2 people, 160 SF/3 people, 200 SF/4 people, 260 SF/6 people).

Eating in Mürren

Many of these restaurants are in or near my recommended hotels. Outside of summer and ski season, it can be hard to find any place that's open (ask around).

Stägerstübli is everyone's favorite Mürren diner. It's the only real restaurant not associated with a hotel. Located in the town center, this 1902 building was once a tearoom for rich tourists, while locals were limited to the room in the back—which is now the nicer area to eat. Sitting on its terrace, you know just who's out and about in town (18-35-SF lunches and dinners, big portions, lovely lamb, daily 11:30-21:00, closed first week of Sept, Lydia).

Hotel Blumental specializes in typical Swiss cuisine, but also serves fish, international, and vegetarian dishes in a stony and woody dining area. It's one of Mürren's most elegant, romantic settings (18-30-SF specials, 21-31-SF fondue served for one or more, 15-SF pastas, daily from 17:00, tel. 033-855-1826).

Edelweiss cafeteria offers lunches and restaurant dinners with the most cliff-hanging dining in town—the views are incredible (pizzas, hearty salads, sandwiches; daily specials around 20 SF, family-friendly, tel. 033-856-5600).

Hotel Bellevue's restaurant is atmospheric, with three dining zones: a spectacular view terrace, a sophisticated indoor area, and the Jägerstübli—a cozy, well-antlered hunters' room guaranteed to disgust vegetarians. This is a good bet for game, as they buy chamois and deer direct from local hunters (lamb or game-34-44 SF, cheaper options as low as 15 SF, mid-June-Oct daily 11:30-14:00 & 18:00-21:00, closed off-season, tel. 033-855-1401).

Supermarket: The **Co-op** is the only grocery store in town, with good picnic fixings and sandwiches (Mon-Fri 8:00-12:00 & 13:45-18:30, Sat until 17:00, closed Sun). Given restaurant prices, this place is a godsend for those on a tight budget.

BERNER OBERLAND

Wengen

Wengen—a bigger, fancier Mürren on the east side of the valley—has plenty of grand hotels, restaurants, shops, diversions, and terrific views. This traffic-free resort is an easy train ride above Lauterbrunnen and halfway up to Kleine Scheidegg and Männlichen. From Wengen, you can catch the Männlichen lift up to the ridge and take the rewarding, view-filled, nearly downhill "Männlichen-Kleine Scheidegg" hike, rated ▲▲▲ and described on page 196.

Wengen's **TI** is two blocks from the station: Go up to the main drag, turn left, and it's on the left. They have info on hiking and sell hiking maps (tel. 033-855-1414, www.mywengen.ch).

The **Co-op grocery,** across the square from the train station, is great for picnic fixings, and is larger than most groceries in the area (Mon-Sat 8:00-18:30, closed Sun).

For an overnight stay, consider **Hotel Falken** (www.hotel falken.com), **Hotel Berghaus** (www.berghaus-wengen.ch), **Hotel Schönegg** (www.hotel-schoenegg.ch), or the cheaper **Bären Hotel** (www.baeren-wengen.ch).

Activities in the Berner Oberland

Scenic Lifts and Trains

Enjoying at least one of the two high-altitude thrill rides described here is an essential Berner Oberland experience.

▲▲▲The Schilthorn and a 10,000-Foot Breakfast

The Schilthornbahn cable car carries skiers, hikers, and sightseers effortlessly to the 10,000-foot summit of the Schilthorn, where the Piz Gloria cable-car station awaits, with its solar-powered revolving restaurant, shop, and panorama terrace. At the top, you have a spectacular panoramic view of the Eiger, Mönch, and Jungfrau mountains, lined up on the horizon.

Ascending the Schilthorn: You can ride to the Schilthorn and back from several points—the cable-car station near Stechelberg on the valley floor (95 SF), Gimmelwald (85 SF), or Mürren (74 SF). Snare a 25 percent discount for early and late rides (roughly before 9:00 and after 15:30) and in spring and fall (roughly May and Oct). If you have a Swiss Pass (50 percent discount) or Eurailpass (25 percent off), you might as well go whenever you like, because you can't double up discounts. Lifts go twice hourly, and the ride from Gimmelwald (including two transfers) to the Schilthorn takes 30 minutes. You can park your car at the valley station near Stechelberg (2 SF/2 hours, 6 SF/day, cash only). For more information, including current weather conditions, see www.schilthorn.ch or call 033-826-0007.

As the cable car floats between Gimmelwald and Mürren you'll see the metal bridge that marks the end of the *via ferrata*. You'll also see fields of wooden tripods, which serve two purposes: They stop avalanches and shelter newly planted trees. Made of wood, they're designed to eventually rot when the tree they protect is strong enough to survive the winter snowpack. From Mürren to Birg, keep an eye on the altitude meter.

At the Top: Head out to the terrace, where information boards identify each peak, and directional signs point hikers toward some seriously steep downhill climbs. Watch paragliders set up, psych up, and take off, flying 45 minutes with the birds to distant Interlaken. Walk along the ridge out back. This is a great place for a photo of the mountain-climber you. Youth hostelers—not realizing that rocks may hide just under the snow—scream down the ice fields on plastic-bag sleds from the mountaintop. (There's an English-speaking doctor in Lauterbrunnen—see page 162.)

Inside, Piz Gloria has a free "touristorama" **film** room. The 20-minute video shows the natural wonders of the area, highlights a few activities—including racing down the famous Inferno

ski run, briefly shares the story of the Schilthornbahn lift itself, and shows a substantial clip from the 1969 James Bond movie, *On Her Majesty's Secret Service.* That movie used the newly completed station as one of its major film sets.

You can ride up to the Schilthorn and hike down, but it's tough. (Hiking *up* from Gimmelwald or Mürren is easier on your knees...if you don't mind a 5,000-foot altitude gain.) For information on **hikes** from lift stations along the

Schilthorn cable-car line, see "Hiking and Biking," later. My favorite "hike" from the Schilthorn is simply along the ridge out back, to get away from the station and be all alone on top of an Alp.

Breakfast at 10,000 Feet: The huge 28-SF "007 Breakfast Buffet" is served 8:00-11:00. The restaurant also serves hot dishes all day at prices that don't rise with the altitude (around 24 SF).

▲▲▲Jungfraujoch

The literal high point of any trip to the Swiss Alps is a train ride through the Eiger to the Jungfraujoch (the saddle between the Mönch and Jungfrau mountains). At 11,300 feet, it's Europe's highest train station. (If you have a heart or lung condition, you may want to check with your doctor before making this ascent.)

Ascending to the Jungfraujoch: Train runs all year to the Jungfraujoch from Lauterbrunnen (166 SF round-trip) and from Kleine Scheidegg (112 SF round-trip). The first trip of the day to the Jungfraujoch is discounted—ask for a Good Morning Ticket and leave the top by 12:30 (first train from Lauterbrunnen—130 SF, leaves about 7:00; from Kleine Scheidegg—90 SF, leaves about 8:00; Nov-April you can get Good Morning rates for the first or second train and return any time that day; confirm all times and prices, 25 percent discount with Swiss Pass and Eurailpass, railpass holders get a better deal than Good Morning Ticket and can't combine discounts). Pick up a leaflet on the lifts at a local TI (www.jungfraubahn.ch). If it's cloudy, skip the trip; for a terse trilingual weather forecast from the Jungfraujoch, call 033-828-7931.

The ride from Kleine Scheidegg takes about an hour (sit on the right side for better views), including two five-minute stops at stations actually halfway up the notorious North Face of the Eiger. You have time to look out windows and marvel at how people could climb the Eiger—and how the Swiss built this train track more than a hundred years ago. The second half of the ride takes you through a tunnel inside the Eiger (some newer train cars run multilingual videos about the history of the train line).

At the Top: Once you reach the top, study the Jungfraujoch chart to see your options (many of them are weather-dependent). There's a restaurant, a history exhibit, an "ice palace" (a cavern with a gallery of ice statues), and a 20-minute video that plays continuously. A tunnel leads outside, where you can summer ski (33 SF for gear and lift ticket), sled (free loaner discs with a 5-SF deposit), or hike an hour across the ice to  Mönchsjochhütte (a mountain hut with a small restaurant). An elevator leads to the Sphinx observatory for the highest viewing point, from which you can see the Aletsch Glacier—Europe's longest, at nearly 11 miles—stretch to the south. Remember that your body isn't used to such high altitudes. Signs posted at the top remind you to take it easy.

You can combine one of the best hikes in the region—from

Männlichen to Kleine Scheidegg—with your trip up to the Jungfraujoch (see page 196).

Hiking and Biking

This area offers days of possible hikes. Many are a fun combination of trails, mountain trains, and cable-car rides. I've listed them based on which side of the Lauterbrunnen Valley they're on: west (the Gimmelwald/Mürren/Schilthorn side) or east (the Jungfrau side).

On the Gimmelwald (West) Side of the Lauterbrunnen Valley

Hikes from the Schilthorn

Several tough trails lead down from the Schilthorn, but most visitors take the cable car round-trip simply for the views (see "Lifts and Trains," earlier). If you're a serious hiker, consider walking all the way down (first hike) or part of the way down (second hike) back into Gimmelwald. Don't attempt to hike down from the Schilthorn unless the trail is clear of snow. Adequate shoes and clothing (weather can change quickly) and good knees are required. (If you want to visit the Sprutz Waterfall on your way to Gimmelwald, see page 194.)

From the Top of the Schilthorn (very difficult)—To hike downhill from the Piz Gloria revolving restaurant at the peak, start at the steps to the right of the cable, which lead along a ridge between a cliff and the bowl. As you pass huge rocks and shale fields, keep an eye out for the painted rocks that mark the scant trail. Eventually, you'll hit the service road (a ski run in the winter), which is steep and not very pleasant. Passing a memorial to a woman killed by lightning in 1865, you come to the small lake called Grauseeli. Leave the gravel road and hike along the lake. From there, follow the trail (with the help of cables when necessary) to scamper along the shale in the direction of Rotstockhütte (to Gimmelwald, see next hike) or Schilttal (the valley leading directly to Mürren; follow *Mürren/Rotstockhütte* sign painted on the rock at the junction).

▲▲Birg to Gimmelwald via Brünli (moderately difficult)— Rather than doing the very long hike all the way back down into Gimmelwald, I prefer walking the easier (but still strenuous) hike from the intermediate cable-car station at Birg. This is efficiently combined with a visit to the Schilthorn (from Schilthorn summit, ride cable car halfway down, get off at Birg, and hike down from there; buy the round-trip excursion early-bird fare, which is cheaper than the Gimmelwald-Schilthorn-Birg ticket, and decide at Birg whether you want to hike or ride down).

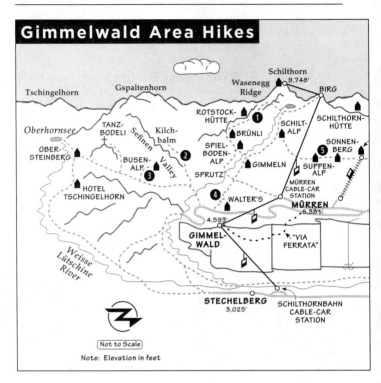

Gimmelwald Area Hikes

Tschingelhorn | Gspaltenhorn | Wasenegg Ridge | Schilthorn 9,748' | BIRG

Oberhornsee

TANZ-BODELI

Kilch-balm

ROTSTOCK-HÜTTE ❶

SCHILT-ALP

SCHILTHORN-HÜTTE

OBER-STEINBERG

BUSEN-ALP ❸

Sefinen Valley ❷

BRÜNLI

SPIEL-BODEN-ALP

SPRUTZ

GIMMELN

SONNEN-BERG

SUPPEN-ALP ❺

HOTEL TSCHINGELHORN

❹ WALTER'S

MÜRREN CABLE-CAR STATION

MÜRREN 5,381'

4,593'

GIMMEL-WALD

"VIA FERRATA"

Weisse Lütschine River

STECHELBERG 3,025'

SCHILTHORNBAHN CABLE-CAR STATION

Not to Scale

Note: Elevation in feet

The most interesting trail from Birg to Gimmelwald is the high one via Grauseeli lake and Wasenegg Ridge to Brünli, then down to Spielbodenalp and the Sprutz Waterfall. Warning: This trail is quite steep and slippery in places, and can take four hours. Locals take their kindergartners on this hike, but it can seem dangerous to Americans unused to alpine hikes. Do not attempt this hike in snow, which you might find at this altitude even in the peak of summer. (Get local advice.)

From the Birg lift station, hike toward the Schilthorn, taking your first left down and passing along the left side of the little Grauseeli lake. From the lake, a gravelly trail leads down rough switchbacks (including a stretch where the path narrows and you can hang onto a guide cable against the cliff face) until it levels out. When you see a rock painted with arrows pointing to Mürren and Rotstockhütte, follow the path to Rotstockhütte (traditional old farm with light meals and drinks, mattress loft with cheap beds), traversing the cow-grazed mountainside.

For a thrill, follow Wasenegg Ridge. It's more scary than dangerous if you're sure-footed and can handle the 50-foot-long "tightrope-with-handrail" section along an extremely narrow ledge with a thousand-foot drop. This trail gets you to Brünli with the least

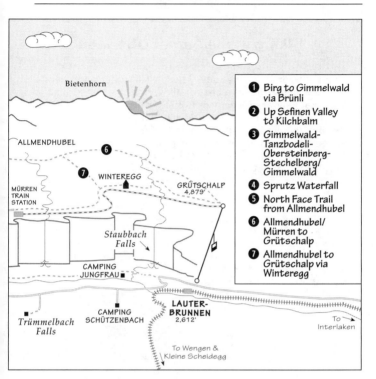

Bietenhorn

ALLMENDHUBEL

MÜREN TRAIN STATION

WINTEREGG

GRÜTSCHALP
4,879'

Staubbach Falls

CAMPING JUNGFRAU

CAMPING SCHÜTZENBACH

LAUTER-BRUNNEN
2,612'

Trümmelbach Falls

To Interlaken

To Wengen & Kleine Scheidegg

❶ Birg to Gimmelwald via Brünli

❷ Up Sefinen Valley to Kilchbalm

❸ Gimmelwald-Tanzbodeli-Obersteinberg-Stechelberg/Gimmelwald

❹ Sprutz Waterfall

❺ North Face Trail from Allmendhubel

❻ Allmendhubel/Mürren to Grütschalp

❼ Allmendhubel to Grütschalp via Winteregg

altitude drop. (The safer, well-signposted approach to Brünli is to drop down to Rotstockhütte, then climb back up to Brünli.) The barbed-wire fence leads you to the knobby little summit, where you'll enjoy an incredible 360-degree view and a chance to sign your name on the register stored in the little wooden box.

A steep trail winds directly down from Brünli toward Gimmelwald and soon hits a bigger, easier trail. The trail bends right (just before the farm/restaurant at Spielbodenalp), leading to Sprutz. Walk under the Sprutz Waterfall, then follow a steep, wooded trail that deposits you in a meadow of flowers at the top side of Gimmelwald.

Hikes from Gimmelwald

▲**Up Sefinen Valley to Kilchbalm (easy)**—The trail from Gimmelwald up the Sefinen Valley (Sefinental) is a good rainy-weather hike, as you can go as far as you like. After two hours and a gain of only 800 feet, you hit the end of the trail and Kilchbalm, a dramatic bowl of glacier fields. Snow can make this trail unsafe, even into the summer (ask locally for information), and there's no food or drink along the way.

From the Gimmelwald fire station, walk about 100 yards

Hiking in the Berner Oberland

This region is a wonderful place to hike, and I've listed my favorite excursions. The super-scenic walk from Männlichen to Kleine Scheidegg is the best of all worlds: It's both dramatic and relatively easy. The hike from Schynige Platte to First is spectacular, but much more challenging, as is the hike from the Birg cable-car station down to Gimmelwald—don't try either of these in bad weather. In case of rain, the lower hikes (North Face Trail from Allmendhubel; the walk from Mürren or Allmendhubel to Grütschalp; the Sefinen Valley hike from Gimmelwald; and the stroll along the Lauterbrunnen Valley) are better bets.

To do any serious hiking, you should invest in a good hiking map. Hikers can get specifics at the Mürren TI or from hoteliers. For a description of six diverse hikes on the west side of Lauterbrunnen, pick up the free *Mürren-Schilthorn Hikes* brochure. This 3-D overview map of the Mürren mountainside makes a useful and attractive souvenir. For the other side of the valley, get the *Wandern Jungfraubahnen* brochure, which also has a handy 3-D overview map of hiking trails (both brochures free at stations, hotels, and TIs).

Once under way, don't mind the fences (although be aware that wires can be solar-powered electric); a hiker has the right of way in Switzerland. Don't forget a water bottle and some munchies. Trails are well-marked, with yellow signs listing destinations and the estimated time it'll take you to walk there. Refer to maps (within this chapter) as you read about the hikes.

Weather Concerns: Locals always seem to know the weather

down the paved Stechelberg road. Leave it on the dirt Sefinental road, which becomes a lane, then a trail. You'll cross a raging river and pass a firing range where locals practice their marksmanship (Fri and Sat evenings; the *danger of fire* sign refers to live bullets). Follow signs to Kilchbalm into a forest, along a river, and finally to the glacier fields.

▲**Gimmelwald-Tanzbodeli-Obersteinberg-Stechelberg/ Gimmelwald (more difficult, for good hikers)**—This eight-hour, 11-mile hike is extremely rewarding, offering perfect peace, very few people, traditional alpine culture, and spectacular views. (There's no food or drink for five hours, so pack accordingly.) The trail can be a bit confusing, so this is best done with a good, locally purchased map.

report (as much of their income depends on it). Clouds can roll in anytime, but skies are usually clearest in the morning. All over the region, TV sets are tuned to the local weather station, with real-time views from all the famous peaks. The same station airs a travelogue on the region each evening at about 21:30. You can also check the weather at www.swisspanorama.com.

In the Berner Oberland, snow can curtail your hiking plans, even in July (the Männlichen lift doesn't even open until the first week in June). Before setting out on any hike, get advice from a knowledgeable local. Well into the spring, and sometimes also in early fall, the high trails (Männlichen to Kleine Scheidegg, Schynige Platte to First, and anything from Schilthorn or Birg) are likely to be impassable.

Wildlife: As hunting is not allowed in the vicinity of any lifts, animals find safe havens in places you're likely to be. Keep an eye out for chamois (called *Gemsen* here)—the sure-footed "goat antelopes" that live at the top of the treeline and go a little lower when hungry. Spotting an ibex—a wild goat with horns, scrambling along the rocky terrain—is another Berner Oberland thrill. You'll also encounter marmots—big alpine mice (like 2-pound squirrels) who get really fat each summer, planning to sleep underground for six months through the winter. These burrowing rodents are fun to watch, and if you sit still, they don't see you. You'll hear them whistle. Your best viewing place is above Allmendhubel, in the meadow above the highest hut in Blumental.

Nordic Walking: You may wonder about the Germans you'll see with their walking sticks *(Alpenstock)*. Enthusiasts claim Nordic walking is an all-body workout, activating 90 percent of your muscles and burning a third more calories than "normal" walking, while cutting way back on the strain on your back and knees when going downhill. To do it right requires proper instruction. Sticks can be rented at some outdoor shops.

BERNER OBERLAND

About 100 yards below the Gimmelwald firehouse, take the Sefinental dirt road (described in previous listing). As the dirt road switches back after about 30 minutes, take the right turn across the river and start your ascent, following signs to *Obersteinberg*. After 1.5 hours of hard climbing, you have the option of a side-trip to Busenalp. This is fun if the goat-and-cow herder is there, as you can watch traditional cheesemaking in action. (He appreciates a bottle of wine from hikers.) Trail markers are painted onto rocks—watch carefully. After visiting Busenalp, return to the main path.

At the *Obersteinberg 50 Min/Tanzbodeli 20 Min* signpost, head for Tanzbodeli ("Dancing Floor"). This is everyone's favorite alpine perch—great for a little romance or a picnic with breathtaking

views of the Obersteinberg valley. From here, you enter a natural reserve, so you're likely to
see chamois and other alpine
critters. From Tanzbodeli, you
return to the main trail (there's
no other way out) and continue
to Obersteinberg. You'll eventually hit the Mountain Hotel

Obersteinberg (see "Sleeping in Obersteinberg," later; American
expat Vickie will serve you a meal or drink).

From there, the trail leads to Mountain Hotel Tschingelhorn
(see "Sleeping in Obersteinberg," later). About an hour later, you
hit a fork in the trail and choose where you'd like your hike to end:
back to Gimmelwald (2 hours total) or Stechelberg (near the bottom of the Schilthornbahn cable car, 1.5 hours total).

▲**Sprutz Waterfall (moderately difficult)**—The forest above
Gimmelwald hides a powerful waterfall with a trail snaking behind
it, offering a fun gorge experience. While the waterfall itself is not
well-signed, it's on the Gimmelwald-Spielbodenalp trail. It's steep,
through a forest, and can be very slippery when wet, but the actual
crossing under the waterfall is just misty.

The hike up to Sprutz from Gimmelwald isn't worth the trip
in itself, but it's handy when combined with the hike down from
Birg and Brünli (described earlier) or the North Face Trail (see
next listing). As you descend on either of these two hikes, the trail
down to Gimmelwald splits at Spielbodenalp—to the right for the
forest and the waterfall; to the left for more meadows, the hamlet
of Gimmeln, and more gracefully back into Gimmelwald.

Hikes from Mürren/Allmendhubel
▲▲**North Face Trail from Allmendhubel (easy and family-
friendly)**—For a pleasant two-hour hike, head out along this

four-mile trail, starting at
6,385 feet and finishing at
5,375 feet (some stretches
can be challenging if you're
not in shape). To reach the
trail, ride the Allmendhubel
funicular up from Mürren
(much cheaper than Schilthorn, good restaurant at top,
see page 182). From there,

follow the well-signed route, which loops counterclockwise around
to Mürren (or cut off at Spielbodenalp, near the end, and descend
into Gimmelwald via the Sprutz Waterfall). As this trail doesn't

technically begin at Allmendhubel, you'll start by following signs to *Sonnenberg*. Then just follow the blue signs. You'll enjoy great views, flowery meadows, mountain huts, and a dozen information boards along the way, describing the fascinating climbing history of the great peaks around you.

Along the trail, you'll pass four farms (technically "alps," as they are only open in the summer) that serve meals and drinks. Sonnenberg was allowed to break the all-wood building code with concrete for protection against avalanches. Suppenalp is quainter. Lean against the house with a salad, soup, or sandwich and enjoy the view. Just below Suppenalp is a little adventure park with zip lines and other kid-pleasing activities.

Notice how older huts are built into the protected side of rocks and outcroppings, in anticipation of avalanches. Above Suppenalp, Blumental ("Flower Valley") is hopping with marmots. Because hunters are not allowed near lifts, animals have learned that these are safe places to hang out—giving tourists a better chance of spotting them.

The trail leads up and over to a group of huts called Schiltalp (good food, drink, and service, and a romantic farm setting). If the poles under the eaves have bells, the cows are up here. If not, the cows are still at the lower farms. Half the cows in Gimmelwald (about 100) spend their summers here. In July, August, and September, you can watch cheese being made and have a snack or drink. Thirty years ago, each family had its own hut. Labor was cheap and available. Today, it's a communal thing, with several families sharing the expense of a single cow herder. Cow herders are master cheesemakers and have veterinary skills, too.

From Schiltalp, the trail winds gracefully down toward Spielbodenalp. From there you can finish the North Face Trail (continuing down and left through meadows and the hamlet of Gimmeln, then back to Mürren, with more historic signposts), or cut off right (descending steeply through a thick forest and under the dramatic Sprutz Waterfall into Gimmelwald—see Sprutz Waterfall, previous page, for details).

▲**Allmendhubel/Mürren to Grütschalp (fairly easy)**— For a not-too-tough two-hour walk with great Jungfrau views, ride the funicular from Mürren to Allmendhubel and walk to Grütschalp (a drop of about 1,500 feet), where you can catch the train back to Mürren. An easier version is the lower Bergweg from Allmendhubel to Grütschalp via Winteregg and its cheese farm. For a super-easy family stroll with grand views, walk from Mürren just above the train tracks either to Winteregg (40 minutes, restaurant, playground, train station) or through even better scenery on to Grütschalp (1 hour, train station), then catch the train back to Mürren.

Hikes on the Jungfrau (East) Side of the Lauterbrunnen Valley

▲▲▲**Männlichen-Kleine Scheidegg (easy and with dramatic views)**—This is my favorite easy alpine hike (2.5 miles, 1-1.5 hours, 900-foot altitude drop to Kleine Scheidegg). It's entertaining all the way, with glorious mountain views. If you missed the plot, it's the Young Maiden (Jungfrau), being protected from the Ogre (Eiger) by the Monk (Mönch). Trails may be snowbound into June; ask about conditions at the lift stations or at TIs (see "Jungfraujoch" listing on page 188).

If the weather's good, start off bright and early. From the Lauterbrunnen train station, take the little mountain train up to Wengen. Sit on the right side of the train for great valley and waterfall views. In Wengen, buy a picnic at the Co-op grocery across from the station, walk across town, and catch the lift to Männlichen, located on top of the ridge high above you. The lift can be open even if the trail is closed; if the weather is questionable, confirm that the Männlichen-Kleine Scheidegg trail is open before ascending. Don't waste time in Wengen if it's sunny—you can linger back here after your hike.

Riding the gondola from Wengen to Männlichen, you'll go over the old lift station (inundated by a 1978 avalanche that buried a good part of Wengen—notice there's no development in the "red zone" above the tennis courts). Farms are built with earthen ramps on the uphill side in anticipation of the next slide. The forest of avalanche fences near the top was built after that 1978 avalanche. As you ascend you can also survey Wengen—the bright red roofs mark new vacation condos, mostly English-owned and used only a few weeks a year.

For a detour that'll give you an easy king- or queen-of-the-mountain feeling, turn left from the top of the Wengen-Männlichen lift station, and hike uphill 10 minutes to the little peak (Männlichen Gipfel, 7,500 feet).

Then go back to the lift station (which has a great kids' area) and enjoy the walk—facing spectacular alpine panorama views—to Kleine Scheidegg for a picnic or restaurant lunch. To start the hike, leave the Wengen-Männlichen lift station to the right. Walk past the second Männlichen lift station (this one leads to Grindelwald, the touristy town in the valley to your left). Ahead of you in the distance, left to right, are the north faces of the Eiger, Mönch, and Jungfrau; in the foreground is the Tschuggen peak, and just behind it, the Lauberhorn. This hike takes you around the left (east) side of this ridge. Simply follow the signs for Kleine Scheidegg, and you'll be there in about an hour—a little more for gawkers, picnickers, and photographers. You might have to tiptoe through streams of melted snow—or some small snow banks, even well into the summer—but the path is well-marked, well-maintained, and mostly level all the way to Kleine Scheidegg.

About 35 minutes into the hike, you'll reach a bunch of benches and a shelter with incredible unobstructed views of all three peaks—the perfect picnic spot. Fifteen minutes later, on the left, you'll see the first sign of civilization: Restaurant Grindelwaldblick (the best lunch stop up here, open daily, closed Dec and May, described on page 199). Hike to the restaurant's fun mountain lookout to survey the Eiger and look down on the Kleine Scheidegg action. After 10 more minutes, you'll be at the Kleine Scheidegg train station, with plenty of lesser lunch options (including Restaurant Bahnhof, described on page 199).

From Kleine Scheidegg, you can catch the train up to "the top of Europe" (see Jungfraujoch listing, earlier), take the train back

down to Wengen, or hike downhill (gorgeous 30-minute hike to Wengernalp Station, a little farther to the Allmend stop; 60 more steep minutes from there into Wengen). The alpine views might be accompanied by the valley-filling mellow sound of alphorns and distant avalanches. If the weather turns bad or you run out of steam, catch the train at any of the stations along the way. After Wengernalp, the trail to Wengen is steep and, though not dangerous, requires a good set of knees. The boring final descent from Wengen to Lauterbrunnen is knee-killer steep—catch the train instead.

▲▲Schynige Platte to First (more difficult)—The best day I've had hiking in the Berner Oberland was when I made this demanding six-hour ridge walk, with Lake Brienz on one side and all that Jungfrau beauty on the other. Start at the Wilderswil train station (just outside Interlaken), and catch the little train up to Schynige Platte (6,560 feet; 2/hour, 55 minutes, 35 SF). The high point is Faulhorn (8,790 feet, with its famous mountaintop hotel). Hike to a small mini-gondola called "First" (7,110 feet), then ride down to Grindelwald and catch a train back to your starting point, Wilderswil. Or, if you have a regional train pass (or no car but endless money), take the long, scenic return trip: From Grindelwald, take the lift up to Männlichen (2/hour, 30 minutes, 36 SF), do the

BERNER OBERLAND

hike to Kleine Scheidegg and down to Wengen (described earlier), then head down into Lauterbrunnen.

For a shorter (3-hour) ridge walk, consider the well-signposted Panoramaweg, a loop from Schynige Platte to Daub Peak.

The alpine flower park at Schynige Platte Station offers a delightful stroll through several hundred alpine flowers (free, June-Sept daily 8:30-18:00, www.alpengarten.ch), including a chance to see edelweiss growing in the wild.

Lowa, a leading local manufacturer of top-end hiking boots, has a promotional booth at Schynige Platte Station that provides free loaners to hikers who'd like to give their boots a try. They're already broken in, but bring thick socks (or buy them there).

If hiking here, be mindful of the last lifts (which can be as early as 16:30). Hiking from First (7,113 feet) to Schynige Platte (6,454 feet) gives you a later departure down and less climbing. The TI produces a great Schynige Platte map/guide narrating the train ride up and describing various hiking options from there (available at Wilderswil Station).

Mountain Biking

Mountain biking is popular and accepted, as long as you stay on the clearly marked mountain-bike paths. You can rent bikes in Mürren (Stäger Sport, see page 179) or in Lauterbrunnen (Imboden Bike, see page 162). The Lauterbrunnen shop is bigger, has a wider selection of bikes, and is likely to be open when the Mürren one isn't. The two shops work together: For an 8-SF surcharge, you can pick up your bike at one location and  leave it at the other. On trains and cable cars, bikes require a separate ticket.

The most popular bike rides include the following:

Lauterbrunnen to Interlaken: This is a gentle downhill ride on a peaceful bike path across the river from the road (don't bike on the road itself). You can return to Lauterbrunnen by train (13 SF total for bike and you). Or rent a bike at either Interlaken station, take the train to Lauterbrunnen, and ride back.

Lauterbrunnen Valley (between Stechelberg and Lauterbrunnen town): This delightful, easy bike path features plenty of diversions along the way (several listed under "Activities in and near Lauterbrunnen" on page 162).

Mürren to Winteregg to Grütschalp and Back: This fairly level route takes you through high country, with awesome mountain views.

Mürren to Winteregg to Lauterbrunnen: This scenic descent, on a service road with loose gravel, takes you to the Lauterbrunnen Valley floor.

Mürren-Gimmelwald-Sefinen Valley-Stechelberg-Lauterbrunnen-Grütschalp-Mürren: This is the best ride, but it's demanding—with one very difficult stretch where you'll likely walk your bike down a steep gulley for 500 yards. While you'll be on your bike most of the time, to complete the loop take the cable car from Lauterbrunnen up to Grütschalp and then bike back to Mürren.

More in the Berner Oberland

I'd sleep in Gimmelwald, Mürren, or Lauterbrunnen. But you could also consider the following places.

Sleeping and Eating at or near Kleine Scheidegg

(6,762 feet)
This high settlement above the timberline is where you catch the train up to the Jungfraujoch. All of these places serve meals. Confirm prices and availability before ascending. Note that the last train down to Wengen leaves Kleine Scheidegg at 18:30.

$$$ Hotel Bellevue des Alpes, lovingly maintaining a 1930s elegance, is a worthwhile splurge. Since the 1840s, five generations of von Allmens have run this classic old alpine hotel (subsidized by the family income from Trümmelbach Falls). The hallway is like a museum, with old photos (Sb-220-260 SF, Db-370-540 SF, includes breakfast and sumptuous four-course dinner, open only mid-June-mid-Sept, tel. 033-855-1212, fax 033-855-1294, www .scheidegg-hotels.ch, welcome@scheidegg-hotels.ch).

$$ Restaurant Bahnhof invites you to sleep face-to-face with the Eiger (dorm bed-53 SF with breakfast, 73 SF also includes dinner; D-135 SF with breakfast, D-170 SF with breakfast and dinner; in the train station building, tel. 033-828-7828, www.bahnhof -scheidegg.ch, info@bahnhof-scheidegg.ch).

$ Restaurant Grindelwaldblick, a 10-minute hike from the train station, is more charming, romantic, and remote than Restaurant Bahnhof (40 SF/bed in 6- to 20-bed rooms, includes sheets and breakfast, closed Nov and May, tel. 033-855-1374, fax 033-855-4205, www.grindelwaldblick.ch). The restaurant, with a great sun terrace and a cozy interior, sells good three-course lunches (15-25 SF) and 25-SF dinners.

Sleeping in Stechelberg
(3,025 feet)

Stechelberg is the hamlet at the end of the road up the Lauterbrunnen Valley; it's about a mile beyond the Schilthornbahn lift that goes up to Gimmelwald, Mürren, and the Schilthorn (it's a five-minute PostBus ride or a 20-minute trail walk between the lift station and the village). Beyond Stechelberg lies the rugged Rear Lauterbrunnen Valley, the edge of the Jungfrau-Aletsch-Bietschhorn nature reserve—the most glaciated part of the Alps.

$$ Hotel Stechelberg, at road's end, is surrounded by waterfalls and vertical rock, with a garden terrace, a good restaurant, and 16 quiet rooms—half in a creaky old building, half in a concrete, no-character new building (D-90-120 SF, Db-138, Db with balcony-170 SF, T-165 SF, Tb-210 SF, Q-210 SF, bus stops here 1-2/hour, free Wi-Fi, tel. 033-855-2921, fax 033-855-4438, www.hotel-stechelberg.ch, hotel@stechelberg.ch, Marianne and Otto).

$ The **Alpenhof** fills a former "Nature Friends' Hut" with cheap beds. Creaking like a wooden chalet built in 1926 should, and surrounded by a broad lawn, it provides a good, inexpensive base for drivers and families (28 SF/bed in 2- to 6-bed rooms, each group gets a private room, breakfast-12 SF, tel. 033-855-1202, www.alpenhof-stechelberg.ch, alpenhof@stechelberg.ch, Diane and Marc). From the Hotel Stechelberg, go up the paved path, go right at the fork, and cross the river; it's on your left.

Sleeping in Obersteinberg
(5,900 feet)

Here's a wild idea: **$$ Mountain Hotel Obersteinberg** is a working alpine farm with cheese, cows, a mule shuttling up food once a day, and an American (Vickie) who fell in love with a mountain man. It's a 2.5-hour hike from either Stechelberg or Gimmelwald. They rent 12 primitive rooms and a bunch of loft beds. There's no shower, no hot water, and only meager solar-panel electricity. Candles light up the night, and you can take a hot-water bottle to bed if necessary (S-85 SF, D-170 SF, includes linen, sheetless dorm beds-68 SF; these prices include breakfast and dinner, without meals S-37 SF, D-74 SF, dorm beds-20 SF; closed Oct-May, tel. 033-855-2033). The place is filled with locals and Germans on weekends, but it's all yours on weekdays. Why not hike here from Gimmelwald and leave the Alps a day later?

ZERMATT
and the MATTERHORN

 There's just something about that Matterhorn, the most recognizable mountain on the planet. Anyone who says, "You've seen one mountain, you've seen them all" hasn't laid eyes on this pointy, craggy peak. The Matterhorn seems to have a nearly mystical draw for people—it's the Stonehenge of Switzerland.

Oh, and there's a town, too. Zermatt, a little burg of about 5,600 people, might well be the most touristy resort in Switzerland. While the village has pockets of traditional charm, virtually everyone you meet in Zermatt earns a living one way or another from those who flock here for a peek at the peak. Aside from the stone quarries you'll pass on the way into town, tourism is Zermatt's only industry.

Be warned that Zermatt is a one-mountain town (for a comparison of Zermatt and the more interesting Berner Oberland, see the sidebar, next page). Many visitors find Zermatt touristy and overrated, especially considering its inconvenient location (at the dead-end of a long valley in the southwest corner of the country). And if you make the long trek and find only cloudy weather, there's little else to do...other than wish for a T-shirt that reads, "I went all the way to Zermatt and didn't even see the lousy Matterhorn."

Planning Your Time

On a two-week trip in Switzerland, I'd suggest two nights and the better part of two days in Zermatt—if the weather's good. (To get the latest weather report, call the Zermatt TI at tel. 027-966-8100, or check the webcams at www.zermatt.ch.) For efficient sightseeing, arrive or leave on the Glacier Express; it's an all-day, cross-country scenic train ride to or from Chur, which has good

Zermatt vs. the Berner Oberland

If your time is limited and you're going to only one alpine hide-away in Switzerland, the Berner Oberland offers far more high-mountain travel thrills than the Zermatt area (see the Gimmelwald and the Berner Oberland chapter). But if you're trying to make up your mind, here are a few comparisons.

The Berner Oberland is relatively easy to reach, thanks to its more central location in the country and its good rail connections to Bern and Luzern. Zermatt is farther off the beaten track, at the end of a dead-end valley near the Italian border, and the final approach by train (from Brig), run by a private company, is only discounted—not covered—by a Eurailpass (though it is covered by a Swiss Pass).

Zermatt is essentially one town focused on a single mountain. The Berner Oberland is an entire alpine region, with many towns and villages to visit—from the bustling administrative center of Interlaken to the tiny, traditional village of Gimmelwald. In Zermatt, most accommodations options are in the town itself. But in the Berner Oberland, you have your choice of places to sleep—in a resort town or humble hamlet...in the valley or on a ledge overlooking the mountains.

connections to Zürich and elsewhere in northeast Switzerland (see the Scenic Rail Journeys chapter). If you arrive on the earlier Glacier Express, you can go straight to the Matterhorn Museum to splice in an hour's visit before it closes (ask nicely, and they'll likely let you leave your bags behind the counter). Unless the weather's cloudy, you'll want to spend your daylight hours up above town.

Orientation to Zermatt

Zermatt (elevation 5,265 feet) lies at the end of the valley called the Nikolaital, along the Matter Vispa River in the shadow of the mighty Matterhorn (14,690 feet, "Cervino" in Italian).

The train station is at the bottom of town, a few steps from the main drag, Bahnhofstrasse. As you stand in front of the station with the tracks at your back, the heart of the village is to your right. Lifts to thrilling Matterhorn viewpoints leave from near the train station: The train up to Gornergrat is across the street; the station for the underground train/gondola/cable car to Rothorn is a few blocks ahead along the river; and the gondola/cable car up to

As for sightseeing, the best part of the Berner Oberland is the Lauterbrunnen Valley, with great high-altitude attractions on both sides (the Jungfraujoch on one side, the Schilthorn on the other), plus other enjoyable lifts, towns, and hikes. Zermatt doesn't have nearly the same diversity. Budget travelers appreciate the Berner Oberland's cheaper accommodations and the discount given on mountain lifts to Eurailpass-holders (unlike Zermatt, which has Eurail discounts only on the Gornergrat train).

Both areas are touristy, but more traditional tidbits of the authentic Swiss countryside survive in the Berner Oberland than in Zermatt. The Berner Oberland also offers a wider variety of activities, where on a rainy day, you can poke around a traditional village (such as Gimmelwald) or the bigger town of Interlaken, or walk through the thundering Trümmelbach Falls.

You can tell where my heart lies. Still, if you've seen the Berner Oberland already, or if you want to sample two different mountain areas of Switzerland, Zermatt is worth a visit. And the Matterhorn is really something else—there's a reason this place is known around the world.

the Matterhorn Glacier Paradise (on the Klein Matterhorn peak) is farther along through the village (about three-quarters of a mile away). Details on all of these are listed in this chapter.

Zermatt brags that its streets are traffic-free. Well, not quite. Electric cars (big golf carts) buzz around the streets like four-wheeled Vespas, some with surprisingly aggressive drivers. Watch your step.

Addresses are generally not used in this small town. To find your hotel, use the map in this chapter, follow the free map from the TI, look for signs, or ask a local.

Tourist Information

Zermatt's TI is right at the train station (mid-June-Sept daily 8:30-18:00; Oct-mid-June Mon-Sat 8:30-12:00 & 13:30-18:00, Sun 9:30-12:00 & 16:00-18:00; tel. 027-966-8100, www.zermatt.ch). They offer two handy, free resources: an extremely detailed map that labels every building in town, and a thick information booklet with lift schedules and prices, hikes, and almost anything you could think to ask about (all info is also posted on their extremely

ZERMATT

thorough website). You can also buy hiking maps here, including a detailed 1:25,000 map for serious hikers (25 SF) and a good hiking guide (also 25 SF). If you're traveling with kids, ask for their booklet of activities for *Kinder*.

Arrival in Zermatt

Zermatt's small train station is conveniently located in the middle of town; the TI is immediately to the right as you leave the tracks, and lines of electric taxis wait right out front. All the hotels I list are within walking distance of the train station, though if you're staying at Hotel Jägerhof or either of the two hostels, you may want to take a taxi or bus (see individual listings for directions).

Cars are not allowed in Zermatt. Drivers can park in the huge lot at Täsch, a few miles before Zermatt (14.50 SF/day), then take the shuttle train into town (runs every 20 minutes 6:00-22:30, then hourly until 1:30 in the morning, Thu-Sun hourly 23:00-6:00, 7.80 SF one-way, www.matterhornterminal.ch).

Getting Around Zermatt

Even though Zermatt is "traffic-free," your feet aren't your only transportation option. Two different electric **bus** lines depart across from the train station: The green Bergbahnen line goes to the valley stations for the Rothorn and Matterhorn Glacier Paradise lifts (about 2/hour, 2.50 SF, or free with lift ticket). The red line goes to the Matterhorn Glacier Paradise lift (but not Rothorn), taking a more roundabout route via the hamlet of Winkelmatten (1-2/hour, 3.20 SF, free with lift ticket Nov-May only). Neither bus is covered by the Swiss Pass. The buses are marked with their destination and make a few stops along the way before heading back to the station (when they're marked *Bahnhof*).

You can also hire your own **electric taxi** (about 12 SF to anywhere in the heart of town, extra charge for luggage and rides at night, taxi stand in front of train station, or call **Taxi Zermatt**, tel. 027-967-3333).

Helpful Hints

Walking Tour: A one-hour village walking tour in English is offered once a week from mid-June through late September (10 SF, usually Tue at 16:30, confirm details at the TI). This is a good rainy-day option.

Internet Access: Coin-op Internet stations aren't hard to find; the going rate is about 12 SF per hour.

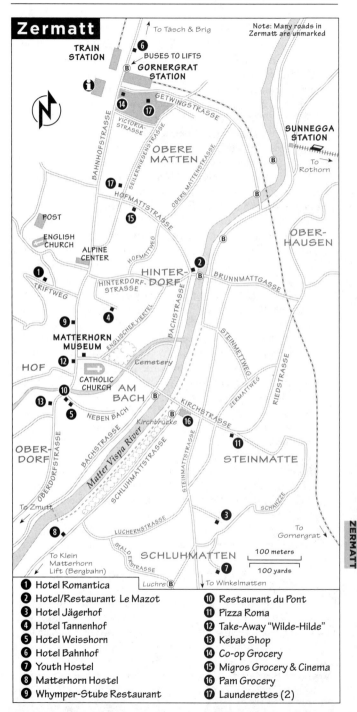

Zermatt

Note: Many roads in Zermatt are unmarked

To Täsch & Brig

TRAIN STATION

❻ BUSES TO LIFTS

Ⓑ GORNERGRAT STATION

ℹ️

🧭 N

BAHNHOFSTRASSE

GETWINGSTRASSE

⑭ ⑰

VICTORIA-STRASSE

SEILERWIESENSTRASSE

OBERE MATTEN

SUNNEGGA STATION

Ⓑ

To Rothorn

⑰

HOFMATTSTRASSE

OBERE MATTENSTRASSE

Ⓑ

POST

⑮

ENGLISH CHURCH

HOFMATTWEG

OBER-HAUSEN

ALPINE CENTER

HINTER-DORF

❷

Ⓑ

BRUNNMATTGASSE

❶

TRIFTWEG

HINTERDORF-STRASSE

BACHSTRASSE

STEINMETTWEG

ZERMATTWEG

RIEDSTRASSE

❾ ❹

ENGLISCHER VIERTEL

MATTERHORN MUSEUM

⑫

Cemetery

HOF

CATHOLIC CHURCH

⑬ ⑩

AM BACH

Ⓑ

KIRCHSTRASSE

❺

NEBEN BACH

Kirchbrücke

Ⓑ

⑯

STEINMATTSTRASSE

⑪

STEINMATTE

OBER-DORF

OBERDORFSTRASSE

BACHSTRASSE

Matter Vispa River

SCHLUHMATTSTRASSE

SCHANZZE

To Zmutt

❽

❸

To Gornergrat

LUCHERNSTRASSE

STALDENSTRASSE

SCHLUHMATTEN

To Klein Matterhorn Lift (Bergbahn)

100 meters

100 yards

❼

Luchre Ⓑ

To Winkelmatten

❶ Hotel Romantica
❷ Hotel/Restaurant Le Mazot
❸ Hotel Jägerhof
❹ Hotel Tannenhof
❺ Hotel Weisshorn
❻ Hotel Bahnhof
❼ Youth Hostel
❽ Matterhorn Hostel
❾ Whymper-Stube Restaurant
⑩ Restaurant du Pont
⑪ Pizza Roma
⑫ Take-Away "Wilde-Hilde"
⑬ Kebab Shop
⑭ Co-op Grocery
⑮ Migros Grocery & Cinema
⑯ Pam Grocery
⑰ Launderettes (2)

ZERMATT

Laundry: Waschsalon Doli is nice and central (20 SF to have them wash and dry a small load, Mon-Sat 8:30-12:00 & 14:00-19:00, closed Sun, tel. 027-967-5100). To find it from the station, take the first left past McDonald's, turn right at the tennis courts, and go down the steps at their sign. **Womy Express** is in the Viktoria Center mall across from train station (Mon-Fri 8:30-12:00 & 13:30-18:30, closed Sat-Sun, tel. 027-967-3242).

Cinema: The **Vernissage Cinema** plays first-run movies, many with English subtitles, as well as a rotating schedule of historical Matterhorn-centric films (Tue-Sat at 18:00 and 20:30, Sun at 20:30 only, closed Mon, Hofmattstrasse 4, tel. 027-967-6636, www.vernissage-zermatt.ch).

Skiing and Snowboarding: Zermatt's high elevation and variety of runs—and the chance to actually ski or snowboard from Switzerland to Italy—make it deservedly popular. Summer skiing is an option at Matterhorn Glacier Paradise (first lift starts at about 8:00, last lift stops around 14:00—after that the snow's too slushy, late April-mid-Oct, limited area in midsummer). A one-day lift ticket will run you about 80 SF; equipment rents for about 45 SF, and snow-wear rental adds another 30-35 SF. Ask at the TI for details.

In the winter, beginners and intermediate skiers head for Gornergrat and the Matterhorn Glacier areas; more advanced skiers prefer Schwarzsee, Rothorn, and especially Stockhorn, with its mogul-filled "freeride" runs (generally open mid-Jan-Easter). The Sunnegga area has a mix of easy and challenging runs.

Rental shops in town include **Matterhorn Sport** (several branches, one near Sunnegga lift, another at Bahnhofstrasse 78, tel. 027-967-2956, www.matterhornsport.ch), **Bayard Sport + Fashion** (also has several branches, including one on Bahnhofplatz, tel. 027-966-4950, www.bayardzermatt .ch), and **Dorsaz-Sport** (near Matterhorn Express lift, tel. 027-966-3810, www.dorsaz-sport.ch). For lift-ticket prices, see www.matterhornparadise.ch; for more tips, read the Switzerland in Winter chapter.

Sights in Zermatt

The town itself is short on attractions. On rainy days, sleep in, linger at the Matterhorn Museum, get your souvenir shopping out of the way, walk up and out of town until you hit the cloud cover (Winkelmatten is a pleasant 20-minute stroll from the Catholic church), catch a movie, and/or take a dip in one of the big hotel pools.

▲**Wander the Town**—Zermatt is charming enough, despite its single-mindedness about catching the tourist dollar. The streets

ZERMATT

may be lined with chalet after chalet, but all the dark wood and overflowing flower boxes lend this super-touristy town an authentic charm.

Just off the main drag, you can find several clusters of traditional shacks, called *mazots,* set on stone stilts (to keep out mice) and topped by stone-slab roofs. Little more than a century ago, the *mazots* and the church were the only buildings standing in this town. A particularly scenic corner is along Hinterdorfstrasse, where several build-ings are labeled according to their former purpose. (You'll also see several *mazots* perched around Hotel Romantica and on the walk up to, and around, the Winkelmatten area).

The big landmark Catholic church (can't miss it on Bahn-hofstrasse) is ringed by mountaineers' tombstones, several inscribed in English. Across the way, the cemetery has lovingly tended graves adorned with flowers and lit by glowing votive lan-terns at night. A smaller English church, built for the many British mountaineers who have flocked to this region, is above and behind the post office, near Hotel Romantica.

▲▲**Matterhorn Museum**—This fun and interesting museum is

the town's best indoor activity, and worth at least an hour on a rainy day. Most of the museum is underground, as it's meant to look like an archeological dig where you can unearth the history of Zermatt and its famous mountain. It focuses on the 19th century, when Zermatt saw the advent of mountaineering and the golden age of tourism. Quite suddenly, what had been a tiny, backwater village became a major destination, known worldwide.

Cost and Hours: 10 SF, covered by Swiss Pass, audioguide-5 SF, July-Sept daily 11:00-18:00, April-June and Oct daily 14:00-18:00, mid-Dec-March 15:00-19:00, closed Nov-mid-Dec, under glass dome at Kirchplatz 11, across from big Catholic church, tel. 027-967-4100, www.matterhornmuseum.ch.

Touring the Museum: Pick up the free English flier, and con-sider paying for the excellent audioguide, which lets you choose to hear Zermatt's history from one of two perspectives: that of native Zermatt alpinist Hannes Taugwalder or British mountaineer Edward Whymper. (No extra cost to hear both versions.)

Whatt's Whatt in Zermatt

Blauherd: Upper station on the Sunnegga-to-Blauherd gondola; lower station on the Blauherd-to-Rothorn cable car, with good access to hikes, including the Marmot hike.

Findelnbach: Station stop on the train from Zermatt up to Gornergrat.

Fluhalp: Small settlement known for its good restaurant, accessible by hike from the Blauherd station.

Furi: Upper station on the gondola from Zermatt; lower station on a different gondola to Schwarzsee and a cable car to Trockener Steg.

Glacier Palace: Free sight at Matterhorn Glacier Paradise; a cavern dug into a glacier with ice sculptures and exhibits.

Gorner Glacier: Glacier that lies between Gornergrat and Klein Matterhorn.

Gornergrat: Viewpoint (10,270 feet) between Klein Matterhorn and Rothorn. At the upper station of a train from Zermatt, it offers views of the Gorner Glacier, Matterhorn, and Monte Rosa.

Gourmetweg ("Gourmet Path"): Hike from Sunnegga down to Zermatt via Findeln through larch forests.

Hinterdorf: Attractive old quarter of Zermatt by the river, with antique chalets and traditional *mazots* (buildings on stone stilts).

Klein Matterhorn: Always snow-covered peak (12,740 feet) with great views of the Alps. The cable-car station just below the summit is called "Matterhorn Glacier Paradise."

Matterhorn: Mountain peak whose shape forms the textbook example of a "horn," indicating that bowl-shaped valleys (cirques) were carved into it by several glaciers on all sides.

Matterhorn Express: Gondola that runs from Zermatt via Schwarzsee to Trockener Steg (with connection to Matter-

Walk downstairs, through the reproductions of an old hotel, church, barn, and other buildings from Zermatt's past. Listen for the fun sound effects. The displays show typical furnishings, tools, and stuffed alpine fauna, as well as exhibits on the city's mountaineering history.

Reliefs of the mountain (and surrounding region) offer a helpful topographic overview. In the mountain guides' hut, press the buttons to see the different routes up the Matterhorn. Consider that even now, only about half the people who attempt this climb make it to the top. To the left, find the picture of local hero Ulrich Inderbinden, who climbed the Matterhorn more than 370 times, the last when he was—no kidding—90 years old. (Inderbinden died in 2004 at age 104; a fountain in the Hinterdorf area of town honors him.)

horn Glacier Paradise).

Matterhorn Glacier Paradise: Europe's highest cable-car station (12,530 feet), just below the Klein Matterhorn peak.

Monte Rosa: Tallest peak in Switzerland (15,200 feet).

Murmelweg ("Marmot Path"): Hike from Blauherd down to Sunnegga through marmot habitat.

Nikolaital: Deepest valley in Switzerland, with the town of Zermatt at its upper end.

Riffelalp: Station stop on the train from Zermatt up to Gornergrat.

Riffelberg: Station stop on the train from Zermatt up to Gornergrat.

Riffelsee: Lake below the Rotenboden station.

Rotenboden: Station stop on the train from Zermatt up to Gornergrat.

Rothorn: Upper station of the Blauherd-to-Rothorn cable car, offering quintessential views of the Matterhorn.

Schwarzsee: Alpine lake at an elevation of 8,470 feet and a gondola station; the closest you can (easily) get to the Matterhorn.

Stafel: Village along the hike from Schwarzsee down to Furi.

Stellisee: Alpine lake along a hike from Blauherd.

Sunnegga: Upper station on the underground funicular from Zermatt and the lower station of the Sunnegga-to-Blauherd gondola; offers good access to hikes.

Trockener Steg: Upper station on the Zermatt-to-Trockener Steg gondola; lower station on the Trockener Steg-to-Matterhorn Glacier Paradise cable car.

Winkelmatten: Cliff-hanging neighborhood above the Matterhorn Express lift station in Zermatt.

Next door is a morbid cabin displaying artifacts found after deadly accidents, with a room dedicated to July 14, 1865—the day the Matterhorn was finally conquered by a team of seven climbers. (Four of them died on the descent, when the least-experienced among them fell, dragging three others to their deaths; you can see the snapped rope in a glass case.) Two 10-minute movies play in the "hotel": one about mountain rescuers, the other with clips from a campy 1937 movie about the first ascent. Be sure to check out the display case (near the WCs) that holds a collection of Matterhorn memorabilia and products.

Goat Parade—Every day in summer, a small flock of furry "black-neck" goats are herded through the center of town on the way to pasture. They're unique to the surrounding Upper Valais region, with a black head and shoulders, a white rear end, and long horns.

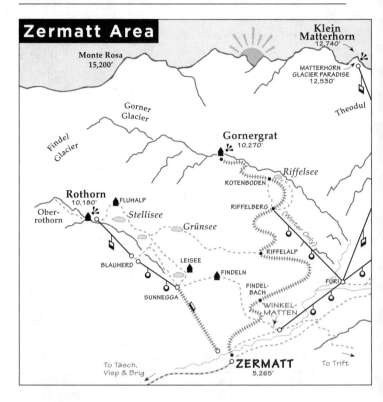

Keep an eye out for this charming and unusual event (daily July-mid-Aug at around 9:00 and back home again at about 17:00).

Indoor Swimming—Several of Zermatt's swankier hotels have pools and saunas, which non-guests can enjoy for a fee—worth paying if you have time to kill in bad weather. In winter, however, most hotels reserve pools for their guests (about 25 SF/day for pool, ask at TI for advice).

High-Mountain Excursions from Zermatt

You have four options for lifts up and out of Zermatt:

1. A cable-car ride to the highest lift station in Europe, the **Matterhorn Glacier Paradise,** near the top of the Klein Matterhorn peak (not the "real" Matterhorn).

2. A side spur off the Matterhorn Glacier Paradise line leading to **Schwarzsee,** with some of the closest views you'll get of the Matterhorn.

3. An underground funicular, then gondola, then cable car to **Rothorn,** with classic Matterhorn views.

4. A train up to **Gornergrat,** for good views down on a glacier.

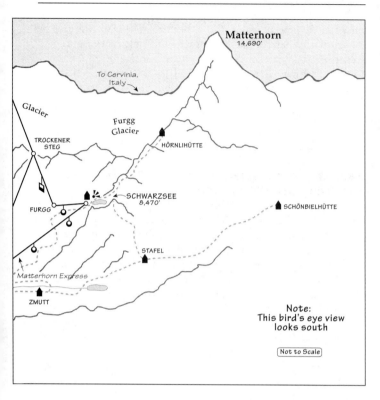

Matterhorn
14,690'

To Cervinia,
Italy

Glacier

Furgg
Glacier

TROCKENER
STEG

HÖRNLIHÜTTE

SCHWARZSEE
8,470'

SCHÖNBIELHÜTTE

FURGG

STAFEL

Matterhorn Express

ZMUTT

Note:
This bird's eye view
looks south

Not to Scale

The first trip leads to a snowy wonderland, year-round skiing slopes, and a cave carved into the ice. The other three will take you to pristine pastures with alpine lakes and Matterhorn vistas. (For more details, see the "Whatt's Whatt in Zermatt" sidebar on pages 208-209.)

Passes: If the weather's clear and your pockets are deep, consider springing for a **Peak Pass,** which gives you unlimited access to all these lifts; unfortunately, the minimum length of the pass is three days, so it's a bad value for a one- or two-day visit (3 days-190 SF, 4 days-216 SF, 5 days-214 SF). The **Panoramic Pass,** available only from mid-June to mid-September, is a better deal for a short visit; it covers Matterhorn Glacier Paradise, Schwarzsee, and Rothorn, but not Gornergrat (1 day-125 SF, 2 days-144 SF). The **Hiking Pass** gives you unlimited access to lifts up to (but not above) Trockener Steg, Schwarzsee, Blauherd, and Riffelberg (3 days-144 SF, or 108 SF with Swiss Pass). You can purchase any of these passes at lift stations or local train stations.

Individual Tickets: Buy individual tickets directly at the lift stations. Some tickets offer afternoon discounts on individual fares to Matterhorn Glacier Paradise, Schwarzsee, or Rothorn, saving you about 20 percent (valid after either 13:30 or 14:30, mid-June or July until mid-Sept or mid-Oct, depending on ticket). Eurailpass holders get a 25 percent discount on the Gornergrat train but not on other Zermatt lifts, while Swiss Pass holders pay half-price on all area lifts. For more information, see www.matterhorn paradise.ch.

Winter Sports: Note that the descriptions and prices in this section apply only to the summer season. If you're a skier or snow-boarder, ask the Zermatt TI about specifics for your visit.

▲▲Matterhorn Glacier Paradise (12,530 feet) and Schwarzsee (8,470 feet)

To really get your high-altitude high, zip up to the highest cable-car station in Europe, the Matterhorn Glacier Paradise, on the peak called Klein ("Little") Matterhorn. From way up here, the Matterhorn is just one of many cut-glass peaks—this is your best chance for a bird's-eye panorama of the Alps without hiking. But some visitors are disappointed by this particular view because it's not the classic Matterhorn profile on all the postcard racks (for that, head to Rothorn, described later).

The trip up to Klein Matterhorn has three parts. First, a small, six-seat gondola takes a six-minute ride over pretty glacier-carved foothills to the Furi station. From Furi, a larger cable car rides up to Trockener Steg. (You can also take a different gondola from Furi to Schwarzsee—described later.) Finally, the last cable car travels up to Klein Matterhorn; on the left are great views down on glaciers and across to the Gornergrat train station. All the way up, you'll see plenty of ski lifts and picturesque little chalets. The area around Klein Matterhorn stays snow-covered all year long, making it a popular place for summer skiers.

Cost: Zermatt to Matterhorn Glacier Paradise costs 100 SF round-trip (64 SF one-way; half-price with Swiss Pass); Zermatt to Schwarzsee is 49 SF round-trip (32 SF one-way, half-price with Swiss Pass, ask about afternoon discount). If you plan to do both, consider the Peak or Panoramic pass, as both cover this combo-trip and more.

Hours: The lifts up to Klein Matterhorn are open daily year-round (generally late June-Aug 6:30-16:20, Sept-late June 8:30-16:05). If the weather's iffy, confirm that the entire route (all the way to the Matterhorn Glacier Paradise) is open before you ascend—upper segments can close if it's too windy. The gondola from Furi to Schwarzsee doesn't run in late spring or late fall (mid-June-Aug 8:00-16:30, Sept-mid-Oct and late Nov-mid-May 8:30-16:30, closed mid-May-mid-June and mid-Oct-late Nov, www .zermatt.ch).

Getting There: The elevator to the Matterhorn Express station is about three-quarters of a mile upriver from the train station (simply walk down Bahnhofstrasse to the church, head toward the bridge, and follow the river; or catch an electric bus marked *Glacier* or *Bergbahnen* in front of the Gornergrat train station, across from the main train station, 2/hour).

At the Top: nonskiers have two sightseeing options—the observation deck and the Glacier Palace. As you leave the lift, follow the hall branching to the left, and take the elevator to the **observation deck** (12,200 feet). Exit the elevator and walk another 100 steps up to stunning panoramas. On a clear day, you can see Italy and France (including Mont Blanc, Europe's highest peak).

If you follow the hall from the lift all the way to the end, you'll reach the Panorama Bar and the exit. Go outside and walk a few

steps downhill to the low-profile entrance of the **Glacier Palace,** marked *Gletschergrotte* (free if you bought a full-price lift ticket, 7.50 SF if you got a Swiss-Pass discount, daily 9:30-15:45). This place brags that it's the "highest glacial grotto in the world"—a claim that must make other high-altitude glacial grottos seethe with envy.

The "Palace" is basically a big hole dug into the glacier, allowing you to walk deep inside. As you wander, you'll see ice sculptures (including the Matterhorn and some flowers encased in ice) and some lackluster exhibits about glaciers, local wines, and "glacier fleas" (a.k.a. "springtails," little bugs that live up here). You can also wriggle into an actual crevasse.

From Furi, rather than going all the way to Klein Matterhorn, you can take a gondola to the alpine lake **Schwarzsee.** Though much lower in elevation (8,470 feet), this area is the closest you can get to the Matterhorn (though it lacks the big-picture alpine panorama that the other lift excursions offer). You can also detour here on your way back down from Klein Matterhorn (when you reach Furi, follow signs to *Schwarzsee* instead of *Zermatt;* 35 SF round-trip for just this segment from Furi to Schwarzsee and back to Furi, 23 SF one-way). Several popular hiking trails lead from here back down to the valley (see below).

Hikes: You won't find any hiking paths from the very top of Klein Matterhorn, since it's covered with snow year-round. The best hike on this series of lifts is at Schwarzsee. From the Schwarzsee lift station, the hike directly down to Furi is quite steep; a longer but easier and more enjoyable route is to hike down to Stafel, then on to Furi. Downhill from Furi is the **Ricola Herb Garden,** one of six company gardens that feature the 13 medicinal herbs in Ricola cough drops. It's a 15-minute walk down from Furi or a 30-minute walk up from Zermatt, in the hamlet of Blatten (always open, best July-Sept, near Restaurant Blatten, www.ricola .ch). From Furi you can catch the gondola back to Zermatt (or continue to Zermatt on foot). Plan on the better part of a day for the full Schwarzsee-Furi-Zermatt hike; easier hikes elsewhere in the region are described later.

▲▲Rothorn (10,180 feet)

While actually farther away from the famous peak than the other lifts I've described, Rothorn offers *the* classic Matterhorn view. It's also less crowded than Gornergrat (described next). The passage up to Rothorn has three parts: first, an underground funicular to Sunnegga (eight cold minutes, bring a sweater), then a gondola to Blauherd, and, finally, a cable car to Rothorn. All along the way are typical glacial lakes, offering a picturesque foreground for your Matterhorn photos.

Cost and Hours: 66 SF round-trip, 43 SF one-way, half-price with Swiss Pass; if going up after 13:30, ask about afternoon discount. You can get to Rothorn or Blauherd only between mid-June and mid-Sept (daily 8:40-16:40, 3/hour); the lower segment, to Sunnegga, opens earlier in June and stays open through mid-October (3-6/hour). The whole shebang is open again December through late April, when the mountain is ready for skiers.

Getting There: The station for the underground funicular to Sunnegga is across the river from the Zermatt train station, just downstream from the Gornergrat train tracks.

Hikes: You have plenty of easy options for walking around the lakes up here. Get details at the TI before you ascend. Perhaps the best is the mostly level hike from the Blauherd station, around the Rothorn peak, past the Stellisee, to the restaurant at Fluhalp, then back again. If only the Sunnegga funicular is open, it's still worthwhile to go for the hiking and a great view of the Matterhorn (16 SF one-way). Try the 40-minute Murmelweg ("Marmot Path") up to Blauherd—for a good chance of spotting these fuzzy mountain mammals—or hike from Sunnegga down to Zermatt. The Gourmetweg hike (allow 1.25 hours) takes you through larch forests, and the path is covered with soft, fragrant pine needles.

▲▲Gornergrat (10,270 feet)

This viewpoint is somewhere between Klein Matterhorn and Rothorn—both geographically and in terms of your experience. A train takes you from Zermatt up to Gornergrat in about 35 minutes, with stops at other stations along the way (Findelbach, Riffelalp, Riffelberg, and Rotenboden). On the way up, sit on the right-hand side for good Matterhorn vistas. At Gornergrat you

can enjoy a sweeping alpine pan-orama with great views of the Matterhorn (though it's not the perfect profile that you see from Rothorn). What's distinctive about Gornergrat is that it offers the best views of the Gorner Glacier that runs between it and Klein Matterhorn. It also gets you up close to the *other* big mountain in the neighborhood, which is actually taller than the Matterhorn: Monte Rosa, the highest point in Switzerland (15,200 feet).

Cost and Hours: 40 SF each way—no round-trip discount, half-price with Swiss Pass, 25 percent discount with Eurailpass. Two or three trains an hour leave mid-June-Sept, starting at about 7:00 and ending at about 19:00 (fewer trains and shorter hours off-season, tel. 027-927-7000, www.gornergrat.ch).

Getting There: The Gornergrat train station is right across the street from Zermatt's train station.

Hikes: The best option is to take the train from Gornergrat back to the Rotenboden station, where you can enjoy the pretty lake called Riffelsee. Then walk down to the Riffelberg station and take the train back into Zermatt.

Other Mountain Activities

Aside from hiking and views, adventure seekers have even more opportunities for alpine thrills near Zermatt. **Tandem paragliding** is an expensive but unforgettable experience, best from Rothorn (about 190 SF; Paragliding Zermatt, tel. 027-967-6744, www.paragliding-zermatt.ch; or Alpine Adventures, mobile 079-643-6808, www.alpine-adventures-zermatt.com). The hills above Zermatt are laced with great **mountain-bike** paths (get specifics from TI). For skiing options, see "Helpful Hints," earlier.

Sleeping in Zermatt

Little Zermatt has more than a hundred hotels—and all of them are expensive. This is a resort town, plain and simple, where even the budget bunks cost big bucks. I've scrutinized the options and presented you with the best deals I could find. I've listed peak summer rates (generally highest July-Aug). You'll pay less at most places in shoulder season (June and Oct), and more during ski season (Dec-late March/early April). When there's a range, higher prices are for busy times, and lower prices are when it's slow (unless otherwise noted). Many hotels close in the shoulder season (as early as mid-April) and stay closed until some time between early

---

Sleep Code

(1 SF = about $1.10, country code: 41)
S = Single, **D** = Double/Twin, **T** = Triple, **Q** = Quad, **b** = bathroom, **s** = shower only. Unless otherwise noted, credit cards are accepted, English is spoken, and breakfast is included.

To help you sort easily through these listings, I've divided the accommodations into three categories, based on the price for a standard double room with bath during high season:

$$$ Higher Priced—Most rooms 150 SF or more.
$$ Moderately Priced—Most rooms between 110-150 SF.
$ Lower Priced—Most rooms 110 SF or less.

Prices can change without notice; verify the hotel's current rates online or by email. For other updates, see www.ricksteves.com/update.

May and late June. Of course, several hotels are open year-round.

$$$ Hotel Romantica, a scenic (and steep) block up from the main street, offers 15 rooms in a flower-dappled chalet surrounded by old-fashioned huts. If you like all those huts, consider sleeping in one—this hotel has converted two of them into accommodations. Both have tiny interiors with two stories: sitting room and modern bathroom downstairs, loft bedroom upstairs. Choose between the very low-ceilinged and rustic hut (cozy and romantic) or the hut with more modern finishes (Sb-85-90 SF, Db-160-210 SF, huts-220 SF, prices depend on room quality and season, free Wi-Fi, elevator, closed roughly Easter-June, tel. 027-966-2650, fax 027-966-2655, www.reconline.ch/romantica, romantica.zermatt @reconline.ch, Cremonini family).

$$$ Hotel Le Mazot has nine cozy, nicely renovated rooms—four with Matterhorn-view balconies worth the extra francs—in a central but quiet location next to the river and above an intimate restaurant (S-55-65 SF, Db-140-170 SF, Db with big view balcony-150-180 SF, extra bed-40 SF, open May-mid-Dec only, free Wi-Fi, Hofmattstrasse 23, tel. 027-966-0606, fax 027-966-0607, www.lemazotzermatt.ch, le.mazot@reconline.ch).

$$$ Hotel Jägerhof has 48 homey rooms and lots of charm. It's a little farther from the center, across the river toward the Matterhorn Express lift station. Its rustic lounge is plenty cozy on rainy days (Sb-88 SF, Db-176 SF, Tb-238 SF, Qb-300 SF, pricier in ski season, some doubles have balconies, elevator, pay Internet access, free Wi-Fi, fitness room, tel. 027-966-3800, fax 027-966-3808, www.hoteljaegerhofzermatt.ch, jaegerhof@zermatt.ch, Perren family). From the train station, walk or take either the green- or red-line bus to the Kirchbrücke stop (across the river from the Catholic church). From there, walk up Kirchstrasse (away from the river) one more block, then hang a right onto Steinmattstrasse; just after the building labeled *Biners Backstube,* take the left fork and look for the small wooden *Hotel Jägerhof* sign on your left.

$$ Hotel Tannenhof is a great value hiding a few steps off the main drag behind a fancy hotel that steals the Matterhorn views. Its 23 rooms are small, tight, and woody, without much character, but the location is good and the place is well-run (S-55 SF, Sb-80 SF, D-100 SF, Db-120-130 SF, T-120 SF, thin walls, pay Internet access and Wi-Fi, Englischer Viertel 3, tel. 027-967-3188, fax 027-967-3173, www.rhone.ch/tannenhof, hotel-tannenhof@rhone.ch, Schaller family).

$$ Hotel Weisshorn offers 16 basic but comfortable rooms over a restaurant, right in the heart of town. The rooms are nothing special (even the three with balconies), but the rates are reasonable (S-61-68 SF, Sb-75-84 SF, D-104-126 SF, Db-130-166 SF, T-147-165 SF, prices vary by season, Am Bach 6, tel. 027-967-1112, fax 027-967-3839, www.holidaynet.ch/weisshorn, welcome @weisshorn-zermatt.ch).

$$ Hotel Bahnhof, with 17 tidy alpine-style rooms (and 3 dorm rooms), is in a 1902 building so completely remodeled that it feels brand-new. The basement features a relaxing lounge, a dining room, and a large guests' kitchen (often dominated by big groups). Rooms without baths have Matterhorn-view balconies. It's well-run, but management is offsite at night—so if the younger crowd comes back late after partying, you're on your own. It's conveniently located across the street from the train station (dorm bed-40 SF, S-70-80 SF, Sb-80-90 SF, D-100-110 SF, Db-110-145 SF, Qb-210-245 SF, breakfast-15 SF, nice showers, handy coin-op laundry facilities, free Wi-Fi, lockers, closed May and mid-Oct-Nov, tel. 027-967-2406, fax 027-967-7216, www.hotelbahnhof.com, welcome@hotelbahnhof.com, Lauber family).

$ Zermatt's official Youth Hostel is sparkling new. It looks over town from a perch high above the river and offers views of the Matterhorn. The hostel is slick and super-modern, with key cards and bathrooms inside most rooms. Travelers of all ages will feel comfortable here. The hostel is an especially good deal since the rates include breakfast and dinner—a real plus in expensive Zermatt (prices per person: in 8-bed room-51 SF, in 6-bed room with bathroom-54-64 SF, in 4-bed room without bathroom-58-68 SF, in 4-bed room with bathroom-62-74 SF, in twin D-68-84 SF, in D with one big bed-76-106 SF, in Db with one big bed-86-111 SF, nonmembers pay 6 SF more, all rates include sheets, pay Internet access, free Wi-Fi, laundry facilities, no age limit, no curfew, Staldenweg 5, tel. 027-967-2320, fax 027-967-5306, www.youthhostel.ch/zermatt, zermatt@youthhostel.ch). From the station, take the bus marked *Winkelmatten* to the Luchre stop (3.20 SF); the hostel is a steep hike up from there (follow the signs with the international hostel symbol). To avoid the steep walk, take the bus one more stop and walk downhill while keeping an eye out for the big, modern, gray building on the right (not signed if walking downhill).

$ Matterhorn Hostel is a more low-key, easygoing place over-looking the river. Its mission is to provide cheap beds in an expensive town, and it delivers. The floor plan is claustrophobic, with not an inch of wasted space: 10 dorm rooms with graffiti decor are upstairs (some with Matterhorn-view balconies); the lounge and showers are in the basement; and a tiny Internet nook (free access) is tucked under the spiral staircase (bed in 6- to 8-bed dorm-36 SF, in 4-bed room-41 SF, in 2- or 3-bed room-46 SF, cash preferred, breakfast-8 SF, towel rental-2 SF, sheets-3.50 SF, free Wi-Fi, closed 10:00-16:00, or 11:00-16:00 in peak season, Schluhmattstrasse 32, tel. 027-968-1919, fax 027-968-1915, www.matterhornhostel.com, info@matterhornhostel.com). It's a 15-minute walk from the train station on the way up to the Matterhorn Express lift station, above the river. Take either the green-line bus to the Kirchbrücke stop (2.50 SF; red line also stops here but costs a little more), then follow Schluhmattstrasse upstream for a few minutes—look for signs for Sparky's restaurant, on the right.

Eating in Zermatt

Zermatt's restaurants are as expensive as its hotels. But cheap snack bar-type places aren't too hard to find, and you can easily assemble a picnic at one of the town's several bakeries and grocery stores. For sit-down meals, simply wander the town and pick the place that looks best; the streets are lined with restaurants featuring garish signs, interchangeable menus, and high prices. I ate well without breaking the bank at the eateries listed here. The first two are obvious and touristy (with Japanese signs outside), but the prices and food are acceptable, and you may see locals mixed in with the out-of-towners.

Whymper-Stube, named for the first brave soul to conquer the Matterhorn, specializes in cheese dishes—that means fondue (about 25 SF/person) and raclette (8 SF/serving, two servings is enough for most). While American, French, and Japanese tourists photograph each other eating fondue, six barstools in the corner are warmed by local regulars. On weekend nights in peak season, reservations are smart (kitchen open daily 12:00-14:00 & 18:00-22:00 but fondue and cold dishes are served daily 11:00-22:00, shorter hours in winter, friendly staff, on Bahnhofstrasse—the main drag, tel. 027-967-2296).

Restaurant du Pont claims to be the oldest restaurant in town. Note that it doesn't claim to be the best. Its ambience—with low ceilings and Swiss folk sayings on the walls—beats the food (fondue for two-44 SF, *Rösti* for about 15 SF, daily 12:00-22:00, cash only, on Bahnhofstrasse at end of square with big Catholic church, tel. 027-967-4343).

Pizza Roma offers a good value, a friendly staff, and an escape from the worst tourist hordes. Dine in the warm, woody interior or outside on the sidewalk (16-22-SF daily specials, good 19-27-SF wood-fired pizzas, 20-25-SF pasta dishes, daily 18:30-22:30; from Bahnhofstrasse, turn up Kirchstrasse—it's on the right a few blocks up the hill after you cross the river; tel. 027-967-3229).

Sandwiches and Kebabs: Smack in the middle of town, across from the Catholic church, sits **Take-Away "Wilde-Hilde,"** a no-frills deli that makes fresh sandwiches on demand (7-11 SF depending on size, Tue-Sun 9:00-19:00, closed Mon, Kirchplatz, tel. 027-967-0209). It's the ground floor of the former home of the two Peter Taugwalders (father and son), mountain guides on the first Matterhorn ascent. Just a few more yards down Bahnhofstrasse is a kebab shop that's open later (daily 11:00-21:00, Oberdorfstrasse 24).

Supermarkets: **Co-op** is across from the train station (Mon-Sat 8:00-19:00, closed Sun), **Migros** is across from the tennis courts on Hofmattstrasse (Mon-Sat 8:30-18:30, closed Sun), and **Pam** is across the river, on Kirchstrasse (Mon-Sat 8:00-12:30 & 14:00-18:30, Sun 16:00-18:30).

Zermatt Connections

Zermatt is at the end of the Nikolai Valley, which you can only reach on the privately operated Matterhorn Gotthard Railway (MGB, www.mgbahn.ch). It connects Zermatt to Visp and Brig hourly (1.25 hours, second-class fares: 34 SF one-way to Visp, 35 SF to Brig, covered by Swiss Pass, 25 percent discount with Eurailpass—buy discounted tickets at counter in station). From Visp and Brig, you can easily connect to destinations all over the country. Swiss Rail (SBB) info: toll tel. 0900-300-300 (1.19 SF/minute) or www.rail.ch.

From Zermatt by Train to: Bern (hourly, 2.25 hours, transfer in Visp), **Zürich** (hourly, 3.25 hours, transfer in Visp), **Montreux** (hourly, 2.5 hours, transfer in Visp), **Lausanne** (hourly, 3 hours, transfer in Visp), **Interlaken Ost** (hourly, 2.25 hours, transfer in Visp and Spiez), **Luzern** (hourly, 3.25 hours, transfer in Visp and Bern).

By Glacier Express to Eastern Switzerland: In summer, four trains depart Zermatt daily and arc scenically on high-altitude tracks over the middle of Switzerland to the east. All of these Glacier Express trains go through **Chur** (6 hours), then continue either to **Davos** or **St. Moritz** (8 hours total to either). In winter, there's one train per day in each direction. These trains don't require a transfer in Visp or Brig. For more details, see the Scenic Rail Journeys chapter.

APPENZELL

Welcome to cowbell country. In the moo-mellow and storybook-friendly Appenzell region, you'll find the warm, intimate side of the land of staggering, icy Alps. With just one percent of Switzerland's territory and one percent of its population, the little canton of Appenzell stubbornly celebrates its way of life. You'll see its symbol everywhere: a scary bear walking upright, yielding its sharp claws and teeth. And yet the people here are mellow and welcoming. You'll savor Appenzell's cozy, small-town atmosphere.

Appenzell is Switzerland's most traditional region...and the butt of jokes because of it. Entire villages meet in town squares such as Appenzell town's Landsgemeindeplatz to vote (an event featured on most postcard racks). Until 1990, the women of Appenzell couldn't vote on local issues. Lately, the region has become more progressive. In 2000, its schools were the first in Switzerland to make English—rather than French—the mandatory second language.

A gentle beauty blankets this region of green, rolling hills, watched over by the 8,200-foot peak of Mount Säntis (Appenzell's highest point). As you travel, you'll enjoy an ever-changing parade of finely carved chalets, colorful villages, and cows moaning, "Milk me." While farmers' bikini-clad daughters make hay, old ladies with scythes walk the steep roads, looking as if they just pushed the Grim Reaper down the hill. When locals are asked about Appenzeller cheese, they clench their fists as they answer, "It's the best." (It is, without any doubt, the smelliest.)

If you're here in late August or early September, there's a good chance you'll get in on (or at least have your road blocked by) the ceremonial procession of flower-bedecked cows and whistling herders in formal folk costumes. The festive march down from the high pastures is a spontaneous move by the herding families, and when they finally do burst into town (a slow-motion Swiss Pamplona), locals young and old become children again, running joyously onto the streets.

Planning Your Time

On a two-week trip through Switzerland, save a day for the Appenzell region. This pastoral area offers a good first look at Switzerland—but would be anticlimactic after the rugged Berner Oberland or Matterhorn. If you have only a week or less in Switzerland, skip the subtle charms of Appenzell and head instead for the high mountains.

In the Appenzell region, I prefer overnighting up on Ebenalp to really get away from it all. But if that mountaintop retreat's rustic accommodations and steep hikes aren't your cup of tea, consider the comfort of sleeping in Appenzell town, which is also a more efficient base for getting around the region.

Getting Around Appenzell

Appenzell is a breeze by **car**—you could see everything in this chapter in one (very busy) day. Notice that the attractions in Stein and Urnäsch and the Kronberg luge ride form a handy little loop to the west of town. The lift up to Ebenalp is just to the south.

Appenzell town is a convenient public-transportation hub. Regional narrow-gauge trains are operated by Appenzeller Bahnen (www.appenzellerbahnen.ch). From Appenzell town, a very handy **train** generally runs twice an hour (except in the early afternoon and after 20:00, when it's hourly), connecting most destinations I describe. It goes from Appenzell south to Wasserauen (base of Ebenalp lift, 11 minutes); the same train runs west from Appenzell, stopping at Gontenbad (one end of the Barefoot Walk, 3 minutes), Jakobsbad (luge ride and other end of the Barefoot Walk, 9 minutes), Urnäsch (folk museum, 16 minutes), then north to Herisau (33 minutes; change here to reach St. Gallen or Luzern), and Gossau (40 minutes; change here to reach Zürich or St. Gallen).

Regional **buses** also connect towns several times a day; for schedules, check with the TI or the post office.

The one destination in this chapter not well covered by public transportation is Stein (with its cheesemaking showcase and

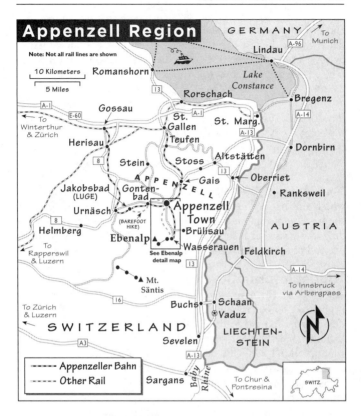

Appenzell Region

Note: Not all rail lines are shown

10 Kilometers
5 Miles

GERMANY — To Munich
A-96
Lindau
Lake Constance
Romanshorn
13
Rorschach
Bregenz
A-14
Gossau
St. Gallen
St. Marg.
A-13
Teufen
Altstätten
Dornbirn
Herisau
Stein
Stoss
Oberriet
Gais
Ranksweil
Jakobsbad (LUGE)
Gonten-bad
Appenzell Town
AUSTRIA
Urnäsch
(BAREFOOT HIKE)
Brülisau
Helmberg
Ebenalp
Wasserauen
Feldkirch
See Ebenalp detail map
A-14
To Rapperswil & Luzern
To Innsbruck via Arlbergpass
Mt. Säntis
16
Buchs
Schaan
To Zürich & Luzern
Vaduz
SWITZERLAND
LIECHTEN-STEIN
A3
Sevelen
A-13
N
—·—·— Appenzeller Bahn
— — — Other Rail
Sargans
Baby Rhine
To Chur & Pontresina
SWITZ.

folk museum). Appenzell's shuttle service, **PubliCar,** takes passengers to locations not serviced by buses (for Appenzell to Stein, figure about 9 SF, or 5 SF with Swiss Pass or Appenzell Card). To reserve, inquire at the TI or post office, or call 0848-553-060.

Appenzell Town

In this authentically Swiss town, kids play "barn" instead of "house,"

while Mom and Dad watch yodeling on TV. The town center is a painfully cute pedestrian zone lined with some of Switzerland's most colorful housefronts. This is a great spot to simply let your pulse slow and enjoy Swiss small-town life. The big square of Landsgemeindeplatz—at the far

APPENZELL

end of Hauptgasse from the town church and TI—is where residents gather the last Sunday of each April to vote on local issues by show of hands. (The rest of the year, it's a parking lot.) A fountain on the square shows an Appenzeller raising his hand to be counted.

Appenzell town is touristy, sure. But from watching the locals robustly greet each other in the streets or laugh over a local beer in the pubs, it's clear this is also a real, living town.

Orientation to Appenzell

Tiny Appenzell town clusters along its main street, Hauptgasse, which runs from the bridge over the Sitter River to the biggest square, Landsgemeindeplatz. From the middle of this colorful drag, Postgasse heads south to the train station. You can walk from one end of town to the other in about 10 minutes.

Tourist Information

The TI is on the main street at Hauptgasse 4 (May-Sept Mon-Fri 9:00-12:00 & 13:30-18:00, Sat-Sun 10:00-12:00 & 14:00-17:00; Oct-April Mon-Fri 9:00-12:00 & 14:00-17:00, Sat-Sun 14:00-17:00; tel. 071-788-9641). For information on the greater Appenzell region, call 071-898-3300 or check out www.appenzell.info.

If you stay for several days in the region, you'll receive an **Appenzell Card** from your hotel that covers all local train trips (on trains operated by Appenzeller Bahnen, as far as St. Gallen), free rides on three different cable cars, free admission to local museums, a free ride on the Kronberg luge, a discounted rate on the PubliCar shuttle service (5 SF), and more (the details of exactly what's covered by this card are subject to change from year to year). The card is free of charge, but only if you're staying three nights or longer. Hotels and some smaller pensions offer the card; ask when you reserve.

Arrival in Appenzell Town

From the **train** station—possibly Switzerland's cutest—walk straight ahead up Postgasse to Postplatz, then follow Poststrasse up to Hauptgasse, where you'll run directly into the TI.

If arriving by **car**, ask your hotel about parking. If you're just day-tripping here, leave your car in the free lot by the brewery (in the blue zone, you're limited to one hour; the white zone is unlimited). Walk across the bridge and veer right onto the main drag, Hauptgasse. You'll see a large church on your right, with the TI and Appenzell Museum just past it.

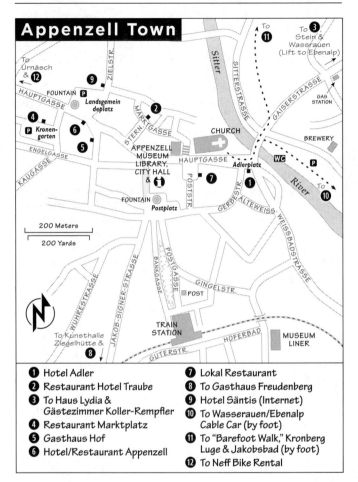

1. Hotel Adler
2. Restaurant Hotel Traube
3. To Haus Lydia & Gästezimmer Koller-Rempfler
4. Restaurant Marktplatz
5. Gasthaus Hof
6. Hotel/Restaurant Appenzell
7. Lokal Restaurant
8. To Gasthaus Freudenberg
9. Hotel Säntis (Internet)
10. To Wasserauen/Ebenalp Cable Car (by foot)
11. To "Barefoot Walk," Kronberg Luge & Jakobsbad (by foot)
12. To Neff Bike Rental

Helpful Hints

Blue Monday: Appenzell's museums are closed on Monday, but hiking and biking are good any day the sun shines. The Kronberg luge (in Jakobsbad) runs every day, unless it's raining.

When the Cows Come Home: If you're here at the right time, you might luck into seeing the festive procession of cows heading up to the high-mountain pastures (*Alpfahrt,* generally late May-early June) or returning from a summer high in the Alps (*Alpabfahrt,* generally late Aug-early Sept). Unfortunately, the cows don't give much advance notice—announcements of the event pop up around town just a few days ahead. If you want to be sure to fit some cows into your itinerary, you can catch them in the Appenzell cattle show, usually the first Tuesday in October. For more on the cow culture of the Swiss Alps, see the sidebar on page 170.

Internet Access: Use the computers at the **library,** which shares a building with the TI and the Appenzell Museum (3 SF/30 minutes, after that 1 SF/15 minutes; Tue and Thu 9:30-11:30 & 14:00-17:00, Wed 14:00-17:00, Fri 16:30-19:30, Sat 9:30-11:30, closed Sun-Mon). **Hotel Säntis** has a stand-up computer in its lobby (5 SF/30 minutes, free for guests, Landsgemeindeplatz 3).

Post Office: It's in front of the train station (Mon-Fri 7:30-12:00 & 13:30-18:00, Sat 8:00-11:00, closed Sun).

Bike Rental: You can rent wheels at the train station (20 SF/half-day, 25 SF/day, return bike by 18:00). Most hotels rent bikes or can arrange a rental for you. For mountain bikes, go to the garage of **Elmar Neff,** a five-minute walk beyond Landsgemeindeplatz (20 SF/half-day, 30 SF/day, Mon-Fri 7:30-12:00 & 13:15-18:30, Sat 7:30-12:00 & 13:15-16:00, closed Sun, Hauptgasse 58, tel. 071-787-3477).

Sights in Appenzell

The Appenzell region has three folk museums—one in Appenzell town, another in Stein, and a third in Urnäsch. All are good, and they're different enough that visiting all three is worth considering if you have ample time and interest. To be more selective, weigh these differences: Stein's is the biggest, most modern, and probably the best-presented (but also the most difficult to reach without a car); Urnäsch's is the most atmospheric, as it's in a creaky old house; and Appenzell town's is the most convenient, giving a good all-around look at the region (it's especially strong on local costumes) but lacking a bit of the charm of the other two.

In Appenzell Town

▲**Appenzell Museum**—The folk moo-seum above the TI pro-vides a fine look at the local cow culture. Buy your ticket, borrow the English trans-lations, and ride the elevator five floors up. From the elevator, detour up the stairs to the attic for a collection of coins, measure-ment instruments, and torture devices. Check out the excellent collection of tra-ditional costumes on the fifth floor, then work your way down, wandering through the rest of the exhibits as you go. You'll see old flags and banners, reconstructed rustic rooms, woodcarvings, 19th-century peas-

ant art, handmade embroidery, and (oddly) an Egyptian coffin. One thought-provoking room displays boards called *Rebretter*, which were used to lay out the body of a recently deceased loved one. The boards were painted with the name and information of the deceased and, after the burial, displayed on the family's house.

Cost and Hours: 7 SF, covered by Swiss Pass; April-Oct daily 10:00-12:00 & 14:00-17:00; Nov-March Tue-Sun 14:00-17:00, closed Mon; Hauptgasse 4, tel. 071-788-9631.

▲**Folk Music**—The accordion never really caught on here, making Appenzell's folk music, which still uses older instruments (violin, dulcimer), unique in Switzerland. Free concerts take place every Thursday (mid-June-mid-Oct) at 18:30 in City Hall, and every Wednesday at 20:00 at Hotel Hof Weissbad (about 2 miles out of town, on the way to Wasserauen, tel. 071-798-8080). You may also find live music at local restaurants—ask at the TI.

Modern Art Museums—Appenzell has two modern/contemporary-art exhibits in great settings: **Museum Liner** is a silver-clad modern building right behind the train tracks (Unterrainstrasse 5, tel. 071-788-1800), and **Kunsthalle Ziegelhütte** is a bit farther out, at Ziegeleistrasse 14 (tel. 071-788-1860).

Cost and Hours: Each one costs 9 SF, but a 15-SF combo-ticket gets you into both; also covered by Swiss Pass; April-Oct Tue-Fri 10:00-12:00 & 14:00-17:00, Sat-Sun 11:00-17:00, closed Mon; Nov-March Tue-Sat 14:00-17:00, Sun 11:00-17:00, closed Mon; www.museumliner.ch.

Hiking

Appenzell makes a good home base for hiking, with gentle hills and pastoral scenery all around. The TI can suggest several easy walks in the region. I recommended two possibilities here.

Appenzell to Wasserauen—This two-hour walk, which takes you to the foot of the Ebenalp cable car (described on page 234), begins near the parish church in Appenzell and leads you along a creek through meadows and forests. The path is well-marked. Once you reach Wasserauen, you can take the cable car up to Ebenalp, or simply hop on the train back to Appenzell.

Barefoot Walk (Barfussweg)—This 1.5-hour walk between Jakobsbad and Gontenbad offers a surprising and unusual experience...yes, with your shoes off. The trail leads over meadows, through creeks, and on stretches of asphalted road, in a tranquil valley roughly parallel to the Appenzell-Urnäsch road and rail line. Two specially designed fountains along the way will refresh your feet. The path was inspired by the philosophy of 19th-century therapist Sebastian Kneipp, who sought to treat medical conditions with water of different temperatures and pressures.

To get from Appenzell to the trailhead, take the train to

Jakobsbad (1-2/hour, 9 minutes, trailhead right across the street from the train station and the Kronberg luge ticket office—described later), and do the barefoot walk to Gontenbad. From Gontenbad, you can ride the train back to Appenzell (3 minutes), or keep on walking (another 45-60 min).

Near Appenzell Town

▲Stein

The unassuming, hill-capping village of Stein has two worthwhile attractions, side by side: A cheese production facility with a visitors center, and arguably the region's best folk museum. Stein is very difficult to reach by public transportation; if you don't have a car, use the PubliCar service (described on page 223).

Appenzeller Demonstration Cheese Dairy (Appenzeller Schaukäserei)—This facility is where the Appenzeller brand—a major local producer—makes its cheese and explains the process to visitors. It's fast, smelly, and user-friendly. As you enter, ask about the next English showing of the 10-minute video (which treads a fine line between informative and promotional). Large, colorful displays trace the cheesemaking process, and you can peer down into the production facility (cheese is generally being made 9:00-17:00—most interesting when they pour the contents of the giant vat into the long line of wheel molds). You'll learn how the special pungent flavor of Appenzeller cheese comes from an age-old, secret-recipe herbal brine mixture that's lovingly rubbed on each wheel as it ages. Down the long hallway, watch hundreds of wheels of cheese silently age. Then head into the tasting area, where you can nibble on the various types of Appenzeller brand cheese. The ladies at the cheese counter love to cut it so you can sample it. Notice how the age affects the aroma and taste. The dairy also sells yogurt and cold drinks, and the restaurant serves powerful cheese specialties.

Cost and Hours: Advance reservations required for free guided tour, 15-SF self-guided iPad tour (can be shared), daily April-Oct 8:30-18:30, Nov-March 8:30-17:30, tel. 071-368-5070, www.showcheese.ch.

Appenzell Folklore Museum (Appenzeller Volkskunde Museum)—This excellent museum offers a modern, well-presented look at the folk culture in these parts. Borrow the essential English translations at the entry, then explore the three floors of exhibits. The ground floor is dedicated to local customs and lifestyles. The replica of the alpine cheesemaking hut is occasionally used for live demonstrations. There's a huge collection of cowbells, which, according to the explanation, are used for various purposes: to scare off evil spirits, to make the lead cow easier to follow in processions, to more easily find a lost cow..."and anyway, cows like them." Upstairs is an art collection entitled "Peasant Painting 1600-1900," with everything from huge murals from the sides of barns to delicate oil paintings to miniature wood carvings—virtually all featuring pastoral countryside scenes of cheesemaking

huts, cows, and rolling meadows. Each of the "naive" (untrained) artists who created these works is explained in a short bio, which brings the collection to life. You'll see great examples of the

brightly painted traditional regional furniture (also easy to find in local hotels and restaurants). The basement shows off more furniture pieces (in the replica of a traditional bedroom, notice how the colorful paint makes the furniture stand out from the plain wooden walls). But the focus here is on two other local crafts: weaving and embroidery. The exhibit explains how embroidery gradually evolved from simple handmade to machine-made, as it went from a craft to an industry. The rustic loom and the giant embroidery machine are sometimes used for demonstrations.

Cost and Hours: 7 SF, covered by Swiss Pass, Tue-Sun 10:00-17:00, closed Mon, tel. 071-368-5056, www.appenzeller-museum .ch.

Demonstrations: A visit to this museum is best on Saturdays and summer Wednesdays, when demonstrations are going on (cheesemaking starts at 13:00, most interesting around 14:45). If you're interested in one of these demos, call ahead to ask when is the best time to come.

▲Urnäsch

This appealing one-street town has Europe's cutest museum.

Museum of Appenzell Customs (Appenzeller Brauchtums-museum)—On the town square, this museum brings this region's folk traditions to life. They are displayed on four floors of two adjacent, different-as-day-and-night buildings. Though the new building is slick and mostly used for temporary exhibits, the 400-year-old, aptly named "Old House" has low ceilings, dramatically sloping funhouse floors, and lots of creaks. Warm and homey,

it's a happy little honeycomb of Appenzeller culture—you'll feel like a local invited you over to his house for a visit. First ask to watch an English showing of the 20-minute movie that explains four of the major regional festivals. The most memorable is Silvesterchläus—the Appenzell New Year, celebrated on January 13 per the old Julian calendar. On this date, local men celebrate by putting on gigantic, cartoonish headdresses and giant cowbells. You'll see some of those costumes—and others—then twist your way up through the tiny halls and staircases, pausing to look at replicas of local rooms, collections of handicrafts and tools, and other slices of Appenzell life. On the top floor of the new building, don't miss the music room, where you can try your hand at traditional musical instruments, including a hammered dulcimer and a coin-in-a-bowl (which, in the right hands, is more musical than you might think). There's no English, and barely any German, but it's still fun to explore.

Cost and Hours: 6 SF, covered by Swiss Pass; April-Oct Mon-Sat 9:00-11:30 & 13:30-17:00, Sun 13:30-17:00; Nov-March Mon-Sat 9:00-11:30, closed Sun; tel. 071-364-2322, www.museum-urnaesch.ch.

Kronberg Luge Ride (Bobbahn)

Between Appenzell and Urnäsch, in the village of Jakobsbad, you can enjoy a bobsled ride that runs on steel rails from May through October. Each sled has seatbelts and can carry two people. Two handles at the side allow you to control the speed: Push to accelerate, pull to brake. Respect the *Bremsen!* signs—which suggest when to brake—and don't come too close to the sled in front of you. The luge doesn't run in rainy weather; if the skies look iffy, call ahead to check. One ride lasts about seven minutes. The same entertainment zone includes a chairlift for hikes, as well as a high-ropes course.

Cost and Hours: 9 SF per sled for adults—two adults can share one sled, 6 SF per sled for kids—ditto, 81 SF/10 rides, 153 SF/20 rides, 270 SF/40 rides, multiple-ride cards are shareable; July-mid-Oct daily 9:00-18:00; May-June and mid-Oct-late Nov Mon-Fri 9:00-17:00, Sat-Sun 9:00-18:00; closed late Nov-April except might run on good-weather weekends—call to ask; tel. 071-794-1289, www.kronberg.ch. Jakobsbad is a very easy side-trip by train from Appenzell (1-2/hour, 9-minute trip, luge just across the tracks from the train station).

APPENZELL

Sleeping in Appenzell Town

Sleep in touristy Appenzell town if you want comfort—but for a rustic, high-altitude thrill, I love the low-tech, no-shower dorms at Ebenalp (described later). Appenzell town is small, and the hotels are central. All hotels offer the Appenzell Card to guests who stay at least three nights. When I've listed a range, it's based on season; the highest prices are for July through September. The *Privatzimmer* are a 10- to 20-minute hike from the town center.

Hotels

$$$ Hotel Adler, above a delicious café/bakery with the best croissants in town (generally Tue-Thu 7:30-19:30, closed Wed), is in a building that dates from 1562 and boasts a historic wine cellar. The hotel has two types of rooms: modern or traditional Appenzeller (with lamps imitating the local farmer headwear). Helpful Franz Leu, proud to be an Appenzeller, has turned the halls and traditional rooms of his hotel into a museum of regional art and culture (Sb-100-120 SF, Db-170-200 SF, "superior" Db-190-220 SF, suite-240-260 SF, closed in Feb, elevator, free Internet access and Wi-Fi, pleasant lounge, Herr Leu can arrange bike rentals for guests, between TI and bridge on Adlerplatz, tel. 071-787-1389, fax 071-787-1365, www.adlerhotel.ch, info@adlerhotel.ch).

$$$ Restaurant Hotel Traube, just off Hauptgasse near Landsgemeindeplatz, rents seven cozy, tastefully decorated, modern rooms above a fine restaurant. The friendly Hunziker family has welcomed guests here for three generations, and they still do it

---

Sleep Code

(1 SF = about $1.10, country code: 41)
S = Single, **D** = Double/Twin, **T** = Triple, **Q** = Quad, **b** = bathroom, **s** = shower only. Unless otherwise noted, credit cards are accepted, English is spoken, and breakfast is included.

To help you sort easily through these listings, I've divided the accommodations into three categories, based on the price for a standard double room with bath during high season:

$$$ Higher Priced—Most rooms 130 SF or more.
$$ Moderately Priced—Most rooms between 50-130 SF.
$ Lower Priced—Most rooms 50 SF or less.

Prices can change without notice; verify the hotel's current rates online or by email. For other updates, see www.ricksteves.com/update.

APPENZELL

with style (Sb-100-120 SF, Db-160-180 SF, free Wi-Fi, Marktgasse 7, tel. 071-787-1407, fax 071-787-2419, www.hotel-traube.ch, info @hotel-traube.ch). Don't confuse Hotel Traube ("grape" in German) with the similarly named Hotel Taube ("dove") nearby.

Privatzimmer

To experience a pleasant Swiss suburban neighborhood, consider the following B&Bs, just east of Appenzell's pedestrian zone. To reach them from the town center (TI/town church), cross the bridge, pass the Mercedes-Esso station, then take the next right. You'll reach Koller-Rempfler first (just a few houses down), then— after another 500 yards or so—Haus Lydia.

   $$ Haus Lydia, a six-room, Appenzell-style home filled with tourist information and a woodsy folk atmosphere, has a garden and a powerful mountain view. (That's Ebenalp on the horizon.) Its crisp, nicely decorated rooms are a fine option if you have a car or don't mind a 20-minute walk from the town center (Sb-68-78 SF, Db-116 SF, great breakfast, pay Internet access and free Wi-Fi, Eggerstandenstrasse 53, tel. 071-787-4233, fax 071-787-8633, www .hauslydia.ch, contact@hauslydia.ch, friendly Frau Mock-Inauen). She also rents two roomy apartments by the week (Db-77-100 SF depending on season, plus 50-90-SF cleaning fee, breakfast extra).

   $$ Gästezimmer Koller-Rempfler is a classic Germanic guesthouse renting four old-fashioned but comfortable rooms (Db-104-110 SF, Tb-156-165 SF, cash only, Wi-Fi, Eggerstandenstrasse 9, tel. 071-787-2117, niklauskoller@hotmail.com, Margaret and Niklaus speak just enough English).

Eating in Appenzell

In Appenzell, menus and prices are similar from place to place— it's fairly expensive but good local cuisine, usually featuring (surprise) the heavenly but oh-so-smelly Appenzeller cheese. The Appenzeller beer is tasty, famous, and about the only thing cheap in the region. Many top restaurants cluster around the big square called Landsgemeindeplatz. All restaurants are open daily from about 8:00 to 24:00 unless otherwise noted.

   Restaurant Hotel Traube, at the recommended hotel of the same name, combines fresh ingredients to create a wide selection of Swiss and Appenzeller meals. Sit outside on the terrace, or in the woody dining room. Their affordable "small dishes," for 10-20 SF, are plenty filling (19-37-SF main dishes, vegetarian options, Tue-Sun 9:00-24:00, closed Mon, Marktgasse 7, tel. 071-787-1407).

   Restaurant Marktplatz is filled with locals playing cards in a genuine Appenzeller atmosphere. Enjoy the beautifully detailed inlaid tables and the wood-carved wall panels (24-44-SF main dishes, Fri-Tue 11:00-14:30 & 17:30-23:00, no midday break on weekends, closed Wed-Thu and early July-early Aug, on small parking lot across from Landsgemeindeplatz fountain, walk around white building with horse head, tel. 071-787-1204). On summer Mondays, the restaurant hosts evening concerts by young dulcimer musicians.

Gasthaus Hof, which feels particularly local, offers a bewildering variety of specials (from "vitamin corner" to cold dishes to the *Fitnessteller*). There's a sprawling beer garden out back, and the cozy dining room is filled with the unforgettable aroma of Appenzeller cheese (most dishes 15-30 SF, Engelgasse 4, tel. 071-787-4030).

Hotel Appenzell fills a formal dining room that feels like a genteel café. They have a seasonal menu and specialize in vegetarian dishes, though they also serve meat dishes (20-33-SF main dishes, Tue closed until 14:00, at corner of square closest to TI, tel. 071-788-1515).

Lokal is modern, Italian, and the opposite of every other eatery in Appenzell. This low-key café serves made-to-order focaccia sandwiches, crêpes, and gelato for takeaway or to eat in the mod interior or out front (6-SF crêpes, 6-11-SF sandwiches, Sun 12:00-19:00, Tue-Sat 9:00-19:00—until 18:00 in winter, Fri-Sat in summer until 22:00, closed Mon, am Schmäuslemarkt, tel. 071-787-0115).

With a View over Town: **Gasthaus Freudenberg** has reasonably priced meals and sweeping panoramas over Appenzell's rooftops from outdoor tables. If you'd like to dine with a view, it's worth the steep, 15-minute uphill walk or short drive from the town center (fixed-price meals from 27 SF, veggie dishes available, closed Wed and Nov; go under train station, turn right, and follow yellow *Freudenberg* signs through a residential zone, then up through the hills; tel. 071-787-1240). Drivers can follow the yellow *Freudenberg* signs from near the train station.

With a Grand Alpine View: If you're heading up to Ebenalp for a hike in the afternoon, consider sticking around for an early dinner at **Berggasthaus Aescher,** which begins serving around 17:30. But carefully note the last lift down; outside of summer, this isn't a practical option if you need to return to Appenzell to sleep (unless you want to hike down). For details on the lift and the restaurant, see the "Ebenalp" section, later.

Appenzell Connections

For taking the train to destinations within this chapter, see "Getting Around Appenzell" on page 222. Remember that for connections beyond the Appenzell region, you'll generally change in either Herisau or Gossau.

From Appenzell Town by Train to: Zürich (2/hour, 1.75 hours with change in Gossau, 2.25 hours with change in St. Gallen), **Chur** (2/hour, 2-2.5 hours, 1-3 changes, easiest via St. Gallen), **Luzern** (2/hour, 2.75 hours, 1-2 changes), **Bern** (hourly, 3 hours, transfer in Gossau), Interlaken (at least hourly, 4-4.5 hours, 2-3 transfers), **Lausanne** (2/hour, 4-4.5 hours, transfer in Gossau or St. Gallen), **Munich** (3/day, 4.5 hours, transfer in St. Gallen). Train info: toll tel. 0900-300-300 (1.19 SF/minute) or www.rail.ch.

Ebenalp

This mountain features wonderful views and a cliff-hanging, family-run hut, providing a "hills are alive" thin-air alternative to Appenzell town. From Wasserauen—five miles south of Appenzell town by road or rail line—ride the lift up

to Ebenalp (5,380 feet), a high, rocky ridge that drops off to vertical cliffs on the southern side. On the way up, you'll get a sneak preview of Ebenalp's cave church and the cliffside boardwalk that leads to the guesthouse (near the top, left side). From the top you'll enjoy a sweeping view north all the way to Lake Constance (Bodensee). Though this excursion is doable in so-so weather, clear skies really enhance the Ebenalp experience—ask in Appenzell before you head up to the mountain, or check the webcam at www.ebenalp .ch. In any weather, sturdy shoes and rain gear are recommended— the weather can change in the blink of an eye.

Leaving the lift, look for *Wildkirchli* and *Aescher* signs pointing to the 12-minute hike down to the mountain hut. First you'll hike steeply down under the cables, then you'll hook right and venture downhill through a prehistoric cave. It's slippery and dimly lit, so watch your step and use the railing—trust me, you'll soon return to daylight. As you emerge into the

light, you'll pass a hermit's home (a tiny museum, always open) and the 400-year-old Wildkirchli cave church (hermit monks lived there 1658-1853), before following the cliff-hugging path to a 170-year-old weathered-shingle guest-house built snugly against the

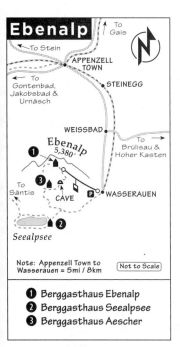

Ebenalp

To Gais
←To Stein
APPENZELL TOWN
← To Gontenbad, Jakobsbad & Urnäsch
STEINEGG
WEISSBAD
To Brülisau & Hoher Kasten
Ebenalp 5,380'
❶
❸
To Säntis
CAVE
P
WASSERAUEN
❷
Seealpsee

Note: Appenzell Town to Wasserauen = 5mi / 8km
Not to Scale

❶ Berggasthaus Ebenalp
❷ Berggasthaus Seealpsee
❸ Berggasthaus Aescher

mountain. Originally a hut housing farmers, goats, and cows, it evolved into a guesthouse for pilgrims coming to the monks for spiritual guidance. Today, the recommended Berggasthaus Aescher welcomes tourists, offering cheap dorm beds and hot, hearty plates of *Rösti*.

The region is a hit with hikers who make the circuit of mountain hotels. There are 24 hotels, each a day's hike apart. All originated as alpine farms. Of these, Berggasthaus Aescher is the oldest and smallest.

From Ebenalp's sunny cliffside perch, you can almost hear the cows munching on the far side of the valley. Only the paragliders, like neon jellyfish, tag your world as 21st century. In the distance, nestled below Säntis peak, are the isolated Seealpsee ("Lake-Alp Lake") and the recommended Berggasthaus Seealpsee.

Hikes from Berggasthaus Aescher: The trail beyond Berggasthaus Aescher leads to a pair of rugged hikes that are worth considering: down to the alpine lake called Seealpsee (and

eventually all the way down to Wasserauen), or up for a steep-but-scenic route back to the Ebenalp lift.

The hike down to **Seealpsee,** which takes a little over an hour, is steep but rewarding: Take a left at the first fork beyond Berggasthaus Aescher. After some initial knee-jarring switchbacks, the trail gets easier, and as it flattens out, a fork to the right leads in about 10 minutes to the lake. To reach Wasserauen (45 minutes) and the train back to Appenzell, retrace your steps till you reach the nearest fork, but this time take the other path (to the right), which turns into a narrow road.

To **return to the Ebenalp lift** from Berggasthaus Aescher, you can retrace your steps through the cave (allow 25 minutes for this uphill hike). Or, for a different and more strenuous return, you can hike up around the back of the mountaintop: As you leave the Berggasthaus, continue straight on the path (skipping the first fork in the trail, which leads down to Seealpsee). After the fork, the path winds you steeply uphill, eventually arriving back at the top of the Ebenalp lift.

Getting There: First, a train takes you from Appenzell to Wasserauen (1-2/hour, 11 minutes). Then, across the road from the Wasserauen station, the Ebenalp lift carries hikers to the summit and back every 15 minutes (19 SF up, 27 SF round-trip, half-price with Swiss Pass, 7-minute trip, daily July-Aug 7:30-19:00 but runs until 21:00 mid-July-early Aug, June and Sept 7:30-18:00, last half of May and Oct 7:30-17:30, mid-Dec-Easter 8:30-17:00, 2-week maintenance closures April-early May and Nov-early Dec—call ahead, free and reportedly safe parking at lift, pick up the free hiking map before you ascend, tel. 071-799-1212, www.ebenalp.ch).

Sleeping and Eating on Ebenalp

Although Appenzell town offers all the predictable comforts, hardy travelers enjoy overnighting on Ebenalp instead. You'll live by the lift schedule (see above), the facilities are limited (only rainwater), and reaching any of these accommodations involves some steep hiking. But it's an unforgettable place to sleep.

$$$ Berggasthaus Seealpsee is on the idyllic alpine Seealpsee, a hike up a private road from the Wasserauen train station (loft dorm beds with sheets-35 SF, D-110 SF, Db-130 SF, showers-3 SF, closed Nov-mid-April, tel. 071-799-1140, fax 071-799-1820, www.seealpsee.ch, berggasthaus@seealpsee.ch, Meier family).

$$ Berggasthaus Ebenalp sits atop the mountains just above the lift. Its refurbished rooms are booked long in advance for Saturdays, but are otherwise empty (4-, 6-, or 8-bed dorms with comforters-40 SF per person; D-124 SF, coin-op rainwater shower-4 SF, closed Nov-mid-May, tel. 071-799-1194, www.gasthaus-ebenalp.ch, infos@gasthaus-ebenalp.ch, Sutter family).

$ Berggasthaus Aescher (see photo on page 234) promises a memorable experience. Built in 1805, the house has only rainwater and no shower. Friday and Saturday nights sometimes have great live music, but are often crowded and noisy, with up to 40 people, and parties going into the wee hours. But on Monday through Thursday, it'll likely feel like a quiet mountain refuge (outside of July and August, which can be a little busy). The hut is actually built into the cliff; its back wall is the rock itself. You can study this alpine architecture from the toilet. Sip your coffee on the deck, sheltered from drips by the gnarly overhang 100 feet above. The guest book goes back to 1940, there's a fun drawer filled with an alpine percussion section, and the comfortable dining/living room is filled with happy hikers dining on *Rösti* and sipping coffee spiked with schnapps and topped with whipped cream. Claudia can show you rock-climbing charts. For a strenuous 45-minute pre-dinner hike, copy the goats: Take the high trail toward the lake, circle clockwise up toward the peak and the lift, then hike down the way you originally came (dorm bed-45 SF, includes breakfast and comforter, no towels or showers available, dinner-20-30 SF, no credit cards but euros and traveler's checks accepted, closed Sun nights and Nov-April, 12 minutes by steep trail below top of lift, tel. 071-799-1142, www.aescher-ai.ch, info@aescher-ai.ch, reservations by phone only, run by Claudia and Beny Knechtle-Wyss and their five adult children—Bernhard, Reto, Lukas, Lilian, and Dominik—plus 35 sheep, 20 rabbits, 5 chickens, 3 pigs, and a dog). Lunch is served roughly 11:30-16:00, and dinner from around 17:30, but you can get a coffee anytime.

Near Appenzell: Liechtenstein

Appenzell is just an hour away from the tiny and touristy country of Liechtenstein. This quirky remnant of medieval feudal politics is truly landlocked, without a seaport, or even an airport.

Liechtensteiners—who number about 36,000—speak German, are mostly Catholic, and have a stubborn independent streak. Women weren't given the vote until 1984.

Liechtenstein is not worth going out of your way for (unless you collect stamps—postal or passport), but it's a no-brainer detour if you happen to be driving south from Appenzell toward Chur or the Upper Engadine (Pontresina/St. Moritz). Heading south on the A13 expressway, the road actually skirts Liechtenstein just across the Rhine (the border). For a 30-minute detour, exit at Buchs and turn toward Schaan. After crossing the border (without stopping, or likely even noticing), you'll wind up in the town of Schaan. Follow signs (south/right) toward Vaduz, the capital of the Principality of Liechtenstein (Fürstentum Liechtenstein, or FL for short on its sleek black license plates).

Low-key Vaduz, with about 5,000 people, feels basically like a midsized Swiss town. Its pedestrianized main drag is lined with modern art and hotels bordering a district of slick office parks. Like other "micro-countries," Liechtenstein offers businesses special tax and accounting incentives. Many European companies establish their official headquarters here to take advantage of its low taxes.

Once in Vaduz, you'll find various parking lots and garages

APPENZELL

along the main street, Äulestrasse. Try to park directly under the looming castle. If you park at the Marktplatz garage, you can simply walk one block up to the pedestrian zone called Städtle, where you'll run right into the TI (at #37, daily 9:00-17:00, a second kiosk is set up at the big bus parking lot the same hours Easter-Sept, tel. from Switzerland 00-423/239-6300, www.tourismus.li). The TI will stamp your passport for 3 SF. If you have more time, go for a stroll along enjoyable Städtle street. Use Swiss francs or euros to buy a postcard and some Liechtenstein stamps to send to the collector in your life (1.90 SF postage for a postcard to the US...but be sure to write and send it before leaving the country).

The billionaire prince, who looks down on his six-by-twelve-mile country, wields more real political power in his realm than any other member of European royalty. The Liechtenstein family purchased this piece of real estate from the Holy Roman Emperor. In 1719, the domain was granted principality status, answering only to the emperor. In 1806, during the age of Napoleon, Liechtenstein's obligations to the Habsburg emperor disappeared, and the country was granted true independence.

The Liechtenstein princes, who lived near Vienna, saw their country merely as a status symbol, and at first didn't even bother to visit. In fact, it wasn't until the 20th century that the first Liechtenstein prince actually lived here. Later, after World War I, tough times forced the principality to enter an economic union with Switzerland. To this day Liechtenstein enjoys a very close working relationship with its Swiss neighbors—functioning in some ways like just another Swiss canton, with the same currency, international diplomacy, bus system, and even soccer league.

The prince's striking castle, a 20-minute hike above Vaduz, is closed to the public, but there's a fine view from the grounds (find the trail near Café Burg). After that visit, you'll quickly run out of things to do. No problem—just head back to Switzerland. Continue south through town on Äulestrasse, turn right at the well-marked *Schweiz* sign, cross back over the Rhine, and you're back in Switzerland (and the A13 expressway)...ready to check another country off your list. Or, if you're headed northeast toward Austria, head back north through Schaan, then up to Feldkirch.

LAKE GENEVA
and FRENCH SWITZERLAND

Lausanne • Château de Chillon • Montreux • Gruyères

Lake Geneva, in the southwest corner of the country, is the Swiss Riviera. Separating France and Switzerland, the lake is surrounded by Alps and lined with a collage of castles, museums, spas, resort towns, and vineyards. Elegant French-style villas—with pastel colors, frilly balconies, and characteristic mansard roofs—give it an air of gentility. Its crowds, therefore, are understandable. This area is so beautiful that Charlie Chaplin and Idi Amin both chose it as their second home.

French is the predominant language at Lake Geneva ("Lac Léman" in French, "Genfersee" in German). To establish a better connection with the locals, see the "French Survival Phrases" in the appendix, *s'il vous plaît.*

Skip the big, dull city of Geneva; instead, sleep in fun, breezy Lausanne. Explore the romantic Château de Chillon and stylishly syncopated Montreux. If time allows, delve deeper into the French Swiss countryside, which offers up chocolates, vineyards, Gruyère cheese, a mountaintop glacier, and a fine folk museum.

Planning Your Time

On a quick trip, you can get a good overview of Lake Geneva's highlights in a day or less. Lausanne makes the best home base. If you're in a hurry, make a beeline for Château de Chillon. With more time, lazily float your way between Lausanne

and Chillon on a scenic boat cruise, and get lost in Lausanne's old town and unique museums (the best are the l'Art Brut and Olympic museums, though the latter is closed for renovation until late 2013).

On a longer trip, the French Swiss countryside to the north (especially around the town of Gruyères) is worth exploring. This is most convenient by car, especially if you're driving between Lake Geneva and points north (Bern, Murten, or the Berner Oberland), but it's doable by train. You can also get a good taste of the countryside on the convenient Chocolate Train that departs from Montreux (described on page 267).

Getting Around Lake Geneva

Trains easily connect towns along Lake Geneva. Take a faster IR train if you're going between larger cities, such as Lausanne or Montreux, or a slower Régional or S train if you're heading for a smaller destination, such as Château de Chillon.

Boats carry visitors to all sights of importance. Daily boat trips connect Lausanne with Vevey (1 hour, 16.50 SF), Montreux (1.25-1.5 hours, 21.10 SF), and Château de Chillon (1.5-2 hours, 22.70 SF). These run about four times per day in each direction from mid-June to mid-September (fewer in shoulder season, virtually none late Oct-Easter). First class costs about a third more and gets you passage on the deck up top, where you should scram-

Château de Chillon

ble for the first-come, first-served chairs. You can sail free with a Eurailpass or Swiss Pass, but it uses up a travel day of a flexipass; to avoid giving up a day just for the cruise, take an afternoon cruise on the same day you arrive by train in the morning (tel. 0848-811-848, www.cgn.ch).

Study the schedule (available at TIs and boat ticket windows) to find a cruise that appeals to you—you have a variety to choose from. For just a quick hop on the water, the 15-minute cruise between Montreux and Château de Chillon is fun (8 SF). The pretty town of Vevey, between Montreux and Lausanne, is enjoyable for a short stop (1 hour from Lausanne, 30-60 minutes from Chillon). Evian-les-Bains, immediately across from Lausanne, is the French spa town famous for its mineral water. The boats there are filled with people ready to enjoy its spa and tour its mineral-water facilities (not quite hourly, 35 minutes, 33 SF round-trip, passport required).

Lausanne

Lausanne is the most interesting city on the lake, proudly dubbing itself the "Olympic Capital" (it's been home to the International Olympic Committee since 1915). Amble along the serene lakefront promenade, stroll through the three-tiered, colorful old town, explore the sculptures at Olympic Park, and visit the remarkable Collection de l'Art Brut. Take a peek at the Gothic Cathedral, and climb its tower for the view.

The Romans founded Lausanne on the lakefront—but with the fall of Rome and the rise of the barbarians, the first Lausanners fled for the hills, establishing today's old town. The Roman site was abandoned (scant ruins today), but in the age of tourism, the waterfront—a district called Ouchy—thrived. So the city has a design problem that goes back 1,500 years: two charming zones separated by a nondescript residential/industrial urban mess. Thankfully, the waterfront and the old town are easily linked by a steep, handy Métro line.

Lausanne has the energy and cultural sophistication of a larger city, but is home to only about 117,000 people (300,000 in the greater area). A progressive city government (with a mayor from the Green Party) that subsidizes art and culture, and a university with plenty of foreign students carbonate the place with a youthful spirit. That spirit shows itself in Lausanne's notoriety as a haven for inline skating and skateboarding.

Orientation to Lausanne

The tourist's Lausanne has two parts: the lakefront **Ouchy** (oo-shee), with a breezy resort ambience and the Olympic Museum; and the **old town district,** with creaky Old World charm and other fine museums, directly uphill from the lake. The "old town district" is divided roughly into two adjacent parts: the true "old town," or *vieille ville* (vee-yay veel), near the cathedral; and the "city center," or *centre-ville,* with my favorite hotels and restaurants. The train station is located between Ouchy and the old town, and everything's connected by the slick Métro.

Be careful to pronounce Lausanne correctly (loh-ZAHN), and don't confuse it with Luzern.

Tourist Information

Lausanne has two TIs: One is in the train station (daily 9:00-19:00), and the other is at the lakefront Ouchy Métro stop, in a blue pavilion (daily April-mid-Sept 9:00-19:00, mid-Sept-March 9:00-18:00, tel. 021-613-7373, www.lausanne-tourisme.ch).

At either TI, ask about **walking tours** in English (10 SF, free for students, 1.5 hours, May-Sept Mon-Sat usually at 10:00 and 14:30, in English only if there's a guide and demand, meet in front of Town Hall at Place de la Palud, call 021-320-1261 to confirm time and language).

If you're here between mid-June and late September—prime time for cultural events—pick up the TI's free *Lausanne Estivale* program. At any time of year, ask about organ concerts at the cathedral.

Arrival in Lausanne

By Train: The train station, with lockers, late-night groceries, and a Métro stop, is midway between the old town and the lakefront. This sounds inconvenient, but the Métro takes you either up to the old town or down to the lake in about two minutes, with constant departures. For most recommended hotels, take the Métro to the Lausanne-Flon stop (details listed under "Sleeping in Lausanne," later). It seems confusing only until you do it. A **taxi** from the train station to your hotel runs about 15 SF.

By Car: Driving is tricky in this nearly vertical city—especially in the twisty old town. Avoid headaches by leaving your car at a park-and-ride (labeled *P+R*); several of these flank the city and are well-connected by Métro to the old town (10 SF/day covers parking and transit into center for 1 person, 0.50 SF extra for each additional person). If you're coming on the freeway from the north (such as from Bern), get off at the Vennes exit. Either stop at the park-and-ride here (use the Vennes Métro stop), or—if you want to head into the city center to find a pricier garage—follow *Centre* signs. Alternatively, you can stay on the freeway as it loops around and down to *Lausanne Sud,* ending at the lakefront Ouchy district, with another handy park-and-ride (Pêcheurs, near the base station of the Métro). If you're coming on the lakeside road from the east (such as from Montreux), follow blue signs along the lakeshore directly into Lausanne.

By Boat: From the dock, veer left toward the plaza with the flagpoles. Beyond the poles is a TI, and across the street is a Métro station.

By Plane: Lausanne and the Lake Geneva area are served by the Geneva airport, at the lake's southwest corner. The airport sits on the western edge of Geneva, straddling the French border. It's straightforward and easy to manage. Exiting from the baggage claim area, you're met by various local tourist information

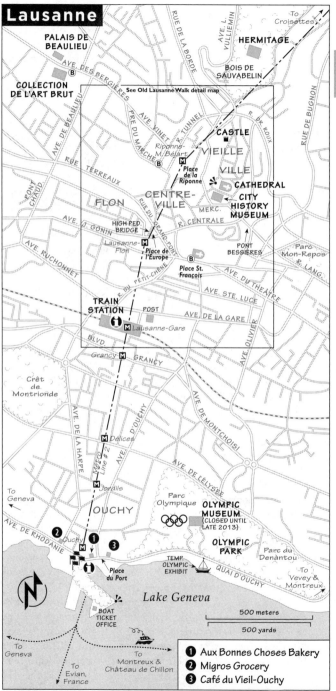

Lausanne

PALAIS DE BEAULIEU

COLLECTION DE L'ART BRUT

AVE. DES BERGIÈRES

RUE DE LA BORDE

AVE. L. VULLIEMIN

To Croisettes

HERMITAGE

BOIS DE SAUVABELIN

RUE DE BUGNON

See Old Lausanne Walk detail map

R. DU. ROUX

AVE. DE BEAULIEU

RUE TERREAUX

PRÉ DU MARCHÉ

AVE. VINET

R. TUNNEL

CASTLE

VIEILLE VILLE

Riponne-M. Béjart

Place de la Riponne

CENTRE-VILLE

CATHEDRAL

CITY HISTORY MUSEUM

PONT CHAUD.

FLON

AVE. J. GONIN

RUE DU GRAND PONT

MERC.

R. CENTRALE

HIGH PED. BRIDGE

Lausanne-Flon

Place de l'Europe

PONT BESSIÈRES

Parc Mon-Repos

R. LANG.

AVE. RUCHONNET

R. DU PETIT-CHÊNE

Place St. François

AVE. DU THÉÂTRE

TRAIN STATION

POST

Lausanne-Gare

AVE. STE. LUCE

AVE. DE LA GARE

AVE. OLIVIER

BLVD.

Grancy

GRANCY

Crêt de Montriond

AVE. DE LA HARPE

Métro Line #2

Délices

Jordils

Parc Olympique

AVE. DE MONTCHOISI

AVE. D'OUCHY

AVE. DE L'ÉLYSÉE

OLYMPIC MUSEUM (CLOSED UNTIL LATE 2013)

OUCHY

To Geneva

AVE. DE RHODANIE

Ouchy

Place du Port

OLYMPIC PARK

Parc du Denantou

TEMP. OLYMPIC EXHIBIT

QUAI D'OUCHY

To Vevey & Montreux

Lake Geneva

BOAT TICKET OFFICE

500 meters

500 yards

To Geneva

To Evian, France

To Montreux & Château de Chillon

❶ Aux Bonnes Choses Bakery
❷ Migros Grocery
❸ Café du Vieil-Ouchy

desks. To the left is a bank of ATMs and beyond that, the airport's train station, with handy connections all over Switzerland. Trains leave for Lausanne about four times each hour (25 SF, 45-55 minutes). Geneva's city-center train station is the first stop on any train departing from the airport; you can get a free ticket for this short hop in the baggage-claim area (before customs—look for machines).

Helpful Hints

Market Days: On Wednesday and Saturday mornings, produce stands fill the pedestrian streets of the old town. Saturday is flea market day on Place de la Riponne.

Internet Access: Freeport Café, in the train station, has free Wi-Fi (daily 8:00-24:00, just off track 1). Free Wi-Fi is also available around town, such as on Place de la Riponne, Place de la Palud, at the waterfront square in Ouchy, and in many cafés. If you're traveling sans wireless device and your hotel doesn't have a public computer, ask at the TI about Internet cafés or see if a nearby hotel will let you use their computer.

Bookstore: Books Books Books has a great selection of English-language books, including literature on Switzerland and a few of my titles (Mon-Sat 9:00-18:00, closed Sun, Rue de la Mercerie 12, tel. 021-311-2584).

Baggage Storage: The train station has lockers and a left-luggage service (daily 9:00-19:00 except closed Sat-Sun 12:00-13:00).

Laundry: Quick-Wash is well-run and handy to the train station (wash-7 SF, dry-about 4 SF, Mon-Fri 8:00-21:30, Sat-Sun 9:00-21:30, self-service only, good English instructions, below train station at Boulevard de Grancy 44, mobile 079-449-3761). Exit behind the train station (down the stairs past track 9), turn right, then head left down Passage de Montriond to the corner.

Late-Night Grocery: The train station's **Aperto** grocery store is open long hours (daily 6:00-24:00).

Bike Rental: A bike is pretty worthless in this steep city, but it's great for exploring the lakefront, vineyards, and nearby villages. It's a three-hour waterfront pedal to Montreux; Ouchy is a good starting point (rent from one of the places listed below, then take the bike with you on the Métro for 2 SF extra; buy ticket from machine in Métro station).

Near the old town, the city offers free rental bikes through **Lausanne Roule,** tucked under the arches in front of the Lausanne-Flon Métro stop (at the right end of Place de l'Europe as you exit the Métro). If you return your bike here (rather than at one of their unmanned stations) within four hours, it's free (otherwise 6 SF/day, leave passport or other ID as deposit; mid-April-Oct daily 8:00-18:00; first 2 weeks of April Mon-Fri 8:00-17:00, Sat 10:00-17:00, closed Sun; closed Nov-March; Place de l'Europe 1b, tel. 021-533-0115, www .lausanneroule.ch).

You can rent a bike year-round at the **train station's** baggage office (25 SF/half-day, 33 SF/day, 5 SF less with Eurailpass or Swiss Pass, Mon-Fri 8:30-18:30, Sat-Sun 9:00-12:00 & 13:00-18:30, tel. 051-224-2162, www.rentabike.ch). It's possible to reserve ahead on popular weekends (at least 48 hours ahead, online only). Ask about dropping off the bike at a different train station (7 SF extra, limited to a few stations).

Getting Around Lausanne

By Public Transport: Lausanne is steeper than it is big, and the nifty **Métro** and **bus** network make it easy to get around. While the Métro has two lines (converging at the Lausanne-Flon stop), only line #2 is useful for travelers. This mostly vertical, 14-stop Métro line climbs up from the lakefront to the old town, then all the way up to the freeway. The key stops are Ouchy (at the lakefront); Lausanne-Gare (at the train station); Lausanne-Flon (at the bottom end of the old town—exit into Place de l'Europe, ride the elevator up to the pedestrian bridge, and stroll straight into the town center); and Riponne-M. Béjart (at the top end of the old town, on Place de la Riponne). When boarding the Métro, watch the direction: Croisettes will take you up, Ouchy will take you down. You're unlikely to need the bus, except to reach the l'Art Brut museum.

If you're sleeping in Lausanne, ask your hotel for a Mobilis Card, which covers local transit and is included in your hotel tax. Otherwise, you'll need to buy tickets, unless you have a Swiss Pass. The city center is covered by one zone (zone 11); if you're headed a bit farther (such as to Lutry or the Vennes park-and-ride), you might cross into zone 12. Tickets are valid on both Métro and buses. A short-ride ticket, valid for 30 minutes and up to three stops, costs 1.90 SF. If you're staying within one zone, a single ticket of up to an hour costs 3 SF, and an all-day ticket (valid 6:00-24:00) costs 8.60 SF. Adding a second zone costs a bit more. Before boarding, buy bus tickets from the TI, ticket windows, or user-friendly ticket machines (with English instructions).

By Taxi: Cabs are pricey—figure 15 SF for a short ride.

Self-Guided Walk

A Stroll Through Old Lausanne

There's no way to see this town without lots of climbing. Locals are used to it (enjoy the firm legs). This self-guided stroll introduces you to both parts of Lausanne's charming old town (*vieille ville,* then *centre-ville*). It's a big counterclockwise circle, taking you from the Church of St. Francis up to the cathedral (and castle just beyond), then more or less back to the starting point. You can begin this walk at the Church of St. Francis (skip down to the "Place St-François" section), but I've started it at the ❶ **Lausanne-Flon Métro station,** where you're most likely to arrive in town.

• *From the Métro stop, ride the elevator up to the high* **pedestrian bridge** *(Passerelle du Flon). Orient yourself from midway across the bridge, which leads to the city's main thoroughfare...*

❷ **Rue du Grand-Pont:** Below you stretches Flon—until recently, a down-and-dirty industrial zone. Now, the old ware-

houses are renovated and throb at night with trendy bars, restaurants, theaters, and discos. The recommended Vinothèque Nomade is immediately below. The only reminder of the mills that once churned here is the name of the hottest dance club in town: MàD (stands for "Moulin à Danse," or "Dance at the Mill," just out of sight at Rue de Genève 23).

• *Walk to where the pedestrian bridge hits the busy street. Head for the green copper spire of the Church of St. Francis (to the right). As you walk along Rue du Grand-Pont, enjoy lovely views of the cathedral on your left. You'll soon reach...*

❸ **Place St-François:** The Church of St. Francis marks the town's center and transportation hub, with the grand post office and banks on the right. The church is Gothic, founded by Franciscans in the 13th century. But in 1536, it went Protestant—and was gutted of decorations. Later, a grand Baroque organ was installed. (Note the stop for bus #2, which goes from the street alongside the church to the Collection de l'Art Brut.)

• *Head uphill (passing to the left of the church) along Lausanne's pedestrianized "Fifth Avenue," Rue de Bourg—home to the finest shops. When the street ends, turn left, continuing uphill and over the bridge toward the cathedral.*

❹ **Pont Bessières:** The railing on the bridge is designed to discourage suicidal people from leaping. While Switzerland seems to have it all, its mind-set can be conservative, the orderliness can be stifling, and life here can be stressful—or even depressing (the country has one of the highest suicide rates in Western Europe). Here in Lausanne, between Christmas and New Year's, social workers are stationed on this bridge with soup and coffee to counsel and comfort the distraught people who congregate here,

LAKE GENEVA

Old Lausanne Stroll

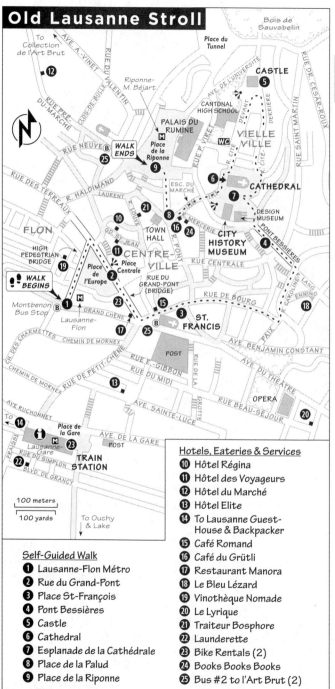

To Collection de l'Art Brut

Bois de Sauvabelin

Place du Tunnel

12 Hôtel du Marché

AVE. A.-VINET

RUE DU VALENTIN

RUE PRÉ-DU-MARCHÉ

CLOS-DE-BULLE

Riponne-M. Béjart

CASTLE **5**

AVE. DE L'UNIVERSITÉ

RUE DR.-CÉSAR-ROUX

CANTONAL HIGH SCHOOL

RUE P. VIRET

DEVANT

DERRIÈRE

RUE NEUVE **B**

RUE DES TERREAUX

R. HALDIMAND

LAURENT

PALAIS DU RUMINE

M

Place de la Riponne

WALK ENDS

25

9

VIELLE VILLE

WC

R. CITÉ

RUE SAINT MARTIN

6 CATHEDRAL

7

DESIGN MUSEUM

ESC. DU MARCHÉ

K. LÖVE

21

8

10

TOWN HALL

16

24

MERCERIE

CITY HISTORY MUSEUM

PONT BESSIÈRES

FLON

HIGH PEDESTRIAN BRIDGE

19

GD. ST JEAN

11

CENTRE-VILLE

Place Centrale

RUE CENTRALE

4

PONT

WALK BEGINS

2 Place de l'Europe

23

RUE DU GRAND-PONT (BRIDGE)

15

RUE DE BOURG

K. CAROLINE LANG

18

PENNING

Montbenon Bus Stop **B**

1

M Lausanne-Flon

GRAND CHÊNE

17

25

B

3 ST. FRANCIS

PAIX

AVE. BENJAMIN CONSTANT

CH. DES CHARMETTES

CHEMIN DE MORNEX

CHEMIN DE MORNEX

RUE DE PETIT-CHÊNE

POST

RUE E.-GIBBON

RUE DU MIDI

13

RUE DE LA GROTTE

AVE. DU THÉÂTRE

AVE. SAINTE-LUCE

RUE BEAU-SÉJOUR

OPERA

20

AVE. RUCHONNET

14

Place de la Gare

Lausanne-Gare **M**

23

POST

AVE. DE LA GARE

FRAISSE

RUE DU SIMPLON

22

TRAIN STATION

BLVD. DE GRANCY

| 100 meters |
| 100 yards |

To Ouchy & Lake

Self-Guided Walk
1 Lausanne-Flon Métro
2 Rue du Grand-Pont
3 Place St-François
4 Pont Bessières
5 Castle
6 Cathedral
7 Esplanade de la Cathédrale
8 Place de la Palud
9 Place de la Riponne

Hotels, Eateries & Services
10 Hôtel Régina
11 Hôtel des Voyageurs
12 Hôtel du Marché
13 Hôtel Elite
14 To Lausanne Guest-House & Backpacker
15 Café Romand
16 Café du Grütli
17 Restaurant Manora
18 Le Bleu Lézard
19 Vinothèque Nomade
20 Le Lyrique
21 Traiteur Bosphore
22 Launderette
23 Bike Rentals (2)
24 Books Books Books
25 Bus #2 to l'Art Brut (2)

contemplating ending it all.

Walking toward the cathedral, you'll notice that Lausanne's old town—filled with administration buildings, offices, schools, and apartments—is subdued compared to most other European old towns, which are lively with lots of eateries.

• *Climb up, with the patch of grass on your left, past the Design Museum, then—after taking a peek at the French Alps—go around the right end of the cathedral (we'll come back later). Continue up the cobbled Rue Cité-Derrière (under the two stone arches) and hike a few short blocks to the summit of the old town, where you'll find the...*

❺ **Castle:** Lausanne's castle is closed to the public, but the view terrace behind it is always open. The statue celebrates Major

Abraham Davel, a local William Tell-like hero. In 1536, the German-speaking Bernese swept into this region (the canton of Vaud) and took over, converting it to Protestantism and ruling for two centuries. In 1723, Davel's heroic attempt to free Lausanne ended in his decapitation. It wasn't until 1798 that the local popula-

tion, inspired by the French Revolution, invited French troops to the region, and with their help, drove the Bernese out. In 1803, the region entered the Swiss Confederation.

Walk downhill on Rue Cité-Devant, toward the big, blocky cathedral tower. Halfway down on your right, you can't miss the **cantonal high school** (*gymnases cantonaux*). One of two great buildings from the Bernese period, it was constructed as a school to train a new kind of Christian leader after the Reformation. This was the first French-speaking Protestant school (c. 1590)—predating similar schools in Geneva (which, under the leadership of John Calvin, was the center of the Swiss Reformation).

• *Continue to the...*

❻ **Cathedral:** More than 300 feet long, this is the biggest church in Switzerland. Step inside for a look (free, April-Aug Mon-Fri 7:00-19:00, Sat-Sun 8:00-19:00, Sept-March daily until 17:30).

This is an Evangelical Reform Church, meaning that it belongs to the tradition of early Protestant reformer John Calvin—and, like its founder, it remains very strict (members aren't allowed to dance, or even to have buckles on their shoes). Iconoclasm, the removal of religious symbols, suited the Calvinists well. The once-ornate cathedral, originally dedicated to Mary, was cleared of all

its statues and decorations. Its frescoes were plastered over, and its colorful windows were trashed and replaced by plain ones (the colored windows were added in the 20th century).

The **pipe organ** above the main door is American-made by Fisk, a Boston company that won the commission and installed it in 2003. Locals love their organ and figure its cost (four million SF) was money well spent. They hold free concerts here, generally on Friday evenings (about 15 times per year—ask about schedule in cathedral welcome center or TI). Look back at its 6,700 pipes: The "stiletto in Oz" design represents the wings of angels. (The old pipes now toot in a church in Gdańsk, Poland.)

The **rose window** in the south (right) transept has the church's only surviving 13th-century glass. The rest of the glass dates from the early 1900s. The north (left) transept has some dreamy blue Art Nouveau scenes. Below the rose window (and just to the left) is the Mary Chapel—once the most elaborate in the church. In 1536, it was scraped clean of anything fancy or hinting of the Virgin Mary. Look at the bits of surviving original paint, and imagine the church in its colorful glory six centuries ago.

The **painted portal** (on the right side of the nave, as you face the altar) was the church's main entrance in the Middle Ages, but is now glassed in to pro-tect its remarkable painted Gothic statuary: Jesus over-seeing the coronation of Mary. The panels beneath Jesus illustrate Mary's death and Assumption.

In the back-right cor-ner of the church, you'll find a **welcome center** and gift shop (Mon-Sat 8:30-11:45 & 13:30-18:00, Sept-March until 17:00; Sun 14:00-17:00). Here you can buy a ticket to climb the 224-step **tower,** which offers a grand view of nearly the entire lake—and lots of Alps (2 SF, last entry 30 min-utes before welcome center closes for lunch and at end of day).

As the city was originally built of wood, it burned down sev-eral times. Since the Middle Ages, a **watchman** has lived in the church's tower. His job: to watch for fires and to call out the hours. The city is made of stone today—so there's little danger of fire—and people now sport watches of their own. Nevertheless, Lausanne's night watchman, the last one of his kind in Switzerland, still calls out the hours. Every night on the hour, from 22:00 to 2:00 in the morning, he steps onto his balcony and hollers. His first announcement: "I am the watchman. I am the watchman. We just had 10 o'clock. We just had 10 o'clock."

• *Back outside, belly up to the fine viewpoint immediately in front of the cathedral.*

❼ **Esplanade de la Cathédrale:** On a clear day, look beyond the spire of the Church of St. Francis to see the French Alps (Chamonix and Mont Blanc, over there somewhere, are just out of sight). Evian-les-Bains, the famous French spa town, is immediately opposite Lausanne. On the right, the soft, rolling Jura Mountains, which mark the border of France and Switzerland, stretch all the way from Lake Geneva to Germany.

• *Notice that the City History Museum is across the square from the cathedral (described later, under "Sights in Lausanne"). Now's a good time to visit.*

A covered wooden staircase (Escaliers du Marché) leads down from the cathedral's front door. At the top of the stairs, a sign points to the **Chemin de St. Jacques.** *This is a stop on one of the many pilgrimage routes across Europe that funnel hikers to the Camino de Santiago across northern Spain (you'll see its stylized seashell icon near the next set of stairs). Head through the tunnel under the busy road. You'll pass Le Barbare ("The Barbarian"), a pub famous for its fine hot chocolate, and the recommended Café du Grütli.*

❽ **Place de la Palud:** This square is marked by its colorful Fountain of Justice (with the blindfolded figure of Justice holding her sword and scales...commanding fairness as she stands triumphantly over kings and bishops). Imagine the neighborhood moms sending kids here to fetch water in the days before plumbing. Behind the fountain is a mechanical clock whose animated figures perform with recorded French narration every hour, on the hour (9:00-19:00). The Town Hall at the bottom of the square, dating from 1685, is, along with the cantonal high school we saw earlier, the other fine Bernese building in town.

• *Uphill from Town Hall, Rue de la Madeleine leads to the vast and modern...*

❾ **Place de la Riponne:** The Palais du Rumine (former university), overlooking the square, now houses a collection of museums (all of which are skippable).

• *Your tour is over. Now enjoy some of Lausanne's fine museums. To reach the Collection de l'Art Brut, you can walk about 10 minutes, or catch bus #2 from Rue Neuve (a block west of Place de la Riponne, across the street from the blocky church). To head down to the lakefront Ouchy district, ride the Métro from the Riponne–M. Béjart stop down to Ouchy. Or simply enjoy poking around more of the old town's twisty lanes.*

Sights in Lausanne

In and near the Old Town

▲**City History Museum (Musée Historique de Lausanne)**—
Facing the cathedral, this museum's fascinating displays trace life

in Lausanne from Roman times to the present. The highlight for many is the 1:200-scale model of Lausanne in the 17th century, downstairs from the ticket counter (when you enter the museum, request to hear the 18-minute recorded English commentary on the model, and they'll book you a time). While you wait for the commentary to begin, head downstairs and follow the one-way route of "Lausanne Through the Ages." Look for the English fliers in each room.

The model, in the last room of the bottom floor, is based on an engraving from 1638 (see copy on wall). You're viewing the town from the perspective of the lakefront district of Ouchy, with the Church of St. Francis in the foreground. You can see river valleys that have since been obliterated by the modern city. The little water mills mark the birthplace of industrial Flon. Though the city's walls are long gone, its vineyards survive. Adjacent rooms show the construction of the Grand-Pont and an interesting collection of historic photos.

Rounding out the collection are several rooms upstairs dedicated to the Bernese epoch (Protestant, 1536-1798), Lausanne silver from the 18th century, a collection of musical instruments, an exhibit about the beginnings of the modern era, and several temporary exhibits.

Cost and Hours: 8 SF, covered by Swiss Pass, Tue-Thu 11:00-18:00, Fri-Sun 11:00-17:00, closed Mon except open 11:00-18:00 July-Aug, Place de la Cathédrale 4, tel. 021-315-4101, www.lausanne.ch/mhl.

▲▲**Collection de l'Art Brut**—This well-displayed, thought-provoking collection shows art produced by untrained artists, many labeled (and even locked up) by society as "criminal" or "insane." The works are displayed (perhaps fittingly) without much rhyme or reason on four floors. Read thumbnail biographies of these outsiders (posted next to their works), and then enjoy their unbridled creativity.

In 1945, artist Jean Dubuffet began collecting art he called "Brut"—untrained, ignoring rules, highly original, produced by people "free from artistic culture and free from fashion tendencies." In the 1970s, he donated his huge collection to Lausanne, which now displays 35,000 works by 500 artists—loners, mavericks, fringe people, prisoners, and mental-ward patients. Dubuffet said, "The art does not lie in beds ready-made for it. It runs away when its name is called. It wants to be incognito." As you tour the thought-provoking

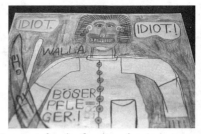

collection and learn about the artists, ponder the fine line that separates sanity and insanity when it comes to creative output.

Cost and Hours: 10 SF, covered by Swiss Pass, Tue-Sun 11:00-18:00, closed Mon except July-Aug, mandatory bag check in lockers (1 SF deposit), Avenue des Bergières 11, tel. 021-315-2570, www.artbrut.ch.

Getting There: The museum is an easy 10-minute walk from the old town (west from Place de la Riponne). Or you can reach it by bus: Bus #2 makes several convenient stops in the old town, including at Place St-François and at Rue Neuve near Place de la Riponne (6/hour on weekdays, 4-5/hour on weekends, direction: Désert, stop: Beaulieu-Jomini). From the train station, take bus #3 or #21 (also very frequent, direction: Bellevaux or Blécherette, stop: Beaulieu-Jomini).

In Ouchy, Lausanne's Waterfront

The lazy resort charm of Lausanne lies on its lakefront. The handy Métro connects Ouchy with the train station and the old town every few minutes. Within 100 yards of the Ouchy Métro stop, you'll find plenty of handy services: TI, boat dock, paddleboat rental, the start of the lakeside promenade, and a park. The place is lively from Easter through October, and dead otherwise.

From the Métro, walk straight out to the water. A big C-shaped **weathervane** stands on the breakwater. Identify which of the four winds is blowing by lining the "C" up with semicircle cutouts in the four granite pillars (crouch). By matching the "C" with the pillar that creates a perfect "O," you learn the prevailing wind.

Nearby, notice the solar-powered **Aquarel tour boats,** which run quietly, smoothly, slowly, and greenly (12 SF, 40-minute tours, www.lausanne.ch/aquarel). Environmentalism is popular in this city, which boasts 300 square feet of green space per inhabitant—more than nearly any city in Europe.

Lake Geneva **cruise boats** leave from the piers just to the left (described on page 240). A five-minute walk beyond those is Ouchy's main attraction...

▲▲**Olympic Museum and Park**—This sight, combining a high-tech museum and beautiful park, celebrates the colorful history

of the Olympic Games. Unfortunately, the museum is closed for renovation until late 2013. During this time, you can still enjoy the park, with beautiful lake views; see the Olympic flame, which flickers atop the park; and visit a floating exhibit, featuring a taste of the museum's collection (moored just across the street from the park).

The exhibit and park celebrate the ideals of Pierre de Coubertin, who in 1894 founded the International Olympic Committee and restarted the games after a 1,500-year lapse. The Olympic spirit is one of peace. Coubertin acknowledged that to ask nations to love one another was naive, but to ask them to respect one another was a realistic and worthy goal.

The museum is a thrill for Olympics buffs—and plenty of fun for those of us who just watch every two years. It features informative English descriptions, thrilling video clips, and mementos from Olympics history, including Jesse Owens' spiked jumping shoes, Katarina Witt's red skating dress, a basketball signed by the 1992 American "Dream Team," and Cathy Freeman's running shoes.

Cost and Hours: Temporary exhibit—likely free, covered by Swiss Pass, April-Oct daily 9:00-18:00, closed Nov-March; when museum reopens, entry fee likely to be at least 15 SF; tel. 021-621-6511, www.olympic.org/museum.

Getting There: From the Ouchy Métro stop, turn left and walk five minutes along the water to the big, white fountain (Quai d'Ouchy 1). On the way, you'll pass the Beau-Rivage Palace, Lausanne's venerable belle époque hotel, which, since 1857, has hosted a glamorous guest list that includes Winston Churchill, Woody Allen, Charlie Chaplin, Dizzy Gillespie, Liz Taylor, and, uh, Richard Nixon. To save yourself the climb to the top of the park, ride the outdoor escalator (with your back to the water, it's to the left of the park).

Near Lausanne:
Lakeside and Vineyard Excursions

Hike to Lutry—A delightful promenade stretches in both directions from the Ouchy Métro stop. The best easy walk is east to Lutry (left as you face the lake, 1.25 hours). From Lutry you can catch the train back to Lausanne (2/hour, 8 minutes). If you hike, bring the TI's *Discover the Terraces of Lavaux* flier (describes several hikes, including this one). The trail is marked with blue plaques explaining in English the flora, fauna, and culture you're enjoying. **Vineyards**—Picturesque vineyards abound along the lake near Lausanne. My favorite plan: a 5- to 10-minute train ride to Chexbres or Grandvaux, then a walk through the villages—following the yellow signs—toward Lutry for stunning views of Lake Geneva. From Lutry, hop the train back to Lausanne.

You can also take the **Lavaux Express,** a cutesy choo-choo train that leaves from Lutry and makes a one-hour loop, affording you an up-close look at the vineyards (13 SF; runs April-Oct on Wed, Fri, and Sun at 13:30, 15:00, and 16:30; also at 10:30 on Sun; 20-SF wine-tasting trip on Fri-Sat evenings, leaves at 18:30 and goes to a wine-cellar *cave*; tel. 021-791-6262, www.lavaux express.ch).

For tips on seeing this area by car, see page 258.

Bike to Morges—The best bike path goes west (after sharing with cars for half a mile, the trail leaves the road and hugs the shoreline all the way to Morges). You'll pass Vidy (with its Roman ruins—just foundations, free), the headquarters of the International Olympic Committee (not open to the public), lots of sports facilities, and finally just peaceful lakefront parkland stretching to Morges (about 6 miles away, easy return by boat or train).

Sleeping in Lausanne

Lausanne hotels are expensive. The only cheap doubles are at the Lausanne GuestHouse—which also has the best lake views but fills up fast in summer (hotels in the old town tend to be less full during this time). Lausanne charges a tourist tax of 2.50 SF per person per night (which is generally not included in the rates listed here). This buys you a Mobilis Card, which gives you free access to the city's public transportation for the duration of your stay (potentially worth far more than the tax). Ask for yours when you check in.

In the Old Town

To find the Régina and Voyageurs, take the Métro to the Lausanne-Flon stop, ride the elevator up to the pedestrian bridge, cross Rue du Grand-Pont, walk up Rue Pichard, and take the first right. For the Marché, continue one more stop up on the Métro to Riponne-M. Béjart, then walk five minutes up Rue Pré-du-Marché. Because the Régina and Voyageurs are buried in Lausanne's old town, they can be challenging for drivers. You are allowed to drive through the pedestrian zone to your hotel to drop

Sleep Code

(1 SF = about $1.10, country code: 41)

S = Single, **D** = Double/Twin, **T** = Triple, **Q** = Quad, **b** = bathroom, **s** = shower only. Unless otherwise noted, credit cards are accepted, English is spoken, and breakfast is included.

To help you sort easily through these listings, I've divided the accommodations into three categories, based on the price for a standard double room with bath during high season:

$$$ **Higher Priced**—Most rooms 170 SF or more.
$$ **Moderately Priced**—Most rooms between 100-170 SF.
$ **Lower Priced**—Most rooms 100 SF or less.

Prices can change without notice; verify the hotel's current rates online or by email. For other updates, see www.ricksteves.com/update.

off your things, but you'll have to park the car at a nearby garage. Get careful instructions, or leave your car at a park-and-ride and arrive by Métro.

$$$ Hôtel Régina, on a steep pedestrian street immersed in old-town charm, is a find: 36 comfy, remodeled rooms, hospitable hosts (Michel and Dora, with help from Anna), and a great location (Sb-138 SF, Db-178 SF, Tb-208 SF, suites-165-325 SF depending on number of people, 10 percent less Fri-Sun for stays of at least 2 nights—email the hotel directly when booking to get these special prices for Rick Steves readers, ceiling fans, elevator, free Internet access and Wi-Fi, Rue Grand Saint-Jean 18, tel. 021-320-2441, fax 021-320-2529, www.hotel-regina.ch, info@hotel-regina.ch).

$$$ Hôtel des Voyageurs has 33 predictable rooms across the street from Hôtel Régina (Sb-140 SF, Db-185 SF, Tb-220 SF, extra bed-40 SF, about 10 percent cheaper July-Aug and on weekends, elevator, pay Internet access, free Wi-Fi, parking-15 SF/day, Rue Grand Saint-Jean 19, tel. 021-319-9111, fax 021-319-9112, www.voyageurs.ch, hotel@voyageurs.ch, friendly Pierre).

$$ Hôtel du Marché isn't cozy, but its 25 rooms are nicely renovated. It's a five-minute walk from Place de la Riponne in the old town, on the way to the l'Art Brut museum (S-80-100 SF, Sb-110-130 SF, D-115-130 SF, Db-135-150 SF, Tb-155-170 SF, Qb-180-200 SF, prices vary with demand—check the hotel's website for deals, breakfast-12 SF, elevator, free Internet access and Wi-Fi, Rue Pré-du-Marché 42, tel. 021-647-9900, fax 021-646-4723, www.hoteldumarche-lausanne.ch, info@hoteldumarche-lausanne.ch).

Near the Train Station

These accommodations are easier for drivers and offer rooms with lake views (unlike most hotels in the old town).

$$$ Hôtel Elite, run by the Zufferey family, is on a quiet, leafy, residential street just above the train station. Its 33 rooms are no-nonsense and not exactly plush, though a few have balconies (Sb-140 SF, Db-180-260 SF depending on size and view, Tb-210-265 SF, elevator, free Internet access, pay Wi-Fi; from station, cross the street and go uphill around McDonald's, take first right to Avenue Sainte-Luce 1; tel. 021-320-2361, fax 021-320-3963, www.elite-lausanne.ch, info@elite-lausanne.ch).

$ Lausanne GuestHouse & Backpacker has to be one of Switzerland's best hostels. This elegant, century-old house, which offers dorm beds and private rooms, turns its back on the train tracks. All of its rooms overlook the lake on the quiet side, and all of the bathrooms face the tracks—which means that even if you have a "private" bathroom, you'll have to cross the hall to reach it. If traveling in summer, it's best to book ahead (bunk in 4-bed dorm-39 SF, D-106 SF, Db-126 SF, Qb family room-146 SF; single-room rates available Nov-April: S-88 SF, Sb-97 SF; prices include sheets and tax, no breakfast, no curfew, reception open 7:30-12:00 & 15:00-22:00, elevator, pay Internet access, free Wi-Fi, lockers, laundry, kitchen, garden, reserve ahead for parking, Epinettes 4, tel. 021-601-8000, www.lausanne-guesthouse.ch, info@lausanne-guesthouse.ch). The hostel is a five-minute walk from the train station: Head to track 9 and follow it with the tracks to your right, pass through the small building on the tracks, then go down the stairs, turn right, and walk until you reach the big, light-yellow building right next to the tracks.

Eating in Lausanne

In the Old Town

Café Romand is a classic Swiss brasserie filled with natives enjoying hearty French Swiss home cooking. The city's students, pensioners, and professionals sit under old-time photos in this characteristic yet simple eatery like they own the place (18-30-SF plates, Swiss white wines by the glass and carafe—see list of what bottles are open above the bar, daily specials, open Mon-Sat 9:00 until late, hot food served until 23:00, closed Sun, Place St-François 2, tel. 021-312-6375).

Café du Grütli, named for the meadow where Switzerland was born, offers typical French Swiss cuisine near Place de la Palud. Choose from three tempting areas to eat: outside on a cozy cobbled lane; ground-floor, circa-1850, Parisian-bistro style; or upstairs, with antlers and the ambience of a 13th-century castle (often closed for special events). The Prutsch family is into hunting, so you'll find game on the menu (27-40-SF plates, Mon-Fri 9:00-14:30 & 18:00-23:00, Sat 9:00-15:30 & 18:00-23:30, closed Sun, Rue de la Mercerie 4, tel. 021-312-9493).

Restaurant Manora is part of a modern, self-service chain offering a quick and healthy series of buffet lines where you grab what looks good, including hot meals and salads (5.10-SF, 8.50-SF, and 11.80-SF plates), along with fancy fruit juices, desserts, and so on (Mon-Sat 6:45-22:00, Sun 7:45-22:00, where Rue du Grand-Pont hits Place St-François).

Le Bleu Lézard has great French cuisine, a typical French atmosphere, and a trendy clientele who appreciate its candlelit, bohemian interior and fun outdoor patio (23-SF salads, good 23-SF veggie options, 25-30-SF meat dishes, daily 7:00 until late, food served 11:30-15:00 & 19:00-23:00, La Cave music club downstairs, Rue Enning 10, tel. 021-321-3830).

Vinothèque Nomade is primarily a wine bar, where you can choose from 40 different wines available by the glass (generally 7-10 SF; many more by the bottle). To order appetizers, see their short "tapas" menu (8-13 SF, three tapas for 26 SF). For a full meal, browse among the many bottles and take your favorite into the restaurant, where they serve tasty and beautifully presented Mediterranean dishes (25-45-SF plates, 19-SF daily specials, strong on vegetables). Locals sip their wine and hang out on the big, modern sun terrace (Mon-Fri 9:00 until late, Sat from 10:00, Sun from 11:30, below the pedestrian bridge and across from Lausanne-Flon Métro stop at Place de l'Europe 9, tel. 021-320-1313).

Le Lyrique is a neighborhood restaurant filled with locals enjoying their *souvlaki, keftedes,* and calamari in a warm, candlelit interior. The traditionally Greek dishes include vegetarian options, and the wine selection is good (20-35-SF main dishes, Mon-Sat 11:45-14:00 & 18:30-22:30, closed Sun, no English menu, Rue Beau-Séjour 29, tel. 021-312-8887).

Traiteur Bosphore is a good option for a quick and inexpensive takeaway lunch or early dinner. Popular with locals who enjoy the better-than-average *döner kebabs* (8 SF), the place has no seating—stand at back counter or walk to the nearby Place de la Louve and find a seat with the other budget eaters (Mon-Fri 9:30-19:00, Sat 8:30-1:00 in the morning, closed Sun, Rue de la Louve 7, across from Manor department store, tel. 021-311-0770).

In Ouchy

The lakeside Ouchy district is *the* place to relax. Immediately in front of the Métro stop is a fun zone with fountains, parks, playgrounds, promenades, and restaurants.

Picnics: The only good, budget eating option is a picnic with the local office gang on any of the many inviting benches or scenic lakeside perches. **Aux Bonnes Choses** is a small bakery with a heart for picnickers, offering good sandwiches, salads, pastries, and drinks to go. This is infinitely better than the lousy kiosk options in the waterfront park (6-SF salads, daily 7:00-19:00, to the left as you exit the Métro, Place de la Navigation 2, tel. 021-617-8857). Another good spot to shop for your picnic is the **Migros** grocery store (Mon 9:00-21:45, Tue-Sun 8:00-21:45, to the right as you exit the Métro on Avenue de Rhodanie).

Café du Vieil-Ouchy, charming and reasonably priced, seems a bit out of place among all the fancy, expensive restaurants. It offers traditional Swiss cuisine, including cheese fondue and hash brown-like *Rösti* (20-30-SF entrées, Thu-Mon 9:00-14:30 & 17:30-22:00, closed Tue-Wed, Place du Port 3, tel. 021-616-2194).

Lausanne Connections

From Lausanne by Train to: Montreux (3/hour, 25 minutes), **Château de Chillon** (hourly, 35 minutes), **Gruyères** (hourly, 1.25 hours, via Palézieux), **Geneva** (5/hour, 35-50 minutes), **Geneva Airport** (4/hour, 45-55 minutes), **Bern** (2/hour, 70 minutes), **Murten** (hourly, 1.5 hours, change in Fribourg, Neuchâtel, or Payerne), **Interlaken** (2/hour, 2.25 hours, transfer in Bern; or go by Golden Pass scenic route, with transfers in Montreux and Zweisimmen—see the Scenic Rail Journeys chapter), **Luzern** (hourly, 2.25 hours direct; more frequent with transfer in Olten and/or Bern; or go by Golden Pass route—see the Scenic Rail Journeys chapter), **Zürich** (2/hour, 2.25 hours, some with change in Biel), **Zermatt** (hourly, 3 hours, change in Visp—not Brig, unless connecting to Glacier Express), **Lyon** (almost hourly, 2.75-3.25 hours, transfer in Geneva), **Chamonix** (every 2 hours, 2.5-3 hours, change in Martigny and/or Le Châtelard-Frontière), **Paris** (6/day, 4 hours, more with change in Geneva). Train info: toll tel. 0900-300-300 or www.rail.ch.

By Boat: For boat connections from Lausanne, see "Getting Around Lake Geneva" near the beginning of this chapter.

Route Tips for Drivers

If connecting the Lake Geneva sights by car, note the various routes. The expressway high above the lake zips you quickly between Lausanne and Montreux; although slower, the lakeside road provides great lake-and-vineyards views for about half of the drive (but also passes through several congested towns along the way).

For an even slower but more scenic approach, consider detouring to the **Corniche de Lavaux.** This rugged, sometimes frightening Swiss Wine Road swerves through picturesque towns and the stingy vineyards that produce Lake Geneva's tasty but expensive wine. It lies roughly between Lausanne and Montreux; to get a taste, detour from the lakeside road between Cully (near Lausanne) and Vevey (near Montreux). Going in either direction, follow signs for Chexbres to find the wine road. The "Route de la Corniche" between Chexbres and Cully is particularly well-known. Note that this isn't a tidy, straightforward route; expect lots of exploring on twisty vineyard roads. Getting lost is the point.

Château de Chillon

This medieval castle, set wistfully at the edge of Lake Geneva on the outskirts of Montreux, is a ▲▲▲ joy. Because it's built on a rocky island, it has a uniquely higgledy-piggledy shape that combines a stout fortress (on the land side) and a residence (on the lake side). Remarkably well-preserved, Château de Chillon (shee-yohn) has never been damaged or destroyed—always inhabited, always maintained. Today it's Switzerland's best castle experience. Enjoy the château's tingly views, dank prison, battle-scarred weapons, simple Swiss-style mobile furniture, and 800-year-old toilets. Stroll the patrol ramparts, then curl up on a windowsill to enjoy the lake.

Getting There

The castle sits at the eastern tip of Lake Geneva, about 20 miles east of Lausanne and about 2 miles east of Montreux. From Lausanne you can connect to the castle using a combination of methods. For a memorable outing, consider mixing and matching these options.

By Train Plus a Short Walk: The S1 regional train (13 SF, hourly, 35 minutes, direction: Villeneuve) takes you to the station at Veytaux-Chillon, a 10-minute walk along the lake (ideal for picnicking) from the castle.

By Train Plus a Bus Ride or Hike: The faster, more frequent IR train whisks you to Montreux (11.40 SF, 2/hour, 20 minutes), where you transfer to a bus that takes you straight to the castle. From the Montreux station, escalate down to Avenue des Alpes, cross the street, and go down the stairs to Grand-Rue (or take the elevator down, marked *Ascenseur public Grand-Rue*). Cross the street and find the blue bus stop on your right, where you can hop bus #201 to Château de Chillon (3 SF, 6/hour, less frequent after 19:00 and on Sun morning, 10 minutes, direction: Villeneuve Gare, stop: Chillon; buy tickets from driver—coins only, covered by Swiss Pass). You can also hike the two miles from Montreux to Château de Chillon (figure about 45 minutes one-way).

To return to Lausanne, simply reverse the above directions (catch the regional train from the Veytaux-Chillon station back to Lausanne—trains leave hourly at :26 past the hour—or hop the bus from Château de Chillon to Montreux, direction: Vevey, stop: Escaliers de la Gare).

By Boat: A slower but more scenic route to Château de Chillon is to cruise there from Montreux (15 minutes), Vevey (30-60 minutes), or even Lausanne (1.5-2 hours). For details, see "Getting Around Lake Geneva" on page 240.

Orientation

Cost and Hours: 12 SF, 6 SF with Riviera Card (see "Sleeping in Montreux," later), free with Swiss Pass, 28-SF family ticket, daily April-Sept 9:00-19:00, March and Oct 9:30-18:00, Nov-Feb 10:00-17:00, last entry one hour before closing, free and easy parking along road above the castle, then walk down to entrance, tel. 021-966-8910, www.chillon.ch.

Audioguide: My self-guided tour hits all of the highlights, but for a bit more depth, rent the excellent 1.5-hour iPod audioguide; bring a splitter and extra headphones to share one with your travel partner (6 SF, leave ID as deposit).

Baggage Storage: The castle has free lockers (1-SF deposit, off the first courtyard in the room with vending machines). The train station and boat dock don't have lockers.

Eating: Food at the castle is expensive, whether from the vending machines inside or the basic garden café outside. This is an ideal place to bring a picnic.

Background

The aristocratic Savoy family (their seal is the skinny red cross on the towers) enlarged Château de Chillon to its current state in the 13th century, when this was a prime location—at a crossroads of a major trade route from England and France to Rome. From the outside, the castle has looked pretty much the same for 800 years. The only major difference: In the Middle Ages, it gleamed with a bright whitewash.

This was the Savoys' fortress and residence, with four big

halls (a major status symbol) and impractically large lake-view windows (because their powerful navy could defend against possible attack from the water). But when the Bernese invaded in 1536, the castle was conquered in just two days, and the new governor made Château de Chillon his residence (and a Counter-Reformation prison). With the help of French troops, the French-speaking Swiss on Lake Geneva finally kicked out their German-speaking Bernese oppressors in 1798. The castle became—and remains—the property of the canton of Vaud. It's been used as an armory, a warehouse, a prison, a hospital, and a tourist attraction. Jean-Jacques Rousseau's writings first drew attention to the castle, inspiring visits by Romantics such as Lord Byron and Victor Hugo, plus other notables, including Dickens, Goethe, and Hemingway.

Self-Guided Tour

When you buy your ticket, ask for the free self-guided English brochure and map. The numbers in my tour correspond to those in the brochure, on the audioguide, and posted at the site.

You'll cross a natural moat (since the château is built on an island) and enter the **first courtyard** (#3). In the room marked #4, you can pick up an audioguide and get oriented with a good model of the castle (in the off-season, audioguides may be in the gift shop—Room #2).

• *Start by heading down the stairs marked 5/9 to a series of...*

Cellars: You can see how the castle was built upon a foundation of jagged natural stone. In Room #8, look up to the right at the stone stairway—a secret escape route for the castle lord, who could hightail it into a waiting boat from this hidden water gate. At the far end is Room #9, **Bonivard's Prison,** named for a renegade Savoyard who was tortured here for five years (lashed to the fifth column from the entrance). When the Romantic poet Lord Byron came to visit, Bonivard's story inspired him to write *The Prisoner of Chillon,* which vividly recounts a prisoner's dark and solitary life ("And mine has been the fate of those/To whom the goodly earth and air/Are bann'd, and barr'd—forbidden fare"; full text available in the gift shop). You can still see where Byron scratched his name in a column (third from entrance, covered by glass).

• *Head back out into the daylight and turn left through the big gate into the **second courtyard** (#12), which is dominated by the towering keep (more on that later). Just before the keep on the left, go into the...*

Constable's Dining Room (#13): This is one of the château's finest halls. The gigantic fireplace was used to roast large animals (including bears and boars) for feasts. The opposite wall has the first of many grand lake-view windows you'll see in the castle. Look up to the six-centuries-old wooden ceiling.

• *Climb up the spiral staircase to the...*

Aula Nova **(#14):** This room has a striking barrel-vaulted ceiling that was restored in the 1920s. The collection of mobile furniture recalls a time when nobility traveled throughout their realm (and took their belongings with them) to keep an eye on things and collect taxes. In fact, in many European languages, the word for "furniture" implies that it's mobile—German *Möbel,* French *mobilier,* and so on. Enjoy the ornate decorations on each traveling chest.

• *Continue up to the...*

Private Quarters (#15-17): The **bedroom** (#16) has a short bed—only about five and a half feet long. Not only were people shorter back then, but they slept half-upright, propped up on pillows. The **coat-of-arms hall** (#18) is usually filled with temporary exhibits. The walls are lined with the family crests of some 50 "bailiffs" who governed this territory during Bernese rule. Capping this hall is another great wooden ceiling reminiscent of a waffle (or maybe I just need lunch).

• *Exit at the far end of the hall, and turn right into the...*

Camera Domini **(#19):** This was the bedroom of the master of the house. Its location—at the farthest end of the castle from the entrance—was particularly secure.

In the corner, notice the spiral stairs (closed to the public) that the lord could use to scamper down to Mass in his private chapel, or up to the ramparts. Under a sumptuous fleur-de-lis ceiling, wall paintings (imitating tapestries) illustrate various animals, including a camel, lion, griffin (with the body of a lion and the head and wings of an eagle), and the trademark Bernese bear. Study the model in the middle of the room, which helps you imagine what this room looked like in all of its original colorful splendor.

• *Exit the room and turn right (following the 20/24 sign), and pass through a few more rooms—making sure not to miss the **medieval latrines** (#21, on the left), a feature that aims to please a certain class of traveler. You'll end up in a **small courtyard** (#23), which leads to that **private chapel** (#24) where the lord's staircase ended up. Leave this room following the signs for 26, and you'll wind up in the...*

Third Courtyard (#25): Notice that the courtyard's irregular shape causes the angled walkways to focus your attention on the grand window of the master's bedroom—the *camera domini* we visited earlier. There's no question who was the king of this castle.

• *Go in the door marked 26/33. The **aula magna** (#26) is yet another grand hall—this one for banquets—with spectacular lake-view windows. Proceed through a few more rooms (including more latrines, #29) to the...*

Domus Clericorum (#31): In this "house of the clerks," the castle bean-counters kept meticulous records of all money and goods that passed through here, creating an invaluable historical record. In Room #32 you'll find a series of **models and illustrations** that explain the gradual construction of the château over time.

• *Climb back up into the third courtyard again, then pass through to the **fourth courtyard** (#34). Remember the grand views from the lakeside windows? Notice the small slits facing the road on the land side, which are more practical for defense.*

*Now's the time to scramble along the **sentry walk**. As you pass through various indoor rooms and outdoor galleries (marked 38/46), pretend that you're defending the château from invaders. Enjoy the castle courtyard and lake views. Circle all the way around to the...*

Keep (#42): This was the last line of defense and final refuge in the event of a siege. Inside are a few interesting exhibits on

medieval weaponry and how it was used (for instance, those big, heavy, long swords were mostly used for cutting, while skinnier, lighter swords were way more lethal and used for stabbing). To climb to the top of the eight-story tower, you can scale 76 claustrophobic steps for views over the castle, lake, and surrounding mountains. From here you can see France (across the lake) as well as three different Swiss cantons.

Our tour is over. You may scramble the ramparts, enjoy the lake views, and play king of the castle at will.

Montreux

This expensive resort—primarily famous for its jazz festival each July—doesn't offer much to see, but its laid-back vibe and lake-view accommodations help you remember that you're on vacation.

Tourist Information: The wonderful Montreux TI has tons of brochures and extensive information about the region, excursions, and a list of moderately priced rooms in the center (mid-May–mid-Sept Mon-Fri 9:00-18:00, Sat-Sun 9:30-17:00; off-season Mon-Fri 9:00-12:00 & 13:00-17:30, Sat-Sun 10:00-14:00; Place de l'Eurovision, tel. 084-886-8484, www.montreuxriviera.com). In summer you can take a two-hour walking tour of the city, though it's not always offered in English (10 SF, April-Sept Wed-Sat at 10:00, no tours Sun-Tue or Oct-March, meet in front of TI, call TI to confirm language).

Arrival in Montreux: The train station is one steep block uphill from the main waterfront road. From the station, descend on the escalator to Avenue des Alpes, then look for signs for the stairs *(escalier)* or elevator *(ascenseur,* free) down to Grand-Rue, where you'll find the TI, boat dock, and my two recommended hotels.

Sights in Montreux: The lakeside promenade takes you along parks, palm trees, *crêperies,* ice-cream stands, modern sculptures, and the Friday produce market. In the center, meet the statue of Freddie Mercury, who had strong bonds with Montreux. His band, Queen, bought the local Mountain Recording Studios in 1978.

For an easy way to see several sights in the French Swiss countryside, including the town of Gruyères and the chocolate factory in Broc, take a ride from Montreux on the **Chocolate Train** (see page 267).

Sleeping in Montreux

(1 SF = about $1.10, country code: 41)

Accommodations in Montreux levy a tourist tax of 3.40 SF per person per night (generally not included in the rates listed below). This buys you a Riviera Card, giving you free use of local buses and discounts on sights (including half off at Château de Chillon), trains, and boats. Demand and room rates shoot up during the July jazz festival.

$$$ Hôtel Splendid claims to be the second-oldest hotel in town, with genteel public spaces and 28 refurbished rooms. The front rooms are bigger and more expensive, with lake views worth the extra cost (Sb-115-160 SF, Db-180-220 SF, Tb-246-280 SF, prices higher during jazz festival, elevator, free Wi-Fi, 5-minute walk from train station, across the street from TI, above Mayfair Café at Grand-Rue 52, tel. 021-966-7979, fax 021-966-7977, www .hotel-splendid.ch, info@hotel-splendid.ch, David).

$$ Hôtel Parc et Lac, just a few doors down from Hôtel Splendid, has seen better days, but its 30 creaky rooms—with worn carpets and old furnishings—have a certain charm. It also has about the cheapest beds you'll find in the town center and sits above a chic, reasonably priced Italian restaurant. Rooms in front are more expensive and come with a nice view of the lake (most with small balconies), but also some street noise (Sb-100-120 SF, Db-150-160 SF, elevator, free Wi-Fi, 5-minute walk from train station to Grand-Rue 38, tel. 021-963-3738, fax 021-963-2317, parc etlac@bluewin.ch).

In Territet: **$ Montreux Youth Hostel** is very institutional, but nicely situated near a lakeside park. Located in the village of Territet, it's actually closer to Château de Chillon than to Montreux, and easily reachable by frequent buses (bunk in 6-bed dorm-34 SF, bunk in 4-bed dorm-38 SF, D-97 SF, 7 SF more per person during jazz festival, includes breakfast and sheets, non-members pay 6 SF extra, 16-SF meals available, check-in 17:00-22:00, closed Dec-Jan, Passage de l'Auberge 8, tel. 021-963-4934, fax 021-963-2729, www.youthhostel.ch/montreux, montreux @youthhostel.ch). From the Territet train or bus stop, follow the main road (Avenue de Chillon), with the lake to your right, for about 100 yards; when the main road curves inland, walk along small Rue du Bocherex downhill for a block, then take the stairs with the thin red banister down to the hostel's front door.

In Vevey: **$ Riviera Lodge,** on the main square in nearby Vevey, offers "chic and cheap" beds in a 19th-century townhouse on the lake (mid-March-Oct: dorm bed-32 SF, D-98 SF; Nov-mid-March: dorm bed-30 SF, D-92 SF, pricier in Dec; sheets included in doubles or 5 SF extra in dorms, breakfast-9 SF, pay Internet access, free Wi-Fi, kitchen, laundry facilities, reception open 8:00-12:00 & 16:00-20:00, 3-minute walk from station—cross Avenue de la Gare and head to the left of the big yellow building down Avenue Paul Cérésole to Place du Marché 5, tel. 021-923-8040, www.rivieralodge.ch, info@rivieralodge.ch).

Montreux Connections

From Montreux by Train to: Lausanne (3/hour, 25 minutes), **Vevey** (4/hour, 6-9 minutes), **Gruyères** (hourly, 1.25 hours), **Bern** (2/hour, 1.5 hours, transfer in Lausanne), **Geneva** (4/hour, 1-1.25 hours, half with change in Lausanne), **Zermatt** (hourly, 2.5 hours, change in Visp). Montreux is also the first/last stop on the Golden

Pass route (see Scenic Rail Journeys chapter).

By Bus: Bus #201 goes to Chillon and Vevey. Catch it on Grand-Rue; facing the lake, the Chillon bus (direction: Villeneuve Gare) is headed to the left, and the Vevey bus to the right (6/hour, less frequent after 19:00 and on Sun morning, 10 minutes to Chillon, 20 minutes to Vevey).

By Boat: The boat connecting Montreux to Lausanne, Château de Chillon, and several other Lake Geneva destinations departs from the big park next to the TI (see page 240).

French Swiss Countryside

The sublime French Swiss countryside is sprinkled with crystal-clear lakes, tasty chocolates, fragrant cheese, and sleepy cows. If you're passing through this enticing region, take time to sample a few of its sights, tastes, and smells.

I've divided these attractions into two groups: in and around Gruyères (easy to reach by car or train), and in the mountains southeast of Lake Geneva (out of the way and worthwhile only with a car).

Around the famous and touristy cheesemaking town of Gruyères, just north of Lake Geneva, you can visit two very different cheesemakers, a tourable chocolate factory, and a workaday town with a fine folk museum. This area is particularly handy if you're traveling between Lake Geneva and points north (e.g., Bern, Murten, or the Berner Oberland). In the mountainous area southeast of the lake, I've pointed out a remote, time-passed cow-herding village and a lift to a mountaintop glacier.

Getting Around the French Swiss Countryside

The Gruyères region is ideal by car. By public transportation, it's a bit more challenging, but workable. The city of Fribourg and the large town of Bulle are the area's transit hubs. Major trains go through Fribourg, from which you can take the bus to Bulle (2/hour, 40 minutes). From Bulle, trains connect easily to Gruyères (hourly, 7 minutes) and to Broc (hourly, 10 minutes to factory). Buses are less useful, but a few routes are worth knowing about, including Gruyères-Moléson (hourly, 15 minutes).

For an easy all-day side-trip from Lake Geneva, consider hopping on the **Chocolate Train** in Montreux. The train carries either panoramic or old-time belle époque coaches. It leaves from Montreux at 9:12 and begins by following the same route as the Golden Pass (described in the Scenic Rail Journeys chapter). You'll be served coffee and a croissant while enjoying the scenic ride. At 10:15, the train lets you off for a visit to the Gruyères cheese factory. From there, a bus takes you up to the picturesque old town of Gruyères for a visit to the castle (included) and some time for lunch (on your own). Then the journey continues to the town of Broc, where you'll tour the Cailler Chocolate Factory (including a film and chocolate tasting). The train returns to Montreux at 18:00 (99 SF, first class only, 49 SF reservation fee with first-class Swiss Pass or Eurailpass, 59 SF fee with second-class Swiss Pass or Eurailpass; runs July-Aug daily; May-June and Sept-Oct Mon, Wed, and Thu only; toll tel. 0900-245-245, from European countries outside Switzerland call 00-41-840-245-245, from the US call 011-41-840-245-245, www.goldenpass.ch/goldenpass_chocolate_train).

The sights to the southeast of Lake Geneva (Taveyanne and the Glacier des Diablerets), though beautiful, aren't worth trying to do on public transit—without a car, I'd skip them.

Gruyères

This ultratouristy town, famous for its cheese, fills its fortified hilltop like a bouquet. Its ramparts are a park, and the ancient buildings serve tourists. Everything is expensive, from the museums to the food, but the town's magical ambience makes it worth a visit.

Orientation to Gruyères

Tourist Information: The helpful TI is at the town entrance (daily May-Sept 9:30-12:00 & 13:00-17:30 but no lunch break July-Aug, April and Oct until 17:00, Nov-March 10:30-12:00 & 13:00-16:30, tel. 0848-424-424, www.la-gruyere.ch). The ATM's conspicuous location (just in front of the TI) strikes a delicate balance between convenience and greed.

Arrival in Gruyères: The town's train station is at the foot of the hill, a steep 15-minute hike up to the village itself. A bus meets each train (just outside station shack, 3 minutes, 2.90 SF, covered by Swiss Pass, get off at first stop: Gruyères Ville). If you're driving, note the three parking lots on the way up to the town—to reduce walking, drive as high up as you can find space.

Sights in Gruyères

Gruyères' main attraction is the charming town itself. Wander around the manicured main square, which feels like a movie set. You'll see the town symbol—the crane (*grue* in French)—everywhere. If you have time to kill and/or a special interest, consider dipping into one of these three sights.

Castle—Gruyères' castle has a fine setting and a ho-hum interior. While tidy and nicely restored, the place feels empty and could use a lively audioguide—it's not quite worth the cost of entry, but it merits a short stop if you have a Swiss Pass. Admission includes a dull 18-minute audiovisual show about the town's history, heavy on myths and legends (you'll be assigned an entry time when you buy your ticket). Then, with the help of the English brochure, you can explore the various halls and rooms of the castle itself. Spend some time poking around the grounds, including the view terrace and the manicured garden.

Cost and Hours: 9.50 SF; combo-tickets available for Giger Museum, Tibet Museum, or La Maison du Gruyère cheese factory (all described later); covered by Swiss Pass; daily April-Oct 9:00-18:00, Nov-March 10:00-16:30; last entry 30 minutes before closing, tel. 026-921-2102, www.chateau-gruyeres.ch.

H. R. Giger Museum—This museum—a spooky, offbeat contrast to idyllic Gruyères—is dedicated to the Swiss artist who designed the monsters in the *Alien* movies. Not for the easily creeped out, this museum shares those movies' dark aesthetic. It also displays temporary exhibits by other out-there artists.

Cost and Hours: 12.50 SF, 17-SF combo-ticket includes castle, covered by Swiss Pass; April-Oct Mon-Sat 10:00-18:00, Sun 10:00-18:30; Nov-March Tue-Fri 13:00-17:00, Sat-Sun 10:00-18:00, closed Mon; below the castle in the Château St. Germain, tel. 026-921-2200, www.hrgiger museum.com.

Tibet Museum—Rounding out Gruyères' oddball attractions is this offbeat but genuinely interesting collection of art and artifacts—statues, paintings, and other objects—from the top of the world. These prized Tibetan possessions of a Swiss collector are thoughtfully displayed inside a former church, making it feel as though the Tibetan deities are squatting in Jesus' old house. Dim lighting and mood music add to the mellow ambience. It's very small—especially considering its high price—but might interest anyone who enjoys Tibetan culture.

Cost and Hours: 10 SF, 15-SF combo-ticket includes castle, covered by Swiss Pass; April-Oct daily 11:00-18:00; Nov-March Tue-Fri 13:00-17:00, Sat-Sun 11:00-18:00, closed Mon; 4 Rue de Château, tel. 026-921-3010, www.tibetmuseum.ch.

▲▲Fromageries near Gruyères

Gruyères is justifiably famous for its Gruyère cheese (no "s" at the end when it's the cheese itself). In fact, since 2001 the cheese has been an A.O.C. product, meaning that to be called Gruyère, it must be made right here, according to exacting standards. In addition to eating the cheese, which you'll find on menus, the breakfast table, and everywhere else, you can actually watch cheese being made. Choose your cheese-production setting: an old farm in the hills outside town or a newer facility handy to the town. If you have time and interest, consider visiting both.

Ye Olde Cheesemaker: Moléson Fromagerie d'Alpage—
Five miles above Gruyères, a dark and smoky 17th-century farm-house in the village of Moléson gives you
a fun look at the traditional, smelly way of
crafting cheese in a huge cauldron over an
open fire. There's no point venturing here
unless you arrive by 10:00 to watch them
make the cheese. Since space at the demos
is limited, it's wise to reserve a slot the
day before (the staff speaks only French—
consider asking your hotelier or the Moléson
TI to reserve for you; TI tel. 026-921-8500).
A slow-moving video (with some English
titles) traces the entire process. Then they
repeat the whole thing in the flesh: First the

milk is brought to the proper temperature and consistency. Then
the cheesemaker skims out the curds with a cloth and packs it into
a frame to drain and compress. Finally he chops it into blocks and
separates it into smaller circular frames that will turn it into wheels
of cheese. They dispense cups of the cheesemaking leftovers (milk
minus curds, a.k.a. whey) for visitors to taste—it's like sweet skim
milk. Then the cheesemaker takes buckets of the whey out to feed
to the pigs. Unfortunately, there's not a word of English during the
presentation, but even for non-Francophones, it's still fascinating.

Cost and Hours: 5 SF, 3.50 SF without cheesemaking
demo—pointless as it's otherwise just a rustic barn with a cheese
shop, May-Sept daily 9:00-19:00, 45-minute demo at 10:00, closed
off-season, Place de l'Aigle 12, tel. 026-921-1044, www.fromagerie
-alpage.ch.

Getting There: From Gruyères, it's about a 10-minute drive
(follow signs to *Moléson*). Park in the giant lot at the entrance to
the village, then hike about five minutes up to the *fromagerie*—
just follow the cartoon cows. Hourly buses connect Gruyères and
Moléson (15 minutes).

Other Sights in Moléson: Aside from the cheesemaker, the
sleepy village of Moléson has a few other high-mountain attractions, as well as a very helpful **TI** (Mon-Sat 8:00-12:00 & 13:30-
18:00, closed Sun, tel. 026-921-8500, www.moleson.ch). A **luge
ride** is on the hillside adjacent to the *fromagerie* (6 SF, mid-June-
mid-Sept daily 11:00-18:00, mid-Sept-mid-Oct Sat-Sun only
11:00-18:00, off-season Sat-Sun 13:00-17:00 in good weather).
From the parking lot, a **lift** carries you in two stages (funicular,
then cable car) to a mountaintop perch, offering you a lovely view
over the Gruyères countryside (27 SF round-trip, departs every
20 minutes, mid-June-Oct daily 9:00-18:00, weekends only mid-

May-mid-June, closed Nov-mid-May).

Cheese Factory: La Maison du Gruyère—This modern cheese-production center at the foot of Gruyères opens its doors to tourists, who're mooooooved by fun cheese facts: A cow consumes 100 kilograms of grass and 85 liters of water each day to produce 25 liters of milk, while 400 liters of milk goes into making one 35-kilogram wheel of cheese. Admission includes a sample of three varieties of Gruyère cheese (aged different lengths of time), plus an audioguide narrated by an English-speaking cow named Cherry, essential for understanding the otherwise sparse exhibits. Punch in the number listed next to each display to learn about the whole process. Smell the various alpine flowers and plants—see if you can discern the subtle flavors they lend the cheese—and hold some cheesemaking tools in your hands. The big windows give you a view down to the production floor (most interesting when cheese production is going on, 9:00-11:00 & 12:30-14:30); the action peaks at the end, when the curds are pulled from the vats (around 10:30 and 14:00). Even if cheesemakers aren't working during your visit, video screens show the process. The finale is the cellar (near the ticket desk), where long rows of cheese wheels age. Watch a robot cheesemaker move up and down the aisles, lovingly flipping and rubbing each wheel just right.

Cost and Hours: 7 SF, 12-SF family ticket, 14.50-SF combo-ticket includes castle, covered by Swiss Pass, daily June-Sept 9:00-19:00, until 18:00 Oct-May, last entry 30 minutes before closing, restaurant, well-stocked gift shop, straight ahead as you come down the road from Gruyères' hilltop, tel. 026-921-8400, www.lamaisondugruyere.ch.

More Sights near Gruyères

The following worthwhile sights—a folk museum and a chocolate factory—are just a short hop north of Gruyères.

Bulle

The biggest town in the region is Bulle (pronounced "bool"), which has a charming, distinctly French ambience and proudly flies banners with its mascot and namesake bull. Unlike the many cutesy time-passed villages in this region, Bulle feels like a real town. On Thursdays the weekly produce-and-craft market fills the center of town. The market gets bigger and more colorful in summer, when many vendors wear their traditional costumes and sell handmade crafts. The castle that dominates the main square, while impressive from the outside, is closed to the public (it houses municipal offices).

The **TI**, which covers the entire region, is located between the castle and the train station (Mon-Fri 9:00-12:00 & 14:00-18:00,

Sat 9:00-12:00, closed Sun, Place des Alpes 26, tel. 0848-424-424, www.la-gruyere.ch).

▲**Musée Gruèrien**—Somehow the unassuming little town of Bulle managed to build a refreshing, cheery folk museum that

teaches you all about life in these parts and leaves you feeling good. A two-minute walk behind the castle (through the grounds and garden), the museum is located in the basement of the library, with thoughtfully selected pieces well-displayed in one large room. The self-guided English tour guidebooklet, available at the entry, helps bring the exhibits to life. In this cheese-crazy region, cows are key—notice the many cowbells displayed and the panels from barns painted with murals of the cows' twice-yearly procession up and down the Alps. When the tour is over, the guidebooklet beseeches, "Don't you think that the Musée Gruèrien offers sufficient material to justify an additional visit? The Golden Book of Visitors awaits your signature and your comments. Thank you for your visit!"

Cost and Hours: 8 SF, Tue-Sat 10:00-12:00 & 14:00-17:00, Sun 14:00-17:00, closed Mon, tel. 026-916-1010, www.musee-gruerien.ch.

Cailler Chocolate Factory

To fight their image of being a boring "old grannies'" chocolate, Cailler invited famous designers to reinvent the brand. One of the happy results of that effort is the factory's fun visitors' experience. The revamped "Maison Cailler" center features a tour through exhibits about the production and shipment of chocolate, a collection of old chocolate molds, and vintage films about chocolate production (for more on Swiss chocolate, see the sidebar on page 30). Taste almonds and hazelnuts, crumble a cocoa bean in the palm of your hand, and touch a block of cocoa butter. In the tasting room, friendly employees are happy to answer questions as visitors sample creations from elegant trays. Peek into the actual working factory, as video screens explain the process, before concluding in the chock-full-of-chocolate gift shop.

Cost and Hours: 10 SF, daily April-Oct 10:30-18:00, Nov-March until 17:00, particularly busy in July-Aug, last entry one hour before closing, located in sweet-smelling town of Broc, follow signs to *Nestlé* and *Broc Fabrique,* tel. 026-921-5960, http://cailler.ch.

Sleeping in and near Gruyères

Hotels in Gruyères are expensive. If you'd like to pay a premium to sleep right on Gruyères' main square, you can do it at **$$$ Hostellerie Saint-Georges,** which has 14 small, old-fashioned rooms above a restaurant (Sb-130 SF, Db-180 SF, 20 SF more for view, 40 SF more for large view room, Tb-230 SF, free Wi-Fi, tel. 026-921-8300, www.st-georges-gruyeres.ch, info@st-georges -gruyeres.ch).

For something more affordable, I prefer **$$ Hostellerie Le Castel,** at the main intersection of the nearby town of Le Pâquier, a five-minute drive or easy train ride from Gruyères (toward Bulle). They offer 10 double rooms and a few studios with kitchenettes (Sb-120 SF, Db-135 SF, 20 SF more for view, Db studio-150 SF, extra bed-60 SF, about 10 SF cheaper off-season, prices don't include 2 SF per person per night tax, breakfast-14 SF, minimum 2-night stay, free Wi-Fi, Rue de la Gare 10, tel. 026-912-7231, www.castel -gruyere.ch, info@ castel-gruyere.ch).

Eating in Gruyères

The main square of Gruyères is surrounded by eateries with indoor and outdoor seating, serving (guess what?) all manner of Gruyère cheese dishes. These places are more or less interchangeable; pick the place that looks best to you. **Chalet de Gruyères** looks like a giant cuckoo clock perched atop the square (on the way to the castle). With stuffy indoor seating or a fine terrace, this restaurant has a good reputation and serves up huge portions (20-40-SF meals, open daily, tel. 026-921-2154).

Countryside Sights Southeast of Lake Geneva

Tucked in the slow-going mountainous countryside just southeast of Lake Geneva, these two places are less convenient than the ones listed above, as they're not in the immediate direction of other recommended destinations. They do, however, give you a French-flavored taste of high-altitude life in *les Alpes suisse.*

▲▲Taveyanne
This remote hamlet is a huddle of log cabins used by cowherds in the summer. Actually part of a nature reserve, Taveyanne is two miles off the main road between Col de la Croix and Villars (a small sign points down a tiny road to a jumble of huts and snoozing cows stranded at 5,000 feet). The hamlet's old bar is a restaurant,

serving a tiny community of vacationers and hikers.

Sleeping in Taveyanne: The town's inn is **$ Refuge de Taveyanne** (from 1882), where the Seibenthal family serves meals in a rustic setting with no electricity, low ceilings, and a huge, charred fireplace. Consider sleeping in their primitive five-mattress loft (15 SF, D-32 SF, cash only, access by a ladder outside, bathroom outside, closed Tue except July-Aug, closed mid-Oct-May, tel. 024-498-1947, www.taveyanne.ch). It's a great opportunity to really get to know prizewinning cows...you'll see, hear, and smell them all around.

Getting There: Taveyanne is perched in the middle of nowhere, on a backcountry, summer-only road that twists from Villars to Col de la Croix. From Lake Geneva (Lausanne or Montreux), head south on expressway 9. From here there are various ways to reach Villars (a.k.a. Villars-sur-Ollon). From Villars, proceed toward Col de la Croix; along this road, watch for the Taveyanne turnoff. Or, for a less straightforward but particularly scenic approach, stay on expressway 9 to the Bex exit. Drive through Bex, then follow signs to Gryon and Villars. You'll twist up through tidy vineyards and villages to the pleasant town of Gryon. Shortly after Gryon (but before Villars), in the town of Barboleusaz, keep an eye out for *Taveyanne* signs, which you'll carefully track on very narrow mountain roads. After visiting Taveyanne, you can go more directly to the main Villars-Col de la Coix. Note that these roads are extremely narrow and winding, through meadows, woods, and along cliffs; Taveyanne is not for fainthearted drivers.

Glacier des Diablerets

For a grand alpine trip to the tip of a 10,000-foot peak, ascend to the Glacier des Diablerets, which does its icy thing high above the charming town of Les Diablerets. Up top you'll not only enjoy views of peaks all around and a vast glacier slowly oozing down below you, but also some fun attractions (such as a mountaintop luge trip, chairlift ride, and chance to ride across the glacier on a "snow bus"). While similar lifts in the Berner Oberland and Zermatt area are more thrilling, this is French

Switzerland's answer to high-altitude fun. Allow about an hour and a half total to get your money's worth.

The handiest approach is from **Col du Pillon,** a 10-minute drive east of Les Diablerets (on the smaller road toward Gstaad). Here you'll load into the cable car, ride five minutes up, switch to another car (follow *Glacier* signs), then ride another five minutes to the summit. In just 15 minutes total, you're standing on a perch overlooking a glacier, with alpine panoramas all around and plenty of activities to keep you entertained.

The top of the lift is called **Scex Rouge.** The boxy gray tower adjacent to the cable car has an elevator zipping you to various services (shop, view terrace, self-service cafeteria, and a sit-down restaurant). Ride the elevator to floor 3 and use the walkway to reach the staircase up to the summit viewpoint, where orientation panels identify the mountain ranges all around you. You can see the Matterhorn and a bit of Mont Blanc, the Alps' highest peak. At your feet sprawls a glacier filled with skiers in cold weather (Oct-May), gray and gloomy in summer.

Just outside the main building are several other options. The most exciting is the **"alpine coaster"**—actually the world's highest luge course, perched on a rocky bluff (9 SF/ride). You'll sit on a plastic sled and shoot down a 1,000-meter-long metal rail, with twists and turns that feel like they're about to send you over the edge (pull back on your handles to brake as needed). At the end, you and your cart are pulled safely back up to the top. A **chairlift** (included in your lift ticket) takes you down to the glacier itself, where you can pay 15 SF to ride a **"snow bus"** across its surface.

Cost and Hours: 77 SF round-trip, 39 SF with Swiss Pass, departs every 20 minutes; daily early May-late-Sept 9:00-16:50, off-season until 16:30 except late-Sept-early-Nov, when it's closed for maintenance; these are last ascent times, tel. 024-492-0923, www.glacier3000.ch.

Getting There: It's easiest for drivers, who will find the base of the Col du Pillon lift about 10 minutes east of Les Diablerets. (If you'd like a scenic drive through the mountains on smaller roads, this combines well with a visit to Taveyanne.) It's doable by public transportation: Take the train to Les Diablerets, where there are eight buses per day to Col du Pillon.

LUGANO

Lugano, the leading city of the Italian-speaking Swiss canton of Ticino, gives you Switzerland with an Italian accent. The town (population 55,000) sprawls luxuriously along the shores of Lake Lugano. Just a short, scenic train ride over the Alps from the German and French regions of Switzerland, Lugano has a splashy, zesty, Mediterranean ambience. It attracts vacationers from the rainy north with its sunshine, lush vegetation, inviting lake, and shopping. While many travelers come here for the fancy boutiques, others make this a base for hiking, cruising the lake, and passing lazy afternoons in its many gardens. Its mountains aren't mighty, its beaches are lousy, the cityscape is nothing thrilling, and it can all feel a little geriatric, but Lugano is the best spot to enjoy palm trees in Switzerland, and its unique charm merits at least a short visit.

Planning Your Time

Lugano lies conveniently at the intersection of the William Tell Express and the Bernina Express—two of Switzerland's more scenic train rides. Blitz sightseers arrive on the William Tell one day and take off on the Bernina Express the next.

If relaxing is on your itinerary, spend two nights and a full day here, arriving and departing on the scenic trains. With a day, spend the morning exploring the old town with my self-guided walk, then do a boat cruise and ascend a mountain lift in the afternoon. Extra time (and you'll have some) can be spent relaxing in gardens and along the lakefront.

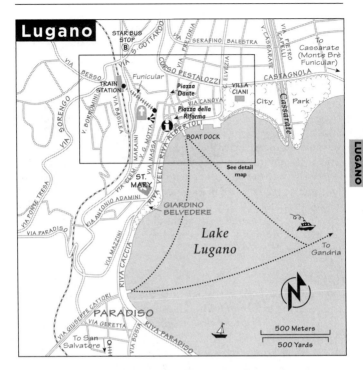

Orientation to Lugano

The old town is on Lake Lugano, which is bordered by promenades and parks. A funicular connects the old town with the train station above. Nearly everything in this chapter (with the exception of the mountain lifts) is within a five-minute walk of the base of the funicular. The town of Lugano fades into other, smaller waterfront communities all around the lake.

Italian is the language of Lugano and its region (Ticino), which is surrounded on three sides by Italy (see "Italian Survival Phrases" in the appendix). In this corner of Switzerland, a *Strasse* (street) becomes a *Via,* and a *Platz* (square) becomes a *Piazza.*

Tourist Information

Lugano's TI faces the boat dock a couple of blocks below the funicular (Easter-mid-Oct Mon-Fri 9:00-19:00, Sat 9:00-18:00, Sun 10:00-18:00; off-season Mon-Fri 9:00-12:00 & 13:30-17:30, Sat 10:00-12:30 & 13:30-17:00, closed Sun; Palazzo Civico, Riva Albertolli, tel. 058-866-6600, www.luganoturismo.ch).

The TI offers free **walking tours** in English four days a week, with a different theme each day (Mon 9:30—classic tour; Thu 9:30—history through architecture; Fri 14:20—to the top of

Monte Brè; Sun 10:00—parks and gardens; all tours leave from TI except Monte Brè, which starts at funicular station at the bottom of the mountain; details for all tours at TI).

Arrival in Lugano

The train station has lockers (in the underground passage and out front, small locker-6 SF, big locker-9 SF), a less convenient and pricier baggage-storage counter (10 SF, short hours), ATMs, a convenient grocery (Piccobello, daily 6:00-22:00), a surprisingly genteel restaurant, and a room-finding service—but no real TI. The easiest way to get to the town below is by funicular (look for *funicolare per il centro* sign in the middle of the station, every 5 minutes, daily 5:20-23:50, 1.10 SF, free with Swiss Pass). The funicular deposits you right in the heart of the old town, at Piazza Cioccaro, a short walk from my recommended accommodations (and at the start of my self-guided walk).

Helpful Hints

Internet Access: A few blocks off Piazza della Riforma is a no-name call center with reasonable rates; look for Lebara Mobile and Western Union signs in the window (6 SF/hour, Mon-Fri 9:00-19:00, Sat 9:00-17:30, closed Sun, Via Canova 9). The **Manora** self-service restaurant, also in the middle of town, has free Wi-Fi for customers (see "Eating in Lugano," later).

Local Guide: Lovely **Christa Branchi** teaches enthusiastically about her city and its history (180 SF/1-3 hours, 220 SF/half-day, 330 SF/day, tel. 091-606-3302, christabranchi@hotmail .com).

Getting Around Lugano

The town center is easily walkable, and the two nearby hilltop excursions, San Salvatore and Monte Brè, start from funicular stations that are each a 20-minute lakeside stroll away from the center. To save time, you can reach both these lifts with bus #1 (4-6/hour). Buy bus tickets from the coin-op machines next to any bus stop (1.60 SF, day pass-5 SF, all Lugano buses covered by Swiss Pass).

Self-Guided Walk

Welcome to Lugano

Little, resorty Lugano hides some interesting history, but let's face it: You're here to relax. Consider taking this short stroll to get yourself oriented...or just grab a gelato and wind your own way through the city center's arcades and lakeside promenade.

To join me on the walk, start on Piazza Cioccaro, at the base of the funicular that connects the train station with the town center.

• *With your back to the funicular, go down the narrow street to the right of the building at the bottom of the square.*

Via Pessina: In this tangled, colorful little corner are several small shops run by Signor Gabbani. Stop in if you'd like to sample some of the best local cheese, bread, salami, and/or wine.

• *Farther down, at Via Pessina 3, is...*

Grand Café al Porto: This venerable institution is both Lugano's best spot for cakes and coffee and the most historic café in town. The *1803* above the fireplace is the date it opened—and also when Ticino joined the Swiss Federation. Once a convent (notice the fine *sgraffito* facade), the café evokes the 19th-century days when Giuseppe Mazzini and fellow Italian patriots would huddle here—safely over the border—planning their next move to unify Italy. Much later, as World War II wound down, US dignitary Allen Welsh Dulles met right here with Nazi and Italian representatives to organize a graceful end to the war and prevent the Germans from ruining Italy with a scorched-earth retreat. And in more carefree times, this is where Clark Gable and Sophia Loren dipped cookies in their coffee.

• *Just past Grand Café al Porto, take a left at the fountain into...*

Piazza della Riforma: This square is Lugano's living room. The city is proudly reformist, as the name of its main square implies.

Its progressive spirit from the days of the Risorgimento (Italian unification) survives today, as Lugano remains one of the most liberal-voting cities in Switzerland. This square—with geraniums cascading on all sides—hosts an open-air cinema, markets (Tue and Fri), and local festivals.

• *Facing the giant, yellow City*

Lugano Center

1. To Hotel International au Lac
2. Hotel San Carlo
3. Hotel/Restaurant Pestalozzi
4. Art Hotel Stella
5. Hotel & Hostel Montarina
6. La Tinera Restaurant
7. Manora Cafeteria
8. Bottegone del Vino
9. Co-op Cafeteria
10. Grand Café al Porto
11. Pizzeria Tango
12. Sass Café
13. Olympia Restaurant
14. Vanini Café
15. Internet Access
16. Paddleboat Rentals (2)
17. Giosy Tours Bus Stop

Hall, make a 90-degree left turn and walk (between the farmacia *and the white bank building) down...*

Via Canova: This street leads directly to the city park. Follow it for a few blocks, watching for the elegant gallery that burrows through a block (on your left). Just after that, on your right, you'll pass the **Cantonal Art Museum** (Museo Cantonale d'Arte), which displays ever-changing art exhibits (main collection-7 SF, with special exhibits-12 SF, covered by Swiss Pass, Wed-Sun 10:00-17:00, Tue 14:00-17:00, closed Mon, Via Canova 10, may move to new LAC center in 2013, tel. 091-910-4780).

Next is the creamy little **Church of San Rocco.** Its rich frescoes celebrate the saint responsible for protecting the city against the plague.

Beyond the Church of San Rocco is the park-like **Piazza Indipendenza.** The giant head on its side is the work of Polish sculptor Igor Mitoraj, who has decorated squares all over Europe with similar sculptures. On your right is the vast, sterile **casino** building. Though its blocky, modern style doesn't quite

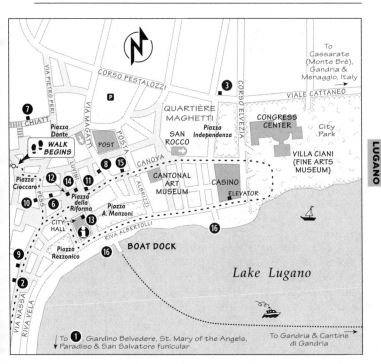

fit the otherwise elegant architecture of this area, it does have an elevator leading up to a fine lake view (lake side of building—we'll pass there later on this walk).

• *Continuing straight across the street from Piazza Indipendenza, pass through the gate to come face-to-face with the pink palace in the...*

City Park (Parco Civico Villa Ciani): The park's centerpiece, the Villa Ciani, houses a fine-arts museum. Sprawling from here

along the lake is a lush park filled with modern art and exotic trees from around the world. Its water gate evokes the 19th century, when this was the private domain of aristocrats. The flower beds are organized to show off maximum color all year long. If the weather's nice, stow your guidebook and remember you're on vacation as you explore this ingeniously landscaped, people-friendly space. It's lit at night and particularly good for a late, romantic stroll (open daily 6:00-23:00, until 21:00 in winter).

• *From the city park, walk back to the town center along the...*

Waterfront: This lovely promenade may get even nicer in

coming years, as the city is considering barring car traffic along this stretch of the lakefront. On the right, the casino's top-floor restaurant overlooks the lake. If it's open, ride the glass *elevatore* up and down for a fun and free view (daily 12:00-15:00 & 19:00-24:00). Then continue strolling through the arcade or under the mulberry trees (a favorite of silk worms, dating from the time when silk was a local industry) until you reach the **TI** and the **boat dock** (for information on lake cruises, see page 286). On the way, you'll pass several places to rent paddleboats (8 SF/30 minutes).

Look across the lake for the village clustered around a huge, blocky, sand-colored building (lit up in bright colors at night). That's the Casinò di Campione, the largest casino in Europe, which enjoys special legal privileges, granted by Mussolini when he saw what casino tourism had done for nearby Lugano. The casino dominates **Campione d'Italia**—a tiny enclave of Italy that's surrounded by Switzerland on all sides; residents use Swiss francs, have Swiss phone numbers and license plates, and pay Swiss taxes... but carry Italian passports.

• *Back at the yellow City Hall building, cross the busy road (notice the pedestrian underpass nearby). A block inland from the TI is Piazza della Riforma again. The first left is...*

Via Nassa: This is one of Lugano's main shopping streets. For the next several blocks, just enjoy the wandering, window-shopping, and people-watching along this gauntlet of boutiques and jewelry shops under typical Lombardi arcades. On the right, at #22, the Co-op department store (closed Sun) has a good selection of chocolates (just inside the door on the left) and a handy, recommended top-floor cafeteria (lunch only, great views).

• *Follow Via Nassa until it dead-ends at the small but historic...*

Church of St. Mary of the Angels (Chiesa Santa Maria degli Angioli): This lakefront church, which dates from 1499, was part of a monastery (next door). Inside the church are the city's best frescoes.

The Passion and Crucifixion of Christ, the artistic highlight of all Ticino and the finest Renaissance fresco in Switzerland, is on the wall that separates the nave from the altar

The Story of Lugano

Lugano's history is tied to its strategic position: where the Italian world is pressed up against the Alps, and just below the most convenient alpine passes. The Celts crossed the Alps here and left their mark. The ancient Romans were here, too—the oldest sacred building in Switzerland is an early Christian baptistery on this lake.

In 1220, when the first road over the Gotthard Pass was built, the Swiss took an interest in acquiring the Italian-speaking region of Ticino, leading to a battle for control. The nearby town of Bellinzona is named not for the Italian *bella* ("beautiful"), but for the Latin *bellum* ("war"), and this truly was a medieval war zone. Several castles in Bellinzona recall a pivotal Swiss victory in 1513. With this success, the Swiss gained a toehold in Ticino.

But the feisty region maintained its independence. In 1798, Ticino even stood up to Napoleon by creating an independent Republic of Ticino. However, the people of Ticino were unable to rule themselves peacefully, and five years later (in 1803) they decided to join the Swiss Federation. With that event, the present-day borders of Switzerland were finally established.

In the 19th century, Lugano—Italian-speaking, just a short trip from Milan, yet safely over the border in Switzerland—provided a refuge and staging ground for intellectual Italian revolutionaries. They'd meet here to plan the Risorgimento, the struggle for Italian unification (c. 1840-1869). Later in the 19th century, tourism arrived and the grand lakefront hotels were built.

Today, Lugano is second among Swiss cities only to Zürich in its number of banks. It's easy for Italians and others with suitcases of hard cash—black money—to swing by and take advantage of the secret bank accounts. (Locals claim George H. W. Bush stops in annually.) But the mentality here remains Italian. Rather than the Zürich model ("live to work"), the people of Lugano brag that they work to live.

area. Milanese Bernardino Luini, who painted it in 1529, is sometimes called the "Raphael of the North" for the gentle expressions and calm beauty of his art. Follow the action as the scenes from Christ's passion are played out, from Jesus being crowned with thorns (left) to the doubting apostle Thomas touching Jesus' wound after his Resurrection (right). The central dominating theme is the Crucifixion. The work is riddled with symbolism. For instance, at the base of the cross, notice the skull and femur of Adam, as well as his rib (from which Eve was created). Worshippers saw this and remembered that without Adam and Eve's first sin, none of the terrible action in the rest of the fresco would have been necessary.

Luini spent a decade working on this. Take an extremely close-up look at the fresco technique.

Facing the giant fresco, look to your left to find the three smaller frames. This is Luini's *Last Supper,* which was sliced off a wall of the monks' dining hall and put on canvas to be hung here.

Finally, wander up to the front of the church. The altar is rich and unusual with its wooden inlay work.

• *Along the lakefront across from the church begins the...*

Giardino Belvedere: This delightful little garden park is an open-air modern-art museum. The building facing it was once a monastery, then the Grand Hotel Palace. This first grand hotel on the lake was radical in that it actually faced the lake. From here, survey the scene. Paradiso, the big hotel zone with its 80-foot-high fountain, is a 15-minute walk along the lakeside. From there, the San Salvatore lift zips sightseers to the summit (described next). The ridge across the lake marks the border of Italy.

• *Our walk is finished. If you've got energy left, continue along the lakefront on the pleasant path to Paradiso; there you can summit San Salvatore, hop on a lake cruise, or do both.*

Sights near Lugano

Mountain Lifts

Lugano is a base from which several relatively small peaks can be conquered, sweat-free, by lifts. At about 3,000 feet, Lake Lugano's mountains are unimpressive compared with the mightier Alps farther north; if you've done some of the higher lifts in the Berner Oberland or Zermatt regions, nothing here will thrill you. Still, the commanding mountaintop views over the lake are enjoyable. Doing more than one is overkill; San Salvatore is best and relatively handy to Lugano town.

▲**San Salvatore**—The easiest and most rewarding peak on the lake, thanks to its fine panoramic views, San Salvatore (2,990 feet) rockets up from the Lugano suburb of Paradiso.

At the top you'll find good viewpoints, as well as a playground, a self-serve cafeteria (13-16-SF meals, closes at 18:00), and an overpriced restaurant (10-20-SF pastas, 30-35-SF main dishes, food served 11:00-15:00, in high season also 19:00-23:00 but after dark you have no views). From the lift, be sure to climb five more minutes to the actual summit. On the way up, pop into the Salvatore Museum, with its small collection of religious art and exhibits on local geology (included in funicular ticket, Wed-Sun 10:00-12:00 & 13:00-15:00, closed Mon-Tue). At the top of the mountain, there's a small church surrounded by a view terrace. For the best panorama, climb to the rooftop of the church (entrance around the right side) for a sweeping, nearly 360-degree view. Unfortunately, the bay directly in front of Lugano is just about the only thing you can't see from up here.

Cost and Hours: 24 SF round-trip, half-price with Swiss Pass, 2/hour—departs on the hour and the half-hour, 12-minute ride, transfer to another funicular midway up, daily June-mid-Sept 9:00-23:00, off-season generally 9:00-18:00, closed early Nov-mid-March, these are last ascent times—last descent generally 30 minutes later, tel. 091-985-2828, www.montesansalvatore.ch.

LUGANO

Getting There: To reach the base of the funicular, either walk along the water (about 20 minutes south of the city center; keep

your eye out for brown signs indicating the funicular), or take bus #1 (direction: Paradiso, get off at Scuole Paradiso stop and go to the right, then take the next left downhill until you see the funicular station on the left; for bus details, see "Getting Around Lugano," earlier).

Monte Brè—Departing from the other end of Lugano, in the suburb of Cassarate, this funicular takes you to arguably the best

view down on the lagoon of Lugano itself (3,005 feet).

Cost and Hours: 23 SF round-trip, half-price with Swiss Pass, 2/hour—generally at :15 and :45 after the hour, daily June-Oct 9:00-19:00, Nov-Dec and March-May until 17:00, closed Jan-Feb, 20-minute trip, tel. 091-971-3171, www.montebre.ch.

Getting There: From Lugano's old town, you can take bus #1 to the Cassarate/Monte Brè stop. Getting off the bus, walk a little farther along the water, then follow brown *funicolare* signs uphill to the left. Don't dawdle—the turnstile gate closes with little warning shortly before the funicular departs.

Monte Generoso—The tallest but farthest from Lugano, Monte Generoso (5,590 feet) is high enough that you can see some of the more distant cut-glass peaks.

Cost and Hours: 39 SF round-trip, half-price with Swiss Pass, April-Oct departs from Capolago train station at :35 past the hour 9:20-15:35, plus 16:35 mid-May-mid-Sept, few or no trains Nov-March, tel. 091-630-5111, www.montegeneroso.ch.

Getting There: You'll take the train (15 minutes) or a much slower boat to Capolago, then ride 35 minutes on a cogwheel train up to Generoso Vetta, the summit; from the Lugano train station, you can reach the top in less than an hour.

Cruising Lake Lugano with a Stop in Gandria

Lake Lugano is made to order for a boat trip. Along with pad-

dleboats and simple cruises from village to village, you have a dizzying array of more elaborate excursions to choose from (a lunch trip, a grand tour, a shopping excursion into Italy, and an evening dinner cruise). Pick up the boat schedule *(orario)* listing your options, and ask the TI or at one of the boat docks for details.

One-Hour Loop Trip: The best basic trip is the one-hour circle from Lugano. This cruise stops at a few desolate restaurants and hamlets along the far side of the lake, visits Gandria (a peaceful and picturesque little fishing town with several romantic view restaurants), then returns to Lugano (24.20 SF round-trip including stopovers, or 14.60 SF for one segment, free with Swiss Pass). You can get off and hike. The far side of the lake has a trail lacing together several little grottos and hamlets (each with a boat stop) with hiking times and directions clearly marked. For information on the hike, ask the TI, your hotel, or even the guys on the boat. Note that if you're hopping on and off the boat, you'll actually cobble together the trip from various longer cruises, each with different itineraries. Some circle the lake clockwise, others counterclockwise, and not every boat makes every stop. Study the boat schedule, carefully noting when the next boat comes by and exactly where it stops (as this can be confusing).

Stops on the Lake: Cantine di Gandria has two traditional trattorias and wine grottos—great for a rustic meal or just a snack and a drink (they close on different days, so at least one is sure to be open on any given day in the summer; they're both closed Nov-April). A five-minute walk from Cantine di Gandria takes you to the **Customs Museum** (Museo Doganale) with underwhelming exhibits on customs and smuggling (free, no English but worth a 10-minute visit, April-mid-Oct daily 13:30-17:30, closed mid-Oct-

March). Boats stop alternately at Cantine di Gandria and Museo Doganale.

Gandria, around the headland on the Lugano side of the lake, is the most intriguing stop. This dense cluster of fishing houses hangs over the lake with a few lazy, romantic hotels and several inviting restaurants. Of the various waterfront options, **Restaurant Miralago Gandria** is immediately above the ferry dock, with an extremely romantic setting (mediocre food, fair prices, 18-20-SF pastas, 30-SF main dishes, open daily, tel. 091-971-4361). You can lob bits of bread to the hungry birds, rewarding the ones who fly high circles by your lakeside table. **Locanda Gandriesi** has better cooking and a smaller, quieter terrace, but is pricier and farther from the boat dock and birds (go left from the dock—it's about a 5-minute walk, just below the church; 18-24-SF pasta and polenta dishes, 35-45-SF main dishes, open daily, tel. 091-971-4181).

If stopping in Gandria, you can walk back to Lugano (great 45-minute lakeside path before hitting the Castagnola suburb of Lugano, then a boring 30-minute walk along streets into town). To skip the boring part of the walk, catch bus #1 from the Castagnola post office back into Lugano.

Note that the last boat of the day from Gandria back to Lugano leaves at 18:15 (or 19:05 in July-Aug); a bus runs after that (bus #490, departing Gandria at 18:25), except on Sundays. If you stay longer and miss the boat and bus, you'll have to walk or fork over 40-50 SF for a taxi.

Half-Day Plan: Here's a pleasant way to spend a late afternoon and evening (schedules are subject to change—confirm boat times before departing):

15:45 Walk from Lugano to Paradiso (20-minute walk, plus time to stroll and snap photos).

16:13 Catch the boat from Paradiso to Gandria and have a drink and appetizer, or an early dinner in Gandria (at Miralago Gandria—early diners always get lakeside tables).

18:15 (or 19:05 in July-Aug) Catch the last boat to Paradiso. Once at Paradiso, walk to the San Salvatore lift, ride the lift to the summit of the mountain (beautiful at twilight but disappointing after dark), ride back down, and walk along the lake from Paradiso back to Lugano.

Sleep Code

(1 SF = about $1.10, country code: 41)
S = Single, **D** = Double/Twin, **T** = Triple, **Q** = Quad, **b** = bathroom, **s** = shower only. Unless otherwise noted, credit cards are accepted, English is spoken, and breakfast is included.

To help you sort easily through these listings, I've divided the accommodations into three categories, based on the price for a standard double room with bath during high season:

$$$ **Higher Priced**—Most rooms 200 SF or more.
$$ **Moderately Priced**—Most rooms between 120-200 SF.
$ **Lower Priced**—Most rooms 120 SF or less.

Prices can change without notice; verify the hotel's current rates online or by email. For other updates, see www .ricksteves.com/update.

Sleeping in Lugano

In the City Center

$$$ Hotel International au Lac is a classic, pricey hotel with 78 rooms, old-school furnishings, some Lake Lugano views, and even a "museum" of relics from the hotel's Victorian past. It's conveniently and scenically located where pedestrian-only Via Nassa hits the lake. Four generations of Schmids have maintained the early-20th-century ambience since 1906, with old photos, inviting lounges, antique furniture, and, it seems, many of their original guests (Sb-120-185 SF, Db-200-315 SF, price depends on size and view, check online for occasional deals, extra adult-40 SF, extra child-20 SF, closed Nov-Easter, family-friendly, air-con, elevator, free Internet access, free Wi-Fi in lobby, pay Wi-Fi in rooms, terrace restaurant, fun view seats on balcony of bar, swimming pool, parking-20 SF/day, Via Nassa 68, tel. 091-922-7541, fax 091-922-7544, www.hotel-international.ch, info@hotel -international.ch).

$$ Hotel San Carlo, also on the pedestrian-only shopping street, but closer to the center, rents 20 small but cheerful rooms. This welcoming place is run by Anna Martina and Beppe. The flamboyant Italian-mod design within its old walls is fun and refreshing, with much of the hand-carved woodwork proudly done by Beppe himself (Ss-95-100 SF, Sb-120-40 SF, Ds-145-150 SF, Db-170-175 SF, Qb-280 SF, cheaper off-season, elevator, no air-con but fans, pay Internet access, free Wi-Fi, Via Nassa 28, tel. 091-922-7107, fax 091-922-8022, www.hotelsancarlolugano.com, sancarlo@ticino.com).

$$ Hotel Pestalozzi, near the city park, is plain and vaguely institutional. It offers 55 fresh, modern, somewhat sterile rooms with a woody Nordic touch and some lake views. Though it's a bit longer walk from the train station funicular, this hotel is a particularly good value (S-68 SF, Sb-104-110 SF, D-116 SF, Db-176-196 SF—pricier rooms have lake view and/or air-con, extra bed-40-50 SF, elevator, pay Internet access and Wi-Fi, recommended and affordable restaurant, Piazza Indipendenza 9, tel. 091-921-4646, fax 091-922-2045, www.pestalozzi-lugano.ch, pestalo@bluewin.ch).

Near the Train Station

$$ Art Hotel Stella, a wonderful little oasis, offers 14 rooms between slick office buildings just behind the train station. Owner Antoinette Burkhard's love of modern art is evident, with statues on the patio and fun paintings throughout. Enjoy the garden and the tiny swimming pool (Sb-120 SF, Db-170 SF, Tb-200 SF, 5 percent discount with this book, some rooms have terraces, air-con, free Internet access and Wi-Fi, Via Francesco Borromini 5, tel. 091-966-3370, fax 091-966-6755, www.arthotelstella.ch, info @arthotelstella.ch). Exit the station to the rear (toward track 4), turn right and follow the tracks for 50 yards, take the first left uphill, then turn left up Via Francesco Borromini.

$-$$ Hotel & Hostel Montarina, a creaky pink mansion in a palm garden overlooking the lake, has to be one of Europe's most

appealing hostels. It's a great hotel option as well. It has 140 dorm beds (27 SF, sheets-3 SF, 5-16 bunks per dorm), as well as 24 private rooms; half of these are antique rooms with classic furniture and shared bathrooms (S-80 SF, D-110 SF), and the other half are modern "comfort" rooms, with private bathrooms (Sb-90 SF, Db-130 SF, extra bed-40 SF). Surrounded by lush tropical gardens and an extremely inviting swimming pool, and with a helpful staff, this place is well worth considering even for non-hostelers (breakfast buffet-12 SF, reception open 7:30-23:00, late-night train noise, lockers, small kitchen, self-service laundry, pay Internet access, free cable Internet, free Wi-Fi in lobby, free parking, Via Montarina 1, tel. 091-966-7272, fax 091-966-0017, www .montarina.ch, info@montarina.ch). At the train station, head to track 4, then walk along the tracks with the station and lake on your left, and go through the parking lot toward the *Continental Parkhotel* sign. Just before the sign and a stone wall, take the sharp uphill turn to the right; halfway up the hill, go left through the gate marked *#1*.

Eating in Lugano

My recommended restaurants are all in the old town. I've empha-sized some more affordable options, with a few splurges (you'll pay a premium to dine on Piazza della Riforma, but it can be worth the expense). Lugano is not the best place for lakeside dining. For better value, cross the lake to the remote little grotto restaurants, or visit the town of Gandria (both options described on page 287). Good news for the wine-curious: You'll pay the same per liter for the little one-deciliter (about 3.5 oz) glasses as you do for the big half-liter (about 17 oz) carafes—so go with the small glasses and try several different wines. Experiment. The Ticino merlot is great.

La Tinera, beloved by locals, serves affordable, traditional Ticinese cuisine. It's tucked away in an old wine cellar, with heavy wooden furniture and decorated with wine bottles and antique copper cookware (20-SF daily specials, 20-30-SF meat dishes, 14-20-SF smaller dishes, Tue-Sat 11:30-15:00 & 17:30-22:30, closed Sun-Mon and Jan, Via dei Gorini, just a block behind Piazza della Riforma, tel. 091-923-5219).

Manora is an enticing self-service restaurant offering afford-able, healthy food. Choose to sit inside or out on the covered ter-race (with a playground). It's near the Manor supermarket on Piazza Dante Alighieri (100 yards from bottom of train station funicular; 10-17-SF main dishes, salad bar, pasta bar, lots more, Mon-Sat 7:30-22:00, Sun 10:00-22:00).

Bottegone del Vino is an expensive little eatery appreciated for its fine wine. The menu is small and rustic, the wine is excel-lent, and the indoor or outdoor ambience is of a quality wine bar. Sitting here, you feel in the know—but order carefully, as prices really add up (20-30-SF dishes, Mon-Sat 11:30-24:00, closed Sun, a block off Piazza della Riforma at Via Magatti 3, tel. 091-922-7689).

Restaurante Pestalozzi, close to the city park, serves reason-ably priced, crank-'em-out meals in an alcohol-free setting (15-20-SF daily specials, open daily 11:00-21:30, Piazza Indipendenza 9, tel. 091-921-4646).

Co-op Cafeteria, midway along the Via Nassa pedestrian mall, has an elegant-as-cafeterias-go dining area on its top floor, with a pretty rooftop terrace (Mon-Sat 11:30-14:30, closed Sun, Via Nassa 22).

Grand Café al Porto isn't the cheapest place in town for cof-fee and pastries, but it's definitely the most elegant, and boasts a rich history (Mon-Sat 8:00-18:30, closed Sun, Via Pessina 3, tel. 091-910-5130; see "Welcome to Lugano" walk, earlier).

Around Piazza della Riforma: Various restaurants offer decent food and great people-watching from outdoor tables on Lugano's main piazza. The ambience here is magical at twilight. I like **Pizzeria Tango,** where a helpful waitstaff serves Italian cuisine with a Ticino influence. While many of its tables face the busy main piazza, its interior and the tables facing a quiet little

square on the back may be more inviting (14-25-SF pizzas, 20-25-SF pastas, 35-40-SF meat dishes, daily 8:00-24:00, Piazza della Riforma, tel. 091-922-2701). Also consider **Sass Café** (classy wine bar with 25-30-SF daily specials, 25-SF pastas, and 50-SF à la carte items), **Olympia** (the mayor's fave, below City Hall, 12-25-SF pizzas, 20-30-SF pastas, 25-50-SF main dishes), and **Vanini Café** (tops for coffee and desserts; try the *marrons glacés*—candied chestnuts).

Lugano Connections

Lugano is a long detour from virtually anywhere else in Switzerland. It's best connected to other Swiss destinations by scenic trains—the **William Tell Express** (train-and-boat combination to Luzern) or the **Bernina Express** (bus-and-train combination to eastern Switzerland). The Bernina Express bus leaves for Tirano near Lugano's train station (200 yards to the left as you leave the station, see chart at station). More details about these trips are in the Scenic Rail Journeys chapter. Train info: toll tel. 0900-300-300 or www.rail.ch.

From Lugano by Train to: Luzern (hourly, 2.5 hours, half with easy change in Arth-Goldau), **Zürich** (hourly, 2.75 hours, half with easy change in Arth-Goldau), **Interlaken Ost** (hourly, 4.75 hours, 1-2 changes), **Bern** (hourly, 3.75 hours, transfer in Luzern or Zürich), **Milan** (hourly, 1 hour).

From Lugano by Bus to St. Moritz: The "Palm Express" bus to St. Moritz leaves only once a day in peak season and just on weekends off-season, but it's handy if you're headed to Italy's Lake Como, because it stops in lakeside Menaggio en route (departs Lugano's train station usually at 11:55 but confirm time in advance; 50 minutes to Menaggio, 3.5 hours to St. Moritz; daily mid-June–mid-Oct, mid-Oct–mid-June runs Sat-Mon only).

From Lugano by Bus to Italy's Lake Como: In addition to the handy Palm Express described above, an Italian-run bus (#C12) goes from Cassarate (a suburb just east of Lugano, served by local bus #1 from Lugano's old town) to Menaggio on Lake Como (departs at least every 2 hours, 1 hour).

From Lugano to Milan's Airports: The closest major airports to Lugano are actually in Italy, near the city of Milan: Malpensa Airport and Linate Airport (www.sea-aeroportimilano.it). The handiest way to reach either is to use the direct shuttle service operated by **Giosy Tours** (7/day, 70 minutes, 35 SF, reserve ahead, departs from in front of train station, tel. 091-858-2326, www.giosytours.ch). Alternatively, you can take the 1-hour train to Milan's Central Station, where cheap and easy shuttle buses leave about every 15 minutes for both Malpensa and Linate.

PONTRESINA, SAMEDAN, and ST. MORITZ

The Romansh Resorts of the Upper Engadine

Pontresina, Samedan, and St. Moritz are a trio of towns that anchor the Upper Engadine region, tucked away in an intriguing and scenic fringe of Switzerland. Here you'll ride a lift to a thrilling mountain-capping hike, stroll with the high rollers in a ritzy resort, explore the unique townscapes of an exotically remote mountain valley, and hear enticing snippets of the obscure Romansh language.

Nestled in the southeast corner of the country, the time-passed Upper Engadine (Engiadin Ota in Romansh, Oberengadin in German) is arguably less thrilling—and certainly more difficult to reach—than the mountain resorts of the Berner Oberland and Zermatt. But this region wedged in the Alps between Italy and Austria, in the canton of Graubünden, offers rough-around-the-edges mountain culture that feels far from Germanic influence, and closer to the Latin roots that run deep beneath this part of Switzerland. For tourists riding the scenic Bernina Express or Glacier Express, this area is an easy stopover.

On first glance, there may not seem to be much history here—but look closer. Celtic people inhabited this region centuries before Christ, and the hillsides are still terraced, recalling the hard work that came with farming up here in ancient times. History is in the region's unique language, too: Romansh evolved from a form of Latin that arrived with the Etruscans, who were chased here as Rome expanded. Town names date back to various invaders. For instance, "Pontresina" comes from "Bridge of the Saracens."

Two valleys meet here, carving out a picturesque region dominated by three very different towns. The most famous is the swanky ski resort of St. Moritz, which, like a too-sweet dessert, is enjoyable only until its glitz makes you sick. Pontresina is a lower-key but still upper-crust resort town with even better access to high-mountain lifts, making it an ideal base for hikers. And humble little Samedan feels more like a real town, with just enough hotels to make it cozy. If you can set aside the jet set comparing tans in St. Moritz, the Upper Engadine feels like a place where workaday Swiss people go to find some high-altitude fun. English-language newspapers are in short supply, an indication that while there are many visitors, most are Swiss.

Planning Your Time

Unless you're passing through on a scenic rail journey, the Upper Engadine is probably too time-consuming to reach to be worth cramming into a busy itinerary. I'd head for the Berner Oberland instead. But with plenty of time to enjoy Switzerland—and a healthy curiosity about its overlooked Romansh corner, not to mention this area's famous resorts—it's worth a visit. Conveniently, the Upper Engadine happens to link two scenic rail trips: the Bernina Express and the Glacier Express (see the Scenic Rail Journeys chapter). Hop off the train here, set up a home base, explore, and then continue on your way.

The three towns in this chapter—Pontresina, Samedan, and St. Moritz—form a convenient little triangle, each about 10 minutes apart by train. With a full day here and some good planning, you can sample all three and throw in a hike to boot.

Like other resort areas, this region has two distinct tourist seasons: summer (June-Oct) and winter (Dec-March). Outside of these seasons, many places are closed and the area can feel dead.

Getting Around the Upper Engadine

There's no need for a car in this region. Pontresina, Samedan, St. Moritz, and Punt Muragl (the base of the funicular to Muottas Muragl) are all well-connected by train and bus.

Trains connect each of the three towns about hourly (about 10 minutes between towns, 5.20 SF).

The local **bus** system is good, but a bit confusing. Pick up the bus schedule *(Fahrplan/Urari)* at a local TI, and study your options. Pay attention to which stop to use in a given town. For example, Pontresina Bahnhof is at the bottom of town, while two other stops are up in the town center: Pontresina Post, near my recommended hotels; and Pontresina Rondo, near the TI. St. Moritz has several stops, including Dorf (charming town center), Bahnhof (train station), and Bad (dull lakeside spa zone). Rides between towns cost 5.20 SF; rides within a town (such as between St. Moritz Bad and St. Moritz Dorf) cost 3 SF.

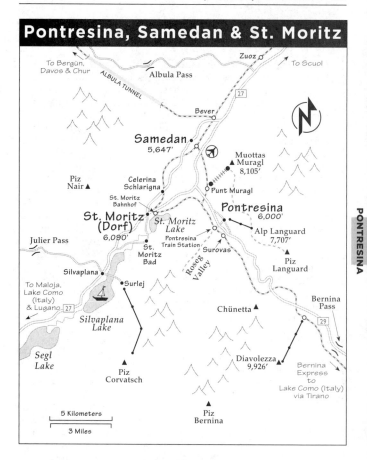

Pontresina, Samedan & St. Moritz

To Bergün, Davos & Chur

ALBULA TUNNEL

Albula Pass

Zuoz

To Scuol

27

Bever

Samedan
5,647'

Muottas
▲ Muragl
8,105'

Piz
Nair ▲

Celerina
Schlarigna

St. Moritz
Bahnhof

Punt Muragl

Pontresina
6,000'

**St. Moritz
(Dorf)**
6,090'

St. Moritz
Lake

Pontresina
Train Station

Alp Languard
7,707'

Julier Pass

St.
Moritz
Bad

Surovas

Piz
Languard

Silvaplana

Surlej

Roseg
Valley

To Maloja,
Lake Como
(Italy)
& Lugano 27

Silvaplana
Lake

Chünetta ▲

Bernina
Pass

29

Segl
Lake

Diavolezza
9,926'

Bernina
Express
to
Lake Como (Italy)
via Tirano

Piz
Corvatsch ▲

Piz
Bernina ▲

5 Kilometers

3 Miles

PONTRESINA

Bus #1 is particularly confusing, as two different routes operate using this same number. One bus #1 goes from Pontresina to Punt Muragl, then on to Samedan (hourly in summer, 1-2/hour rest of year, 15 minutes). A different bus #1 goes from Pontresina to Punt Muragl, then to St. Moritz Bahnhof and St. Moritz Bad (but skips Samedan; hourly, figure 10-15 minutes from Pontresina to St. Moritz). Carefully check the schedule and the destination posted on the bus before boarding.

Other bus lines are more straightforward:

Bus #2 links Pontresina, Punt Muragl, and St. Moritz Dorf (2/hour).

Bus #3 connects St. Moritz Bahnhof with St. Moritz Dorf (4/hour).

Buses #5 and **#6** connect Samedan with St. Moritz Dorf (each 2/hour).

Allegra (Welcome) to Graubünden

Pontresina, Samedan, St. Moritz, and the rest of the Upper Engadine belong to Switzerland's biggest canton, Graubünden. Isolated by high mountain ranges, this canton is also one of the country's most conservative. The name Graubünden goes back to 1395, when a group of farmers wearing gray clothes organized themselves in the "Gray League" to fight for their autonomy. This fiercely independent region didn't join the Swiss Confederation until 1803.

People in Graubünden believe the best way to control nature is to obey it. Passionate about their environment, they purify all dirty water before returning it to the rivers. Engineers are currently going through the expensive process of removing canals (built to direct streams and rivers) and allowing the water to choose its own course once again. The natives love their beautiful countryside and cherish their customs—consistently voting against EU membership and other issues that might compromise Swiss neutrality and self-determination.

Graubünden cuisine is hearty. Try *Pizokel,* a *Spätzle*-like creation of cheesy flour dumplings. In fall you might find *Pizokel* made from chestnut flour and served with wild mushroom stew. The Graubünden's air-dried beef, *Bündnerfleisch*—very expensive and sliced paper-thin—is popular throughout Switzerland. *Capuns* are cabbage leaves stuffed with a mix of dough, leeks, bacon, onion, and air-dried beef. *Bündner Gerstensuppe* is a creamy barley and vegetable soup. For a Graubünden dessert, it's got to be *Nusstorte,* a rich walnut cake.

Graubünden has three official languages: German, Italian, and Romansh (an ancient dialect that comes directly from Latin). You'll overhear conversations where one person speaks Italian, the other replies in German, a third butts in with Romansh...and everybody understands each other. On the trains, the announcements are in German and Romansh (which sounds a bit like Italian).

Most tourists here speak German (others Italian, others English), but if you'd like to please your Romansh hosts, try these phrases:

Welcome.	*Allegra.*	ah-LEY-grah
Hello (Good day).	*Bun di.*	boon dee
Good evening. (after 17:00)	*Buna saira.*	BOO-nah SIGH-rah
Please.	*Per plaschair.*	pehr plah-ZHAIR
Thank you. (very much)	*Grazcha.* *(fich)*	GRAHTS-chah (feech)
Goodbye.	*Arevair.*	ah-reh-VAIR

Helpful Hints

Altitude Alert: Even the valley floor here is at a high elevation (more than 6,000 feet), and you might feel dizzy and tired, especially on your first day. Top athletes from all over the world come here for altitude training before the Olympics.

Guest Card: If you're staying at least two nights in the Upper Engadine region in the summer, your hotel may give you a free Engadin Card, which can save you plenty (10-SF deposit). Sometimes this card covers local public transportation (including trains and buses), sometimes it covers mountain lifts, but usually it covers both (as well as guided hikes). Hoteliers can choose to opt in or out of the various versions—ask when you reserve.

Winter Activities: If you're here in winter and want to ski some of the most famous slopes in the world, head for Corviglia, the largest ski area in the region, which offers varied terrain, mostly intermediate runs, and good snowboarding (convenient from St. Moritz, or a bus ride from Pontresina). Other areas to consider are Corvatsch-Furtschellas (great views) and Diavolezza-Lagalb (smaller, less crowded, great for non-skiers who want views). Both cater mainly to intermediate and expert skiers. See www.bergbahnenengadin.ch for more information and to buy lift tickets in advance. Winter isn't just about hitting the slopes, though—the area has more than 100 miles of cross-country skiing trails, great sledding, Nordic walking, and spectator sports such as polo in the snow (horses and all). Ask at any TI for information; for more tips, see the Switzerland in Winter chapter.

PONTRESINA

Pontresina

A popular winter and summer mountain resort with about 2,000 residents, Pontresina makes a good Upper Engadine home base. At 6,000 feet above sea level on a wind-protected terrace overlooking the Bernina Valley, Pontresina faces southwest and enjoys plenty of sunshine. Popular trails through its larch forests offer spectacular views of the 13,000-foot Piz Bernina peak and the immense Morteratsch glacier.

Pontresina's first tourists, mostly German and British, arrived in the 1850s. For a while, it was a summer-only destination. But by the early 1900s, the Muottas Muragl railway was inaugurated, the first grand hotels were built, and tourists began showing up in winter, too. Although a bit sterile and resorty—with not quite enough local charm or character—Pontresina is handier than Samedan and not as glitzy as St. Moritz, making it the best compromise home base in this region.

Orientation to Pontresina

Pontresina sits on a ledge overlooking a valley where the Bernina and Roseg rivers meet, forming the Flazbach River. Virtually everything of interest is along Via Maistra (may-strah), which means "Main Street" in Romansh. The post office and my recommended hotels are at the top end of Via Maistra, and the TI is near the bottom end. The train station sits in the valley floor just below.

Tourist Information

The TI is in the heart of town in the slick Rondo Culture and Congress Center, right on Via Maistra. Pick up a pile of handy, free brochures: town map, local bus schedule *(Fahrplan/Urari)*, *Panorama* map showing the lifts and hiking trails, and biweekly *Information for Visitors* guide. The TI is happy to suggest tips for hikes and mountain lifts around the region (mid-June-mid-Oct and mid-Dec-mid-April Mon-Fri 8:30-18:00, Sat 8:30-12:00 & 15:00-18:00, Sun 16:00-18:00; mid-April-mid-June and mid-Oct-mid-Dec Mon-Fri 8:30-12:00 & 14:00-18:00, Sat 8:30-12:00, closed Sun; tel. 081-838-8300, www.pontresina.ch).

Arrival in Pontresina

The train station lies at the foot of the town. You can hike about 10 minutes steeply uphill to the town center, following the white signs to *Pontresina*. Or take bus #2 to Pontresina Post, near my recommended hotels, or Pontresina Rondo, near the TI (2/hour, 3 SF, free with Swiss Pass, buy ticket at counter inside train station or on board bus). Walking the 10 minutes from Pontresina back down to the train station on Via da Mulin offers spectacular gorge views along the way.

Helpful Hints

Internet Access: Most hotels offer Internet access to their guests (generally for a fee). You'll find Wi-Fi and public Internet terminals in the lobby of **Hotel Post** (2 SF/30 minutes for Internet access or Wi-Fi, daily 8:00-21:00, closed in May, Via Maistra 160) and at the **Bellavita** pool and spa complex (5 SF/hour, described later).

Ski Rental: Try **Gruber Sport** (at Via Maistra 190, across from Hotel Schweizerhof, tel. 081-842-6236) or **Engadina Sport** (also on the main drag at Via Maistra 41, tel. 081-842-6262).

Sights in Pontresina

Church of St. Mary (Begräbniskirche Sta. Maria)—Above town, just beyond the five-sided, 13th-century Spaniola Tower,

stands this remarkable little church. Inside, the wooden ceiling is entirely original. Faded 13th-century, Byzantine-inspired frescoes survive on the west wall. The other walls and ceiling were richly decorated by an Italian workshop (1497). The frescoes depict the legend of Mary Magdalene and (above) the story of Lazarus' resurrection. Imagine this church five centuries ago, packed with illiterate villagers who worshipped by following along with the pictures.

Cost and Hours: Free entry, but limited hours: generally July-mid-Oct Mon-Fri 15:30-17:30; mid-Dec-mid-April Mon, Wed, and Fri 14:30-16:00; most of June Mon, Wed, and Fri 15:30-17:30; closed mid-Oct-mid-Dec and mid-April-early June; no photos.

Alpine Museum (Museum Alpin)—This little museum is worth a quick visit. Situated on three floors of an old Engadine town house, it offers exhibits on the development of alpine mountain climbing and skiing, the regional mining industry (with plenty of mineral samples), hunting, local animals, and replicas of traditional rooms (bedroom, kitchen, living room). About 130 of the 250 different bird species found in the Upper Engadine are shown here. Listen to the recorded songs of 60 different birds on the primitive aviary jukebox. The 20-minute slideshow is in German and makes you feel like a wimp. Still, it's interesting for its images of "the mountain experience." Rounding out the space are temporary exhibits. Be sure to pick up the brief English descriptions when you enter.

Cost and Hours: 6 SF, not covered by Swiss Pass, June-Oct and mid-Dec-mid-April Mon-Sat 16:00-18:00—or from 15:00 in bad weather, closed Sun, closed mid-April-May and Nov-mid-Dec, Via Maistra, tel. 081-842-7273, www.pontresina.ch/museumalpin.

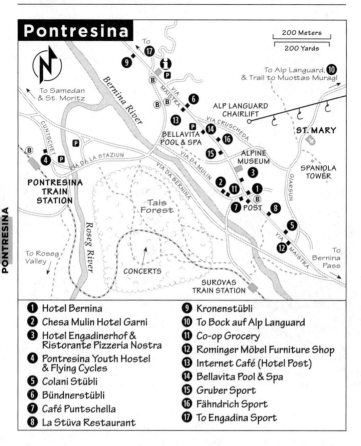

Pontresina

200 Meters
200 Yards

To Samedan
& St. Moritz

To Alp Languard, ⑩
& Trail to Muottas Muragl

Bernina River

ALP LANGUARD
CHAIRLIFT

VIA MAISTRA

VIA CRUSCHEDA

ST. MARY

BELLAVITA
POOL & SPA

ALPINE
MUSEUM

SPANIOLA
TOWER

VIA DA LA STAZIUN

VIA DA MULIN

VIA DA BERNINA

GIARSUN

PONTRESINA
TRAIN
STATION

*Tais
Forest*

POST

To
Bernina
Pass

Roseg River

VIA MAISTRA

To Roseg
Valley

CONCERTS

SUROVAS
TRAIN STATION

PONTRESINA

❶ Hotel Bernina	❾ Kronenstübli
❷ Chesa Mulin Hotel Garni	❿ To Bock auf Alp Languard
❸ Hotel Engadinerhof & Ristorante Pizzeria Nostra	⓫ Co-op Grocery
❹ Pontresina Youth Hostel & Flying Cycles	⓬ Rominger Möbel Furniture Shop
❺ Colani Stübli	⓭ Internet Café (Hotel Post)
❻ Bündnerstübli	⓮ Bellavita Pool & Spa
❼ Café Puntschella	⓯ Gruber Sport
❽ La Stüva Restaurant	⓰ Fähndrich Sport
	⓱ To Engadina Sport

Biking—Several sports stores rent bicycles, inline skates, tennis rackets, and other gear. Riding the train to the Bernina Pass and biking nine miles back into town is just one of many fun biking options. In the town center, **Fähndrich Sport** rents good mountain bikes with various suspensions (25-30 SF/half-day, 35-45 SF/day, helmets-7 SF/half-day or 10 SF/day, cheaper for multiple days, Mon-Fri 8:00-12:00 & 14:00-18:30, Sat until 17:00, closed Sun except July-Aug, at Hotel Allegra on Via Maistra, tel. 081-842-7155, www.faehndrich-sport.ch). Across the street from the train station, in the lower level of the big youth hostel building, **Flying Cycles** rents a huge selection of mountain bikes and fun, easy-to-learn electric-powered bikes (mountain bikes-25 SF/half-day, 33 SF/day; electric bikes-35/half-day, 50 SF/day; tandem bikes available, free loaner helmets, mid-June-mid-Sept daily 9:00-12:00 & 13:00-18:00, shorter hours and closed Sun-Mon in shoulder season, closed in winter, tel. 081-842-6844).

Music—Free summer classical music concerts are offered in the Tais Forest across the river, and (on rainy days) in the Rondo Center or in the church next door (daily at 11:00, mid-June-mid-Sept, confirm and get details at TI).

Bellavita Pool and Spa—This delightful pool complex is an ideal place to relax in any weather. The fun indoor-outdoor swimming-pool complex includes an enclosed 250-foot-long spiral waterslide and an outdoor pool that stays at 93 degrees Fahrenheit year-round. There's also an indoor water playground for kids and a spa with a series of saunas, steam baths, and more. (The spa is usually mixed-gender, adults-only, and clothing optional; it's women-only Mon 13:00-17:00 and Thu after 17:00; kids under 16 allowed with parents Sat-Sun 12:00-16:00.)

Cost and Hours: Pool only-11 SF, pool and spa-26.50 SF; pool open Mon-Fri 10:00-22:00, Sat-Sun until 20:30; spa open Mon 13:00-22:00, Tue-Fri 10:00-22:00, Sat-Sun 10:00-21:00; public pay Internet terminal in lobby, smack-dab in the middle of Via Maistra, tel. 081-837-0037, www.pontresina-bellavita.ch. You can rent a swimsuit for 10 SF, or buy one in the shop.

Hiking

Pontresina is a hiker's paradise. The town boasts one of Switzerland's largest mountaineering schools and has a good reputation for adventure sports. Shops lining Via Maistra rent and sell all kinds of sports gear. The TI will help you find just the right hike. Their great, free foldout *Panorama* map is marked with hiking trails and lists details about each one. They also hand out a leaflet describing a few popular routes. (Most hikers agree that the Muottas Muragl-Alp Languard route is tops.)

Upper Engadine trails come with high altitudes. Hikers should bring the appropriate gear (solid shoes, sun protection, windbreaker, hat, and water). Even in summer, with cold winds blowing down from the snow-capped mountains, it can get cold—especially on chairlifts. The sun is strong and the air is thin, so use sunscreen. Hiking trails are marked according to their difficulty. Yellow signs indicate easy hikes and walks. White-and-red signs signal more demanding hikes, where real hiking boots are in order. Blue signs are for alpine routes that require serious gear (these dangerous trails include rock climbing and glacier crossings).

Some flowers in the Alps are protected; pick one, and you may be fined. Some meadows are also protected for haymaking. Signs ask you to stick to the trails, as trampled grass is hard to cut.

Pontresina to Muottas Muragl to Alp Languard—For maximum alpine thrills per calorie burned, take this three-hour hike. It comes with grand views and takes you gradually down 1,000 feet in altitude. It's also possible to extend your mountain visit with an overnight stay in Muottas Muragl.

This impressive alpine perch overlooking Samedan and the valley is accessible by foot (from Pontresina) or by funicular. To reach the funicular, take either bus #1 or #2 from Pontresina, or catch the train between Pontresina and Samedan and get off at Punt Muragl (it's a request-only stop—press the green button, or it won't stop). The funicular dates from 1907 (24 SF one-way, 33 SF round-trip, June-Oct 2/hour from 8:00-23:00—round-trip ticket lets

you return on this funicular or on the Alp Languard lift described below).

Up top on Muottas Muragl (8,105 feet), you can hike, rent a deck chair, have a meal (self-service or pricey but good restaurant), or start your hike over to Alp Languard (7,710 feet). Midway, there's a great soup or coffee-and-cakes stop (ask for the WC key for a fun alpine memory). Keep your eyes open for ibex, bighorn stags, and marmots. For extra credit, consider the more challenging upper trail that climbs the mountainside above the main one. Each year a different appreciation-of-nature theme is displayed along this trail. If you're up for this more serious hike, ask for details at the TI.

At Alp Languard, a chalet serves reasonably priced traditional meals (see page 305). From here, hike or ride the lift down to Pontresina (15 SF one-way, 22 SF round-trip, June-Oct 8:30-17:30, also covered by round-trip Muottas Muragl funicular ticket).

Sleeping at Muottas Muragl: **$$$ Alpine Hotel Muottas Muragl** offers a secluded overnight high in the Alps. When the funicular takes the last tourist down, things become as peaceful as the Alps can be (open mid-June-mid-Oct and mid-Dec-mid-April only, Db-240-320 SF depending on view and size of room, cheaper for 3 or more nights, includes funicular ticket, Wi-Fi, free parking at base of funicular, tel. 081-842-8232, www.muottasmuragl.ch, info@muottasmuragl.ch).

Other Hikes—A fun way to explore the nearby Roseg Valley and marvel at its glacier (from a distance) is to hike two hours up the valley and take the **horse-drawn "omnibus"** back to Pontresina (reservations required, June-Oct departures at fixed hours, 18 SF one-way, 28 SF round-trip, tel. 081-842-6057, Luigi Costa). You can also rent a private carriage (110 SF one-way, 160 SF round-trip).

Consider taking the train up to the **Bernina Pass** (7,000 feet), hike around for a couple of hours, then take the train back—or, to get even higher, ride the cable car from the Bernina Pass up to **Diavolezza** (9,930 feet, 24 SF one-way, 33 SF round-trip, 2/hour, daily 8:30-17:00, until 17:30 in July-Aug).

The TI offers various guided hikes with themes, such as "Experiencing Wilderness with Marmots and Ibex" (free, cable-car ride costs 15 SF one-way, 22 SF round-trip, 3-4 hikes per week, reservations required). The hikes are guided in German; for a fee, you can hire an English-speaking mountaineer through the TI.

Shopping in Pontresina

Many sports and souvenir shops line Via Maistra. A typical product from the Upper Engadine is furniture carved from Arven pine (a.k.a. Scotch pine). The pine, special to this region, starts out light, darkens with time, and has spots where the branches used to be. Look for the tree's characteristic five-needle clusters when hiking.

Rominger Möbel, a local furniture store, makes the Arven pine furniture it sells. Its upstairs showroom is like a modern Engadine home show—walking among hand-carved beds, tables, and dressers gives you a sense of good living high in this remote corner of Switzerland (Mon-Fri 8:30-12:00 & 14:00-18:00, Sat until 17:00, closed Sun, 5-minute walk from town center on Via Maistra in the direction of Bernina Pass, tel. 081-842-6263, www .rominger.ch).

Sleeping in Pontresina

$$$ Hotel Bernina, a well-run and woody three-star place, feels high-quality, from the free and friendly pickup at the station (let them know what time you'll arrive) to the traditionally clad wait-resses who serve your breakfast coffee. Its 41 traditional and neat rooms are a fine value for this area (Sb-110-135 SF, Db-210-260 SF, price depends on room and season, elevator, sauna, free Internet access, free Wi-Fi in some parts of hotel, good restaurant serving Engadine specialties, Via Maistra 207, tel. 081-838-8686, fax 081-838-8687, www.hotelbernina.ch, info@hotelbernina.ch).

$$$ Chesa Mulin Hotel Garni, below the main street, offers 30 modern, bright, and comfortable rooms, each with a painting depicting a local legend, and almost all with new bathrooms. The inviting sitting area with open fireplace and library makes bad weather tolerable. The friendly Isepponi-Schmid family takes good care of their guests (Sb-117 SF, Db-206 SF, a bit more for stays of less than 3 nights, discounts sometimes available for guests over 60, great breakfast, elevator, sauna, sundeck, free access to Bellavita pool and spa with 2-night stay, free cable Internet, Via da

Sleep Code

(1 SF = about $1.10, country code: 41)

S = Single, **D** = Double/Twin, **T** = Triple, **Q** = Quad, **b** = bathroom, **s** = shower only. Unless otherwise noted, credit cards are accepted, English is spoken, and breakfast is included.

To help you sort easily through these listings, I've divided the accommodations into three categories, based on the price for a standard double room with bath during high season:

$$$ Higher Priced—Most rooms 180 SF or more.

$$ Moderately Priced—Most rooms between 130-180 SF.

$ Lower Priced—Most rooms 130 SF or less.

Most hotels in this region have a strict cancellation policy (30 days in advance with no penalty, but, thereafter, you'll generally have to pay for the entire period you reserved).

Prices can change without notice; verify the hotel's current rates online or by email. For other updates, see www.ricksteves.com/update.

Mulin 15, tel. 081-838-8200, fax 081-838-8230, www.chesa-mulin.ch, info@chesa-mulin.ch).

$$ Hotel Engadinerhof, while less cozy, can be a good value. Its 85 rooms gather around a sprawling and classic Old World lounge. The cheaper sink-only rooms ("Category A") are clean and have well-preserved furniture from the 1930s (S-75 SF, D-125 SF). "Category B" offers the same old-fashioned rooms, plus antique bathrooms (Sb-95 SF, Db-175 SF). "Category C" gets you modern rooms (Sb-105 SF, Db-195 SF; all rooms a bit cheaper in spring/fall and a bit more in winter, elevator, free Internet access, free pickup from train station if staying at least 3 nights, Via Maistra 203, tel. 081-839-3100, fax 081-839-3200, www.engadinerhof.com, info@engadinerhof.com).

$ Pontresina Youth Hostel, across the street from the train station, rents 130 beds. There's no curfew, and guests have 24-hour access (though check-in is limited to 16:00-18:30 & 19:30-21:00—or 16:00-22:00 in high season; dorm bed-54-72 SF depending on season and number of beds in room, S-97 SF, D-156-161 SF; price includes sheets, breakfast, three-course dinner, discount at Bellavita spa, and—if staying at least 2 nights—Engadin Card; 14.50 SF less for breakfast only, nonmembers pay 6 SF more per day, pay Internet access, free Wi-Fi, self-serve restaurant, game and TV room, closed May and Nov, tel. 081-842-7223, fax 081-842-7031, www.youthhostel.ch/pontresina, pontresina@youthhostel.ch).

Eating in Pontresina

Virtually all restaurants in Pontresina are part of a hotel, apart from a few bakeries that serve reasonably priced meals. Picnickers will seek out the **Co-op** grocery, just below Via Maistra on Via da Mulin (Mon-Fri 8:00-12:15 & 14:00-18:30, Sat 8:00-17:00, closed Sun).

Ristorante Pizzeria Nostra serves wood-fired pizzas as well as some local dishes in two pleasantly low-key rooms of what was once a stone farmhouse (14-24-SF pizzas and pastas, 25-40-SF meat dishes, daily 11:00-14:00 & 18:00-22:30, only pizza after 21:30, at Hotel Engadinerhof, Via Maistra 203, tel. 081-839-3333).

Colani Stübli, a cozy eatery, serves regional and seasonal specialties (20-SF local dishes such as *Krautpizokel* and *Capuns*, 30-40-SF entrées, 40-60-SF fixed-price meals, daily 11:30-14:00 & 18:00-21:00, limited menu available in the afternoon and after 21:00, at Hotel Steinbock, Via Maistra 219, tel. 081-839-3626).

Bündnerstübli dishes up hearty, traditional meals with fish and game in a woody, smartly upscale setting with great views from its front room. Many dishes are available in a cheaper "starter" size for a light meal. Consider being adventurous with the traditional appetizers, which work as main plates (30-50-SF fish and game, 12-17-SF salads, daily 18:00-22:00, at Hotel Rosatsch, Via Maistra 71, tel. 081-838-9800).

Café Puntschella is a bakery with great desserts and take-away lunches (daily 8:00-18:30, Via da Mulin, tel. 081-838-8030).

Elegant Five-Star Hotel Dining Rooms: Pontresina's two top hotels have wonderful restaurants in sumptuous dining rooms. **La Stüva Restaurant,** in the cellar of the fanciful faux-castle Hotel Walther at the top end of town, is expensive and exclusive, with a flair for serving inventive and light regional and international cuisine. Their five-course fixed-price meal for 85-105 SF is a good splurge, but you'll be amazed at how well you can eat with only their 15-SF salad bar and a cheese plate (40-55-SF main dishes, June-Sept and Jan-Easter Wed-Sun 19:00-22:30—kitchen closes at 21:30, closed Mon-Tue as well as Easter-May and Oct-Dec, Via Maistra 215, tel. 081-839-3636). **Kronenstübli** is in the Grand Hotel Kronenhof, which dominates the bottom end of town and has public rooms fit for a Vienna palace. It's less accommodating to anyone concerned about price, but if you've got francs to burn, its five-course fixed-price meal for 150 SF is a memorable splurge (100-SF three-course-meal, 45-60-SF main dishes, Tue-Sat 19:00-21:30, closed Sun-Mon, Via Maistra, tel. 081-830-3030).

Eating Above Pontresina: **Bock auf Alp Languard,** at the top of the lift (7,710 feet up—see page 302), serves affordable meals with unbeatable views (19-SF daily special, June-mid-Oct daily 8:30-17:00, tel. 079-719-7810).

Samedan

Little Samedan (sah-MAY-den) offers a convenient peek at Upper Engadine village culture and buildings. This town, which has the most traditional Engadine architecture of the three destinations in this chapter, is the historic capital of the valley. Romansh remains its first language. Though charming, Samedan is also humble and a bit rough around the edges—it feels like the backwater cousin of ritzy St. Moritz and Pontresina.

Orientation to Samedan

Samedan is gently spread over a hill that rises from the Inn River. It's steeper than it is big. The train station is at the bottom of town; the town center clusters just above. The characteristic cobbled street called Via Plazzet runs through the middle of town, parallel to the river. All the streets seem to converge at the Protestant church on the square called Plaz.

Tourist Information: Samedan's TI is at Via Plazzet 21, across from the giant, pink Hotel Bernina (Mon-Fri 8:45-12:00 & 13:30-18:00, Sat until 17:30, closed Sun, also closed Sat off-season, tel. 081-851-0060, www.samedan.ch).

Arrival in Samedan: Whether you come by bus or train, you'll wind up at the train station (though some buses do go up into the town itself—ask). From here, just hike up the hill, bearing left (on Via Mulin) to reach the main square, or right (on Via Retica) to reach the TI.

Self-Guided Walk

Samedan Town Stroll

There's little to do in Samedan other than relax and enjoy a pleasant walk with nice views. The route described here takes you steeply up through town to a perch overlooking Samedan's magnificent setting.

Begin at the **main square (Plaz),** where all of Samedan's cobbled streets meet. Just downhill, the blocky, modern building with

Traditional Engadine Architecture

Samedan and Pontresina both have fine old traditional houses. A short stroll in either town shows plenty of traditional ele-

ments and medieval ingenuity intended to keep inhabitants warm in the harsh mountain weather. Walls are thick—typically two feet—for insulation. Notice how windows are like the narrow end of a funnel—originally covered with animal skin rather than glass. Bay windows gathered maximum precious light and came with built-in seats where women sat to do handwork.

Even though they're thoroughly modernized, the structural essence of these grand farmhouses survives. You can still see the big lower door for animals and the big upper door for hay and the carriage—with a smaller door built into it for people to get in and out while minimizing heat loss. People had the animals sleep below in the hope their rising body heat would warm the living space above. Proud noble family coats of arms still decorate buildings; many local families can trace their heritage to the Middle Ages.

Look for the traditional Engadine *sgraffito* ornamentation on exterior walls. To make *sgraffito*, facades are covered with a layer of dark plaster, which is then covered with white or colored plaster. Before the white plaster dries, decorative designs are scratched into it, so that the dark background appears. These rustic and crude decorations—much more durable than painted facades—look modern, but have a long history.

the colorful window frames is Samedan's "vertical spa," with several levels of pools (www.mineralbad-samedan.ch). As you face the church, a left on the main drag, Via Plazzet, would take you to the Chesa Planta mansion and the TI (both described later).

But to begin our hike, let's walk uphill on Surtuor, following the white sign for *Kath. Kirch.* After a few blocks, on the right, the 13th-century, castle-like **stone tower** was the private tower of a noble family. From its wooden balcony, they'd oversee festivities in their little domain.

The next house up, at **#12**, dates from 1656. This X-shaped house is in the form of a St. Andrew's cross, made of extended roof beams. This was a popular way to bless homes here. Notice the sturdy beam ends—roofs were built to support heavy stones and snow. Houses come with Romansh names, for example, you'll see houses marked *Chesa Juzi* (Juzi's House) and *Chesa dals 3 Frers* (House of the Three Brothers).

The **Catholic Church** (Neo-Romanesque from 1910, with a bell dating back to 1505) stands at the top of the town. From here, survey the surrounding slopes and their ancient terracing, a vestige from Celtic peoples.

Continue uphill, passing the ski lift. Where the road swings right, pause at the yellow bench for the gorgeous **view.** Samedan lies at the point where the two valleys of the Inn and Flazbach rivers merge. From here, the Inn River continues through Innsbruck before joining the Danube.

Huff and puff the thin air (you're at 6,000 feet) to the dramatically situated Protestant **Church of St. Peter.** The Romanesque

bell tower (c. 1100) predates today's late Gothic church (c. 1480; now a burial church, generally closed to tourists). Benches line the cemetery walls and offer sunny, wind-protected picnic spots. Beneath you stretches the highest-altitude airport in Europe, a favorite among gliders (launched by a yellow truck with a huge winch, rather than an airplane). When you've had your fill of the views, head back down into town.

Sights in Samedan

Chesa Planta—This interesting old mansion, just a block from the main square, shows off upper-crust lifestyles of the 18th and

19th centuries. This former residence of the wealthy local Planta family is preserved just as it was when they lived here. It can only be visited with a 1.5-hour German tour (with an English handout), but the fascinating interior makes it worth considering if you happen to be here at the

right time. You'll see some gorgeous wood-carved rooms, a beautifully painted dining room, original granite slab floors, and fancy ceramic stoves. Upstairs, the same building houses a Romansh library *(biblioteca rumauntscha),* where scholars collect Romansh literature. A copy of any new book published in the Romansh language is sent to this library.

Cost and Hours: 10 SF; mid-June–mid-Oct Tue-Thu tours at 16:30, mid-July-Aug tours available Tue-Sat 15:00-18:00; tel. 081-852-1272, www.chesaplanta.ch.

Sleeping and Eating in Samedan

(1 SF = about $1.10, country code: 41)
While Pontresina has more eating and sleeping options, Samedan hoards the lion's share of this valley's Graubünden quaintness.

$$$ Hotel Palazzo Mÿsanus is a nicely renovated historic hotel just a block below the main square. The building also houses the "smallest whisky bar on Earth." Of the 16 rooms, the cheaper "comfort" rooms come in two types: cozy pine-wood rustic or modern, all with tiny bathrooms (Sb-97 SF, Db-194 SF). The pricier "superior" rooms are all modern (Sb-122 SF, Db-244 SF; surcharges added Jan-April, mid-July-mid-Aug, Nov-Dec, and for stays shorter than 3 nights; free Wi-Fi, parking-6 SF, Crappun 26, tel. 081-852-1080, fax 081-852-1079, www.palazzomysanus.ch, info@palazzomysanus).

$$ Gasthaus zum Weissen Kreuz/Croce Bianca is your budget option, with 20 tight, basic, old-fashioned rooms with new bathrooms above a restaurant just downhill from the main square D-120 SF, Db-145 SF, cash only, tel. 081-852-5353, www.croce samedan.ch, info@crocesamedan.ch).

Eating: The **Bernina Pizzeria,** in the grand Hotel Bernina, is a good value.

St. Moritz

The oldest and perhaps best-known winter resort in the world, St. Moritz has long been the winter haunt of Europe's rich and famous. Its American sister city says it all: Vail.

It's said that in 1864, St. Moritz hotel pioneer Johannes Badrutt invented winter tourism in the Alps. To allay his British guests' skepticism, he offered them free accommodations if the

winter weather was bad. They came and enjoyed fine weather. He liquored them up, they had fun...and they brought their friends along the next year. St. Moritz hosted the Winter Olympics in

1928 and 1948.

Although St. Moritz might have once been a real town, today it's little more than a cluster of luxury hotels and designer boutiques. (Think of it as the anti-Gimmelwald.) But it's still fun to spend a couple of hours exploring its highly manicured cobbles, and nightlife-seekers find St. Moritz livelier than the surrounding towns. For the jet set, winter is prime time in St. Moritz. Summer is quieter and popular with sporty types and nature lovers. While celebrity-spotting drops way, way off in the summer, prices are more reasonable. It's also a great time for hiking and adventure sports. Visitors enjoy inline skating, polo, golf, paragliding, horseback riding, strolling around the lake, and evening concerts. Cable cars zip you to some great mountaintops.

Orientation to St. Moritz

St. Moritz has two centers: the town *(Dorf)* and the spa *(Bad)*. St. Moritz Dorf is on a steep slope, with the train station *(Bahnhof)*

at its base. St. Moritz Bad sprawls on a level plain along the lake; it has some sport facilities (covered pool, tennis courts, ice-skating hall, horseback riding, and so on), but it's mostly a characterless concrete town. Most visitors spend their time in St. Moritz Dorf—and should. Aside from the chance to walk around the lake, St. Moritz Bad is pretty, well, bad.

Connecting the two zones is easy: Convenient bus #3 does a loop between the train station *(Bahnhof)*, St. Moritz Dorf, and St. Moritz Bad (4/hour, 3 SF).

Tourist Information

The slick TI is in the center of St. Moritz Dorf, just a block off the main square (mid-June-mid-Oct Mon-Fri 9:00-18:30, Sat 9:00-12:30 & 13:30-18:00, closed Sun; off-season Mon-Fri 9:00-12:00 & 14:00-18:00, Sat 9:00-12:00, closed Sun; Plaza Mauritius, tel. 081-837-3333, www.engadin.stmoritz.ch).

Arrival in St. Moritz

St. Moritz's train station is near the lake, just below the Dorf. The station has lockers, a left-luggage desk, WCs, and an information desk (pick up a free map, Mon-Sat 9:00-13:30 & 16:00-18:30, closed Sun, tel. 081-832-1007), but no bike rental. The train station café is a rare budget option in this pricey town (10-17 SF dishes, Mon-Sat 6:00-20:00, Sun 6:30-20:00).

To reach the Dorf, it's about a 15-minute steep uphill hike, or you can hop on bus #3. If walking, to save some sweat, exit the station to the left and walk to the Serletta parking garage. Inside the garage, find the art-lined escalator (Switzerland's longest) that zips you up next to the Palace Hotel. From there, it's a relatively quick walk up to the center of St. Moritz Dorf.

Helpful Hints

Supermarkets: You'll find two **Co-op** stores in St. Moritz. In St. Moritz Dorf, the basic Co-op grocery right on the main square (Plaza da Scoula) is the only budget eating option I've found in this part of town (Mon-Fri 8:00-12:15 & 14:00-18:30, Sat 8:00-17:00, closed Sun). A giant Co-op supermarket/department store is on Via dal Bagn, at the entrance to St. Moritz Bad (Mon-Thu 8:00-18:30, Fri 8:00-20:00, Sat 8:00-17:00, closed Sun).

Ski Rental: In St. Moritz Dorf, **Ender Sport** is one of many rental shops (closed Sun and for lunch 12:30-14:00, just uphill from TI and recommended hotels at Via Maistra 26, tel. 081-833-3536). In St. Moritz Bad, **Boom Sport** has a knowledgeable staff, good selection, and handy location (closed Sun and for lunch 12:15-14:00, Via Tegiatscha 5, tel. 081-832-2222).

Sights in St. Moritz

▲▲**Segantini Museum**—This museum is dedicated to the ultimate painter of alpine life. Giovanni Segantini (1858-1899) came here to get away from the misty air of Milan. The crisp alpine atmosphere was great for capturing the bright, sharp, crystal-clear mountain light. Painting in the open air with brushstrokes that invigorated his fascinating scenes, Segantini created works reminiscent of the French Impressionists. The tiny museum, which looks like a Neo-Byzantine church, is actually based on Segantini's design of the Swiss Pavilion for the 1900 World's Fair in Paris—but made of local stone rather than the originally intended steel. Segantini died young (at age 41, in 1899), and money ran out before this grandiose pavilion

could be built. Segantini's masterpiece, the *Alpine Triptych,* was painted for the World's Fair, but also never completed. Segantini's ill-fated vision—both his pavilion and his life's major work—is now here, near where he settled in his 30s.

The paintings are exhibited on two floors. Begin by climbing the stairs to the round room on the top floor, where you can view the haunting *Alpine Triptych:* three paintings representing (left to right) life, nature, and death. Notice how, even in the death scene—as the body of a newly deceased loved one is brought out to a horse cart while mourning women look on—there's a glimmer of hope and faith in the swirling clouds above. Segantini even designed the *Triptych's* frames, ornamented with the local five-needled Arven pine.

Then head back to the entry level, and spend some time with the many smaller canvases here. Particularly notable is *Ave Maria at the Crossing,* as a man rowing a simple boat—laden with a flock of sheep and a mother and baby—pauses to pray at sunset as the church bells toll.

Cost and Hours: 10 SF, worthwhile 30-minute audioguide-3 SF, mid-May-mid-Oct and mid-Dec-mid-April Tue-Sun 10:00-12:00 & 14:00-18:00, closed Mon, closed mid-Oct-mid-Dec and mid-April-mid-May, Via Somplaz 30, tel. 081-833-4454, www.segantini-museum.ch.

Getting There: The museum is perched on the road above the lake about a 15-minute walk southwest of St. Moritz (well-marked from the central roundabout). Rather than walking on the road itself, look for the "Segantiniweg" path that cuts through the woods just above the road. Or you can take bus #2 or #5 to the Segantini Museum stop. Drivers will find metered roadside parking just before the museum.

Engadiner Museum—The historic, domestic, and social cultures of the Engadine region are displayed in this museum. The building (from 1905) houses interiors and furniture from throughout the Engadine (such as a patrician living room, a smoky farm kitchen, and a four-poster bed), as well as an exhibit on the discovery of the spa water that put St. Moritz on the vacation map.

Cost and Hours: 8 SF, Sun-Fri 10:00-12:00 & 14:00-17:00, closed Sat, closed May and Nov, Via dal Bagn 39, take bus #3 to Via Aruons, tel. 081-833-4333, www.engadiner-museum.ch.

Berry Museum—Dedicated not to delicious little fruits, but to local painter Peter Robert Berry (1864-1942), this museum introduces visitors to another talented alpine artist. While Berry enjoyed neither the talent nor the fame of Segantini, and the entry price is steep, this is a suitable rainy-day activity for art-lovers.

Cost and Hours: 15 SF, includes audioguide, mid-June-mid-Oct and mid-Dec-mid-April Wed-Mon 10:00-13:00 & 16:00-

19:00, closed Tue and mid-Oct–mid-Dec and mid-April–mid-June, just below the center of St. Moritz Dorf at Via Arona 32, tel. 081-833-3018, www.berrymuseum.com.

Walk Around the Lake—The charming lake below St. Moritz is a delightful place for a stroll—especially on sunny summer days, when it's filled with sailboats. It takes about an hour to walk all the way around.

Sleeping in St. Moritz

(1 SF = about $1.10, country code: 41)
I prefer sleeping in Pontresina or Samedan, but St. Moritz has a certain allure. I've ignored the giant, overpriced hotels in favor of these smaller, cozier options, which have more character. The first two hotels are in St. Moritz Dorf, just uphill from the TI. The youth hostel is down below and across the lake, at the far end of St. Moritz Bad.

$$$ Hotel Eden is a classy-feeling small hotel renting 34 rooms. The public spaces are a mix of old-style and modern, and the breakfast room is quite something. This place seems to offer all the little extras, such as free afternoon tea in a grand lounge (Sb-117-158 SF, Db-188-272 SF; bigger "superior" rooms with views: Sb-149-171 SF, Db-256-346 SF; higher prices are for weekends, pricier in ski season, elevator, free Wi-Fi, lovely rooftop terrace, parking-12 SF, Via Veglia 12, tel. 081-830-8100, fax 081-830-8101, www.edenstmoritz.ch, info@edenstmoritz.ch).

$$$ Hotel Languard, next door, is a bit cozier and friendlier, with 22 pine-wood rooms (Sb-100-130 SF, Db-195-220 SF; "superior" rooms with views: Sb-125-165 SF, Db-210-315 SF; higher prices are for July-Aug, much pricier in ski season, 10 percent more for stays of 1 or 2 nights, elevator, free Wi-Fi, free parking, Via Veglia 14, tel. 081-833-3137, fax 081-833-4546, www.languard-stmoritz.ch, hotel@languard-stmoritz.ch).

$ Youth Hostel Stille is at the boring, residential eastern end of St. Moritz Bad—one of the last buildings before the woods. Despite its inconvenient location, it offers 306 beds and all the services, activities, games, and lavish extras a top-end hostel can have (dorm beds-53 SF, D-134 SF, Db-173 SF, family rooms, price includes breakfast and four-course dinner, prices about 10 SF per person higher in winter, nonmembers pay 6 SF more, reception open 7:00-23:00 except May and Nov 8:00-10:00 & 17:00-21:00, pay Internet access, free Wi-Fi, parking-10 SF, 10-minute walk from bus stop on Via Sela, Via Surpunt 60, tel. 081-836-6111, fax 081-836-6112, www.youthhostel.ch/st.moritz, st.moritz@youthhostel.ch).

Eating in St. Moritz

Similar to Pontresina, most of St. Moritz's restaurants are in hotels, but here are a few stand-alone options.

Restaurant Hauser is the standard stop for local workers who know where to find the best-value meal in town. Centrally located in St. Moritz Dorf, this place has everything: restaurant, café, pastry shop, indoor and outdoor seating, and a vast menu (most meals 17-27 SF, weekday lunch specials under 20 SF, daily 7:00-23:00, below Hotel Hauser at Via Traunter Plazzas 7, tel. 081-837-5050).

In St. Moritz Bad: **Veltlinerkeller,** decorated with a huge stuffed moose head, is a casual-feeling eatery that serves a variety of grilled meats and Italian specialties (20-25-SF pastas, 25-45-SF main dishes, Mon-Sat 9:00-14:00 & 17:00-23:00, closed Sun, in St. Moritz Bad at Via dal Bagn 11, tel. 081-833-4009).

Upper Engadine Connections

By Train: St. Moritz, Pontresina, and **Samedan** are all connected to each other by train (hourly, 10 minutes, 5.20 SF). From these towns, trains go to **Chur** (hourly, 2 hours), **Tirano** (hourly, 2.5 hours), and **Zürich** (hourly, 3.75 hours, transfer in Chur). From Pontresina, you may have to change in Samedan. For details on the Bernina Express and Glacier Express, see the Scenic Rail Journeys chapter. Train info: toll tel. 0900-300-300 (1.19 SF/minute) or www.rail.ch.

By Bus: For details on getting around the region by bus, see page 294. If connecting to **Lugano** in the Italian-Swiss canton of Ticino, consider the "Palm Express" bus (departs St. Moritz train station at 12:20, stops at Menaggio on Italy's Lake Como en route, arrives at Lugano's train station at 16:20; daily mid-June-mid-Oct, Sat-Mon only mid-Oct-mid-June, www.postauto.ch/alpen).

SCENIC RAIL JOURNEYS

Golden Pass • William Tell Express • Bernina Express • Glacier Express • Chur

Switzerland has one of the world's best rail networks, and many of its tracks run through dramatic and beautiful scenery. While just about any train ride in Switzerland is photogenic, four are aggressively marketed as the most spectacular: the Golden Pass, the William Tell Express, the Bernina Express, and the Glacier Express. If you're looking for a scenic day enjoying the Alps from the window of your train, and would like to do it in a "panoramic" car (offering huge windows that sweep halfway across the ceiling), these journeys can be great experiences. Though they aren't quite as "fantastic with countless highlights" as they're advertised to be (the high lifts in the mountains themselves are much higher and more breathtaking), the trains are a fun way to do some sightseeing while getting from point A to point B.

This chapter provides you with all the logistical, nuts-and-bolts information you'll need to splice each journey into your itinerary. I've described highlights along each route, written in the direction that most travelers are likely to go. If you travel in the opposite direction, the same information still applies—just hold the book upside-down.

This chapter also includes information about Chur, a town that's not really worth a visit, except that it lies at the intersection of the Bernina Express and Glacier Express routes. Chur makes for a handy pit stop or overnight if connecting these trips; better yet, stay in Pontresina and take at least a day to explore the Upper Engadine Valley (see Pontresina, Samedan, and St. Moritz chapter).

Tickets

Schedules Can Change: In this chapter, I've listed specific departure and arrival times, but these schedules are always subject to change, so it's essential to confirm the times before you travel. Timetables for most of these trains appear on the Swiss Rail website: www.rail.ch. (Also try Germany's all-Europe rail site, www.bahn.com—use http://bahn.hafas.de/bin/query.exe/en to go directly to an English-language search page; or call the Swiss Rail info line at 0900-300-300, 1.19 SF/minute.) Any train station in Switzerland can provide you with free schedules. Each scenic rail line also operates its own website, with even more details (listed in each section, below).

Buying Tickets: Tickets and reservations for all these scenic rail lines can be purchased at any train station in Switzerland. In the US, you'll pay more (about $20 per order) to get tickets and reservations through your travel agent or at www.raileurope.com. Getting your reservations before you go limits your flexibility, as reservations made through US agents are nonchangeable and nonrefundable—unlike reservations made at train stations in Europe. Most of these trips are covered by both Swiss Passes and Eurailpasses, though reservations (required on some trains) cost extra (the Glacier Express is the biggest exception, with stretches not covered by Eurailpasses; see page 340).

Reservations: On these journeys, "reservations" are essentially scenic-train supplements that happen to come with a reserved seat. You can book these as early as three months ahead, or as late as the day before, at any Swiss train station or on the various websites (but be warned that many sell out several days ahead in high season). You can even wait until you've boarded to buy your reservation (though you'll pay a little extra—and risk finding no available seat). The Glacier Express requires reservations. If you want to take the official tourist package for the William Tell Express (not recommended) or ride in the panoramic cars on the Bernina Express (somewhat recommended), reservations are also required. Reserve the Golden Pass only if you want a front-row VIP seat. To save money and maximize your flexibility, you can take standard regional trains (without panoramic cars) on all scenic routes without a reservation (though the bus segment of the Bernina Express requires a reservation, it's easy to purchase from the bus driver). These alternatives are explained in each section below.

If you're set on taking a panoramic train and your itinerary is already fixed, it makes sense to book your scenic-train seats as soon as you can. On most routes at most times, however, individual travelers usually book just a few days in advance—usually after they've seen a weather report. If your itinerary is flexible, I'd recommend you do the same: Keep an eye on the weather, pick a good travel

Scenic Swiss Rail Routes

GERMANY

FRANCE

AUSTRIA

Zürich
Luzern
BOAT
TRAIN Flüelen
Landquart
Wassen
Chur
Inter-laken
Disentis
Davos
Spiez
Andermatt
Filisur
Lausanne
Zweisimmen
Airolo
St. Moritz
Gstaad
Pontresina
Montreux
Brig
Poschiavo
Geneva
Visp
Bellinzona
Locarno
Tirano
Zermatt
Lugano
Sorico
Menaggio
BUS

ITALY

- - - - - - - Golden Pass —————— William Tell Express
- - - - - - - Glacier Express —————— Bernina Express

SCENIC RAIL JOURNEYS

day, and then reserve your seats at any train station. From mid-July to mid-August, trains (especially the über-promoted Glacier Express) book up farther ahead.

Eurailpass and Swiss Pass: Two major types of railpasses can be useful in Switzerland: A Eurailpass (Global Pass or Selectpass that includes Switzerland) and a Swiss Pass. These railpasses cover most of your travel on the scenic rail journeys. But seat reservations always cost extra, and some trips aren't fully covered by a railpass. However, traveling the same route on standard regional trains, rather than on the designated tourist trains, is fully covered by a railpass; on the Glacier Express, two different segments of the trip are free with a Swiss Pass, but not covered by a Eurailpass (see page 340 for details).

When buying your ticket or making reservations, be sure the ticket agent understands what type of pass you have (if any) and exactly what trip you're taking. Confirm that you've gotten all the reservations and other tickets you need to complete your trip. While rail agents generally know what railpasses cover, sometimes they don't, which can lead to frustrating run-ins with conductors who insist that you've only paid for part of your trip.

Train Types

Various types of trains, with various types of cars, run these routes. Here are the key distinctions to look for:

Classes: Most trains have both first- and second-class cars. The difference between the first- and second-class cars is generally the same on tourist trains as on standard trains (first class has somewhat wider seats, a little more legroom, and fewer passengers; second-class cars offer the same scenery, go just as fast, and usually still have plenty of room). On some of the tourist trains (such as portions of the Golden Pass), panoramic cars are only available in first class. If you have a second-class railpass, you can always pay extra to sit in first on any given train. In bigger train stations, a digital panel on the tracks indicates departure time, destination, and at which part of the platform you'll find the first- or second-class cars.

Standard vs. Tourist Trains: In many cases, standard trains operated by Swiss Rail run these same routes—more frequently, and usually less expensively  (though you'll sacrifice things such as fancy dining cars and souvenir key chains). Because local commuters use standard trains, they may stop at more stations along the route than the designed-for-tourists panoramic trains. Many travelers enjoy the flexibility of following the scenic route on standard trains, enabling them to hop off and explore a village, then hop on the next standard train that comes through—without the headache of reservations (which are rarely necessary on standard trains).

Panoramic vs. Standard Cars: All the tourist trains on the routes in this chapter offer special panoramic cars, usually in both first and second class, so there's no need to splurge for first class.

Panoramic cars have huge wraparound windows, allowing you to see through part of the ceiling and most of the walls. The  Golden Pass trains go one better: The driver sits in a little bubble upstairs, leaving the very front of the train open for VIP seating with completely unobstructed views of what's coming up. The windows in the panoramic cars generally can't open, meaning that photographs often suffer from glare, and the interior (even with air-conditioning) can heat up on sunny days.

Since nonpanoramic cars have a smaller field of vision than the panoramic cars, these require a little more bobbing and weaving to enjoy the views. Aside from being cheaper, the chief advantage of the standard cars is that the windows generally can be opened, for cool air and photos without reflections. Passengers in panoramic cars are free to walk to the standard cars to open a window and snap a photo.

Golden Pass

The exceptionally picturesque Golden Pass train route cuts a swath diagonally across the pristine center of Switzerland, connecting Luzern with Lake Geneva. Of all the rail journeys in this chapter, its central location—lacing together many of Switzerland's top sights—makes the Golden Pass the one you're most likely to take.

Orientation to the Golden Pass

The Route

The Golden Pass officially runs between Luzern and Lake Geneva's Montreux, though you could easily connect onward to Zürich or Geneva with standard trains. With less time, you could hone in even more on the very best stretch, from Interlaken to Montreux.

Because the tracks change from narrow to standard gauge to narrow again, two train changes are required (at Interlaken Ost and Zweisimmen). On each stretch, you can choose between the official Golden Pass tourist train with panoramic cars (on the last stretch, you can also opt for a Golden Pass train with vintage rail cars) and more frequent standard trains without panoramic cars. Here's the breakdown.

Luzern to Interlaken Ost: Tourist trains (5/day, 2 hours); standard trains (hourly, 2 hours).

Interlaken Ost to Zweisimmen: Direct tourist trains (5/day, 1.25 hours); standard trains (at least hourly, 1.25-1.5 hours, change in Spiez).

Zweisimmen to Montreux: Tourist trains (6/day including 2 with VIP cars, 1.75 hours); "classic" Golden Pass trains with vintage rail cars (2/day, 1.75-2 hours); standard trains (roughly hourly, 1.75-2 hours). This is the stretch most likely to fill up, so consider reserving ahead for either of the two tourist-train options.

Planning Your Time: Because it connects so many knockout Swiss destinations (Luzern, Interlaken, and Lake Geneva), and because it goes in both directions, the Golden Pass can be spliced into your itinerary in many different ways. I'd focus on the best stretch, using it to connect Interlaken and Lake Geneva (3 hours total, including the lovely 2-hour segment from Zweisimmen to Montreux).

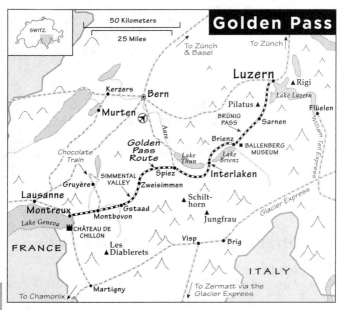

Golden Pass trains—all with panoramic cars and some with front-row VIP seating—depart several times each day. Before choosing your departure, check schedules along the way and plan your layovers strategically to maximize time on the panoramic cars. For example, if traveling from Luzern to Lake Geneva, consider taking the 7:55 panoramic train from Luzern to Interlaken Ost (arriving at 9:55), then wander Interlaken and have lunch before catching the 13:08 panoramic train to Montreux (change trains in Zweisimmen at 14:17, arrive Montreux at 16:13).

Cost and Schedule

The Golden Pass trip from Luzern to Montreux costs 70 SF second class; the "best of" segment from Interlaken to Montreux is 49 SF. The entire ride is covered by a Eurailpass or Swiss Pass. Reservations, while not required, are recommended for summer midmorning departures and the super-scenic front seats (15 SF for front-row VIP seats, 5-10 SF for other seats in panoramic cars; more details under "Seating," below).

Information: Most of the route is part of the Swiss Rail network. Golden Pass panoramic trains on the section between

Zweisimmen and Montreux are operated by MOB (toll tel. 0900-245-245 within Switzerland, 1 SF/minute, from elsewhere in Europe dial 00-41-840-245-245, from the US call 011-41-840-245-245, www.goldenpass.ch). BLS runs some panoramic trains between Interlaken and Zweisimmen (tel. 058-327-2727, www.bls.ch). A free booklet available on the train describes the route and includes a complete schedule.

Seating: Some panoramic cars have special VIP seats. On these cars, the conductor drives the train from a little domed area upstairs—leaving both the front and back of the train open for passengers. The first two rows of VIP seats offer an unobstructed view of the pristine alpine scenery coming right at you. Even if you haven't reserved a VIP seat in advance, you can grab any that's open and pay the conductor on the spot.

The nonsupplement seats just behind the VIP seats give you a bit of the grand front view (and cheapskates have been known to grab a few free minutes up front).

Note that on the Luzern-Interlaken section, you'll need to choose between panoramic (first class) and nonpanoramic (second class) cars.

Eating on the Golden Pass: The Luzern-Interlaken stretch is the only section with a restaurant car, but it may be closed on trains running early or late in the day. Snacks and bar service may be available on other sections of the trip, but the menu is limited and pricey. Save your money and eat fresh by packing a picnic.

Self-Guided Tour

The Golden Pass

I've described only the best and most visually exciting portion of the Golden Pass journey, the five-hour stretch from Luzern to Lake Geneva, focusing on the *crème de la crème*—the two hours between Zweisimmen and Montreux (described from north to south).

As you leave Luzern (sit on the right side), you'll go along the lake to Alpnachstad, the starting point for the cogwheel train that climbs to the top of Mount Pilatus (the massive bulk on the right, see page 95). Then the train follows the Sarner Aa River through farmland, passing through the town of Sarnen and running along Lake Sarnen. Beyond the end of the lake is the town of Giswil, where the train begins its gradual ascent to the **Brünig Pass.** Eventually the train runs above the beautiful turquoise waters of the Lungernsee reservoir. After passing the resort of Lungern, the train climbs gradually through the forest to the summit station of Brünig-Hasliberg (keep an eye out for fake animal cutouts—lynx, ibex, deer—placed whimsically in the woods at eye level). After cresting the pass, the train descends to the Aare River Valley, with its sheer cliffs and waterfalls. The arrow-straight river channel, straightened by the ever-efficient Swiss, slices through the broad valley. (Sir Arthur Conan Doyle chose the town of Meiringen and nearby Reichenbach Falls as the setting for the death of Sherlock Holmes.) The train then follows the river to beautiful **Lake Brienz** (Brienzersee). From the town of Brienz, a bus runs to the remarkable open-air museum at Ballenberg (see page 153). Beyond Brienz, the train follows the lakeshore to Interlaken.

As the train pulls out of Interlaken, you cruise along the south bank of **Lake Thun** (Thunersee). Interlaken ("between the lakes") is situated between the big lakes of Thun and Brienz. Before long, at the town of Spiez, you'll split off and head southwest to Zweisimmen.

Leaving Zweisimmen, you'll roll through the **Simmental** valley, famous among American farmers for its top-end cows. Big farmhouses lie scattered in the lush meadows—an indication that the farmland is good here. The large wooden buildings are typical of Bernese farm architecture: housing the barn, sheltering the crops, and storing agricultural machines, all under one huge roof. Farming is heavily subsidized in Switzerland, and farmers form the strongest economic lobby. Trying to increase their modest income, many farmers have switched to exotic crops (like melons) or animals. Ostriches, yaks, bison, and highland cattle have become a common sight in the Swiss Alps lately.

Between Saanenmoser and Schonried, the train reaches its highest point (about 4,000 feet) and stops at the famous resort town of **Gstaad.** Although known as a favorite hangout for well-known rustic mountain folk such as Julie Andrews, Monaco's Princess Caroline, and Roman Polanski, the town does not offer many exciting sights. In winter, the modest ski slopes are less crowded than the town's flashy nightspots. Sipping their cocktails, the *après*-skiers eye each other and discuss the latest trends in ski gear fashion. In summer, Gstaad hosts the Swiss Open tennis, polo, and golf tournaments, as well as high-quality music festivals.

Just south of Gstaad, say *auf Wiedersehen* to the German-speaking part of Switzerland and *bonjour* to **French Switzerland.** The mountains are jagged. In fact, many are called *dents*, French for "teeth." With the change in language comes a change in culture and architecture. French-style gray stone houses are replacing half-timbered, woody, German-style chalets. The mountain airstrips—generally made for the Swiss Air Force during World War II—are used today for sightseeing flights around the Alps. The cute village of Rougemont, with its traditional chalets, is famous among the Swiss as the place where the wealthy send their girls to boarding school.

Happy **cows** spend their summers on the Alps, wandering freely and munching the fragrant herbs of these lush alpine meadows. The resulting milk is the secret ingredient for tasty Gruyère cheese. On steep hillsides here, the grass is still cut by hand. It dries in the summer sun, then is collected and stored in the barns to serve as cow salads through the winter (see "Swiss Cow Culture" sidebar on page 170).

You might consider interrupting your journey in **Château d'Oex,** known for its Hot-Air Ballooning Week (last week of January). Bertrand Piccard and Brian Jones took off from here on March 1, 1999, and sailed their balloon all the way around the world. Below the train station, Le Chalet restaurant gives insight on Gruyère cheese production.

South of Château d'Oex, the valley narrows to a deep gorge. Up on the hillsides, the damage of the devastating 1999 winter storm "**Lothar**" can still be seen. Entire forests were leveled, aggravating an already precarious avalanche situation. Trees on steep slopes stop snow from sliding down and burying the villages, but once the trees are gone, they don't grow back—artificial avalanche barriers need to be erected. Landslides and floods have been relatively common in recent years—an unfortunate consequence of uncontrolled deforestation and construction of vacation homes in areas that traditionally served as pastures and forestlands.

The small **lake** is dammed and used for hydroelectric power. Switzerland makes good use of its Alps for production of electricity. Although it has some nuclear power plants, 60 percent of Switzerland's energy is hydroelectric. The country exports its electricity to France and Italy.

Montbovon is the place to change trains if you're going to Bulle or Gruyères (see page 266). After the first tunnel, an inscription on the barn to the right welcomes you to the Gruyère region: *La Gruyère vous salue.*

The train winds its way uphill with more curves and tunnels than before. Passing through the **Jaman Tunnel,** you're engulfed in nearly two miles of darkness. When you emerge, you're in another world—you've left the feudal Middle Ages and entered the 19th-century belle époque. At the village of Les Avants, one of Switzerland's oldest winter resorts, the first glimpses of Lake Geneva sprawl deep underneath you. Beginning a steep descent, the train passes through a series of sharp bends in tunnels before delivering you from the mountains to lake level.

The architecture has even more of a French flair now that you've entered the **"Swiss Riviera."** Palm trees, vines, and many sanatoriums indicate that this is a warmer climate. You're surrounded by the vineyards of the Lavaux region, famous for its white wine. The view broadens to include the French Alps of Savoy across the lake, the lakeshore of the Swiss Riviera to the west, and the broad Rhône Valley to the east. As you approach Montreux—with its grand hotels—the train meanders its way intimately through private gardens.

Montreux has the only train station in Europe with three different rail gauges: regular, narrow (which you're on), and very skinny (for the Rochers de Naye train, taking sightseers to a nearby peak with views less exciting than those you've just enjoyed).

From here, it's an easy train trip to Lausanne, or a quick bus ride or about a two-mile lakefront hike to Château de Chillon (see page 259).

Golden Pass Connections

From Luzern by Train to: Zürich (2/hour, 1 hour), **Zürich Airport** (2/hour, 1.25 hours, most change in Zürich), **Bern** (2/hour, 1-1.5 hours), **Interlaken Ost** (2/hour, 2-2.5 hours), **Lausanne** (hourly direct, 2.25 hours), **Appenzell** (2/hour, 2.75 hours, change in Herisau or in Zürich and Gossau), **Lugano** (hourly, 2.5 hours, half with change in Arth-Goldau), **Chur** (hourly, 2.25 hours, change in Thalwil).

From Interlaken Ost by Train to: Lauterbrunnen (2/hour, 20 minutes), **Spiez** (3/hour, 25 minutes), **Brienz** (1-2/hour, 20 minutes), **Bern** (2/hour, 55 minutes), **Zürich** and **Zürich Airport** (2/hour, 2-2.25 hours, most transfer in Bern or Spiez), **Luzern** (2/hour, 2-2.5 hours), **Lugano** (hourly, 4.75 hours, 1-2 changes), **Zermatt** (hourly, 2.25 hours, transfer in Spiez and Visp).

From Montreux by Train to: Lausanne (3/hour, 25 minutes), **Vevey** (4/hour, 6-9 minutes), **Gruyères** (hourly, 1.25 hours), **Bern** (2/hour, 1.5 hours, transfer in Lausanne), **Geneva** (4/hour, 1-1.25 hours, half with change in Lausanne), **Zermatt** (hourly, 2.5 hours, change in Visp).

William Tell Express

A trip on the William Tell Express is half by boat and half by train, from Luzern to the Italian-speaking region of Ticino (the towns of Lugano and Locarno). The journey carries the most famous name in Switzerland. Tell exists only in legend, but his story—being forced to shoot an apple off his son's head because he refused to bow to the Habsburg hat—helped inspire the Swiss to rebel against their Austrian rulers. The boat ride passes the place where the first Swiss cantons pledged "all for one and one for all," the birthplace of the Confoederatio Helvetica in 1291.

Don't go out of your way to do this trip. The boat ride is more pastoral than thrilling, and the train ride is more interesting as a lesson in Swiss engineering than impressive for its views. (Because the train cuts through the highest mountains inside the Gotthard Tunnel, it only reaches 3,600 feet above sea level.)

But if you're connecting Luzern and Italian Switzerland anyway, this route is undeniably scenic. You can book the official "William Tell Express" trip (or the over-the-top "Premium" version), but I wouldn't—really. Unless you enjoy overpaying for a forgettable lunch and a tiny Swiss Army knife souvenir, you miss nothing by simply buying regular tickets. Save money and gain flexibility by just riding the boat and train on regular departures and skip the much-promoted tourist package. Even if you don't spring for the official package, you'll still have access to the fancy panoramic train (no extra charge if you have a first-class railpass or ticket, but those with a second-class railpass must pay for a seat upgrade).

Orientation to the William Tell Express

The Route

The William Tell Express begins with a slow boat trip along the length of Lake Luzern from the city of Luzern to Flüelen (2.75 hours). There you'll switch to the train, and cut down into the Italian-speaking canton of Ticino (2 hours). In the town of Bellinzona, you'll choose between two end points: Lugano or Locarno (I prefer Lugano).

The boat trip from Luzern to Flüelen is lazy and very pretty. As the traditional steamer blows its old-time horn, you glide by idyllic lakeside resort towns and under mighty peaks. If you've already taken a boat trip on the lake, you won't see much more by taking the William Tell boat (it's more efficient to zip to Flüelen in an hour by train); conversely, if you're planning on doing the whole William Tell trip on your way out, don't bother doing a boat trip while in Luzern.

Whether you ride the boat or train from Luzern, in Flüelen you can join the William Tell Express panoramic train (departs Flüelen at 12:15 and 14:15). In Bellinzona, you can either transfer to a nonpanoramic train to Lugano or stay on the same train to Locarno.

Another option is to skip Flüelen entirely. Standard regional trains (without panoramic cars) make the very scenic Luzern-Lugano trip along the same route hourly in each direction (2.5 hours total, www.rail.ch).

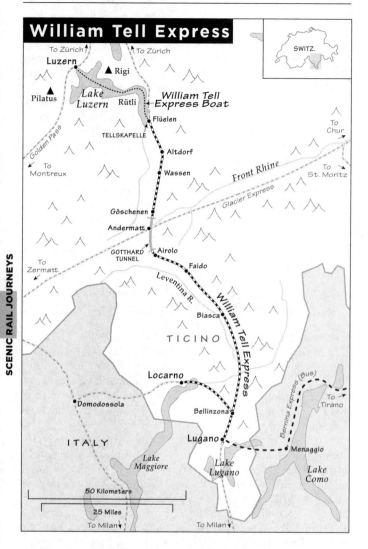

William Tell Express

SWITZ.

To Zürich
To Zürich

Luzern

▲ Rigi

▲ Pilatus

Lake Luzern   Rütli

William Tell Express Boat

Flüelen

TELLSKAPELLE

To Chur

Golden Pass

To Montreux

Altdorf

Wassen

Front Rhine

Göschenen

Andermatt

Glacier Express

To St. Moritz

GOTTHARD TUNNEL

Airolo

Faido

To Zermatt

Leventina R.

Biasca

William Tell Express

TICINO

Locarno

Domodossola

Bellinzona

Bernina Express (Bus)

To Tirano

ITALY

Lugano

Menaggio

Lake Maggiore

Lake Lugano

Lake Como

50 Kilometers

25 Miles

To Milan
To Milan

SCENIC RAIL JOURNEYS

Cost and Schedule

The value of buying the official William Tell Express tourist trip is dubious (174 SF, first-class only). The only things that come "extra" with this pricey package are a mediocre lunch on the boat, a reserved seat on the panoramic train, a brochure about the route, and a souvenir Swiss Army knife key chain. Travelers using a first-class Eurailpass or Swiss Pass pay a 39-SF reservation fee (86 SF with a second-class pass) to buy this official trip, but you're better off skipping the package altogether—your railpass already covers the entire route, including the boat.

Two official William Tell Express trips depart daily in each direction in summer (mid-April–mid-Oct). Going north to south: The boat leaves Luzern at 9:12 and 11:12, docks in Flüelen where the panoramic train departs at 12:15 and 14:15, and arrives in Lugano at 14:27 and 16:27. Going south to north: The train departs Lugano at 9:30 and 11:30, meets the boat and leaves Flüelen at 12:00 and 14:00, and arrives in Luzern at 14:47 and 16:47. In winter, boats and trains depart once a day in each direction (boats from Luzern leave at 10:12, trains from Lugano leave at 10:30). As always, be sure to confirm all times.

Information: The official William Tell Express departures are operated by the Lake Lucerne Navigation Company (tel. 041-367-6767, www.lakelucerne.ch). For more information, see www.wilhelmtellexpress.ch.

Helpful Hints

Boat Ride: If you're doing the full William Tell Express route, board the boat at pier 1 across from the Luzern train station. Present your ticket (and, if you've purchased the package deal, pick up your lunch voucher and information flyers). There's no real baggage check on the boat; travelers just stack their backpacks and suitcases in a corner.

Train Trip: As the train approaches the platform in Flüelen, watch for the car that corresponds to your reservation (the official William Tell Express packet includes a sheet showing you where to stand for your car). If you have no reservation, take any seat without a reservation marker.

Self-Guided Tour

Here's what you'll see if you're doing the entire William Tell Express route. If you're taking only the train, skip to that section.

William Tell Boat Trip

The boat trip crisscrosses the **Vierwaldstättersee** (the "Lake of Four Forest Cantons"—let's call it "Lake Luzern"). The trip is popular with the older generation of European tourists, who eat and drink their way through the lazy route. On a sunny day, you can sit on the deck and enjoy the mountain views. Survey the boat before you settle on a seat—consider sun, shade, and wind.

After two hours, you sail into the **canton of Uri,** and the landscape gets rougher, the slopes steeper, and the villages fewer and more rustic. This is William Tell country. The legendary Swiss national hero represents the essence of the country's spirit, still felt today: the desire for independence from foreign rule. William Tell has been a popular muse: Schiller wrote a play about him based on ancient Swiss chronicles, and Rossini set the legend to music in an 1829 opera.

Swiss patriots get excited as the boat approaches **Rütli.** The meadow above is the birthplace of the Swiss Confederation. In 1291, representatives of the three founding cantons met here and swore allegiance to each other, against their oppressive neighbors. More than 700 years later, Switzerland is still a confederation—but now its cantons number 26.

Some hikers choose to disembark at Rütli and head for the mystical meadow marked by a big Swiss flag. Then they follow the **Weg der Schweiz** ("Path of Switzerland"), a trail leading around the lake. Along the way, they contemplate stone signs representing each of the 26 cantons in the order they joined the union. The canton markers are spaced according to each canton's population (the 20-mile-long trail is designed to have exactly 5 millimeters for each Swiss citizen).

Later, the boat stops at **Tellskapelle.** This 16th-century frescoed chapel marks another legendary spot: where William Tell jumped ship on the way to prison and swam to freedom.

The last stop is **Flüelen,** where the panoramic train awaits.

William Tell Train Trip

From Flüelen, the train climbs from 1,540 feet up to 3,600 feet, at the Gotthard Tunnel—the primary north-south transportation route through the Alps. You enter a classic alpine world of snow-capped mountains towering above wild valleys, with narrow gorges carved over eons by angry white water. Wooden chalets, pine forests, and lush meadows dotted with munching cows complete this image of picture-perfect Central Switzerland.

The train tracks are protected from avalanches, landslides, and waterfalls by concrete galleries. Gazing out the window, you'll see some of the greatest accomplishments of Swiss road and railroad engineering. **Wassen,** marked by its striking chapel, is the climax for trainspotters—with more trains passing per minute than just about anywhere else. First, the chapel is on your right. Then the train loops around the tiny town, and the chapel is on your left. Your train disappears into a tunnel, and when you emerge, the same chapel is still there. The train actually spirals up the slopes.

Göschenen (where you can transfer to Andermatt and on to the Glacier Express—see page 339) is the last stop before the

9.5-mile-long **Gotthard Tunnel.** After 10 minutes of rocketing through darkness, you emerge in a whole different world—a different climate (warmer), canton (Ticino), and language (Italian). Since the 13th century—long before this tunnel was built—the Gotthard Pass has been *the* major trade route over this part of the Alps, connecting northern and southern Europe. The trade continues to rumble under rather than over the pass. These days, heavy truck traffic brings pollution and traffic jams—but little money—to Switzerland. But by 2017, an ambitious new high-speed train tunnel (the Gotthard Base Tunnel), currently under construction, will allow shippers to transport merchandise by train and get trucks off the roads.

Welcome to **Ticino,** Switzerland's botanical garden. While the weather around Lake Luzern is often iffy, Ticino feels Mediterranean—warm and southern—making it a favorite weekend destination for the Swiss. Rather than cuckoo-clock-like chalets, the houses are now plain, square, and made of stone. Instead of conifers, the forests are full of chestnut trees. You'll see vineyards, oleander, and even palm trees. And the upcoming train stops are announced in Italian now: "*Prossima fermata....*"

While life seemed almost too good in the pristine and touristic Lake Luzern region, here in the valley of **Leventina,** the economy is tougher. Unemployment rates are high, young folks have to commute into the cities farther south for a job, houses and roads aren't as well maintained, and window boxes no longer come with so many flowers.

As you approach **Biasca,** notice a modern square building with pebble walls on your left-hand side. This is the information center for the new 30-mile-long Gotthard Base Tunnel and other Alps transit projects (Tue-Sat 9:00-18:00, closed Sun-Mon; 12-40 SF guided tours of work sites possible, call or book reservation on website; tel. 091-873-0550, www.infocentro.ch). You'll see industrial buildings and factories around Biasca.

If heading to Lugano, you'll probably need to change trains in **Bellinzona.** (The official William Tell train continues to Locarno.) The train to Lugano passes the northern tip of Lake Maggiore and goes through a quiet, lush valley lined with picturesque villages and chestnut trees. Enjoy your time in Italian Switzerland!

William Tell Express Connections

From Luzern by Train to: Zürich (2/hour, 1 hour), **Zürich Airport** (2/hour, 1.25 hours, most with change in Zürich), **Bern** (2/hour, 1-1.5 hours), **Interlaken Ost** (2/hour, 2-2.5 hours), **Lausanne** (hourly, 2.25 hours direct), **Appenzell** (2/hour, 2.75 hours, change in Herisau or in Zürich and Gossau), **Chur** (hourly,

2.25 hours, change in Thalwil).

From Lugano by Train to: Zürich (hourly, 2.75 hours, half with easy change in Arth-Goldau), **Interlaken Ost** (hourly, 4.75 hours, 1-2 changes), **Bern** (hourly, 3.75 hours, transfer in Zürich or Luzern). From Lugano, you can continue on to the **Bernina Express.**

Bernina Express

The Bernina Express is one of the most exciting train rides through the Swiss Alps, thanks to its diversity: starting with the sunny palm-tree ambience of Lugano, getting a taste of Italy along beautiful Lake Como, climbing up and over the twisting Bernina Pass, and seeing mountain towns like Pontresina before finishing up in eastern Switzerland. The little red train with panoramic cars spirals up to 7,380 feet, passing steep mountains and cliffs, glaciers, waterfalls, and a wild, rugged landscape.

Orientation to the Bernina Express

The Route

The Bernina Express combines a bus trip through Italy with a train ride up and into the mountains. The bus begins in Lugano, but soon crosses the border to run along the west side of Italy's Lake Como, eventually arriving at Tirano, where the route continues by train. From Tirano, the train crosses back into Switzerland and twists north up the steep mountainside, mastering a very steep grade on regular tracks (no cogwheels) en route to the most spectacular stretch: over the Bernina Pass. Then the train winds back down the other side, stops in mountain towns, and finally deposits you in your choice of towns: either Chur or Pontresina/St. Moritz/Davos.

The route can be reversed (Chur or Davos/St. Moritz/Pontresina to Tirano by train, then bus to Lugano). In fact, this way arguably provides an even better experience: Approaching Pontresina from the north is breathtaking, and it gets even better when the train gets to the Bernina Pass.

Planning Your Time: The trip is spectacular but long. It helps to break it up with an overnight or two in the Pontresina area (see the Pontresina, Samedan, and St. Moritz chapter). The Bernina Express is especially enjoyable in July and August (and, if you're lucky, in early September), when you may be able to take an open-top yellow train car between Tirano and St. Moritz (depending on the weather).

If you have more time, consider taking a standard regional train along this route (rather than the official Bernina Express train with panoramic cars). That way, you can get off as you like for hiking and exploring (see "Skipping the Official Panorama Train" under "Helpful Hints," later).

Cost and Schedule

A one-way trip on the Bernina Express from Lugano to Chur costs 82 SF second class, 120 SF first class. If you're only going as far as Pontresina, it's cheaper (52 SF second class, 69 SF first class). The entire trip (including the bus) is covered by a Eurailpass or a Swiss Pass, though supplements for the panorama cars cost extra.

If you do the official Bernina Express trip, **seat supplements** (which come with reservations) are required for both the bus and the panoramic train (12 SF each for train and bus, 9 SF in winter, buy easy-to-get bus reservation from driver as you board). Remember, you can do the same stretch on a regular regional train without reservations (optional seat reservation-5 SF; no such option for bus).

The bus leaves daily at 10:00 in summer (mid-May–mid-Oct) from outside Lugano's train station and heads for Tirano (facing the lake with the station at your back, walk about 100 yards to the left; bus stop has yellow sign for St. Moritz and Tirano).

At 13:00, you'll arrive in Tirano. From here, trains continue north over the mountains. All trains follow the same tracks for a while, but eventually fan out to two different end points: to Chur (departs Tirano 14:04, arrives Chur 18:27) or to Davos (departs Tirano 14:22, arrives Davos 18:08; this train also stops en route in Pontresina at 16:26 and in St. Moritz at 16:39). Note that official Chur-bound Bernina Express trains pass by—but don't stop in—Pontresina and St. Moritz; but more frequent standard, regional, Chur-bound trains do make those stops.

If you're doing it the other way around, here are some options: From Chur, the train leaves at 8:32 and arrives in Tirano at 12:38. From Davos, the train departs at 8:12 (from St. Moritz at 9:29 and from Pontresina at 9:52), arriving in Tirano at 12:03. The bus from Tirano leaves at 14:25 and arrives in Lugano at 17:30. Remember to confirm all times.

From Tirano, you can also break off the official Bernina Express route and head south to **Varenna**, a favorite stop on Lake Como. Direct Italian regional trains (about €4) take 1.5 hours, departing Tirano at 13:10, 15:10, 17:10, and 19:10.

In winter (late-Oct–mid-May), the bus service stops, but the Bernina Express train still runs from Tirano to St. Moritz and Chur; to reach Davos, you'll change in Filisur. (Standard regional trains continue on all those routes.)

Information: The Bernina Express is operated by Rhaetian Railway (tel. 081-288-6565, www.berninaexpress.ch). You can buy an English guidebook about the Bernina Express on the train or at gift shops along the way (11 SF). A recorded English commentary plays on the train's loudspeaker.

Helpful Hints

Bus Trip: Make yourself comfortable on the Lugano-Tirano bus leg of the Bernina trip. The seats recline, and the footrests, armrests, and individual fans give you more comfort than on a standard transit bus. There are no WCs or food on the bus, so buy your snacks and drinks before boarding (a convenient spot is the Aperto shop at Lugano's train station). The bus stops for a WC and snack break in Italy (Swiss francs accepted). Bags can be put under the bus. The bus trip is almost entirely through Italy.

Train Trip: Once you reach Tirano, you'll switch to a train. For the first part of the ride, views are somewhat better on the right (though the left is better for seeing the train curve around the famous spiral viaduct at Brusio). After Poschiavo, views are better on the left.

Topless Trains: If traveling in July, August, or early September, ask about sitting in the yellow "convertible" train cars with flip seats and no roof (but be aware that these go only on certain segments of the trip). The railway decides the day before—depending on the weather—whether to add these cars to the train (available in both first and second class).

Skipping the Official Panorama Train: The train segment of the Bernina Express can be done on a standard regional train (with smaller windows that open, and possibly a car with larger-view windows). These trains stop at all stations, allowing you to hop off and walk around in the beautiful surroundings. You can get off at Poschiavo for a quick visit, or at the Bernina Pass for hiking, or at Diavolezza to do a cable-car trip. Alp Grüm and Ospizio Bernina are starting points for several great hikes (at Ospizio Bernina, you can leave your bags at the restaurant near the station). Take advantage of the frequent and easy train connections, and make as many short stops as time and interest allow. Not only do you save yourself the panoramic train supplement, but you have the flexibility of traveling without a seat reservation. The panoramic cars are indeed great—and this stretch is particularly well-suited for a panoramic car—but the trip is still very rewarding on a standard train (especially because your panoramic-car supplement doesn't stop some jerks from pulling down the sun shades and ruining your view).

SCENIC RAIL JOURNEYS

Self-Guided Tour

Bernina Express Bus

The bus trip is more scenic than relaxing. Lakes Lugano and Como are almost fjord-like, lined with little Italian getaways. For the best views, sit on the right-hand side (seat numbers on your "reservation" don't seem to matter).

At first, the bus takes you around Lake Lugano on narrow, windy roads, frequently honking its horn to warn oncoming traffic at tight passages. Leaving Lugano, you'll pass the town of Gandria (fun to visit from Lugano by boat—see page 286). Shortly after Gandria, you cross the border into **Italy** (it's a nonevent—bus doesn't stop, no need to show passports). You may notice a change in architecture: Whereas the Swiss love meticulously manicured gardens and painstakingly renovated houses, the Italians take things a bit easier.

Once the bus leaves Lake Lugano, the road broadens and takes you through modern Italian villages before hitting picturesque

Lake Como (Lago di Como). Above the town of Menaggio are your first views of the lake. The village across the lake on the right (by the funny hump of land) is the *real* Bellagio (not the Las Vegas casino). At the nearby village of Dongo, the Italian fascist dictator Mussolini was captured at the end of World War II. Tunnels occasionally disrupt your views, but you can catch glimpses of the lush lakefront. In Gravedona, the street narrows, and getting the bus through is a tight squeeze. Posh private villas and gardens line the street; look for the 12th-century Romanesque Church of Santa Maria del Tiglio. From here, the trip takes you to the tiny harbor town of Domaso, a touristy area with plenty of campgrounds, hotels, and swimming pools.

Shortly before noon, the bus stops for 15 minutes in **Sorico,** at the northern tip of Lake Como. You'll have a chance to use the WC and buy a snack or drink (Swiss francs accepted).

The bus then crosses the **"Pian di Spagna"**—famous for a tense standoff between Spanish and Swiss troops during the religious wars of the Counter-Reformation. The trip continues up the fertile **Valtellina Valley,** where some of northern Italy's white wine is produced. The sunny slopes on the left side are reserved for vineyards, the right lower slopes are for woodland, and the bottom of the valley is occupied by apple plantations. For centuries (from 1512 until Napoleon in 1797) this region belonged to Switzerland's largest canton, Graubünden. This region is Italian today, but many Swiss still think of the local Veltlin wine as their own.

Tirano is our last stop in Italy. In the old town, the bus passes an impressive Renaissance church (Madonna di Tirano, on the left) before arriving at the train station at 13:00. You have time for lunch and some sightseeing before hopping on the Bernina Express train (in summer departs at 14:04 to Chur, or at 14:22 to Pontresina, St. Moritz, and Davos). Both trains follow roughly the same route through Filisur, where they split; remember, the official Chur-bound Bernina Express train passes near Pontresina and St. Moritz, but does not stop at either place. Or, to cram in more sightseeing, take an earlier departure on a regional train to gain time for a stopover in the fine town of Poschiavo (described later), and catch your Bernina Express train from there later (confirm times at the Tirano station information window).

If you're interested in the Poschiavo side-trip, read ahead to the "Poschiavo" section.

Bernina Express Train, Part One: Tirano to Poschiavo

From Tirano, the train crosses the center of town before climbing up to **Brusio.** Here the train takes the famous circular viaduct, the only one in the world—an ingenious construction allowing the train to reach higher altitudes without the help of a cogwheel mechanism. As the train spirals up, you can see the front and back cars curving in front of and behind you, riding over the viaduct.

Sit back and enjoy the most scenic part of the trip. You'll

pass dark old pine forests with needle-and-moss-covered boulders. Chestnut forests, tobacco plantations, and vineyards contribute to the lush tableau. Wildflowers along the track include bright-orange lilies and mountain azaleas. The train slaloms up the steep mountain and offers more and more views of waterfalls, steep cliffs, and the Poschiavo valley and lake far below you.

If you're not stopping in Poschiavo, skip down to "Part Two."

Poschiavo

If you detour for a quick break in this cute town, check the time of the next train (posted on the wall) before you leave the station.

Deposit your bags at the station's luggage counter (3 SF), just beyond the TI, where you can pick up a free map and the English translation for a short orientation walk (TI tel. 081-844-0571).

The best quick visit to Poschiavo includes a stroll to the main square (Piazza Comunale), with the Museo Casa Console and near the town's main church (St. Ignazio). From the station, walk straight out and down the main street until it ends at the river, then turn left, following signs for *Museo Casa Console*. Cross the river over the pedestrian bridge and continue left, then right, then left, following the *Museo* signs.

The main square, **Piazza Comunale**, is lined with Neoclassical and Neo-Gothic buildings, including an impressive Catholic church (Chiesa di San Vittore Mauro). A church stood here as early as 703, but the building has been rebuilt and renovated several times: The bell tower dates from 1202, and the Baroque front door was carved in the 1700s. Don't miss the little yellow building just before the church, with the intricate wrought-iron grills. Have a peek inside, and don't be startled by the skulls lining the walls—you're standing in front of the local ossuary.

In the old Town Hall, below the 12th-century church tower,

is the tiny **Museo Casa Console**. It has a nice collection of Romantic-era paintings of this region—the sort that helped kick off the tourism boom and, in a sense, brought you here. (Before becoming glamorized in the Romantic era, mountains were seen more as obstacles than objects of beauty.) However, the museum is overpriced—unless you have a Swiss Pass, skip it (10 SF, covered by Swiss Pass, Tue-Sun 11:00-16:00, closed Mon and Nov-mid-Dec, tel. 081-844-0040).

Go from the main square a block north and find the **Church of St. Ignazio.** It's ironic that this Protestant church's namesake, St. Ignatius of Loyola, was the founder of the militant Jesuit order, whose main purpose was to fight "heretic" Protestants. Notice the inscription above the central pulpit, which is fervently Protestant: *Chiesa cristiana vangelica riformata da gli errori e superstizioni umane* ("Christian evangelical church, reformed from human errors and superstitions").

Then it's back to the station...you've got a train to catch.

Bernina Express Train, Part Two: Poschiavo to Pontresina

Thirty minutes after leaving Poschiavo, and before you reach the Bernina Pass, you'll spot the first glacier, **Palü Gletscher** (behind the little lake of Palüsee on the left). It lies nestled between the peak Piz Varuna (11,330 feet) on the left and the eastern summit of Piz Palü on the right (12,790 feet).

The groaning of the gears is a reminder that this is the only train crossing over the Alps without a tunnel. It goes right over the summit. Ospizio Bernina—at the **Bernina Pass**—marks the highest point of this trip (7,380 feet). You'll see the White Lake (Lago Bianco), whose color comes from the snowmelt, also called "glacier milk." A watershed sign (yellow, reading *Wasserscheide*) explains that this is a European continental divide: From here, rivers flow either north (toward the Inn and Danube rivers, and finally to the Black Sea) or south (to the Adriatic Sea via the Adda and Po rivers).

Behind the White Lake, you can see the glaciers of **Sassal Masone** and **Piz Cambrena.** This mountain pass not only separates European drainage basins, but also cultures. Back when the train line was more susceptible to bad-weather closures, the Italian-speaking valley of Poschiavo was often cut off from Switzerland in the winter, and turned itself toward its southern neighbor, the valley of Veltlin (where you were just riding the bus).

The train crosses the barren landscape and descends into the **Engadine** valley. Tourists and convalescents discovered this part of Switzerland at the end of the 19th century. Imagine the gorgeous skiing here in the winter, which still attracts the rich and famous.

After the railroad opened this secluded valley to the world, the first hotels and sanatoriums were built (the air and sunshine supposedly helped fight various diseases). Poets found their muse in the wild, romantic landscape, while painters flocked in, attracted by the quality of the light. Keep an eye out for typical Engadine architecture—small windows set in thick walls, etched *sgraffito* decorations, and carved wooden doors (for more on this architecture, see page 307).

The **Montebello curve** offers you the best views over the Morteratsch glacier on the left, with impressive peaks in the background. From left to right: the Bellavista Range (12,770 feet), Crest Agüzza (12,690 feet), and the highest peak in the canton, Mount Bernina (13,280 feet). Mount Bernina was first climbed in 1850 by a team led by rangers from the village of Schanf. Their gear consisted only of thick woolen pants, a shirt and jacket, hobnailed shoes, and a hat with a black veil to shade them from the strong sunshine.

As you continue, the tracks are lined by more and more larch trees. The milky-white waters from Lago Bianco and the Morteratsch glacier run wild in a broad riverbed alongside the tracks, as satisfied cows chew away in the meadows while waterfalls tumble down the cliffs. From the Morteratsch station, there's a fine one-hour hike to the edge of the glacier, past posts tracking the glacier's recent retreat.

Next stop: **Pontresina.** This town is a good place to break the journey (see the Pontresina, Samedan, and St. Moritz chapter). Consider spending a night or two in Pontresina, exploring the quaint village of Samedan, visiting the glitzy resort of St. Moritz, and maybe doing some hiking before continuing on your way.

If you're going to **St. Moritz,** your train trip is nearly over (about 10 minutes after Pontresina). But on the way to **Chur** or **Davos,** there's more to see.

Bernina Express Train, Part Three: Pontresina to Filisur

Although you're leaving the glaciers behind, your trip will still lead you through magnificent mountain scenery, with steep cliffs and deep gorges. (Note that this section of the trip overlaps with the Glacier Express.)

First, you'll slide through the broad and mellow valley around Samedan, following the shortest river in Switzerland, the Flazbach. On the right, look for the funicular heading up to **Muottas Muragl,** a viewpoint overlooking the valleys that come together in Samedan (for details, see page 301). Samedan is home to Europe's highest airport. It serves glider enthusiasts and vacationers in St. Moritz.

After Samedan, in **Bever,** the train leaves the valley and climbs to another spectacular leg of its journey. The section between Bever and Bergün boasts amazing engineering work. Technicians from all over the world come here to admire the diversity of spiral tunnels, looping viaducts, galleries, and bridges that span the Albula Gorge.

The train works its way up along a cheerfully splashing mountain creek, between the Arven pine and larch trees and some isolated farmhouses. The **Albula Tunnel,** the highest subterranean alpine crossing in Europe, takes you up to 5,970 feet. This pass serves as another barrier between cultures and climate—the weather is often quite different on either side of the tunnel. Hikers can follow the tracks and read the information panels about the construction of the train line. Every winter, the street along the tracks is closed to cars, and 100,000 sled enthusiasts enjoy the ride of their lives on a windy three-mile stretch.

From **Preda,** the train loops down through five spiral and two straight tunnels, crosses nine viaducts, and goes under two galleries—it's considered the most ingenious railway line ever built. It covers almost eight miles and descends more than 1,365 feet in altitude. The village of **Bergün** will be visible three separate times as you loop around the valley. Bergün greets you with a modern, public open-air swimming pool and an onion-shaped 17th-century "Roman tower." As the train continues winding down the pretty valley, you may be able to see other parts of the track below or next to you. Any track you see is one you've either already been on—or will soon be on.

You'll pass through **Filisur**, where the two Bernina Express routes split: northwest to Chur or northeast to Davos. If you're riding to Chur, continue to "Part Four."

Bernina Express Train, Part Four: Filisur to Chur

After Filisur, the train enters a tunnel, and an announcement reminds you to ready your camera and position yourself on the left side. Just after the tunnel, you'll cross the famous **Landwasser viaduct.** A masterpiece of engineering, its pillars were built without scaffolding. Iron towers, which formed the center of each pillar, were built first. With the help of cranes set up atop each pillar, materials were hoisted up and the brick was laid. The 425-foot-long viaduct curves elegantly in a radius of 330 feet. Below, the wild Albula River carves the dramatic gorge; above, your train's panoramic windows allow you to see the steep, rugged cliffs looming over the tracks (a particularly beautiful stretch is right after Solis). Notice how nicely the dark limestone masonry matches the surrounding landscape (it was quarried right here).

Thusis is the commercial hub of the broad and lush Domleschg valley. The trip takes you down along the Hinterrhein ("Back-Rhine") River. Notice the many fortresses, castles, towers, and ruins along the river, a reminder that taxes were levied on the traders traveling this major route between northern and southern Europe. One of Switzerland's most popular mineral waters originates in Rhäzüns. The 13th-century castle above the town now belongs to a local chemical company.

Reichenau marks the confluence of two arms of the Upper Rhine (the Hinterrhein and the Vorderrhein—"Front-Rhine"). This town became wealthy from the taxes it got from the passing merchants. The 17th-century Reichenau Castle, right where the rivers converge, was once used as a school, but is now a hotel.

The train follows the Rhine at the foot of Calanda Mountain to our final stop, **Chur.** You can catch the Glacier Express (explained next) from Chur or from St. Moritz.

Bernina Express Connections

From Lugano by Train to: Luzern (hourly, 2.5 hours, half with change in Arth-Goldau), **Zürich** (hourly, 2.75 hours, half with change in Arth-Goldau), **Interlaken Ost** (hourly, 4.75 hours, 1-2 changes), **Bern** (hourly, 3.75 hours, transfer in Zürich or Luzern).

From Pontresina by Train to: St. Moritz (hourly, 11 minutes), **Samedan** (hourly, 6 minutes; 2 buses/hour, 15 minutes), **Zürich** (hourly, 3.5 hours, transfer in Samedan and Chur), **Tirano** (hourly, 2.25 hours; up to 3 panoramic trains per day in summer).

From Chur by Train to: Zürich (2/hour, 1.25-1.5 hours), **Luzern** (hourly, 2.25 hours, transfer in Thalwil), **Appenzell** (hourly, 2-2.5 hours, 1-3 changes, half-hour longer but easier via St. Gallen). To reach destinations in western Switzerland—such as Bern, Interlaken, or Lake Geneva—you'll transfer in Zürich (see "Zürich Connections" on page 67).

Glacier Express

This most promoted of the Swiss scenic rail routes travels between Zermatt in the southwest of Switzerland and various resort towns in eastern Switzerland (St. Moritz, Chur, and Davos). If you stay on for the whole ride, you'll spend almost eight hours crossing 291 bridges, going through 91 tunnels, and reaching an altitude of 6,670 feet.

While it's an impressive and famous journey, the Glacier Express is not necessarily the be-all and end-all of Swiss rail trips.

Much of the journey is down in valleys (as opposed to along the sides of cliffs), meaning that high-altitude views are a little lacking. But the stark landscape, carved by the glaciers that gave the train its name, is striking. The trip offers a dramatic way to connect eastern Switzerland with tucked-away-in-the-mountains Zermatt (see the Zermatt and the Matterhorn chapter).

Orientation to the Glacier Express

The Route

"Glacier Express" is a misnomer—it's hardly an express. Not only does it take its time (traveling at about 20 mph to make the full trip in almost 8 hours), but it also makes several stops along the way. The route cuts along the southern part of Switzerland, between St. Moritz/Chur/Davos (in the east) and Zermatt (in the west). You can ride in either direction.

Planning Your Time: The most distinctive stretch of the trip is the high-mountain pass between Disentis and Brig. If you don't want to commit to the whole eight hours, you can try to connect a trip with this segment only (about 3 hours). Remember that you can join or leave the trip whenever you like (for example, Chur in the east and Brig in the west link conveniently into Swiss rail lines to other major destinations).

Cost and Schedule

You'll pay 134 SF for second class, or 222 SF for first class, between St. Moritz and Zermatt. The entire trip is covered by the Swiss Pass (except the reservation fee, described below). But a Eurailpass covers only part of the journey; two segments (Disentis-Brig and Brig-Zermatt) are privately run by the Matterhorn Gotthard Railway and not covered by Eurail (roughly 70 SF total in second class, 100 SF for first class, buy at station or pay 10 SF extra to buy on board, www.mgbahn.ch). If you're riding the full length of the Glacier Express *sans* railpass, the cost is high enough to warrant a look at the Half-Fare Travel Card, which can quickly pay for itself (110 SF for 1 month—see page 378).

All Glacier Express trains have panoramic first- and second-class cars with air-conditioning, headsets for commentary, and the option of an in-seat meal. Second-class seating can get extremely crowded in summer, so consider splurging on first class.

In addition to your train ticket or pass, you'll have to pay a **reservation fee** (33 SF, or 13 SF off-season). If you're not starting or ending in St. Moritz, or if you're getting off along the way, you can choose cheaper standard regional trains. But if you want to take a direct train between St. Moritz and Zermatt, the pricier Glacier Express is your only option.

SCENIC RAIL JOURNEYS

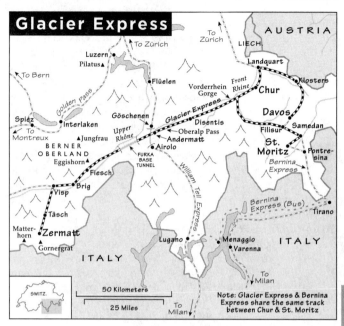

Glacier Express

To Zürich · To Zürich · AUSTRIA · LIECH.
Luzern · Pilatus▲ · Landquart
To Bern · Flüelen · Vorderrhein Gorge · Front Rhine · Chur · Klosters
Spiez · Göschenen · Glacier Express · Davos
To Montreux · Interlaken · Upper Rhône · Disentis · Filisur · Samedan
BERNER OBERLAND · ▲Jungfrau · Oberalp Pass · Andermatt · St. Moritz · Pontre-sina
Eggishorn · FURKA BASE TUNNEL · Airolo · Bernina Express
Fiesch · Brig · Visp · William Tell Express · Bernina Express (Bus)
Täsch · Tirano
Matter-horn · Zermatt · Lugano · Menaggio · Varenna · ITALY
Gornergrat · ITALY · To Milan

SWITZ.
50 Kilometers
25 Miles
To Milan

Note: Glacier Express & Bernina Express share the same track between Chur & St. Moritz

From mid-May through mid-October, four trains run daily in each direction. Going from east to west, the train begins either in St. Moritz (two depart at 9:17, and another at 10:02) or in Davos (departs at 10:41); all trains stop in Chur along the way (at either 11:27 or 12:27). Going from west to east, the trains depart Zermatt at 9:00, 9:13, and two at 10:00. Off-season, frequency drops to one per day in each direction (east to west: departs St. Moritz at 9:02; west to east: departs Zermatt at 10:00). Official Glacier Express trains often stop running in fall (mid-Oct-mid-Dec) to allow for maintenance, but regular regional train service continues.

The train takes almost six hours to connect Zermatt and Chur, or almost eight hours for Zermatt to St. Moritz or Davos. Confirm all times before your trip.

Information: The Glacier Express is operated jointly by the Matterhorn Gotthard Bahn (MGB), based in Brig (tel. 027-927-7777, www.glacierexpress.ch or www.mgbahn.ch), and the Rhätische Bahn (RhB), based in Chur (tel. 081-288-6565, www.rhb.ch). For more detail than found here or in the headset narration, consider picking up a guidebook before you board, or buy the (overpriced) official guide (17 SF on board).

Helpful Hints

Picking the Best Seat: For most of the trip—including the most dramatic stretch, between Disentis and Brig—it's slightly preferable to sit on the south-facing side of the train (generally seat numbers ending in 1 or 2, and in second class, seats ending in 3 or 8, on the aisle; coming from the east, even-numbered seats face forward). Keep in mind: Trains change directions in Brig and in Chur—if you start on the left side in Zermatt, Davos, Samedan, or St. Moritz, you'll be on the right side for most of the train trip (or vice versa).

Luggage: You'll keep your luggage with you (they don't check it through)—just slip it between the backs of the seats.

No-Show Bridges: Most promotional materials show the Glacier Express train venturing across ancient aqueducts and old stone bridges. It makes for picturesque publicity. But realize that you can barely see these bridges from the train itself... because you're on them.

Eating on the Glacier Express: The train has a fancy restaurant car that offers lunch, which is handy if you're in for the full eight hours. For 43 SF, you get a salad (summer) or soup (winter), a main dish, and a dessert; 30 SF buys you just the main dish (drinks cost extra). Their trademark gizmo: a tilted wine glass. Since lunch is generally served when the train is going up a steep incline (11:00-13:30), these gimmicky glasses always get a laugh.

To save a few francs, it's fine to bring your own **picnic,** and most seats have tables—perfect for a grocery-store feast.

Self-Guided Tour

The Glacier Express

All Glacier Express trains—whether they begin in St. Moritz or Davos—go through Chur. I'll describe the route starting at Chur and heading toward Zermatt. (For details on most of the trip from St. Moritz to Chur, see "Bernina Express Train, Part Three: Pontresina to Filisur," earlier.)

Just outside Chur (near where the St. Moritz train line hits the Chur line), you'll be following the **Vorderrhein Gorge,** nicknamed "the Swiss Grand Canyon." It was carved by the Rhine River (though way up here in the Alps, this little "Front-Rhine" is not navigable). After about nine miles, the train diverges from the Rhine and enters a pastoral region called Surselva, centered on the town Ilanz. This is Romansh country, where the fourth official language of Switzerland is kept alive—barely—in communities like this one (see sidebar on page 298). After headset commentary #33, keep an eye out on the right side of the train for three doors, under small brown roofs, tucked into a stone wall beneath a road along the bottom of the hillside. They're part of Switzerland's military defenses; access to this pass can be blown up on short notice

SCENIC RAIL JOURNEYS

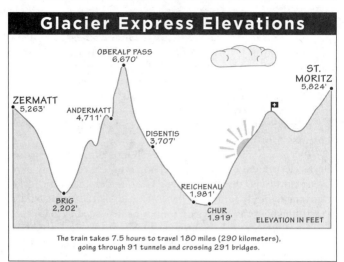

Glacier Express Elevations

OBERALP PASS
6,670'

ST.
MORITZ
5,824'

ZERMATT
5,263'

ANDERMATT
4,711'

DISENTIS
3,707'

REICHENAU
1,981'

BRIG
2,202'

CHUR
1,919'

ELEVATION IN FEET

The train takes 7.5 hours to travel 180 miles (290 kilometers),
going through 91 tunnels and crossing 291 bridges.

(see sidebar on page 102). From this valley (Reichenau, roughly 2,000 feet above sea level and the lowest altitude of the route), the big climb begins.

As you approach **Disentis,** the tracks begin to twist along the edge of a canyon—making the scenery more dramatic (a taste of what's to come). Thirty years ago, those mountains above you were covered in snow year-round—but no longer. You'll pull into Disentis, with its big 17th-century Benedictine monastery looming in your window (first on the left side, then on the right). Your car will jiggle as a cogwheel engine is attached. This locomotive has gears that can lower to latch onto the cogs of an extra rail with grippable teeth. At 10 percent incline (that's 100 meters of gain per kilometer, or about 500 feet per mile), conventional train wheels start to slip. The solution: a cogwheel (a.k.a. rack-and-pinion drive).

You'll work your way up the mountain alongside the Front-Rhine River. Just west of Sedrun is the staging ground for the excavation of the Gotthard Base Tunnel (which will run 30

miles under the mountain from Erstfeld to Bodio when it opens—*Gott* willing—in 2017). Just past Rueras, the track steepens and the train slows to allow its gears to latch into the cog rail. After Tschamut, the last inhabited place before Oberalp Pass, you enter a long series of snow sheds—designed to protect the tracks (and trains) in case an avalanche strikes.

You'll emerge from the sheds at **Oberalp Pass,** the literal high point of this journey (6,670 feet), and glide along the Oberalp Lake. Notice the extensive network of avalanche fences high above you—a reminder of the many generations of Swiss farmers who have learned to live on the land. The reddish streaks you might see on the snow? Believe it or not, that's sand from the Sahara Desert. It gets caught up in high-altitude winds and carried all the way to the Swiss Alps.

As you descend from the pass, you'll travel over, then through, the modern town of **Andermatt,** home to a Swiss Army base. Deep below you is the 9.5-mile-long Gotthard Tunnel, which takes trains unscenically from Göschenen to Airolo. The huge boulders seen throughout this desolate terrain were deposited by glaciers.

Soon after, you'll go through the 9.5-mile-long Furka Base Tunnel. While it might seem like a view-killer, realize that this tunnel—finished in 1982—makes it possible for the Glacier Express to continue running through the winter. Automobiles are allowed onto the train to ride smoothly and safely between Realp and Oberwald. This is especially handy in the winter, when the road is closed.

You'll emerge into the region of **Goms,** with more pretty villages. The up-close view of the village of Reckingen is particularly fun as the train snakes through a narrow passage between the dark-wood houses. Along this stretch, the train joins up with another of Europe's great rivers, the **Rhône.** Just a bubbly little mountain stream here (originating from the once-mighty Rhône Glacier nearby), the Rhône flows all the way to Marseille, France, where it meets the Mediterranean. Some of the construction you may see in this area is part of a project to "correct" (channel and control) this upper stretch of the powerful river, which has a long history of flooding the valley.

As the valley gets rockier, consider that you're on the "back" side of the Berner Oberland. If you climbed up high enough to the north, you'd see the Jungfrau, Mönch, and Eiger mountains (from the village of Fiesch/Kühboden you can do just that, with the help of a cable car up to Eggishorn, which boasts views of the Matterhorn and Mont Blanc to boot).

Finally, you'll arrive at **Brig,** an ugly industrial town with good connections to other train lines (transfer here if you're not continuing to Zermatt). From Brig, it's 20 miles to Zermatt and the Matterhorn, following the craggy Nikolai Valley. You'll feel the tug as the train's cogwheel attaches again for another steep climb. Keep an eye out for vineyards—the highest in Europe. We're out of milk country and into wine country. At Stalden, a road leads up another valley to the resort of Saas-Fee. Along this section, the route closely follows the Vispa River as it scenically tumbles over rapids. Shortly before the village of Randa, you pass a cone of rubble left by a huge avalanche that wiped out two miles of road and track here in 1991.

At **Täsch,** vast parking lots mark the end of the road for drivers. From here it's train-only into the traffic-free terminus of this line, Zermatt. Think about how much the terrain has changed since you started the trip: from remote valleys to fertile farmlands, to tundra above the tree line, to this rough and rocky terrain.

As you continue along the valley lined with quarries, you'll begin to get your first glimpses (provided the weather's clear) of the unmistakable shape of the **Matterhorn**—a fitting exclamation point marking the end of this long journey. **Zermatt**—with its bunker-like, avalanche-proof train station—lies just around the bend.

Glacier Express Connections

From Chur by Train to: Zürich (2/hour, 1.25-1.5 hours), **Luzern** (hourly, 2.25 hours, transfer in Thalwil), **Appenzell** (hourly, 2-2.5 hours, 1-3 changes, half-hour longer but easier via St. Gallen). To reach destinations in western Switzerland, such as Bern or Interlaken, you'll transfer in Zürich (see "Zürich Connections" on page 67).

From Zermatt: Zermatt is connected to the outside world by an 80-minute train ride to Visp or Brig. Brig is a handy place to bail out of the Glacier Express route, if you're coming from the east and not going all the way to Zermatt. If you're coming from or going to Lausanne or Montreux, you'll save time changing trains in Visp, which is located between Zermatt and Brig (Zermatt-Lausanne via Visp: hourly, 3 hours).

From Brig by Train to: Bern (1-2/hour, 1 hour), **Lausanne** (1-2/hour, 1.75 hours), **Interlaken Ost** (1-2/hour, 1.25 hours, transfer in Spiez), **Luzern** (1-2/hour, 2.25-2.75 hours, transfer in Bern or Olten), **Zürich** (1-2/hour, 2.25 hours, some transfer in Bern).

Chur

The routes of the Glacier Express and the Bernina Express both pass through Chur—supposedly Switzerland's oldest and warmest town. It's a handy transportation hub for these two scenic train lines and has a charming-enough old town. Overall, Chur (pronounced "khoor") is just a typical Swiss burg—fine for passing through, but not worth a detour. If you've got time to kill, you can wander up through the cobbled old town to two big churches (the Romanesque cathedral and the Gothic Church of St. Martin), some remains of the medieval city wall, and the town museum (Rätisches Museum, 6 SF). Follow the handy red signs pointing you to the attractions. Public WCs are next to the cathedral.

Orientation to Chur

Chur fans out over the foothills from the Rhine River. The train station is at the bottom (north end) of the town center.

Tourist Information: The TI, downstairs in the train station (next to the railway *Reisebüro*), offers a free town map marked with sights, hotels, and restaurants. If you're here for longer, you can also pick up their free *City Guide* brochure detailing museums and attractions, and the *Accommodations Guide* (Mon-Fri 7:30-20:00, Sat-Sun 8:00-18:00, tel. 081-252-1818, www.churtourismus.ch).

Arrival in Chur: Chur's train station sits atop a long underground concourse, where you'll find the TI, shops, the handy Bahnhofplatz parking garage, and other services. To get to the old town, follow *Stadtzentrum* signs up the escalator, then walk straight up Bahnhofstrasse. In two blocks, you'll reach the big roundabout at Postplatz. The old town is straight ahead.

Internet Access: The **train station** has pay Internet terminals. In the town center, the **library** *(Kantonsbibliothek)* has free access, but it's limited to 15 minutes (Mon-Fri 9:00-17:30, Sat 9:00-16:00, closed Sun, Karlihofplatz, tel. 081-257-2828).

Sleeping in Chur

(1 SF = about $1.10, country code: 41)
Chur is about halfway between Appenzell and the Pontresina area, both of which are more appealing for an overnight stay. Sleep in

Chur only if you must, in order to connect to one of the scenic rail lines. These moderately priced places are in the atmospheric old town, an easy 10- to 15-minute walk from the train station.

Hotel Restaurant Rebleuten, in a 500-year-old building, overlooks a quiet little square a block off Kornplatz. The 13 small rooms are cozy and comfortable. The hotel is warmly run by the Stöhr family (Ss-74 SF, Sb-89 SF, D-128 SF, Db-148 SF, Q-216 SF, a little cheaper in winter, Pfisterplatz 1, tel. 081-255-1144, fax 081-255-1145, www.rebleuten.ch, contact@rebleuten.ch).

Hotel Freieck has a mod lobby and 39 rooms over a low-key café. Their cheaper standard rooms, with old-fashioned furniture, are plenty nice; you'll pay more for a modern "superior" room (Sb-90-150 SF, Db-150-220 SF, Tb-180-240 SF, prices depend on type of room and season—highest May-mid-Oct, elevator, pay Internet access, free cable Internet in rooms, Reichsgasse 44, tel. 081-255-1515, fax 081-255-1516, www.freieck.ch, hotel@freieck.ch, Stockmann family).

Hotel Franziskaner, charming and well-located, rents reasonably priced rooms above a popular restaurant (S-65 SF, D-125 SF, Db-168 SF, free Wi-Fi, Kupfergasse 18, tel. 081-252-1261, fax 081-252-1279, www.hotelfranziskaner.ch, info@hotelfranzis kaner.ch).

Chur Connections

Chur is a convenient spot to catch either the Glacier Express or the Bernina Express. It also offers speedy, frequent connections to Zürich.

From Chur by Train to: Zürich (2/hour, 1.25-1.5 hours), **Luzern** (hourly, 2.25 hours, transfer in Thalwil), **Appenzell** (hourly, 2-2.5 hours, 1-3 changes, half-hour longer but easier via St. Gallen). To reach destinations in western Switzerland—such as Bern, Interlaken, or Lake Geneva—you'll transfer in Zürich (see "Zürich Connections" on page 67).

SCENIC RAIL JOURNEYS

SWITZERLAND
in WINTER

One of my favorite Swiss memories happened one winter night on the snowy slopes of the Berner Oberland. My friend Walter (who runs Hotel Mittaghorn in Gimmelwald) and I, warmed by hot chocolate laced with schnapps, decided to go sledding between mountain-high villages. We strapped flashlights to our heads, miner-style, and zoomed through the crisp, moonlit night.

That said, this is a summertime book. I've included plenty of tips on hiking, while mostly ignoring the winter-sports scene. But winter activities are an important part of the Swiss culture (and tourist industry).

Just a century ago, clever entrepreneurs in the Swiss Alps realized that skiing (which began as a method of wintertime transportation in Scandinavia 4,000 years ago) could be a profitable extension of their resorts' spring and summer seasons. Telemark (cross-country) skiing came first, then alpine (downhill) skiing, and, more recently, snowboarding. Generations of Swiss skiers have honed their skills on these slopes. Big names include Erica Hess, Vreni Schneider, Maria Walliser, Carlo Janka, and the venerable 1948 Olympic champion Karl Molitor (whose family currently runs a ski rental shop in Wengen in the Berner Oberland).

You don't have to be a skier or snowboarder to enjoy Switzerland in the winter. Ski resorts offer plenty of other activities, including snowshoeing, sledding, ice skating...and shopping.

Or just ride up a lift, rent a chair in the sun, and warm up with a glass of *Pflümli* (plum liqueur).

Top Winter Destinations

The winter-sports season begins in early December and runs through Easter. Peak time hits at Christmas and New Year's—during this period, hotel prices in resort towns surpass summer highs.

While Switzerland's resorts vary greatly, they share a rich ski culture, an astounding variety of terrain, relatively mild temperatures (compared to many American destinations), and a lively après-ski scene. For those who can afford them, the best winter activities are in the Berner Oberland (Mürren, Wengen, Grindelwald, and Gstaad); the southern canton of Valais (Zermatt, Saas-Fee, Crans-Montana, and Verbier); and the eastern canton of Graubünden (St. Moritz, Davos, Klosters, and Arosa).

The **Berner Oberland** offers the ultimate diversity of terrain and character, as well as great sledding and stellar views

(see the Gimmelwald and the Berner Oberland chapter). The cliff-hanging town of Mürren is relatively uncrowded and a good home base for expert skiers, with the 10,000-foot Schilthorn peak as the backbone of its ski area. Across the valley, Wengen offers skiing for all skill levels, fine accommodations, and shopping, with a complex lift system connecting it to Kleine Scheidegg, Männlichen, and Grindelwald. Grindelwald, a little closer to Interlaken, is a bit pricier, but has the world's longest sled run and easy access to more than 100 miles of downhill trails, including the area's best range of beginners' runs. For a complete overview of these ski regions, see www.myjungfrau.ch.

The canton of **Valais** ("valley"), known for its excellent wine-making along the banks of the Rhône, is also a popular skiing destination (www.valais.ch). Connected to Italy by several high-mountain passes, Valais is home to Switzerland's best-known sight: the Matterhorn (see the Zermatt and the Matterhorn chapter). The area around the Matterhorn, including the villages of Zermatt and Saas-Fee, enjoy a high elevation and good skiing.

The **Graubündner Alps** contain 14 different passes (www.graubuenden.ch). **St. Moritz,** situated in the Upper Engadine valley, is so well-known that it's a registered trademark (see the Pontresina, Samedan, and St. Moritz chapter). This resort town offers designer boutiques, luxury accommodations, a natural mineral-spring spa...oh, and ski slopes, too (www.stmoritz.ch). In addition to skiing, winter visitors to St. Moritz play polo and cricket on snow, go bobsledding on natural ice, or try skijoring—skiing while being pulled by riderless horses.

Tips for Winter Sports

Expect to spend 60-80 SF a day on lift tickets. You may find cheaper prices in the off-peak season (before mid-Dec and after

Easter), if you buy a multiple-day pass, or if you have a Swiss Pass. Prices may also be lower for seniors, teenagers, and kids (exact age cutoffs vary). Most ski areas offer half-day afternoon passes.

Rental prices are a bit higher than what you'd find in the US. Depending on the fanciness of the gear, you'll pay 45-75 SF for skiing or snowboarding equipment. If you haven't packed ski wear, you'll pay about 45 SF to rent ski pants, a jacket, and gloves.

Many rental shops in Switzerland belong to the Intersport rental network (www.intersportrent.ch), which sets fairly high standards for its member shops. Places outside this network can be cheaper, but Intersport shops are generally a safe bet and offer a useful bonus: Many of them let you pick up rental gear at one ski area and drop it off at another in the region for no charge (an especially handy option in the Berner Oberland).

Always ask your hotelier if they've arranged any special rental deals through local shops. Rental prices don't vary much (since so many shops are part of the Intersport network), so choose a place that's close to your hotel or convenient for getting up the mountain.

Swiss ski resorts are deservedly popular, and slopes can get crowded. Peak crowd times are Christmas, New Year's, mid-February to mid-March (when European school holidays hit), and Easter. The Berner Oberland also fills up in mid-January for world-class racing. Hit the slopes as soon as they open—the hordes don't usually arrive until 10:00 or later. This is especially true in swankier resorts, where well-heeled tourists enjoy long nights and short ski days.

For more in-depth information on the winter scene, see the winter sports section of the Swiss tourism website (www.my switzerland.com).

Christmas Celebrations

Switzerland is an ideal place to celebrate the winter holidays. Imagine spending your days exploring Christmas markets in cozy

Swiss cities, sipping hot mulled wine *(Glühwein)*, picking out your favorite handmade ornaments, then relaxing at night in a warm little chalet, making figure-eights with your cube of bread through a steaming pot of cheese fondue.

Swiss Christmas markets are a treat, whether in big cities (such as Bern, Zürich, and Basel) or smaller towns (Interlaken, Appenzell, Chur, and many others). While some of the bigger markets start at the beginning of December and run through Christmas Eve, smaller towns host markets for just one week or weekend. The Swiss Tourist Board's website lists details (www.my switzerland.com/christmas).

You'll find all cities festively decorated, but Zürich's remarkable display of tasteful, twinkling lights is arguably Switzerland's best. This being the land of Calvin—the most austere of Protestant Reformers— most Christmas decorations are relatively understated here, but they're still charming.

In the village of Gimmelwald, residents in each home adorn a window for Advent. Just as children open a different little paper window each day on an Advent

calendar, Gimmelwald residents reveal a new decorated house window on a different house each day. The debut of a new Advent window often comes with a party. Under a cold sky, with stars reflecting off the snow and the moon inside a halo, the village gathers. In a kind of roving block party, neighbors emerge to meet friends and enjoy grilled sausages, hot mulled wine, and folk music on the accordion. Men take sections of logs (the size of a four-foot chunk of telephone pole), cut the ends into a point, and plant them upright in the snow. Coated with tar, they're set ablaze—torches to light and warm the cozy yet frigid occasion. In the distance, children ride old-time wooden sleds, going up and down, up and down.

For the Swiss, a communal pot of fondue is purely a winter specialty. Invitations to a cozy Swiss party include the word *FIGUGEGL* (fee-GOO-geck-ul), which stands for *Fondue isch guet und git e gueti Lune*—"Fondue is good and gives a good mood." According to tradition, if you drop your bread into the pot, you must kiss the person to your left.

Each Christmas season, usually on St. Nicholas Day (December 6), Swiss children receive a visit from Samichlaus—that's Swiss German for St. Nicholas. With his black-clad, soot-faced henchman, Schmutzli, by his side, Samichlaus goes door to door, visiting the town's children. He knocks on the door, and when the frightened-but-excited kids answer, Samichlaus consults his big book of sins—co-authored by village parents—and does some lighthearted moralizing. Schmutzli stands by as a menacing enforcer, traditionally holding either a stick or switch for beating bad children, and a sack for carrying them away to be eaten (nowadays he only eats the really bad children). Then Samichlaus asks the kids to earn a little forgiveness by reciting a poem. After the poems and assurances of reform, Samichlaus allows them to reach deep into his bag for a smattering of tangerines, nuts, gingerbread, and other treats.

Cutting and decorating the Christmas tree—traditionally done on December 24—is a family affair. Real candles, kept upright by dangling ornamental counterbalances, are attached, then lit by the children. (Locals are bold with their candles; to me, it feels as if their pine houses, with open beams, are ready to go up in flames.) Presents are opened while the candles burn. The tree stays up after Christmas; candles are lit again on New Year's Eve for good luck. Some traditional rural Swiss churches also light candles on their trees for Christmas Eve services.

Other Festivities

Second only to Christmas is *Fasnacht*, the Germanic equivalent of Mardi Gras or Carnival. Traditionally celebrated in the days before or after Ash Wednesday, *Fasnacht* features a parade of locals in traditional masks and garish, larger-than-life costumes.

 Quirky traditions vary from town to town (for example, in Basel—home to Switzerland's most outlandish *Fasnacht*—celebrations begin promptly at 4:00 in the morning, and feature roving fife-and-drum bands). This pre-Christian ceremony likely dates from a pagan tradition to frighten away evil winter spirits and welcome the renewal of springtime. The most famous *Fasnacht* celebrations in Switzerland occur in Basel (www.fasnacht.ch), Bern (www.fasnacht.be), and Luzern (www.luzerner-fasnacht.ch). If you'll be in Switzerland at this time of year, it's worth the effort to catch one of these weird and wonderful celebrations.

SWITZERLAND: PAST and PRESENT

Switzerland has a unique and impressive story, forging unity from diversity and somehow remaining above the fray when Europe goes ballistic. Despite four languages, diverse geography, ill-defined borders, and many religious sects—and despite being surrounded by continental Europe's four big powers (France, Germany, Austria, and Italy)—the Swiss cantons banded together to form an independent federal system that still works today.

Even if you're not going to Switzerland for the history (who would?), you'll encounter it. You can play gladiator inside a fighting arena from Roman times or tour medieval castles and battlegrounds, left over from when the Swiss wrestled their independence from foreign rulers. Stripped-down cathedrals attest to the religious violence of the Reformation that almost tore the country apart. You'll ride the ingenious cogwheel trains and cliff-climbing funiculars of Switzerland's progressive 18th and 19th centuries, when the country was at the forefront of the emerging Industrial Age. The specters of Nazi Germany and the Soviet Union arise in underground fortresses and bomb shelters now open to the public. And finally, you'll see the Switzerland of today—gleaming cities, state-of-the-art transportation, and happy citizens. I love to go a-wandering along the history path, so strap on your rucksack, and let's go.

Early History: Celts and Romans (c. 500 B.C.-A.D. 500)

The Alps mountain range—Switzerland's star attraction—was born 500 million years ago, when the ocean floor was rocked by earthquakes that folded the earth upward, creating this long string of peaks (for details, see the sidebar on page 40). This landscape shaped the history and character of the Swiss people. It kept early populations physically isolated, leading to still-present cultural divisions and fostering an ethos of independence. Switzerland's location at the heart of Western Europe forced it to be international in outlook, yet the impregnable mountains allowed it to remain apart and neutral.

The first Swiss (c. 500 B.C.) were a Celtic tribe called the Helvetii. Their memory survives today in the country's official name, Confoederatio Helvetica. "Helvetia," the female symbol of Switzerland, appears dressed in robes and armed with a spear and shield, on coins, stamps, and statues.

In 58 B.C., the Helvetii were defeated by Julius Caesar, the Roman general and future ruler. The Romans established a capital at

Avenches (where evocative ruins remain—see page 138); built the cities of Zürich, Geneva, Basel, and Lausanne; and assimilated the Helvetii into their Europe-wide empire. Roman culture thrived in Switzerland for almost 500 years.

As Rome fell (c. A.D. 400), Germanic tribes swarmed in. In the north, the Alemanni snuffed out Roman culture in north-central Switzerland and established their Germanic language. In the west, the Burgundians adopted Latin, which eventually evolved into French. But these tribes never penetrated the nooks and crannies of the most remote mountain areas, and in these regions, particularly in the southeast, people still converse in Romansh, a language that's changed little from the colloquial Latin spoken by Roman-era occupiers. South of the Alps, Swiss Latin speakers gradually switched to modern-day Italian. These linguistic/cultural divides remain today.

The Middle Ages: The Holy Roman Empire (c. 500-1291)

Like most of Europe during the dark medieval centuries, Switzerland was poor, feudal, and swept by barbarian invasions. The mostly pagan Swiss were slowly converted to Christianity by traveling Irish monks, including St. Gallus (seventh century), who gave his name to the canton of St. Gallen. Swiss lands became part of Charlemagne's empire (c. 800) and its successor to the east—the Germanic kings of the Holy Roman Empire.

Around the turn of the first millennium, Switzerland began to prosper. Cities such as Bern and Luzern were founded, welcoming skilled craftsmen and traders. High in the Alps, clever engineers built bridges and catwalks to open a vital north-south highway through the St. Gotthard Pass (see page 329). This trade route proved so prosperous that the Holy Roman Emperor ensured access to it by granting the Swiss a measure of independence *(Reichsfreiheit)*. Switzerland got a taste of freedom, and when the Habsburg emperor tried to bring the country under tighter control, the Swiss had had enough.

The Old Confederacy (1291-1500)

On August 1, 1291 (celebrated today as the country's national day), Swiss citizens gathered together and swore an oath. "We will be a single nation of brothers..." they asserted, and rose up against Habsburg rule. The three cantons of Uri, Schwyz, and Unterwalden united, proclaiming independence and democratic institutions. In a legend of the time, the Swiss William Tell refused to bow to the Habsburg hat, a symbol of their power. As punishment, he was forced to shoot an apple off his own son's head. His son lived to see another haircut, and Tell led the rebellion.

The Swiss had to battle the powerful Habsburg family for two full centuries to completely drive them out. In the west, the Swiss fought Burgundy, trouncing them at the pivotal Battle of Murten. One by one, other cantons and cities (Luzern, Zürich, Bern) joined the confederacy, as these areas won more and more concessions from neighboring rulers.

During these centuries of warfare, the Swiss earned a reputation as Europe's fiercest warriors. Swiss mercenaries became a lucrative export, hired by foreign kings to fight their wars and defend their palaces (including the Swiss Guards, who still protect the Vatican today).

By 1499, Switzerland had won independence from the Habsburgs and Burgundians—in fact, if not yet in name.

Reformation and Enlightenment (c. 1500-1700)

The Protestant Reformation split Switzerland in two. In Zürich, Ulrich Zwingli preached Protestantism (see sidebar on page 52), John Calvin brought his French flock to Geneva, and the Dutch humanist Desiderius Erasmus taught at Basel. While the cities went Protestant, the more rural cantons stayed true to the Catholic faith, plunging the country into religious warfare (1529-1531). Angry rioters stormed Catholic cathedrals, stripping them of their "graven images" and leaving the austere interiors travelers see today (including Zürich's Grossmünster, Bern's Münster, and Lausanne's cathedral).

While Europe suffered through a century of religious wars, Switzerland's struggles were relatively short-lived. Swiss mercenaries fought other countries' wars...and Switzerland grew rich. When peace came to Europe with the Treaty of Westphalia

(1648), the agreement also officially recognized Switzerland as a fully independent nation.

1700s and 1800s

Through the Age of Enlightenment, Switzerland had bucked the European trend toward absolute monarchs. As the country steadily advanced economically and technologically, it moved in a firmly democratic direction.

On August 10, 1792, a revolutionary mob in Paris stormed the palace, arrested the king of France, and slaughtered his body-

guards—800 Swiss mercenaries died. This pivotal event in European history is memorialized in Luzern's Lion Monument to fallen Swiss Guards (see page 84).

Riding the wave of the French Revolution, Napoleon Bonaparte occupied Switzerland (1798) and tried (unsuccessfully) to establish a strong central government. With Napoleon's defeat (and the 1815 Congress of Vienna), the European powers restored Switzerland's freedom. They also set it on its future political course—neutrality in all conflicts.

In 1848, amid a Europe-wide wave of liberal reforms, Switzerland's tradition of democracy was finally set down in a constitution. The new Confederation was modeled after America's form of government, but with an even stronger "federalist" (i.e., decentralized) emphasis. The country's national capital was established in the low-key town of Bern.

As a neutral country, Switzerland built a reputation as a leader in international relations. The world's diplomats descended on Geneva (1863-1864), producing two landmark institutions: the International Red Cross (still run from Geneva) and the Geneva Conventions of conduct during war (which were updated significantly in 1949). When the modern Olympic Games were founded in 1894, Lausanne became the movement's world headquarters.

It was also around this time that the country began to welcome hordes of tourists, beginning with French, English, and German aristocrats on the "Grand Tour," who passed through Switzerland on their way to Italy. Next came the British mountaineers, whose

reverence for the Alps was part of the Romanticist outlook on nature—for the first time, Europeans looked at mountains as objects of beauty and inspiration, rather than as frustrating obstacles. Visitors marveled at the mountain scenery and the "sublime" rush it gave them. In this heyday of European travel, Switzerland virtually invented mass tourism as we know it—pioneering ways of marking its mountains, offering the first organized vacations, investing in a well-oiled infrastructure, and establishing a reputation for efficiency, cleanliness, quality, and ease (even inventing English-language names for places whose local names were considered too intimidating for foreign visitors). Switzerland's system of high-altitude trains, funiculars, and mountain lifts was built to carry 19th-century tourists to previously unheard-of heights. Today's visitors stay in the same resort towns (Interlaken, Zermatt, Luzern, St. Moritz), ride the same kind of lifts, and see echoes of themselves in the stylized travel advertisements from that Romantic age.

20th Century: World Wars

Switzerland entered the 20th century on the cutting edge of progress. Its trains and communications systems were top-notch. The artist Paul Klee (1879-1940), with his playful, eccentric style, would contribute to the Modernist movement (see his works at the Rosengart Collection in Luzern and at the Paul Klee Center in Bern). Carl Jung (1875-1961) pioneered the blossoming field of psychoanalysis. And in the quiet city of Bern, an anonymous patent clerk named Albert Einstein

(1879-1955) was rewriting humankind's understanding of how the universe worked (see page 116).

In World War I (1914-1918), Switzerland declared itself neutral and escaped the devastation that hit the rest of Europe. After the war, Geneva served as the seat of the League of Nations, a short-lived forerunner to the United Nations.

When World War II broke out (1939-1945), Swiss neutrality was not taken for granted. As Nazi Germany and fascist Italy flanked the country, 850,000 Swiss men grabbed their rifles and mobilized to protect the borders. Switzerland avoided invasion by military readiness and by trading with the Nazis—some would say "appeasing" the Nazis. Switzerland sheltered refugees and acted as a mediator between the Allies and the Axis.

Today, critics charge that, though neutral in the war, Switzerland actually helped the Nazi effort by continuing to do business with them. (It's no secret that a significant number of German-speaking Swiss weren't all that opposed to the Nazi regime.) They exchanged Swiss francs (the only currency accepted throughout Europe) for Nazi gold—knowing full well that the gold had been stolen from other nations and Holocaust victims. In the 1990s, Swiss banks were sued to account for the ill-gotten bullion in their vaults. A 2002 commission formed by the Swiss government agreed that Switzerland could have done more to resist the Nazis and to help Jewish refugees...but restitution has been slow in coming.

After the war, Switzerland's policy of neutrality led the country to refuse membership in various international alliances and organizations, including the United Nations, NATO, and the European Union.

Switzerland Today

Switzerland maintains a delicate balance between its traditional, neutral past and the high-tech, global future.

As it has been for 700 years, the government is a federalist democracy that gives maximum autonomy to each canton. On the national level, the bicameral parliament is strong, the executive branch is handled by committee, and the president is a figurehead. The federal government handles foreign affairs, national defense, currency, and the federal courts—and leaves most everything else to the 26 cantons. The man-on-the-street can always make his voice heard thanks to frequent referenda, wherein citizens gather enough signatures to require a public vote on an issue. This form of government is often called "direct democracy" because of the power it invests in the individual. Unlike in most modern democracies, Swiss citizens have a direct say in many political matters and leave fewer decisions to elected representatives.

Four political parties (Liberal, Conservative, Social Democrat, People's Party) rule in an ever-changing array of coalitions, as they have since World War II. No single point of view dominates, and collaboration is essential. There's also a universal understanding that, whatever your politics, the good of Switzerland comes first.

The Swiss economy has been sluggish since 2008. Still, Zürich remains a global center of banking and finance. Stability is enhanced by strong social security and a collaborative approach to settling labor disputes between unions and employers.

In foreign affairs, Switzerland remains neutral...but ever-vigilant. Every able-bodied man serves in the army and stays in the reserves. Each house has a gun and a fully stocked bomb shelter. (Swiss vacuum-packed emergency army bread, which lasts two years, is also said to function as a weapon.) Switzerland bristles with 600,000 rifles in homes and 12,000 heavy guns in place. Airstrips are hidden inside mountains, accessed by camouflaged  doors. With the push of a button, all road, rail, and bridge entries to Swiss territory can be destroyed, sealing off the country from the outside world. Sentiments are changing, though, and Switzerland has come close to voting away its entire military. Today, you can visit once-hidden military installations, now open to the public as museums (for example, Fortress Fürigen—see page 101).

Swiss neutrality is not so simple in our increasingly interconnected global economy. For example, Switzerland is home to the European community's high-tech particle accelerator laboratory, called CERN (also the place where the World Wide Web was created). Of the country's hot-button topics, the question of whether to join the European Union has been at the forefront, dominating political discussion for the last decade. In 2002, the Swiss made a big step away from total neutrality when voters approved a referendum to join the United Nations. In 2008, Switzerland joined the Schengen Agreement, opening its borders to its neighboring countries and most of the EU. Is EU membership next? Referendum after referendum shows the Swiss still evenly divided on the issue, as they weigh the huge potential gains with significant potential costs.

While it's nice to think of Swiss neutrality as born of pacifism, many realists argue that it's more about money: Switzerland's neutrality policy is key to one of its main sources of income. Many Swiss banks allow foreigners to deposit money there with few questions asked. Critics charge that these secret bank accounts harbor the dirty money of mobsters, terrorists, dictators, guidebook authors, tax evaders, and sleazy businessmen. In 2009, Switzerland's biggest bank (UBS) responded to pressure from the US, agreeing to release names of formerly secret US clients accused of tax evasion. Switzerland also has a reputation as a safe haven from prosecution, harboring a long list of foreigners (from alleged Communist Charlie Chaplin to Ugandan dictator Idi Amin).

Another big issue in Switzerland is how to deal with the rising tide of immigrants. The country's high standard of living makes it an appealing place to live, and Switzerland has more foreign-born citizens than most countries (about 23 percent, compared with 13 percent in the US). But many of those immigrants are wealthy Europeans enjoying the country's easy tax laws. It's the less-desirable immigrants who have drawn fire—those who arrive with little wealth and then feed off the generous social services.

Opinions on this and many other issues are generally divided along geographic/linguistic lines. City dwellers, along with French and Italian speakers, tend to favor immigrants' rights, EU membership, and other progressive issues; rural German speakers are more likely to be conservative. In 2009, when Switzerland voted to ban the construction of new minarets—sparking controversy across Europe—only four cantons opposed the initiative, all of them in French-speaking areas.

With 2,500 years of history, Switzerland has seen many shifts—from Celts to Romans to Habsburgs, from wars to neutrality to technological progress. But what's striking is how little Switzerland has changed. The Alps are still there, and they're still big and rugged. The government, after 700 years in existence,

remains a model of democracy and international cooperation. Switzerland is fully modern, but you'll also encounter quaint pockets of the past. Take time to see Swiss history alive today—from the cow parades of Appenzell to the Roman ruins in Avenches, and from the turrets of Château de Chillon to the farmers of Gimmelwald, who still make hay while the sun shines.

Notable Swiss People

William Tell (c. 1280-1354): On November 18, 1307, William (Wilhelm) Tell, a Swiss peasant, refused a bailiff's order to bow to a symbol of the Habsburg emperor. As punishment, Tell was forced to aim his crossbow at an apple resting on his son's head. He shot cleanly through the apple without injuring his son, and later ambushed and killed the bailiff—launching a revolt for Swiss independence. Though historians say the famous hero is fictional (a similar Danish legend predates the Swiss one), don't "tell" the Swiss—up to 60 percent still believe there was a real William Tell.

PAST AND PRESENT

Huldrych Zwingli (1484-1531): The son of a farmer, Huldrych Zwingli started out as a Catholic true believer, but under the influence of Renaissance humanists, turned into a religious revolutionary. Known as the "third man of the Protestant Reformation" (the other two were Martin Luther and John Calvin), he used his position as the top pastor in Zürich to challenge Rome, insisting that Christians study the Bible to guide their beliefs. Many Protestant faiths, including the United Church of Christ and the Presbyterian Church, trace their theology back to Zwingli.

Jean-Jacques Rousseau (1712-1778): One of the most influential writers of the 18th century, Jean-Jacques Rousseau ran away from his humble Geneva home for France when he was 16, but he always considered himself Swiss, not French. His writings celebrated nature and human passion (over cold reason), unleashing forces that would result in the French Revolution, Romantic literature, and even a return to breastfeeding. Publishers couldn't print his books fast enough, so they rented them out by the day. Rousseau's descriptions of the Swiss countryside helped start the 19th-century craze for visiting the Alps.

Madame Tussaud (1761-1850): An entertainment empire began when Swiss-born Anna Maria Grosholtz moved to Paris and learned how to sculpt wax. It was an auspicious time and place—she was able to create figures of Voltaire, Jean-Jacques Rousseau, and Benjamin Franklin. Later, during the French Revolution, she made death masks from decapitated heads. After marrying François Tussaud (becoming "Madame Tussaud"), she moved to London and eventually opened a museum of wax figures, which still shows some of her original work.

Henri Dunant (1828-1910): In 1859, Geneva businessman Henri Dunant witnessed one of the bloodiest battles of the 19th century—the Battle of Solferino in northern Italy, where about 40,000 soldiers were killed or wounded. He wrote a book that not only described the carnage, but also proposed a neutral organization that would care for those wounded in wartime. His leadership led to the founding of the International Red Cross and the Geneva Conventions, which put humanitarian limits on the waging of war. He won the first Nobel Peace Prize in 1901.

Carl Jung (1875-1961): After Freud, Carl Jung had the greatest impact on modern psychology; there probably wouldn't be a New Age movement or the Myers-Briggs personality test without him. The Zürich psychologist popularized such terms as "introvert/

extrovert," "personality complex," and "collective unconscious." He once said that the Swiss are a "primitive" people (their love of cows reminded him of African animalism), and that under their legendary efficiency is a deeply buried "earth mysticism."

Hermann Hesse (1877-1962): German-born Hesse, who became a Swiss citizen in 1923, was into psychoanalysis, India, and Buddhism before they were cool. His writing was banned by the Nazis and later beloved by 1960s hippies for its themes of self-discovery and enlightenment. His best-known works—among them *Steppenwolf, Siddhartha,* and *Narcissus and Goldmund*—are still widely read today. He was particularly publicity-shy—upon winning the Nobel Prize for Literature in 1946, he wrote to a friend, "To hell with this damn business."

Paul Klee (1879-1940): Paul Klee's mastery of color and tone created highly individual art that critics have described as "musical" and "childlike." Born and raised in Bern, Klee became a teacher at the famous Bauhaus school in Weimar, Germany, but when Hitler came to power in 1933, he was fired. He returned to Switzerland as the Nazis stripped his paintings from museums and classified them as "degenerate." You can see his work at museums in Bern and Luzern—then decide for yourself.

Le Corbusier (1887-1965): "The house is a machine for living in." With this and other edicts, architect Charles-Edouard Jeanneret-Gris, better known as Le Corbusier, changed the shape of 20th-century cities. His plan for Paris' Marais district was emblematic—rows of identical towers set between freeways, replacing public squares and winding streets. The Parisians turned him down, but many office and housing projects in Europe and America followed his precepts. Le Corbusier was one of the most influential architects of his time, though today many regard his International Style as sterile and socially destructive.

Jean Piaget (1896-1980): According to *Time* magazine, Geneva psychologist Jean Piaget was "the first to take children's thinking seriously." Before the publication of his groundbreaking work, parents and teachers regarded children as empty vessels into which they poured knowledge. By studying his own three kids, Piaget deduced that children are constantly testing their own theories of how the world works, asserting that "children have real understanding only of that which they invent themselves."

Elisabeth Kübler-Ross (1926-2004): She grew up in a strict, Protestant family, but Elisabeth Kübler-Ross defied tradition and got her M.D. in 1957. A year later, she left Zürich for the US, where she was appalled by the way doctors and hospitals treated the dying. The five stages of grief she first explained in *On Death and Dying*—denial, anger, bargaining, depression, and acceptance—have become a modern touchstone, now commonly applied to any catastrophic personal loss.

Ursula Andress (born 1936): When the bikini-clad Andress walked out of the ocean in the first James Bond movie, *Dr. No*, the indelible image of the "Bond heroine" was born. Tough, smart, and outrageously beautiful, Andress was a great match for Sean Connery's 007, even though the producers dubbed her voice to mask her Swiss-German accent. Though many of her subsequent films were subpar, the list of her leading men is not: Laurence Olivier, Frank Sinatra, Marcello Mastroianni, Peter Sellers, and even Elvis Presley.

Roger Federer (born 1981): This Swiss ace was born and raised near Basel. By the age of 29, Federer had won a record 16 Grand Slam tennis titles, including all four majors. From 2003-2007, he reeled off five straight Wimbledon wins, then captured a sixth title two years later. He also pulled off a five-peat at the US Open (2004-2008), making it clear why many regard him as one of the greatest tennis players of all time.

APPENDIX

Contents

Tourist Information

Tourist Offices

The Swiss national tourist office in the US is a wealth of information. Before your trip, download or request printed brochures (including regional and city maps, festival schedules, and hiking information). Call 877-794-8037 or visit www.myswitzerland.com (info.usa@myswitzerland.com).

In Switzerland, your best first stop in every town is generally the tourist information office—abbreviated **TI** in this book. Throughout Switzerland, you'll find TIs are usually well-organized and always have an English-speaking staff. Most TIs are run by the government, which means their information isn't colored by a drive for profit.

A TI is a great place to get a city map and information on public transit (including bus and train schedules), walking tours, special events, and nightlife. Many TIs have information on the entire country or at least the region, so try to pick up maps for destinations you'll be visiting later in your trip. If you're arriving in town after the TI closes, call ahead or pick up a map in a neighboring town.

Although TIs offer room-finding services, they're a good deal only if you're in search of summer and weekend deals on business hotels. The TIs can help you with small pensions and private homes, but you'll save both yourself and your host money by going direct with the listings in this book.

Communicating

Hurdling the Language Barrier

Switzerland has four official languages: German, French, Italian, and Romansh (an obscure Romantic tongue). Most of the destinations in this book are in the German-speaking territory. No matter where you are, most young or well-educated people—especially those in larger towns and the tourist trade—speak at least some English. Still, you'll get more smiles by using the local pleasantries. See the German, French, and Italian survival phrases at the end of the appendix.

In German-speaking Switzerland, locals speak singsongy *Schwyzertütsch* (Swiss German) around the house, but in schools and at work, they speak and write in the same standard German used in Germany and Austria (called "High" German, *Hochdeutsch*—though many Swiss prefer to call it *Schriftdeutsch*, "Written German"). The standard greeting is a hearty *Grüezi* (GRIT-see). "Thank you" is derived from French, but pronounced a little differently: *Merci* (MUHR-see). They also sometimes use the more German-like *Dankche* (DAHN-kheh with a very guttural "kh"). The exact pronunciation (and even spelling) of Swiss German words varies substantially by region.

English—like Dutch, Danish, Swedish, and Norwegian—is a Germanic language, making German easier on most American ears than Romance languages (such as Italian and French). German is a phonetic language—its pronunciation rules are set in stone, and there are no silent letters.

These tips will help you pronounce German words: The letter *w* is always pronounced as "v" (e.g., the word for "wonderful" is *wunderbar*, pronounced VOON-dehr-bar). The vowel combinations *ie* and *ei* are pronounced like the name of the second letter—so *ie* sounds like the letter *e* (as in *hier* and *Bier*, the German words for "here" and "beer"), while *ei* sounds like the letter *i* (as in *nein* and *Stein*, the German words for "no" and "stone"). The vowel combination *au* is pronounced "ow" (as in *Frau*). The vowel combinations *eu* and *äu* are pronounced "oy" (as in *neu, Deutsch,* and *Bräu,* the words for "new," "German," and "brew"). To pronounce *ö* and *ü,* purse your lips when you say the vowel; the other vowel with an umlaut, *ä,* is pronounced the same as *e* in "men." (In written German, these can be depicted without an umlaut as the vowel followed by an *e: oe, ue,* and *ae,* respectively.) Written German always capitalizes all nouns.

Give it your best shot. The locals will appreciate your efforts.

Telephones

Smart travelers use the telephone to reserve or reconfirm rooms, get tourist information, reserve restaurants, confirm tour times, or phone home. Generally the easiest, cheapest way to call home is to use an international phone card purchased in Switzerland. This section covers dialing instructions, phone cards, and types of phones (for more in-depth information, see www.ricksteves.com /phoning).

How to Dial

Calling from the US to Switzerland, or vice versa, is simple—once you break the code. The European calling chart later in this chapter will walk you through it.

Dialing Domestically Within Switzerland

Switzerland has a direct-dial phone system (no area codes). To call anywhere within Switzerland, just dial the number. For example, the number of one of my recommended Gimmelwald hotels is 033-855-1658. To call it from Zürich's train station, just dial 033-855-1658. If you call it from Gimmelwald's cable-car station, it's the same: 033-855-1658. All Swiss phone numbers are 10 digits, including the initial zero.

Dialing Internationally to or from Switzerland

If you want to make an international call, follow these three steps:

• Dial the international access code (00 if you're calling from Europe, 011 from the US or Canada).

• Dial the country code of the country you're calling (41 for Switzerland, or 1 for the US or Canada).

• Dial the local number, keeping in mind that calling many countries requires dropping the initial zero of the area code or local number (the European calling chart lists specifics per country).

Calling from the US to Switzerland: To call a recommended Gimmelwald hotel from the US, dial 011 (the US international access code), 41 (Switzerland's country code), then 33-855-1658 (the hotel's number without its initial 0).

Calling from any European country to the US: To call my

European Calling Chart

Just smile and dial, using this key:
AC = Area Code, LN = Local Number.

European Country	Calling long distance within ...	Calling from the US or Canada to ...	Calling from a European country to ...
Austria	AC + LN	011 + 43 + AC (without the initial zero) + LN	00 + 43 + AC (without the initial zero) + LN
Belgium	LN	011 + 32 + LN (without initial zero)	00 + 32 + LN (without initial zero)
Bosnia-Herzegovina	AC + LN	011 + 387 + AC (without initial zero) + LN	00 + 387 + AC (without initial zero) + LN
Britain	AC + LN	011 + 44 + AC (without initial zero) + LN	00 + 44 + AC (without initial zero) + LN
Croatia	AC + LN	011 + 385 + AC (without initial zero) + LN	00 + 385 + AC (without initial zero) + LN
Czech Republic	LN	011 + 420 + LN	00 + 420 + LN
Denmark	LN	011 + 45 + LN	00 + 45 + LN
Estonia	LN	011 + 372 + LN	00 + 372 + LN
Finland	AC + LN	011 + 358 + AC (without initial zero) + LN	999 (or other 900 number) + 358 + AC (without initial zero) + LN
France	LN	011 + 33 + LN (without initial zero)	00 + 33 + LN (without initial zero)
Germany	AC + LN	011 + 49 + AC (without initial zero) + LN	00 + 49 + AC (without initial zero) + LN
Gibraltar	LN	011 + 350 + LN	00 + 350 + LN
Greece	LN	011 + 30 + LN	00 + 30 + LN
Hungary	06 + AC + LN	011 + 36 + AC + LN	00 + 36 + AC + LN
Ireland	AC + LN	011 + 353 + AC (without initial zero) + LN	00 + 353 + AC (without initial zero) + LN

European Country	Calling long distance within ...	Calling from the US or Canada to ...	Calling from a European country to ...
Italy	LN	011 + 39 + LN	00 + 39 + LN
Montenegro	AC + LN	011 + 382 + AC (without initial zero) + LN	00 + 382 + AC (without initial zero) + LN
Morocco	LN	011 + 212 + LN (without initial zero)	00 + 212 + LN (without initial zero)
Netherlands	AC + LN	011 + 31 + AC (without initial zero) + LN	00 + 31 + AC (without initial zero) + LN
Norway	LN	011 + 47 + LN	00 + 47 + LN
Poland	LN	011 + 48 + LN	00 + 48 + LN
Portugal	LN	011 + 351 + LN	00 + 351 + LN
Slovakia	AC + LN	011 + 421 + AC (without initial zero) + LN	00 + 421 + AC (without initial zero) + LN
Slovenia	AC + LN	011 + 386 + AC (without initial zero) + LN	00 + 386 + AC (without initial zero) + LN
Spain	LN	011 + 34 + LN	00 + 34 + LN
Sweden	AC + LN	011 + 46 + AC (without initial zero) + LN	00 + 46 + AC (without initial zero) + LN
Switzerland	LN	011 + 41 + LN (without initial zero)	00 + 41 + LN (without initial zero)
Turkey	AC (if there's no initial zero, add one) + LN	011 + 90 + AC (without initial zero) + LN	00 + 90 + AC (without initial zero) + LN

- The instructions above apply whether you're calling a land line or mobile phone.

- The international access code (the first numbers you dial when making an international call) is 011 if you're calling from the US or Canada. It's 00 if you're calling from virtually anywhere in Europe (except Finland, where it's 999 or another 900 number, depending on the phone service you're using).

- To call the US or Canada from Europe, dial 00, then 1 (the country code for the US and Canada), then the area code and number. In short, 00 + 1 + AC + LN = Hi, Mom!

office in Edmonds, Washington, from anywhere in Europe, I dial 00 (Europe's international access code), 1 (the US country code), 425 (Edmonds' area code), and 771-8303.

Note: You might see a + in front of a European number. When dialing the number, replace the + with the international access code of the country you're calling from (00 from Europe, 011 from the US or Canada).

Prepaid Phone Cards

To make calls from public phones, you'll need a prepaid phone card. There are two different kinds of phone cards: insertable (best for local calls, but work only in public pay phones) and international (best for calling home). If you have a live card at the end of your trip, give it to another traveler to use up.

Insertable Phone Cards: An insertable, prepaid Taxcard allows you to dial from any public pay phone, as some Swiss phone booths no longer accept coins. Simply take the phone off the hook, insert the card, wait for a dial tone, and dial away. The price of the call is automatically deducted while you talk, and at the end of the call, the phone will helpfully beep to remind you to remove your card and will show the card balance.

These cards are sold at post offices and many newsstand kiosks and gas stations in 5-SF, 10-SF, and 20-SF denominations (because cards work only in Switzerland—and are occasionally duds—avoid the pricier ones).

International Phone Cards: These are the cheapest way to make international calls from Europe—with the best cards, it costs literally pennies a minute. They can be used from any type of phone (but if calling from a hotel, make sure you won't be charged for a toll-free call). These cards also work for local calls, but aren't likely to beat the local rates you'll get at a pay phone.

The cards are sold all over; look for them at many post offices, newsstands, mini-marts, and exchange bureaus. Ask the clerk which of the various brands has the best rates for calls to America. Some cards are rechargeable (you can call up the number on the card, give your credit-card number, and buy more time). Some shops also sell cardless codes, printed right on the receipt. Since you don't need the actual card or receipt to use the account, you can write down the access number and code and share it with friends.

To use the card, scratch to reveal your code (or locate the code on your receipt), then dial the toll-free access number. Following the recorded instructions, enter your code, then dial the number you're calling. Usually the prompts are in fairly concise English, but if not, experiment: Dial your code, followed by the pound sign (#), then the number, then pound again, and so on, until it works. Sometimes the star (*) key is used instead of the pound sign.

US Calling Cards: These cards, such as the ones offered by AT&T, Verizon, or Sprint, are the worst option. You'll save a lot of money by using an international phone card you've purchased in Switzerland.

Types of Phones
Public Pay Phones

Swisscom public pay phones are easy to find, especially at train stations and post offices. Most take only insertable phone cards, though some take coins as well. Local calls cost 0.50 SF for the first minute, then 0.04-0.08 SF/minute after (calls are cheapest outside business hours; calling mobile phones is pricier). International calls aren't much more expensive (about 0.11 SF/minute), so if you don't mind making your calls to home from a phone booth, an insertable Taxcard may be all you need.

Hotel-Room Phones

Calling from your hotel-room phone can be cheap for local calls (ask for the rates at the front desk first), but is often a rip-off for long-distance calls, unless you use an international phone card (explained earlier). Some hotels charge a fee for dialing supposedly "toll-free" numbers, such as the one for your international phone card—ask before you dial. A few hotels have cheap direct-dial rates for North America; but again, always check rates at the front desk before calling. Incoming calls are free, making this a cheap way for friends and family to stay in touch (provided they have a good long-distance plan for calls to Europe—and a list of your hotels' phone numbers). In-room phones are rare in guest houses and private homes.

Mobile Phones

Many travelers enjoy the convenience of traveling with a mobile phone.

Using Your Mobile Phone: Your US mobile phone works in Europe if it's GSM-enabled, tri-band or quad-band, and on a calling plan that includes international calls. Phones from AT&T and T-Mobile, which use the same GSM technology that Europe does, are more likely to work overseas than Verizon or Sprint phones (if you're not sure, ask your service provider). Most US providers charge $1.29-1.99 per minute while roaming internationally to make or receive calls, and 20-50 cents to send or receive text messages.

You'll pay cheaper rates if your phone is electronically "unlocked" (ask your provider about this); then in Europe, you can simply buy a tiny **SIM card,** which gives you a European phone number. SIM cards are sold at mobile-phone stores (Swisscom and

Orange are the dominant Swiss providers) for about $5-15; this generally includes some prepaid domestic calling time, and you can buy more if you need it (25 SF gives you about 75 minutes). Some newsstand kiosks sell SIM cards by Lebara (likely cheaper rates than Swisscom and Orange, especially for international calls). When you buy a SIM card, you may need to show ID, such as your passport. Insert the SIM card in your phone (usually in a slot on the side or behind the battery), and it'll work like a European mobile phone. When buying a SIM card, always ask about fees for domestic and international calls, roaming charges, and how to check your credit balance and buy more time. When you're in the SIM card's home country, domestic calls are reasonable, and incoming calls are free. You'll pay more if you're roaming in another country.

Buying a European Mobile Phone: Mobile-phone shops all over Europe sell basic phones. The mobile-phone desk in a big department store is another good place to check. Phones that are "locked" to work with a single provider start around $40; "unlocked" phones (which allow you to switch out SIM cards to use your choice of provider) start around $60. You'll also need to buy a SIM card and prepaid credit for making calls (explained above). If your phone is "unlocked," you can swap out its SIM card for a new one when you travel to other countries.

Renting a European Mobile Phone: Car-rental companies and mobile-phone companies offer the option to rent a mobile phone with a European number. While this seems convenient, hidden fees (such as high per-minute charges or expensive shipping costs) can really add up—which usually makes it a bad value. One exception is Verizon's Global Travel Program, available only to Verizon customers.

Data Downloading on a Smartphone: Many smartphones, such as the iPhone, Android, and BlackBerry, work in Europe (note that some older Verizon iPhones don't work abroad). For voice calls and text messaging, smartphones work the same as other US mobile phones (explained earlier). But beware of sky-high fees for data downloading (checking email, browsing the Internet, streaming videos, and so on).

The best solution: Disable data roaming entirely, and only use your device when you find free Wi-Fi. You can ask your mobile-phone service provider to cut off your account's data-roaming capability, or you can manually turn it off on your phone (look under the "Network" menu).

If you want Internet access without being limited to Wi-Fi, you'll need to keep data roaming on, but you can take steps to reduce your charges. Consider paying extra for a limited international data-roaming plan through your carrier, then use data roaming selectively (if a particular task gobbles bandwidth, wait until you're on Wi-Fi). In general, ask your provider in advance how to avoid unwittingly roaming your way to a huge bill. If your smartphone is on Wi-Fi, you can use certain apps to make cheap or free voice calls (see "Calling over the Internet," next).

Calling over the Internet

Some things that seem too good to be true...actually are true. If you're traveling with a wireless device (such as a laptop or smart-phone), you can use VoIP (Voice over Internet Protocol) to make free calls over the Internet to another wireless device (or you can pay a few cents to call from your computer to a telephone). If both devices have cameras, you can even see each other while you chat. The major providers are Skype (www.skype.com, also available as a smartphone app) Google Talk (www.google.com/talk), and FaceTime (this app comes standard on newer Apple devices). If you have a smartphone, you can get online at a hotspot and use these apps to make calls without ringing up expensive roaming charges (though call quality can be spotty on slow connections).

Useful Phone Numbers

Emergencies
Dial 112 (medical or other emergencies) or 117 (police).

Embassies in Bern
United States: Jubilaeumsstrasse 93, Mon-Fri 9:00-11:30, closed Sat-Sun, tel. 031-357-7011 or 031-357-7777, http://bern.usembassy.gov

Canada: Kirchenfeldstrasse 88, Mon-Thu 13:00-17:00, Fri 8:00-12:00, closed Sat-Sun, tel. 031-357-3200, http://switzerland.gc.ca

Travel Advisories
US Department of State: tel. 202/647-5225, www.travel.state.gov
Canadian Department of Foreign Affairs: Canadian tel. 800-267-6788, www.dfait-maeci.gc.ca
US Centers for Disease Control and Prevention: tel. 800-CDC-INFO (800-232-4636), www.cdc.gov/travel

Directory Assistance
Dial 111 for domestic numbers, or dial 191 for international numbers.

Train Information
Dial 0900-300-300 (1.19 SF/minute).

Internet Access

It's useful to get online periodically as you travel—to confirm trip plans, check train or bus schedules, get weather forecasts, catch up on email, blog or post photos from your trip, or call folks back home (explained earlier, under "Calling over the Internet").

Some hotels offer a computer in the lobby with Internet access for guests. If you ask politely, smaller places may sometimes let you sit at their desk for a few minutes just to check your email. If your hotel doesn't have access, ask your hotelier to direct you to the nearest place to get online. Most of the towns where I've listed accommodations also have Internet cafés. Many libraries offer free access, but they also tend to have limited opening hours, restrict your online time, and may require reservations.

Traveling with a Laptop or Other Wireless Device: You can get online if your hotel has Wi-Fi or a port in your room for plugging in a cable. Some hotels offer Wi-Fi for free; others charge by the minute or hour. A cellular modem—which lets your laptop access the Internet over a mobile phone network—provides more extensive coverage, but is much more expensive than Wi-Fi.

Warning: Anytime you access the Internet—especially over a public connection (such as a Wi-Fi signal or at an Internet café)—you're running the risk that someone could be looking over your shoulder, literally or virtually. Be careful about storing personal information (such as passport and credit-card numbers) online. If you're not convinced it's secure, avoid accessing any sites (such as online banking) that could be sensitive to fraud.

Mail

Even when post offices are closed, you're never too far from a yellow mailbox with an automated stamp dispenser (most train stations have one). Type in the value of stamp you want (postcard or letter to the US: 1.60 SF economy, 1.90 SF priority), insert coins, and press the pound key. These machines don't give change, so if you have any amount left in the machine, print out a stamp for that amount and use it toward your next postcard.

While you can arrange for mail delivery to your hotel (allow 10 days for a letter to arrive), phoning and emailing are so easy that I've dispensed with mail stops altogether.

You can mail one package per day to yourself worth up to $200 duty-free from Europe to the US (mark it "personal purchases"). If you're sending a gift to someone, mark it "unsolicited gift." For details, visit www.cbp.gov and search for "Know Before You Go."

Transportation

By Car or Public Transportation?

Because Switzerland's train network is excellent, I recommend using public transportation here. Only a few areas—like the Appenzell region and the French Swiss countryside—are better by car. Cars are an expensive headache in the bigger cities.

Trains

Trains are generally slick, speedy, and punctual, with synchronized connections. They're also clean, roomy, and, in Switzerland, entirely  non-smoking. Virtually all Swiss stations have luggage lockers. Few places in Switzerland are out of reach of the train system, though some frustrating schedules make the more out-of-the-way recommendations (such as Taveyanne in the French Swiss countryside) not worth the time and trouble for the less determined.

Swiss trains and stations are marked "SBB CFF FFS." All those letters mean the same thing ("Swiss Federal Railways"), in three different languages: German, French, and Italian.

Schedules

Switzerland has a 24-hour train-info number you can dial from anywhere in the country: toll tel. 0900-300-300 (1.19 SF/minute). For Swiss timetables, visit the Swiss site, www.rail.ch, or Germany's excellent all-Europe timetable, www.bahn.com (use http://bahn .hafas.de/bin/query.exe/en to go directly to an English-language search page). At most train stations, attendants and/or machines will print out a step-by-step itinerary for you, free of charge. Major stations also have handy travel offices offering general help.

Tickets

If you're traveling without a railpass, get train tickets at the station—either at the ticket windows, or at the easy-to-use machines. You need to get a ticket before boarding or risk being fined 90 SF (though under special circumstances, a ticket inspector can waive this fine and sell you a ticket on board with a 10-SF service charge).

Swiss Railpasses

Because of high ticket prices, railpasses are a good deal in Switzerland, even for just a three-day trip. But for such a little

Public Transportation

Note: Not all transportation routes shown.

50 Kilometers
50 Miles

Legend:
— Rail
††††† Mountain Rail
····· Boat
- - - Bus

Comparing Swiss Pass Coverage

All passes that include Switzerland cover national network trains, boat trips on Swiss lakes, and many sightseeing and private rail discounts.

Here are the key routes where coverage varies:

Route or Bonus	Eurail/ Select or Two-Country Passes	Swiss Card or Transfer Ticket	Swiss Pass or Flexipass
Swiss Family Card (kids travel free)	No	Applies	Applies
Postal buses	No	Covered	Covered
Urban transport in 40 cities ($2/trip)	No	No	Covered
Swiss museum admissions	No	No	Covered
Brig-Disentis section of the Glacier Express scenic route ($45 2nd class, reservation extra)	25% discount	Only if it's fastest, most direct route (from south border to south destination)	Covered
Brig-Zermatt private train to see the Matterhorn ($35 2nd class)	25% discount	Only if Zermatt is final destination	Covered
Jungfrau Region Railways (e.g., from Interlaken: $7 to Lauterbrunnen, $10 to Grindelwald, $13 to Wengen; $180 round-trip to Jungfraujoch)	25% discount above Interlaken	50% discount with Swiss Card; Jungfraujoch not covered on in- and outbound round-trip	50% discount above Mürren, 25% discount above Grindelwald or Wengen
Many high mountain lifts (e.g., Stechelberg-Schilthorn $90 round-trip/$70 off-peak)	No	50% discount with Card, not with Transfer Ticket	50% discount
50% transport discount between fully covered flexi travel days	No	50% discount with Swiss Card	50% discount with Flexipass
Le Châtelard, Switzerland to Chamonix, France ($14)	Need France on pass	Covered (e.g., entering our exiting country via Chamonix)	Covered (no 50% discount option)
Passholder rate on international night trains	Applies	No	Applies
7 p.m. rule for night trains	Applies	No	No
All "covered" services start use of a travel day on a flexipass, but discounts do not.			

country, Switzerland has a dizzying array of train passes and deals. I've listed the most popular ones here. For the latest prices, see www.ricksteves.com/rail.

The **Swiss Pass** is the basic version, covering all trains, boats, and buses, plus admission to most Swiss museums (see above), and offering a half-price discount on most high-mountain trains and lifts. It comes in both consecutive-day and flexipass versions. Both versions completely cover the cost of any transportation for a specified number of days (but do not cover seat or overnight-train reservations).

If you're traveling with at least one other person, get the "Saver" version of the pass, which is 15 percent cheaper than individual passes. Second class (available to any age) is 33 percent cheaper than first class.

The **Half-Fare Travel Card** gives you a 50 percent discount on all national and private trains, postal buses, lifts, and steamers (110 SF for one month, sold only in Switzerland). This can save you money if your Swiss travel adds up to more than $220 in point-to-point tickets. The **Swiss Card** is a variation on this, sold only in the US and at a few border stations. It includes the same 50 percent discount and adds two train rides: one ride from any point of entry (such as the German border or Zürich's airport) to any other point in Switzerland, and one back from that point to any border ($266 first class, $190 second class).

Regional passes cover all trains, buses, and boats in a particular area, such as the Berner Oberland (Berner Oberland Regional Pass, see page 143), Zermatt area (see page 211), or Central Switzerland, around Luzern (Tell-Pass, see page 93). Buy these (in Switzerland, not the US) only if you're very focused on a single region, but note that there's usually no need to have both a regional pass and an all-Switzerland pass (or Eurailpass).

Other deals include the **Swiss Family Card,** allowing children under 16 to travel free with their parents (30 SF per child at Swiss stations, or free with Swiss train passes when requested with purchase in the US).

Eurailpasses

If you're also traveling to other countries, consider a Eurail Selectpass, which gives you up to 15 travel days (within a 2-month period) in three, four, or five adjacent countries: Choose among Switzerland, Germany, Austria, France, Italy, and most other European countries (allow about $400 for 5 days in 3 countries, and up to about $900 for 15 days in 5 countries). A 23-country Eurail Global pass is cost-effective only if you're doing a whirlwind trip of Europe (allow roughly $850 for 3 weeks). These rates are per person for two or more adults traveling together; solo travelers age 26 or older will pay about 15 percent more (unlike with the Swiss Pass, if you're over 26, you have to buy a first-class pass).

If you're combining your trip to Switzerland with travel in France, Germany, or Austria, you may want to consider a **two-country pass.**

Railpass Bonuses and Discounts

If you buy a railpass, know what extras are included—for example, boat cruises on the big Swiss lakes are covered by most railpasses.

Lift Lingo

The Swiss have come up with a variety of ways to conquer peaks and reach the best viewpoints and trailheads with minimum sweat. Known generically as "lifts," each of these contraptions has its own name and definition. Use the right terms, and impress your new Swiss friends.

Cogwheel Train: A train that climbs a steep incline using a gear system, which engages "teeth" in the middle of the tracks to provide traction. Also known as "rack-and-pinion train" or "rack railway." In German, it's a *Zahnradbahn* (*train à cremaillère* in French and *ferrovia a cremagliera* in Italian).

Funicular: A car that is pulled by a cable along tracks up a particularly steep incline, often counterbalanced by a similar car going in the opposite direction (meaning you'll pass the other car exactly halfway through the ride). Funiculars, like cogwheel trains, are in contact with the ground at all times. In German, it's a *Standseilbahn* (*funiculaire* in French and *funicolare* in Italian).

Cable Car: A large passenger car, suspended in the air by a cable, which travels between stations without touching the ground. A cable car holds a large number of people (sometimes dozens at a time), who generally ride standing up. When a cable car reaches a station, it comes to a full stop to allow passengers to get on and off. In German, it's a *Seilbahn* (*téléphérique* in French and *funivia* in Italian).

Gondola: Also suspended in the air by a cable, but smaller than a cable car—generally holding fewer than 10 people, who are usually seated. Gondolas move continuously, meaning that passengers have to hop into and out of the moving cars at stations. Also, while cable-car lines usually have two big cars—one going in each direction—gondolas generally have many smaller cars strung along the same cable. In German, it's a *Gondel* (*télécabine* in French and *telecabine* in Italian).

Confusingly, the "car" compartment of a cable car is sometimes referred to as a "gondola."

In addition, Swiss railpasses can get you free entry to many museums and discounts on many mountain lifts. Always ask. Note that while Eurailpasses include some deals in Switzerland beyond simple trains (such as on some mountain lifts), the discounts and coverage of these passes generally aren't as extensive as the Switzerland-only passes (for example, lifts in Zermatt are discounted and postal buses nationwide are free with a Swiss Pass,

Railpasses

Prices listed are for 2011 and are subject to change. For the latest prices, details, and train schedules (and easy online ordering), see my comprehensive *Guide to Eurail Passes* at www.ricksteves.com/rail.

"Saver" prices are per person for two or more people traveling together. "Youth" means under age 26.

SWISS PASS AND SWISS FLEXIPASS

	Individual 1st Class	Individual 2nd Class	Saver 1st Class	Saver 2nd Class	Youth 1st Class	Youth 2nd Class
4 consecutive days	$406	$270	$345	$230	$305	$203
8 consecutive days	587	391	499	333	441	294
15 consecutive days	709	473	603	402	533	355
22 consecutive days	817	545	695	463	613	409
1 month	901	600	765	510	676	450
3 days in 1 month flexi	390	260	332	221	N/A	N/A
4 days in 1 month flexi	472	314	402	267	N/A	N/A
5 days in 1 month flexi	546	364	464	310	N/A	N/A
6 days in 1 month flexi	620	413	527	352	N/A	N/A

Covers all trains, boats, buses, and most museums plus 50 percent off high mountain rides, and—if you have a flexipass—50 percent off any ride taken between your counted "flexi" days. Kids under 16 free with parent, otherwise half of full fare.

SWITZERLAND–AUSTRIA PASS

	Individual 1st Class	Saver 1st Class	Youth 2nd Class
4 days in 2 months	$400	$341	$281
Extra rail days (max 6)	45	38	31

The fare for children 4–11 is half the adult individual fare or Saver fare. Kids under age 4 travel free.

GERMANY–SWITZERLAND PASS

	Individual 1st Class	Saver 1st Class	Youth 2nd Class
5 days in 2 months	$450	$384	$316
6 days in 2 months	496	422	349
8 days in 2 months	585	501	412
10 days in 2 months	677	578	476

The fare for children 4–11 is half the adult individual fare or Saver fare. Kids under age 4 travel free.

Map key:
Approximate point-to-point one-way second-class rail fares in US dollars. First class costs 50 percent more. Add up fares for your itinerary to see whether a railpass will save you money.

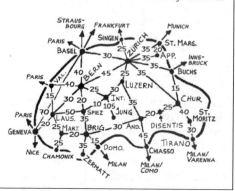

FRANCE–SWITZERLAND PASS

	Individual 1st Class	Saver 1st Class	Youth 2nd Class
4 days in 2 months	$422	$358	$297
Extra rail days (max 6)	46-50	38-44	29-34

Covers many Swiss boats as well as trains. The fare for children 4–11 is half the adult individual fare or Saver fare. Kids under age 4 travel free.

SWISS TRANSFER & SWISS CARD

The **Swiss Transfer Ticket** gives you one train ride in from any Swiss airport or border station to any point in Switzerland, then one trip out from that same point to any airport or border for $200 in first class or $133 in second class. Each direction must be completed in a day by the fastest, most direct route and both trips must occur within a month. Sold only outside Switzerland.

The **Swiss Card** includes one trip in and out within a month as above, plus 50% discounts between those two trips on all Swiss railways, lake steamers, postal buses, and high mountain lifts for $266 in first class or $190 in second class. Also sold at a few Swiss airports and border stations.

but both are full price with a Eurailpass).

If your railpass is a flexipass (it covers a certain number of days in a given span, rather than consecutive days), it's worth knowing when, and when not, to activate your flexi-days. Trips that are merely discounted, rather than free with the pass—most notably many mountain lifts—are valid even if you don't have a flexi-day activated. However, any time you use the pass for a fully covered ("free") trip, it starts the use of a flexi-day. This can be fine and cost-effective if you're already using the pass to cover other transportation that day. But if you've got no other use for your pass that day than your "free" trip (such as a short boat or train ride), it can make sense to pay out of pocket for it rather than use up a valuable day of your flexipass.

If you have a Swiss flexipass (rather than a Eurailpass), note that when you're *not* using a travel day, your pass gets you a 50 percent discount on all rides taken before the use of your last travel day. Unlike flexipasses for most other countries, a Swiss flexipass expires once you've used up all your travel days—even if that's well before the end of the one-month time frame noted on your pass. It can be smart to use your first travel day near the beginning of your trip, and your last travel day near (or at) the end of your trip; then you can use your flexipass throughout your entire trip for transportation discounts on the days you're not using travel days. It's confusing, but once you figure out the system, you can make it work to your advantage.

Train Notes

Scenic Rail Journeys: In addition to being convenient for transportation, many of Switzerland's trains are also breathtakingly scenic. Several trips are particularly beautiful and billed as special "theme" routes for tourists. For many visitors, these are a Swiss highlight, and I've devoted an entire chapter to them (see page 315).

Private Lines: Switzerland has some privately owned train lines. For instance, a large segment of the Glacier Express scenic journey is private. Most private lines are covered by Swiss rail-passes, but not covered by Eurailpasses (though Eurailpasses can get you discounts on certain trips). If your railpass doesn't cover an entire journey, pay for the "uncovered" portion at the station before you board the train.

Check Your Bags: If you're town- or mountain-hopping through Switzerland by train, a great way to lighten your load is by sending your baggage ahead (drop it off at the station, pay 10 SF with ticket or railpass, maximum 55 pounds). Your bag will show up at the designated station within 24 hours of your arrival (usually faster) and will be held for two days (after that, you're charged a few francs a day). For twice the price, you can have same-day service to certain stations (in by 9:00, delivered by 18:00 or so).

Bike 'n' Rail: Hundreds of local train stations rent bikes for 33 SF a day and sometimes have easy "pick up here and drop off there" plans (40 SF/day; see www.switzerlandmobility.ch). For mixing train and bike travel, ask at stations for information booklets, or see www.rent-a-bike.ch.

Renting a Car

If you're renting a car in Switzerland, your US driver's license is all you need. If you're also planning to drive in Austria or Italy, you're also technically required to have an International Driving Permit—a translation of your driver's license (sold at your local AAA office for $15 plus the cost of two passport-type photos; see www.aaa.com). While that's the letter of the law, I've often rented cars in all of these places without having—or being asked to show—this permit.

To rent a car in Switzerland, you must be at least 20 years old with a valid license (age requirements vary by rental company). Drivers under the age of 25 may incur a young-driver surcharge.

Research car rentals before you go. It's cheapest to arrange most car rentals from the US. Call several companies and look online to compare rates, or arrange a rental through your hometown travel agent. Most of the major US rental agencies (such as Alamo/National, Avis, Budget, Dollar, Hertz, and Thrifty) have offices throughout Europe. It can be cheaper to use a consolidator, such as Auto Europe (www.autoeurope.com) or Europe by Car (www.ebctravel.com), which compares rates at several companies to get you the best deal. However, my readers have reported problems with consolidators, ranging from misinformation to unexpected fees; because you're going through a middleman, it can be more challenging to resolve disputes that arise with the rental agency.

Regardless of the car-rental company you choose, always read the contract carefully. The fine print can conceal a host of common add-on charges—such as one-way drop-off fees, airport surcharges, or mandatory insurance policies—that aren't included in the "total price," but can be tacked on when you pick up your car. You may need to query rental agents pointedly to find out your actual cost.

For the best rental deal, rent by the week with unlimited mileage. To save money on gas, ask for a diesel car. I normally rent the smallest, least-expensive model with a stick shift (cheaper than an automatic). An automatic transmission adds about 50 percent to the car-rental cost over a manual transmission. Almost all rentals are manual by default, so if you need an automatic, you must request one in advance; beware that these cars are usually larger models (not as maneuverable on narrow, winding roads).

For a two-week rental, allow about $600 per person (based on 2 people sharing the car) for a small economy car with unlimited mileage, including gas, parking, and insurance. For longer trips, look into leasing; you'll save money on insurance and taxes (explained later).

You can sometimes get a GPS unit with your rental car or leased vehicle for an additional fee (around $15/day; be sure it's set to English and has all the maps you need before you drive off). Or, if you have a portable GPS device at home, consider taking it with you to Europe (buy and upload European maps before your trip). GPS apps are also available for smartphones, but downloading maps on one of these apps in Europe could lead to an exorbitant data-roaming bill.

Big companies have offices in most cities; ask whether they can pick you up at your hotel. Small, local rental companies can be cheaper but aren't as flexible. Compare pickup costs (downtown can be cheaper than the airport), and explore drop-off options. Returning a car at a big-city train station can be tricky; get precise details on the car drop-off location and hours. Note that rental offices usually close from midday Saturday until Monday.

When picking up the car, check it thoroughly and make sure any damage is noted on your rental agreement. Find out how your car's lights, turn signals, wipers, and gas cap function, and know what kind of fuel the car takes. When you return the car, make sure the agent verifies its condition with you.

If you drop your car off early or keep it longer, you'll be credited or charged at a fair, prorated price. Always keep your receipts in case any questions arise about your billing.

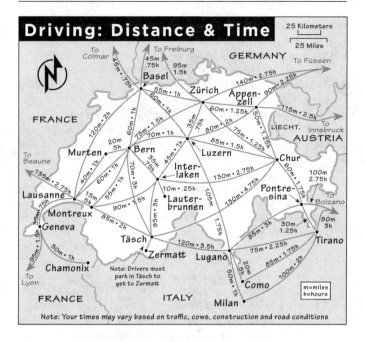

Driving: Distance & Time

Note: Your times may vary based on traffic, cows, construction and road conditions

Car Insurance Options

When you rent a car, you are liable for a very high deductible, sometimes equal to the entire value of the car. Limit your financial risk by choosing one of these three options: Buy Collision Damage Waiver (CDW) coverage from the car-rental company, get coverage through your credit card (free, if your card automatically includes zero-deductible coverage), or buy coverage through Travel Guard.

CDW includes a very high deductible (typically $1,000-1,500). Though each rental company has its own variation, basic CDW costs $15-25 a day (figure roughly 25 percent extra) and reduces your liability, but does not eliminate it. When you pick up the car, you'll be offered the chance to "buy down" the basic deductible to zero (for an additional $15-30/day; this is sometimes called "super CDW").

If you opt for **credit-card coverage,** there's a catch. You'll technically have to decline all coverage offered by the car-rental company, which means they can place a hold on your card (which can be up to the full value of the car). In case of damage, it can be time-consuming to resolve the charges with your credit-card company. Before you decide on this option, quiz your credit-card company about how it works.

Finally, you can buy collision insurance from **Travel Guard** ($9/day plus a one-time $3 service fee covers you for up to $35,000,

$250 deductible, tel. 800-826-4919, www.travelguard.com). It's valid everywhere in Europe except the Republic of Ireland, and some Italian car-rental companies refuse to honor it. Note that various states differ on which products and policies are available to their residents.

For more on car-rental insurance, see www.ricksteves.com/cdw.

Leasing

For trips of two and a half weeks or more, consider leasing (which automatically includes zero-deductible collision and theft insurance). By technically buying and then selling back the car, you save lots of money on tax and insurance. Leasing provides you a new car with unlimited mileage and a 24-hour emergency assistance program. You can lease for as little as 17 days to as long as six months. Car leases must be arranged from the US. One of many reliable companies offering affordable lease packages is Europe by Car (US tel. 800-223-1516, www.ebctravel.com).

Driving

You can get anywhere quickly on Switzerland's fine road system, the world's most expensive per mile to build.

Road Rules: Use your headlights day and night like the Swiss do; the Swiss government strongly recommends doing so, and headlights are required when driving through tunnels. Seat belts are required, and two beers under those belts are enough to land you in jail. Children under 12 (yes, 12) need to ride in a child-safety seat. Be aware of typical European road rules; for example, many countries forbid drivers from talking on mobile phones without a hands-free headset. Ask your car-rental company about these rules, or check the US State Department website (www.travel.state.gov, click on "International Travel," then specify your country of choice and click "Traffic Safety and Road Conditions").

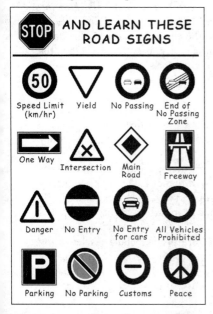

STOP AND LEARN THESE ROAD SIGNS

Speed Limit (km/hr) — Yield — No Passing — End of No Passing Zone

One Way — Intersection — Main Road — Freeway

Danger — No Entry — No Entry for cars — All Vehicles Prohibited

Parking — No Parking — Customs — Peace

Tolls: Drivers pay an annual, 40-SF fee for a permit to use Swiss autobahns.

Check to see if your rental car already has one of these windshield stickers, called a "vignette" (if not, buy it at border crossings, gas stations, post offices, or car-rental agencies). Anyone caught driving on a Swiss autobahn (indicated by green signs with a white expressway symbol) without this tax sticker is likely to be stopped and slapped with a steep fine (100 SF plus the 40-SF fee).

Fuel: Gas is expensive—often around $8 per gallon. US credit and debit cards won't work at pay-at-the-pump stations, but are generally accepted (with a PIN code) at staffed stations. Diesel rental cars are common; make sure you know what type of fuel your car takes before you fill up.

Signage: Know the universal road signs (shown in this chapter and explained in charts in most road atlases and at service stations). *Dreieck* (literally, "three corners") means a Y in the road; *Autobahnkreuz* is an intersection (*carrefour* in French). Exits are spaced about 20 miles apart and often have a gas station (*bleifrei/ sans plomb* are German/French for "unleaded"), a restaurant, a mini-mart, and sometimes a tourist information desk. Exits and intersections refer to the next major city or the nearest small town. Look at your map and anticipate which town names to watch out for. Know what you're looking for—miss it, and you're long autobahn-gone. When navigating, you'll see *nord, süd, ost, west,* or *mitte* (*nord, sud, est, oest,* or *centre* in French).

To get to the center of a city, follow signs for *Zentrum* or *Stadtmitte* (or *centre-ville* in French). Ring roads go around a city.

Parking: Pick up the blue "cardboard clock" (*Parkscheibe,* available free at TIs, gas stations, police stations, and *Tabak* shops) and display your arrival time on the clock and put it on the dashboard, so parking attendants can see you've been there less than the posted maximum stay. Many parking areas require you to display this clock.

Cheap Flights

While trains are usually the best way to connect places that are close together, if your trip extends beyond Switzerland, you may save time and money by flying.

Good comparison search engines for international flights include www.kayak.com and www.hipmunk.com. For comparing inexpensive flights within Europe, try www.skyscanner.com. If you're not sure who flies to your destination, check its airport's website for a list of carriers.

Well-known cheapo airlines in Europe include easyJet (www .easeyjet.com), RyanAir (www.ryanair.com), and BMI Baby (www.bmibaby.com). Those based in Switzerland are Flybaboo (www.flybaboo.com) and Helvetic (www.helvetic.com).

Be aware of the potential drawbacks of flying on the cheap: nonrefundable and nonchangeable tickets, minimal or nonexistent customer service, treks to airports far outside town, and stingy baggage allowances with steep overage fees. If you're traveling with lots of luggage, a cheap flight can quickly become a bad deal. To avoid unpleasant surprises, read the small print before you book.

Resources

Resources from Rick Steves

Rick Steves' Switzerland is one of many books in my series on European travel, which includes country guidebooks, city guide-

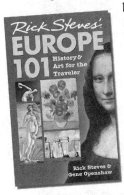

books (Rome, Florence, Paris, London, etc.), Snapshot guides (excerpted chapters from my country guides), Pocket Guides (full-color little books on big cities), and my budget-travel skills handbook, *Rick Steves' Europe Through the Back Door.* Most of my titles are available as ebooks. My phrase books—for Italian, French, German, Spanish, and Portuguese—are practical and budget-oriented. My other books include *Europe 101* (a crash course on art and history), *Mediterranean Cruise Ports* (how to make the most of your time in port), and *Travel as a Political Act* (a travelogue sprinkled with tips for bringing home a global perspective). A more complete list of my titles appears near the end of this book.

Video: My public television series, *Rick Steves' Europe,* covers European destinations in 100 shows, including three episodes that explore Switzerland. To watch episodes, visit www.hulu.com/rick -steves-europe; for scripts and other details, see www.ricksteves .com/tv.

Audio: My weekly public radio show, *Travel with Rick Steves,* features interviews with travel experts from around the world. All of this audio content is available for free at Rick Steves Audio Europe, an extensive online library organized by destination. Choose whatever interests you, and download it for free to your computer or mobile device via www.ricksteves.com /audioeurope, iTunes, or the Rick Steves Audio Europe smartphone app.

Begin Your Trip at www.ricksteves.com

At ricksteves.com, you'll discover a wealth of free information on European destinations, including fresh monthly news and helpful tips from thousands of fellow travelers. You'll find my latest guidebook updates (www.ricksteves.com/update), a monthly travel e-newsletter (easy and free to sign up), my personal travel blog, and my free Rick Steves Audio Europe smartphone app (if you don't have a smartphone, you can access the same content via podcasts). You can even follow me on Facebook and Twitter.

Our **online Travel Store** offers travel bags and accessories that I've specifically designed to help you travel smarter and lighter. These include my popular carry-on bags (roll-aboard and backpack versions), money belts, totes, toiletries kits, adapters, other accessories, and a wide selection of guidebooks, planning maps, and DVDs.

Choosing the right **railpass** for your trip—amid hundreds of options—can drive you nutty. We'll help you choose the best pass for your needs and ship it to you for free, plus give you a bunch of free extras.

Rick Steves' Europe Through the Back Door travel company offers **tours** with more than three dozen itineraries and 450 departures reaching the best destinations in this book... and beyond. Our Germany, Austria & Switzerland tours include "the best of" in 14 days. You'll enjoy great guides, a fun bunch of travel partners (with small groups of generally around 24-28), and plenty of room to spread out in a big, comfy bus. You'll find European adventures to fit every vacation length. For all the details, and to get our Tour Catalog and a free Rick Steves Tour Experience DVD (filmed on location during an actual tour), visit www.ricksteves.com or call us at 425/608-4217.

APPENDIX

Maps

The black-and-white maps in this book are concise and simple, designed to help you locate recommended places and get to local TIs, where you can pick up more in-depth maps of cities and regions (usually free). Better maps are sold at newsstands and bookstores. Before you buy a map, look at it to be sure it has the level of detail you want. For drivers, I recommend a 1:400,000-scale map of the whole country, or even larger-scale maps of particular regions. Train travelers can usually manage fine with the freebies they get with their railpass and from the local tourist offices.

Other Guidebooks

If you're like most travelers, this book is all you need. But if you'll be traveling beyond my recommended destinations, $40 for extra maps and books is money well-spent. For several people traveling by car, the extra weight and expense of a few books are negligible.

The following books are worthwhile, though most are not updated annually; check the publication date before you buy.

Lonely Planet's guide to Switzerland is thorough, well-researched, and packed with good maps and hotel recommendations for low- to moderate-budget travelers. The similar *Rough Guide to Switzerland* is written by insightful British researchers.

If you'll be spending a lot of time on the train, consider *Switzerland Without a Car* (Bradt), which provides helpful descriptions of what you'll see out the window.

Dorling Kindersley publishes snazzy Eyewitness Travel Guides, including one on Switzerland. Though pretty to look at, these books weigh a ton and are skimpy on actual content.

The popular, skinny *Michelin Green Guide: Switzerland* is excellent, especially if you're driving. Michelin Guides are known for their city and sightseeing maps, dry but concise and helpful information on all major sights, and good cultural and historical background. English editions are sold in Europe at gas stations and tourist shops.

Recommended Books and Movies

To get in the mood for your trip, consider these books and films, which take place partly or entirely in Switzerland.

Nonfiction

For a look at how this diverse nation holds itself together, try *Why Switzerland?* (Steinberg), which explains how a country with four official languages can still have a common culture. *Swiss History in a Nutshell* (Nappey) has information that's concise and enjoyable, yet not dumbed-down. *La Place de la Concorde Suisse* (McPhee) follows a mountain unit of the Swiss Army on patrol, exploring how mandatory military service (for men) keeps Switzerland from breaking apart (despite its French title, it's written in English).

Mark Twain's *A Tramp Abroad* is a humorous account of Twain's 1878 "walking tour" through the Alps. For more about mountains, try *The White Spider* (Harrer), which chronicles the first successful ascent of the Eiger's north face; *The Climb Up to Hell* (Olsen) about an ill-fated 1957 Eiger climb; and Jon Krakauer's collection of mountaineering essays, *Eiger Dreams*.

Fiction

The most famous novel about Switzerland (and the source of many Swiss clichés) is the children's classic *Heidi* (Spyri). A refreshing antidote is Max Frisch's 20th-century riddle *I'm Not Stiller*.

Nobel Prize-winning author Thomas Mann was German, but his masterpiece, *The Magic Mountain*, takes place in a sanatorium high in the Swiss Alps, where troubled patients are trying to recover from tuberculosis as World War I is about to start. Another Nobel laureate—Ernest Hemingway—set the climax of his antiwar epic *A Farewell to Arms* on Lake Maggiore and in Lausanne.

In *Hotel du Lac* (Brookner), the heroine is sent by her friends to a Swiss hotel to recover from a misguided love affair, but her stay turns out to be much more than a simple rest cure. A different Swiss inn is the setting for John le Carré's thriller *The Night Manager*, where a fussy hotel worker is recruited by British intelligence to bring down a millionaire gunrunner. *The Watchers* is a detective/fantasy thriller set in the cobbled streets of Lausanne's old town (Steele).

Einstein's Dreams (Lightman) plays with preconceptions of space and time while painting an evocative picture of turn-of-the-century Bern. While several novels and movies recount the story of William Tell, the most enduring version of the legend is by German poet/philosopher/playwright Friedrich Schiller, whose now-classic play broadened the tale into a rallying cry against tyranny.

Films

Hollywood has largely typecast Switzerland as little more than a range of high mountains. (One exception is 2002's *The Bourne Identity*, which set key scenes in urban Zürich...but filmed them mostly in Prague.) Clint Eastwood directed and starred in *The Eiger Sanction* (1975), a spy thriller partially shot in Kleine Scheidegg. The James Bond film *On Her Majesty's Secret Service* (1969) includes stunning action sequences on the slopes of the Schilthorn, in the Piz Gloria revolving restaurant, and down a bobsled run (see page 187). *Five Days One Summer* (1982) is a Sean Connery flick with some breathtaking climbing sequences sandwiched between soap-opera scenes about an incestuous love triangle. The excruciatingly realistic *North Face* (2008) imagines the disastrous 1936 attempt by an Austrian/German team to scale the Eiger's "wall of death."

For Switzerland beyond the mountains, try some foreign-language films. Krzysztof Kieslowski's *Red* (1994), the last part of his *Three Colors* trilogy, is set in Geneva. Alain Tanner is Switzerland's most acclaimed director, and his 1975 French-language film, *Jonah Who Will Be 25 in the Year 2000,* takes a Big-Chill look at former student activists living in Geneva. Xavier Koller's Oscar-winning *Journey of Hope* (1990) follows three members of a Kurdish family in search of a better life in Switzerland.

The Swissmakers (1978), a multilingual comedy about foreigners trying to get Swiss citizenship, is the most popular Swiss movie ever made (but may still be hard to find in the States). Or, if you're in the mood for something completely different, many of India's "Bollywood" movies use Swiss scenery as a stand-in for Himalayan locales (driving increasing numbers of Indian tourists to Switzerland). The romance *Dilwale Dulhania Le Jayenge* (literally *The Brave Heart Will Take the Bride,* 1995), which ran for a record 11 years in Indian movie theaters, was shot in Swiss locations with its actors speaking a mixture of Hindi and English.

Holidays and Festivals

This list includes many—but not all—big festivals in major cities, plus national holidays observed throughout Switzerland. Many sights and banks close down on national holidays—keep this in mind when planning your itinerary. However, not all holidays are celebrated in every canton (particularly religious ones); if you find yourself in a town closed down for an unexpected holiday, consider going on to your next stop (call ahead), where everything may well be in full swing. Before planning a trip around a festival, make sure you verify its dates by checking the festival's website or TI sites (US tel. 877-794-8037, www.myswitzerland.com, info.usa @myswitzerland.com).

For sports events, see www.sportsevents365.com for schedules and ticket information.

Jan 1	New Year's Day
Jan 2	Berchtoldstag (St. Berchtold Day), Harder Potschete (parade), Interlaken
Jan 6	Epiphany (closings)
Mid-Jan	Lauberhorn ski race, Wengen; Inferno ski race, Mürren (www.inferno -muerren.ch)
Feb	Fasnacht (Carnival), especially celebrated in Luzern, Zürich, and Bern

APPENDIX

March 19	Josefstag (St. Joseph's Day)
March-May	International Jazz Festival (www .jazzfestivalbern.ch), Bern
Late March	International Easter Music Festival (1 week, www.lucernefestival.ch), Luzern
Good Friday	April 6 in 2012, March 29 in 2013
Easter	April 8 in 2012, March 31 in 2013
Easter Monday	April 9 in 2012, April 1 in 2013
Third Monday in April	Sechseläuten (Spring Festival, 2 days, www.sechselaeuten.ch), Zürich
Last Sun in April	Open-Air Parliament (public selection of delegates), Appenzell
May 1	Labor Day
Ascension	Christi Himmelfahrt (May 17 in 2012, May 9 in 2013)
Whitsunday	May 27 in 2012, May 19 in 2013
Whitmonday	Pfingstmontag (May 28 in 2012, May 20 in 2013)
Corpus Christi	Fronleichnam (June 7 in 2012, May 30 in 2013)
Early June	Berner Tanztage (dance festival, www .tanztage.ch), Bern
Mid-June-Early July	Zürich Festival (3 weeks, www.zuercher -festspiele.ch)
Late June-early Sept	William Tell Performance (open-air theater, www.tellspiele.ch), Interlaken
Early July	Estival Jazz (free open-air festival, www .estivaljazz.ch), Lugano
Early July	City Festival (www.festivalcite.ch), Lausanne
Early July	Montreux International Jazz Festival (2 www.montreuxjazz.com)
Mid-July	Gurten Open-Air Rock Festival (4 days, www.gurtenfestival.ch), Bern
Aug 1	Swiss National Day (parades and fireworks)
Early Aug	Street Parade (city-wide rave, 1 day, www.streetparade.ch), Zürich
Aug 15	Assumption of Mary (Maria Himmelfahrt)
Mid-Aug-Mid-Sept	Lucerne Festival in Summer (5 weeks, classical, www.lucernefestival.ch)
Early Oct	Festa d'Autunno (food and wine festival, 3 days, www.lugano-tourism.ch), Lugano

Nov 1	All Saints' Day
Late Nov	Lucerne Festival at the Piano (1 week, www.lucernefestival.ch)
Late Nov	Traditional Onion Market Fair (1 day), Bern
Dec	Christmas fairs
Dec 6	St. Nicholas Day
Dec 8	Immaculate Conception
Dec 25	Christmas
Dec 26	St. Stephen's Day (Boxing Day)

Conversions and Climate

Numbers and Stumblers

- Europeans write a few of their numbers differently than we do. 1 = 1, 4 = 4, 7 = 7.
- In Europe, dates appear as day/month/year, so Christmas is 25/12/2013.
- Commas are decimal points and decimals commas. A dollar and a half is 1,50, one thousand is 1.000, and there are 5.280 feet in a mile.
- When counting with fingers, start with your thumb. If you hold up your first finger to request one item, you'll probably get two.
- What Americans call the second floor of a building is the first floor in Europe.
- On escalators and moving sidewalks, Europeans keep the left "lane" open for passing. Keep to the right.

Metric Conversions (approximate)

A kilogram is 2.2 pounds, and 1 liter is about a quart, or almost 4 to a gallon. A kilometer is six-tenths of a mile. I figure kilometers to miles by cutting them in half and adding back 10 percent of the original (120 km: 60 + 12 = 72 miles, 300 km: 150 + 30 = 180 miles).

1 foot = 0.3 meter	1 square yard = 0.8 square meter
1 yard = 0.9 meter	1 square mile = 2.6 square kilometers
1 mile = 1.6 kilometers	1 ounce = 28 grams
1 centimeter = 0.4 inch	1 quart = 0.95 liter
1 meter = 39.4 inches	1 kilogram = 2.2 pounds
1 kilometer = 0.62 mile	32°F = 0°C

Clothing Sizes

When shopping for clothing, use these US-to-European comparisons as general guidelines (but note that no conversion is perfect).

- Women's dresses and blouses: Add 30
  (US size 10 = European size 40)
- Men's suits and jackets: Add 10
  (US size 40 regular = European size 50)
- Men's shirts: Multiply by 2 and add about 8
  (US size 15 collar = European size 38)
- Women's shoes: Add about 30
  (US size 8 = European size 38-39)
- Men's shoes: Add 32-34
  (US size 9 = European size 41; US size 11 = European size 45)

Switzerland's Climate

First line, average daily high; second line, average daily low; third line, average days without rain. For more detailed weather statistics for destinations in this book (as well as the rest of the world), check www.worldclimate.com.

J	F	M	A	M	J	J	A	S	O	N	D
Bern											
38°	42°	51°	59°	66°	73°	77°	76°	69°	58°	47°	40°
29°	30°	36°	42°	49°	55°	58°	58°	53°	44°	37°	31°
20	19	22	21	20	19	22	20	20	21	19	21

Temperature Conversion: Fahrenheit and Celsius

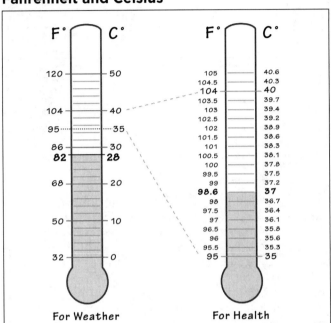

Europe takes its temperature using the Celsius scale, while we opt for Fahrenheit. For a rough conversion from Celsius to Fahrenheit, double the number and add 30. For weather, remember that 28°C is 82°F—perfect. For health, 37°C is just right.

Hotel Reservation

To: _____   _____
            hotel   *email or fax*

From: _____   _____
            name   *email or fax*

Today's date: _____ /_____ /_____
                    day   *month*   *year*

Dear Hotel _____ ,
Please make this reservation for me:

Name: _____

Total # of people: _____   # of rooms: _____   # of nights: _____

Arriving: _____ /_____ /_____   My time of arrival (24-hr clock): _____
              day *month* *year*   (I will telephone if I will be late)

Departing: ____ /____ /____
               day *month* *year*

Room(s): Single____   Double ____   Twin ____   Triple ____   Quad____

With: Toilet ____   Shower ____   Bath ____   Sink only____

Special needs: View____   Quiet____   Cheapest ____   Ground Floor____

Please email or fax confirmation of my reservation, along with the type of room reserved and the price. Please also inform me of your cancellation policy. After I hear from you, I will quickly send my credit-card information as a deposit to hold the room. Thank you.

_____
Name

_____
Address

_____
City   *State*   *Zip Code*   *Country*

Before hoteliers can make your reservation, they want to know the information listed above. You can use this form as the basis for your email, or you can photocopy this page, fill in the information, and send it as a fax (also available online at www.ricksteves.com/reservation).

Packing Checklist

Whether you're traveling for five days or five weeks, here's what you'll need to bring. Pack light to enjoy the sweet freedom of true mobility. Happy travels!

- ❑ 5 shirts: long- and short-sleeve
- ❑ 1 sweater or lightweight fleece
- ❑ 2 pairs pants
- ❑ 1 pair shorts
- ❑ 1 swimsuit
- ❑ 5 pairs underwear and socks
- ❑ 1 pair shoes
- ❑ 1 rainproof jacket with hood
- ❑ Tie or scarf
- ❑ Money belt
- ❑ Money—your mix of:
  - ❑ Debit card (for ATM withdrawals)
  - ❑ Credit card
  - ❑ Hard cash (in easy-to-exchange $20 bills)
- ❑ Documents plus photo-copies:
  - ❑ Passport
  - ❑ Printout of airline eticket
  - ❑ Driver's license
  - ❑ Student ID and hostel card
  - ❑ Railpass/car rental voucher
  - ❑ Insurance details
- ❑ Daypack
- ❑ Electronics—your choice of:
  - ❑ Camera (and related gear)
  - ❑ Computer/mobile devices (phone, MP3 player, ereader, etc.)
  - ❑ Chargers for each of the above
  - ❑ Plug adapter
- ❑ Empty water bottle

- ❑ Wristwatch and alarm clock
- ❑ Earplugs
- ❑ Toiletries kit
  - ❑ Toiletries
  - ❑ Medicines and vitamins
  - ❑ First-aid kit
  - ❑ Glasses/contacts/sunglasses (with prescriptions)
- ❑ Sealable plastic baggies
- ❑ Laundry soap
- ❑ Clothesline
- ❑ Small towel
- ❑ Sewing kit
- ❑ Travel information (guide-books and maps)
- ❑ Address list (for sending postcards)
- ❑ Postcards and photos from home
- ❑ Notepad and pen
- ❑ Journal

If you plan to carry on your luggage, note that all liquids must be in 3.4-ounce or smaller containers and fit within a single quart-size sealable baggie. For details, see www.tsa.gov/travelers.

German Survival Phrases for Switzerland

When using the phonetics, pronounce ī as the long I sound in "light."

English	German	Phonetics
Hello.	Grüezi.	grit-see
Do you speak English?	Sprechen Sie Englisch?	shprehkh-ehn zee ehng-lish
Yes. / No.	Ja. / Nein.	yah / nīn
I (don't) understand.	Ich verstehe (nicht).	ikh fehr-shtay-heh (nikht)
Please.	Bitte.	bit-teh
Thank you.	Merci.	mur-see
I'm sorry.	Es tut mir leid.	ehs toot meer līt
Excuse me.	Entschuldigung.	ehnt-shool-dig-oong
(No) problem.	(Kein) Problem.	(kīn) proh-blaym
(Very) good.	(Sehr) gut.	(zehr) goot
Goodbye.	Ciao.	chow
one / two	eins / zwei	īns / tsvī
three / four	drei / vier	drī / feer
five / six	fünf / sechs	finf / zehkhs
seven / eight	sieben / acht	zee-behn / ahkht
nine / ten	neun / zehn	noyn / tsayn
How much is it?	Wieviel kostet das?	vee-feel kohs-teht dahs
Write it?	Schreiben?	shrī-behn
Is it free?	Ist es umsonst?	ist ehs oom-zohnst
Included?	Inklusive?	in-kloo-zee-veh
Where can I buy / find...?	Wo kann ich kaufen / finden...?	voh kahn ikh kow-fehn / fin-dehn
I'd like / We'd like...	Ich hätte gern / Wir hätten gern...	ikh heh-teh gehrn / veer heh-tehn gehrn
...a room.	...ein Zimmer.	īn tsim-mer
...a ticket to ____.	...eine Fahrkarte nach ____.	ī-neh far-kar-teh nahkh
Is it possible?	Ist es möglich?	ist ehs mur-glikh
Where is...?	Wo ist...?	voh ist
...the train station	...der Bahnhof	dehr bahn-hohf
...the bus station	...der Busbahnhof	dehr boos-bahn-hohf
...tourist information office	...das Touristen- informationsbüro	dahs too-ris-tehn- in-for-maht-see-ohns-bew-roh
...toilet	...die Toilette	dee toh-leh-teh
men	Herren	hehr-rehn
women	Damen	dah-mehn
left / right	links / rechts	links / rehkhts
straight	geradeaus	geh-rah-deh-ows
When is this open / closed?	Um wieviel Uhr ist hier geöffnet / geschlossen?	oom vee-feel oor ist heer geh-urf-neht / geh-shloh-sehn
At what time?	Um wieviel Uhr?	oom vee-feel oor
Just a moment.	Moment.	moh-mehnt
now / soon / later	jetzt / bald / später	yehtst / bahld / shpay-ter
today / tomorrow	heute / morgen	hoy-teh / mor-gehn

In a German-speaking Restaurant

I'd like / We'd like...	Ich hätte gern / Wir hätten gern...	ikh **heh**-teh gehrn / veer **heh**-tehn gehrn
...a reservation for...	...eine Reservierung für...	ī-neh reh-zer-**feer**-oong fewr
...a table for one / two.	...einen Tisch für ein / zwei.	ī-nehn tish fewr īn / tsvī
Non-smoking.	Nichtraucher.	**nikht**-rowkh-er
Is this seat free?	Ist hier frei?	ist heer frī
Menu (in English), please.	Speisekarte (in Englisch), bitte.	**shpī**-zeh-kar-teh (in **ehng**-lish) **bit**-teh
service (not) included	Trinkgeld (nicht) inklusive	**trink**-gehlt (nikht) in-kloo-**zee**-veh
cover charge	Eintritt	**īn**-trit
to go	zum Mitnehmen	tsoom **mit**-nay-mehn
with / without	mit / ohne	mit / **oh**-neh
and / or	und / oder	oont / **oh**-der
menu (of the day)	(Tages-) Karte	(**tah**-gehs-) **kar**-teh
set meal for tourists	Touristenmenü	too-**ris**-tehn-meh-**new**
specialty of the house	Spezialität des Hauses	shpayt-see-ah-lee-**tayt** dehs **how**-zehs
daily special	Tageshit	**tah**-gehs-hit
appetizers	Vorspeise	**for**-shpī-zeh
bread	Brot	broht
cheese	Käse	**kay**-zeh
sandwich	Sandwich	**zahnd**-vich
soup	Suppe	**zup**-peh
salad	Salat	zah-**laht**
meat	Fleisch	flīsh
poultry	Geflügel	geh-**flew**-gehl
fish	Fisch	fish
seafood	Meeresfrüchte	**meh**-rehs-**frewkh**-teh
fruit	Obst	ohpst
vegetables	Gemüse	geh-**mew**-zeh
dessert	Nachspeise	**nahkh**-shpī-zeh
mineral water	Mineralwasser	min-eh-**rahl**-vah-ser
tap water	Leitungswasser	**lī**-toongs-vah-ser
milk	Milch	milkh
(orange) juice	(Orangen-) Saft	(oh-**rahn**-zhehn-) zahft
coffee	Kaffee	kah-**fay**
tea	Tee	tay
wine	Wein	vīn
red / white	rot / weiß	roht / vīs
glass / bottle	Glas / Flasche	glahs / **flah**-sheh
beer	Bier	beer
Cheers!	Prost!	prohst
More. / Another.	Mehr. / Noch ein.	mehr / nohkh īn
The same.	Das gleiche.	dahs **glīkh**-eh
Bill, please.	Rechnung, bitte.	**rehkh**-noong **bit**-teh
tip	Trinkgeld	**trink**-gehlt
Delicious!	Lecker!	**lehk**-er

For more user-friendly German phrases, check out *Rick Steves' German Phrase Book and Dictionary* or *Rick Steves' French, Italian & German Phrase Book*.

French Survival Phrases

When using the phonetics, try to nasalize the <u>n</u> sound.

English	French	Phonetics
Good day.	**Bonjour.**	boh<u>n</u>-zhoor
Mrs. / Mr.	**Madame / Monsieur**	mah-dahm / muhs-yur
Do you speak English?	**Parlez-vous anglais?**	par-lay-voo ah<u>n</u>-glay
Yes. / No.	**Oui. / Non.**	wee / noh<u>n</u>
I understand.	**Je comprends.**	zhuh koh<u>n</u>-prah<u>n</u>
I don't understand.	**Je ne comprends pas.**	zhuh nuh koh<u>n</u>-prah<u>n</u> pah
Please.	**S'il vous plaît.**	see voo play
Thank you.	**Merci.**	mehr-see
I'm sorry.	**Désolé.**	day-zoh-lay
Excuse me.	**Pardon.**	par-doh<u>n</u>
(No) problem.	**(Pas de) problème.**	(pah duh) proh-blehm
It's good.	**C'est bon.**	say boh<u>n</u>
Goodbye.	**Au revoir.**	oh vwahr
one / two	**un / deux**	uh<u>n</u> / duh
three / four	**trois / quatre**	twah / kah-truh
five / six	**cinq / six**	sa<u>n</u>k / sees
seven / eight	**sept / huit**	seht / weet
nine / ten	**neuf / dix**	nuhf / dees
How much is it?	**Combien?**	koh<u>n</u>-bee-a<u>n</u>
Write it?	**Ecrivez?**	ay-kree-vay
Is it free?	**C'est gratuit?**	say grah-twee
Included?	**Inclus?**	a<u>n</u>-klew
Where can I buy / find...?	**Où puis-je acheter / trouver...?**	oo pwee-zhuh ah-shuh-tay / troo-vay
I'd like / We'd like...	**Je voudrais / Nous voudrions...**	zhuh voo-dray / noo voo-dree-oh<u>n</u>
...a room.	**...une chambre.**	ewn shah<u>n</u>-bruh
...a ticket to ___.	**...un billet pour ___.**	uh<u>n</u> bee-yay poor
Is it possible?	**C'est possible?**	say poh-see-bluh
Where is...?	**Où est...?**	oo ay
...the train station	**...la gare**	lah gar
...the bus station	**...la gare routière**	lah gar root-yehr
...tourist information	**...l'office du tourisme**	loh-fees dew too-reez-muh
Where are the toilets?	**Où sont les toilettes?**	oo soh<u>n</u> lay twah-leht
men	**hommes**	ohm
women	**dames**	dahm
left / right	**à gauche / à droite**	ah gohsh / ah dwaht
straight	**tout droit**	too dwah
When does this open / close?	**Ça ouvre / ferme à quelle heure?**	sah oo-vruh / fehrm ah kehl ur
At what time?	**À quelle heure?**	ah kehl ur
Just a moment.	**Un moment.**	uh<u>n</u> moh-mah<u>n</u>
now / soon / later	**maintenant / bientôt / plus tard**	ma<u>n</u>-tuh-nah<u>n</u> / bee-a<u>n</u>-toh / plew tar
today / tomorrow	**aujourd'hui / demain**	oh-zhoor-dwee / duh-ma<u>n</u>

In a French-speaking Restaurant

I'd like / We'd like...	Je voudrais / Nous voudrions...	zhuh voo-dray / noo voo-dree-ohn
...to reserve...	...réserver...	ray-zehr-vay
...a table for one / two.	...une table pour un / deux.	ewn tah-bluh poor uhn / duh
Non-smoking.	Non fumeur.	nohn few-mur
Is this seat free?	C'est libre?	say lee-bruh
The menu (in English), please.	La carte (en anglais), s'il vous plaît.	lah kart (ahn ahn-glay) see voo play
service (not) included	service (non) compris	sehr-vees (nohn) kohn-pree
to go	à emporter	ah ahn-por-tay
with / without	avec / sans	ah-vehk / sahn
and / or	et / ou	ay / oo
special of the day	plat du jour	plah dew zhoor
specialty of the house	spécialité de la maison	spay-see-ah-lee-tay duh lah may-zohn
appetizers	hors-d'oeuvre	or-duh-vruh
first course (soup, salad)	entrée	ahn-tray
main course (meat, fish)	plat principal	plah pran-see-pahl
bread	pain	pan
cheese	fromage	froh-mahzh
sandwich	sandwich	sahnd-weech
soup	soupe	soop
salad	salade	sah-lahd
meat	viande	vee-ahnd
chicken	poulet	poo-lay
fish	poisson	pwah-sohn
seafood	fruits de mer	frwee duh mehr
fruit	fruit	frwee
vegetables	légumes	lay-gewm
dessert	dessert	duh-sehr
mineral water	eau minérale	oh mee-nay-rahl
tap water	l'eau du robinet	loh dew roh-bee-nay
milk	lait	lay
(orange) juice	jus (d'orange)	zhew (doh-rahnzh)
coffee	café	kah-fay
tea	thé	tay
wine	vin	van
red / white	rouge / blanc	roozh / blahn
glass / bottle	verre / bouteille	vehr / boo-teh-ee
beer	bière	bee-ehr
Cheers!	Santé!	sahn-tay
More. / Another.	Plus. / Un autre.	plew / uhn oh-truh
The same.	La même chose.	lah mehm shohz
The bill, please.	L'addition, s'il vous plaît.	lah-dee-see-ohn see voo play
tip	pourboire	poor-bwar
Delicious!	Délicieux!	day-lee-see-uh

For more user-friendly French phrases, check out *Rick Steves' French Phrase Book and Dictionary* or *Rick Steves' French, Italian & German Phrase Book*.

Italian Survival Phrases

Good day.	Buon giorno.	bwohn JOR-noh
Do you speak English?	Parla inglese?	PAR-lah een-GLAY-zay
Yes. / No.	Si. / No.	see / noh
I (don't) understand.	(Non) capisco.	(nohn) kah-PEES-koh
Please.	Per favore.	pehr fah-VOH-ray
Thank you.	Grazie.	GRAHT-seeay
You're welcome.	Prego.	PRAY-go
I'm sorry.	Mi dispiace.	mee dee-speeAH-chay
Excuse me.	Mi scusi.	mee SKOO-zee
(No) problem.	(Non) c'è un problema.	(nohn) cheh oon proh-BLAY-mah
Good.	Va bene.	vah BEHN-ay
Goodbye.	Arrivederci.	ah-ree-vay-DEHR-chee
one / two	uno / due	OO-noh / DOO-ay
three / four	tre / quattro	tray / KWAH-troh
five / six	cinque / sei	CHEENG-kway / SEHee
seven / eight	sette / otto	SEHT-tay / OT-toh
nine / ten	nove / dieci	NOV-ay / deeAY-chee
How much is it?	Quanto costa?	KWAHN-toh KOS-tah
Write it?	Me lo scrive?	may loh SKREE-vay
Is it free?	È gratis?	eh GRAH-tees
Is it included?	È incluso?	eh een-KLOO-zoh
Where can I buy / find...?	Dove posso comprare / trovare...?	DOH-vay POS-soh kohm-PRAH-ray / troh-VAH-ray
I'd like / We'd like...	Vorrei / Vorremmo...	vor-REHee / vor-RAY-moh
...a room.	...una camera.	OO-nah KAH-meh-rah
...a ticket to ____.	...un biglietto per ____.	oon beel-YEHT-toh pehr
Is it possible?	È possibile?	eh poh-SEE-bee-lay
Where is...?	Dov'è...?	DOH-veh
...the train station	...la stazione	lah staht-seeOH-nay
...the bus station	...la stazione degli autobus	lah staht-seeOH-nay DAYL-yee OW-toh-boos
...tourist information	...informazioni per turisti	een-for-maht-seeOH-nee pehr too-REE-stee
...the toilet	...la toilette	lah twah-LEHT-tay
men	uomini, signori	WOH-mee-nee, seen-YOH-ree
women	donne, signore	DON-nay, seen-YOH-ray
left / right	sinistra / destra	see-NEE-strah / DEHS-trah
straight	sempre diritto	SEHM-pray dee-REE-toh
When do you open / close?	A che ora aprite / chiudete?	ah kay OH-rah ah-PREE-tay / keeoo-DAY-tay
At what time?	A che ora?	ah kay OH-rah
Just a moment.	Un momento.	oon moh-MAYN-toh
now / soon / later	adesso / presto / tardi	ah-DEHS-soh / PREHS-toh / TAR-dee
today / tomorrow	oggi / domani	OH-jee / doh-MAH-nee

In an Italian-speaking Restaurant

I'd like...	**Vorrei...**	vor-REHee
We'd like...	**Vorremmo...**	vor-RAY-moh
...to reserve...	**...prenotare...**	pray-noh-TAH-ray
...a table for one / two.	**...un tavolo per uno / due.**	oon TAH-voh-loh pehr OO-noh / DOO-ay
Non-smoking.	**Non fumare.**	nohn foo-MAH-ray
Is this seat free?	**È libero questo posto?**	eh LEE-bay-roh KWEHS-toh POH-stoh
The menu (in English), please.	**Il menù (in inglese), per favore.**	eel may-NOO (een een-GLAY-zay) pehr fah-VOH-ray
service (not) included	**servizio (non) incluso**	sehr-VEET-seeoh (nohn) een-KLOO-zoh
cover charge	**pane e coperto**	PAH-nay ay koh-PEHR-toh
to go	**da portar via**	dah POR-tar VEE-ah
with / without	**con / senza**	kohn / SEHN-sah
and / or	**e / o**	ay / oh
menu (of the day)	**menù (del giorno)**	may-NOO (dayl JOR-noh)
specialty of the house	**specialità della casa**	spay-chah-lee-TAH DEHL-lah KAH-zah
first course (pasta, soup)	**primo piatto**	PREE-moh peeAH-toh
main course (meat, fish)	**secondo piatto**	say-KOHN-doh peeAH-toh
side dishes	**contorni**	kohn-TOR-nee
bread	**pane**	PAH-nay
cheese	**formaggio**	for-MAH-joh
sandwich	**panino**	pah-NEE-noh
soup	**minestra, zuppa**	mee-NEHS-trah, TSOO-pah
salad	**insalata**	een-sah-LAH-tah
meat	**carne**	KAR-nay
chicken	**pollo**	POH-loh
fish	**pesce**	PEH-shay
seafood	**frutti di mare**	FROO-tee dee MAH-ray
fruit / vegetables	**frutta / legumi**	FROO-tah / lay-GOO-mee
dessert	**dolci**	DOHL-chee
tap water	**acqua del rubinetto**	AH-kwah dayl roo-bee-NAY-toh
mineral water	**acqua minerale**	AH-kwah mee-nay-RAH-lay
milk	**latte**	LAH-tay
(orange) juice	**succo (d'arancia)**	SOO-koh (dah-RAHN-chah)
coffee / tea	**caffè / tè**	kah-FEH / teh
wine	**vino**	VEE-noh
red / white	**rosso / bianco**	ROH-soh / beeAHN-koh
glass / bottle	**bicchiere / bottiglia**	bee-keeAY-ray / boh-TEEL-yah
beer	**birra**	BEE-rah
Cheers!	**Cin cin!**	cheen cheen
More. / Another.	**Ancora un po.' / Un altro.**	ahn-KOH-rah oon poh / oon AHL-troh
The same.	**Lo stesso.**	loh STEHS-soh
The bill, please.	**Il conto, per favore.**	eel KOHN-toh pehr fah-VOH-ray
tip	**mancia**	MAHN-chah
Delicious!	**Delizioso!**	day-leet-seeOH-zoh

For more user-friendly Italian phrases, check out *Rick Steves' Italian Phrase Book & Dictionary* or *Rick Steves' French, Italian, and German Phrase Book*.

INDEX

C

Cable cars: 379
Cailler Chocolate Factory (Bulle): 272
Camping: 26–27. *See also* sleeping
Car rental: driving information, 385–386; driving map, 384; general information, 12, 382–383; insurance options, 384–385; road signs and rules, 385
Casino Kursaal (Interlaken): 152
Castles: Gruyères, 268-269; Hünegg Castle, 156; Lausanne, 248; Oberhofen Castle, 156; Thun Castle, 155-156
Catholic Church (Samedan): 308
Celts: 354–355
Chapel Bridge (Luzern): 74–76
Château de Chillon: 259-263
Chesa Planta (Samedan): 308-309
Chocolate: 30–31, 272
Chocolate train: 267
Christmas celebrations: 351–352
Chur: 339, 346–347
Church of St. Ignazio (Poschiavo): 336
Church of St. Mary of the Angels (Lugano): 282–284
Church of St. Mary (Pontresina): 299
Church of St. Peter (Samedan): 308
Churches: Bern Cathedral, 115-116; Catholic Church (Samedan), 308; Church of St. Ignazio (Poschiavo), 336; Church of St. Mary of the Angels (Lugano), 282-284; Church of St. Peter (Samedan), 308; Fraumünster (Zürich), 55-56; French Church (Murten), 130; German Church (Murten), 131; Grossmünster (Zürich), 54-55; Jesuit Church (Luzern), 76-77; Lausanne Cathedral, 248-250; St. Peter's Chapel (Luzern), 80; St. Peter's Church (Zürich), 51-52
Cinema: Luzern, 72; Murten, 135; Zermatt, 206
City History Museum (Lausanne): 251
Climate: 394; temperature conversion, 395

Climbing: 155
Clothing sizes: 394
Cogwheel trains: 379
Collection de l'Art Brut (Lausanne): 251–252
Contemporary Switzerland: 359–361
Costs: 5–7
Cows: 170–171
Credit cards: 13–14, 15–17
Cruises: 57–58; Lake Lugano, 286–287; Murten, 133–134. *See also* boating
Currency: 37
Customs: 19

D

Debit cards: 13–14, 15–17
Depot History Museum (Luzern): 82
Discounts: 13; in the Berner Oberland, 147; Berner Oberland Regional Pass, 143; Engadin Card, 297; Eurail Pass, 317, 378; Jungfraubahnen Pass, 146; Junior Card, 143; LucerneCard, 70-71; Swiss Pass, 70, 317, 377-378; Tell-Pass, 93; Visitors Card, 70; Zermatt, 211; ZürichCARD, 45
Disentis: 343
Drug policy: 47
Dunant, Henri: 362

E

Eating: Appenzell, 232-233; Bern, 123-126; chocolate, 30-31; costs, 6; Ebenalp, 236-237; Gimmelwald, 177; Gruyères, 273; Interlaken, 159-160; Lausanne, 256-258; Lauterbrunnen, 167; Lugano, 290-291; Luzern, 90-92; Mürren, 185; Murten, 136-137; restaurant phrases, 400, 402, 404; restaurants, 27-28; Samedan, 309; St. Moritz, 314; Swiss cuisine, 28-32; tipping, 17; Zermatt, 218-219; Zürich, 65-67
Ebenalp: 234–237
Economy: 36–37
Eiger: 144

MAP INDEX

Audio Europe

Rick's Free Travel App

Get your FREE **Rick Steves Audio Europe**™ app to enjoy…

- Dozens of self-guided tours of Europe's top museums, sights and historic walks

- Hundreds of tracks filled with cultural insights and sightseeing tips from Rick's radio interviews

- All organized into handy geographic playlists

- For iPhone, iPad, iPod Touch, Android

With Rick whispering in your ear, Europe gets even better.

Find out more at ricksteves.com

Join a Rick Steves tour

Enjoy Europe's warmest welcome... with the flexibility and friendship of a small group getting to know Rick's favorite places and people. It all starts with our free tour catalog and DVD.

Great guides, small groups, no grumps.

Rick Steves

www.ricksteves.com

EUROPE GUIDES

Best of Europe
Eastern Europe
Europe Through the Back Door
Mediterranean Cruise Ports
Northern European Cruise Ports

COUNTRY GUIDES

Croatia & Slovenia
England
France
Germany
Great Britain
Ireland
Italy
Portugal
Scandinavia
Spain
Switzerland

CITY & REGIONAL GUIDES

Amsterdam, Bruges & Brussels
Barcelona
Budapest
Florence & Tuscany
Greece: Athens & the Peloponnese
Istanbul
London
Paris
Prague & the Czech Republic
Provence & the French Riviera
Rome
Venice
Vienna, Salzburg & Tirol

SNAPSHOT GUIDES

Berlin
Bruges & Brussels
Copenhagen & the Best of
  Denmark
Dublin
Dubrovnik
Hill Towns of Central Italy
Italy's Cinque Terre
Krakow, Warsaw & Gdansk
Lisbon
Madrid & Toledo
Milan & the Italian Lakes District
Munich, Bavaria & Salzburg
Naples & the Amalfi Coast
Northern Ireland
Norway
Scotland
Sevilla, Granada & Southern Spain
Stockholm

POCKET GUIDES

Athens
Barcelona
Florence
London
Paris
Rome
Venice

Rick Steves guidebooks are published by Avalon Travel,
a member of the Perseus Books Group.

NOW AVAILABLE:
eBOOKS, DVD & BLU-RAY

TRAVEL CULTURE

Europe 101
European Christmas
Postcards from Europe
Travel as a Political Act

eBOOKS

*Nearly all Rick Steves guides
are available as eBooks. Check
with your favorite bookseller.*

RICK STEVES' EUROPE DVDs

11 New Shows 2013–2014
Austria & the Alps
Eastern Europe
England & Wales
European Christmas
European Travel Skills & Specials
France
Germany, BeNeLux & More
Greece, Turkey & Portugal
Iran
Ireland & Scotland
Italy's Cities
Italy's Countryside
Scandinavia
Spain
Travel Extras

BLU-RAY

Celtic Charms
Eastern Europe Favorites
European Christmas
Italy Through the Back Door
Mediterranean Mosaic
Surprising Cities of Europe

PHRASE BOOKS & DICTIONARIES

French
French, Italian & German
German
Italian
Portuguese
Spanish

JOURNALS

Rick Steves' Pocket Travel Journal
Rick Steves' Travel Journal

PLANNING MAPS

Britain, Ireland & London
Europe
France & Paris
Germany, Austria & Switzerland
Ireland
Italy
Spain & Portugal

Rick Steves books and DVDs are available at bookstores
and through online booksellers.

Credits

To help update this book, Rick relied on...

Researcher
Gretchen Strauch

In 1999, Gretchen quit her Seattle job to live in Switzerland for a year—which became three (on the Swiss/German border). Teaching English in Konstanz enabled her frequent forays into the land of snowy peaks, melted cheese, and unpronounceable German. She now works as a Rick Steves guidebook editor, and doesn't recommend being unemployed in Switzerland, even with lovely friends who'll let you crash for months.

Contributor
Gene Openshaw

Gene is the co-author of ten Rick Steves books. For this book, he wrote material on art, history, and contemporary culture. When not traveling, Gene enjoys composing music, recovering from his 1973 trip to Europe with Rick, and living everyday life with his daughter.

Acknowledgments

Thanks to Susana Minich for writing the original version of the Zürich, Central Switzerland, Lugano, Pontresina/Samedan/St. Moritz, and Scenic Rail Journeys chapters; and to Cameron Hewitt for writing the original versions of the Luzern and Zermatt chapters.

Images

The following list identifies the chapter-opening images and credits their photographers.

Location	Photographer
Front color matter: Gimmelwald	Dominic Bonuccelli
Front color matter: Lauterbrunnen Valley	David C. Hoerlein
Introduction: Above Grindelwald	Rick Steves
Zürich: View of Zürich from Limmat River	Cameron Hewitt
Luzern and Central Switzerland: Chapel Bridge	Cameron Hewitt
Bern and Murten: Bern Overview	Rick Steves
Gimmelwald and the Berner Oberland: Gimmelwald	Dominic Bonuccelli
Zermatt and the Matterhorn: The Matterhorn	Susana Minich
Appenzell: Appenzell	Cameron Hewitt
Lake Geneva and French Switzerland: Château Chillon	Cameron Hewitt
Lugano: Lake Lugano	Cameron Hewitt
Pontresina, Samedan, and St. Moritz: Samedan	Cameron Hewitt
Scenic Rail Journeys: Bernina Express	Rick Steves
Switzerland in Winter: Mürren	Cameron Hewitt
Switzerland Past and Present: Gimmelwald	Dominic Bonuccelli

Rick Steves' Guidebook Series

City, Regional, and Country Guides

Rick Steves' Amsterdam,
    Bruges & Brussels
Rick Steves' Best of Europe
Rick Steves' Budapest
Rick Steves' Croatia
    & Slovenia
Rick Steves' Eastern Europe
Rick Steves' England
Rick Steves' Florence
    & Tuscany
Rick Steves' France
Rick Steves' Germany
Rick Steves' Great Britain
Rick Steves' Greece: Athens
    & the Peloponnese
Rick Steves' Ireland

Rick Steves' Istanbul
Rick Steves' Italy
Rick Steves' London
Rick Steves' Paris
Rick Steves' Portugal
Rick Steves' Prague
    & the Czech Republic
Rick Steves' Provence
    & the French Riviera
Rick Steves' Rome
Rick Steves' Scandinavia
Rick Steves' Spain
Rick Steves' Switzerland
Rick Steves' Venice
Rick Steves' Vienna,
    Salzburg & Tirol

Snapshot Guides

Excerpted from country guidebooks, the Snapshots Guides cover many of my favorite destinations, such as *Rick Steves' Snapshot Barcelona, Rick Steves' Snapshot Scotland,* and *Rick Steves' Snapshot Hill Towns of Central Italy.*

Pocket Guides

My new Pocket Guides are condensed, colorful guides to Europe's top cities, including Paris, London, Rome, and more. These combine the top self-guided walks and tours from my city guides with vibrant full-color photos, and are sized to slip easily into your pocket.

Rick Steves' Phrase Books

French
French/Italian/German
German
Italian
Portuguese
Spanish

More Books

Rick Steves' Europe 101: History and Art for the Traveler
Rick Steves' Europe Through the Back Door
Rick Steves' European Christmas
Rick Steves' Mediterranean Cruise Ports
Rick Steves' Postcards from Europe
Rick Steves' Travel as a Political Act